The Future of Intermodal Freight Transport

TRANSPORT ECONOMICS, MANAGEMENT AND POLICY

Series Editor: Kenneth Button, *University Professor, School of Public Policy, George Mason University, USA*

Transport is a critical input for economic development and for optimising social and political interaction. Recent years have seen significant new developments in the way that transport is perceived by private industry and governments, and in the way academics look at it.

The aim of this series is to provide original material and an up-to-date synthesis of the state of modern transport analysis. The coverage embraces all conventional modes of transport but also includes contributions from important related fields such as urban and regional planning and telecommunications where they interface with transport. The books draw from many disciplines and some cross disciplinary boundaries. They are concerned with economics, planning, sociology, geography, management science, psychology and public policy. They are intended to help improve the understanding of transport, the policy needs of the most economically advanced countries and the problems of resource-poor developing economies. The authors come from around the world and represent some of the outstanding young scholars as well as established names.

Titles in the series include:

Globalisation, Policy and Shipping
Fordism, Post-Fordism and the European Union Maritime Sector
Evangelia Selkou and Michael Roe

Cost–Benefit Analysis and Evolutionary Computing
Optimal Scheduling of Interactive Road Projects
John H.E. Taplin, Min Qiu, Vivian K. Salim and Renlong Han

The Future of Automated Freight Transport
Concepts, Design and Implementation
Edited by Rob Konings, Hugo Priemus and Peter Nijkamp

Telecommunications, Transportation and Location
Kenneth Button and Roger Stough with Michelle Bragg and Samantha Taylor

Competition in the Railway Industry
An International Comparative Analysis
Edited by José A. Gómez-Ibáñez and Ginés de Rus

Globalized Freight Transport
Intermodality, E-Commerce, Logistics and Sustainability
Edited by Thomas R. Leinbach and Cristina Capineri

Decision-Making on Mega-Projects
Cost–Benefit Analysis, Planning and Innovation
Edited by Hugo Priemus, Bent Flyvbjerg and Bert van Wee

Port Privatisation
The Asia-Pacific Experience
Edited by James Reveley and Malcolm Tull

The Future of Intermodal Freight Transport
Operations, Design and Policy
Edited by Rob Konings, Hugo Priemus and Peter Nijkamp

The Future of Intermodal Freight Transport

Operations, Design and Policy

Edited by

Rob Konings

Senior Researcher Freight Transport Systems, OTB Research Institute for Housing, Urban and Mobility Studies, Delft University of Technology, The Netherlands

Hugo Priemus

Professor of System Innovation and Spatial Development, Faculty of Technology, Policy and Management, Delft University of Technology, The Netherlands

Peter Nijkamp

Professor of Regional, Urban and Environmental Economics, Faculty of Economics and Business Administration, Free University, Amsterdam, The Netherlands

TRANSPORT ECONOMICS, MANAGEMENT AND POLICY

Edward Elgar

Cheltenham, UK • Northampton, MA, USA

Published by
Edward Elgar Publishing Limited
The Lypiatts
15 Lansdown Road
Cheltenham
Glos GL50 2JA
UK

Edward Elgar Publishing, Inc.
William Pratt House
9 Dewey Court
Northampton
Massachusetts 01060
USA

Reprinted 2013

A catalogue record for this book
is available from the British Library

Library of Congress Control Number: 2008926574

ISBN 978 1 84542 238 7

Printed in Great Britain by Berforts Information Press Ltd

Contents

PART III IMPLEMENTATION AND POLICY

Contributors

Fredrik Bärthel, Division of Logistics and Transportation, Department of Technology Management and Economics, Chalmers University of Technology, Göteborg, Sweden

Lata Chatterjee, Department of Geography and Environment, Center for Transportation Studies, Boston University, United States

Klaus-Peter Franke, Faculty of Manufacturing Engineering and Management, Institute for Business Operations and Logistics, Ulm University of Applied Sciences, Germany

Mariëlle den Hengst, Business Unit Work and Employment, Quality of Life, The Netherlands and Organisation for Applied Scientific Research and Section Systems Engineering, Faculty of Technology, Policy and Management, Delft University of Technology, The Netherlands

José Holguín-Veras, Department of Civil and Environmental Engineering, Rensselaer Polytechnic Institute, Troy, United States

Arne Jensen, Logistics and Transport Research Group, Department of Business Administration, Göteborg University, Sweden

Rob Konings, OTB Research Institute for Housing, Urban and Mobility Studies, Delft University of Technology, The Netherlands

Ekki Kreutzberger, OTB Research Institute for Housing, Urban and Mobility Studies, Delft University of Technology, The Netherlands

T.R. Lakshmanan, Department of Geography and Environment, Center for Transportation Studies, Boston University, United States

Toshinori Nemoto, Graduate School of Commerce and Management, Hitotsubashi University, Tokyo, Japan

Peter Nijkamp, Department of Spatial Economics, Faculty of Economics and Business Administration, Free University of Amsterdam, The Netherlands

Theo Notteboom, Institute of Transport and Maritime Management Antwerp (ITMMA), University of Antwerp, Belgium

Robert Paaswell, University Transportation Research Center, City University of New York, United States

Anthony Perl, Department of Political Science, Simon Fraser University, Burnaby, Canada

Hugo Priemus, Faculty of Technology, Policy and Management, Delft University of Technology, The Netherlands

Piet Rietveld, Department of Spatial Economics, Faculty of Economics and Business Administration, Free University of Amsterdam, The Netherlands

Joan Rijsenbrij, Transport Engineering and Logistics Section, Faculty of Mechanical Engineering and Marine Technology, Delft University of Technology, The Netherlands

Florian Schwarz, Department for Transportation Logistics, Fraunhofer Institute for Material Flow and Logistics, Dortmund, Germany

Bryan Stone, Stone Intermodal Consulting, Basel, Switzerland

Eiichi Taniguchi, Department of Urban Management, Kyoto University, Japan

Dimitrios Tsamboulas, Department of Transportation Planning and Engineering, National Technical University of Athens, Greece

Bart Wiegmans, OTB Research Institute for Housing, Urban and Mobility Studies, Delft University of Technology, The Netherlands

Johan Woxenius, Department of Business Administration, School of Business, Economics and Law, University of Gothenburg, Sweden

Preface

The importance of freight transport for our society is beyond dispute, but transport volumes are ever growing and the problems to accommodate freight flows in an efficient and sustainable way become increasingly alarming. Traffic congestion is rapidly growing and the quality of freight transport is not able to keep pace with the rising ambitions: shippers want higher reliability, lower prices, faster deliveries, more flexibility and higher service levels. In addition the side-effects of freight transport, such as the environmental deterioration, inefficient use of energy, space restrictions and traffic accidents, become more and more acknowledged as serious problems. In light of these problems there is a great challenge to achieve a breakthrough in the improvement of the performance of freight transport systems.

Learning from experiences in the field of passenger transport, intermodal transport offers interesting opportunities to improve the performance of a transport system.

This volume gives an overview of the current operations, design, modelling tools, policy and other issues related to intermodal freight transport.

The book is a collection of contributions of researchers from the research program Freight Transport Automation and Multimodality (FTAM), carried out at Delft University of Technology, together with experts in this field from many different countries. Delft University of Technology has also financially supported this research programme and this book project.

THE AUDIENCE FOR THE BOOK

The book is written from a multidisciplinary perspective, because of the complexity and diversity of relevant issues. Such an approach has the great advantage of presenting a more or less integral view on the theme of multimodal freight transport, which in our opinion really helps to understand the opportunities and threats related to multimodal freight transport. A disadvantage could be that it leads to a set of contributions dealing with rather diverse topics, that could limit the value of the book to a reader having a very specific background or interest. However, since we have attempted to avoid contributions going into very much technical detail and using extensive mathematical formulations, we believe the book is readable for a broad audience. The book is intended to be read by people in the academic world, but it could also appeal to policymakers as well as practitioners in the transport industry, who are involved in the operations, design, modelling, implementation and policies for intermodal freight transport.

COMPANION VOLUME

The idea for this book project was born from the completion of a five-year research programme on Freight Transport Automation and Multimodality (FTAM) at Delft University of Technology. The goal of this research programme was to provide knowledge and tools to design and develop technologies and organizational structures for an integrated, highly automated transport system for inland intermodal transport at different geographical levels. In addition to these scientific ambitions the programme of course also intended to contribute to improving the quality of freight transport, reducing its negative external effects and, finally, increasing its scope.

The richness of both themes and our wish to present a coherent book structure and to avoid fragmentation led us to decide to produce two volumes: this volume dealing with intermodal freight transport, and a companion volume focusing on freight transport automation. Both intermodal transport and transport automation will become increasingly important solutions to cope with ever-increasing transport volumes in an efficient and sustainable way. Although both themes are treated separately it is obvious that they are also strongly related, for example with regard to developments in automated transport at intermodal terminals. The relationship between the books is expressed by the same general structure and comparable titles of both volumes.

For the composition of both volumes a selected number of researchers from the FTAM research programme together with experts in these fields from many different countries have been invited to contribute. The chapters have been reviewed thoroughly by external experts.

Although it is impossible to cover all aspects of freight transport automation and intermodal transport in full breadth, we think that the collections in both volumes give a useful overview of the latest developments and tools regarding design and evaluation of innovations in these fields, as well as a fruitful discussion on the implementation issues. The different chapters of the books can themselves be viewed as an introduction to the specific topics. The recommendations for further readings may be a useful guide for readers to go beyond the scope of these volumes. Finally, we hope that both books will contribute to the further scientific, societal and political debates on freight transport innovations.

ACKNOWLEDGEMENTS

This book project has been financially supported by Delft University of Technology within the framework of its multiyear research programme Freight Transport Automation and Multimodality (FTAM). This support is gratefully acknowledged. Hugo Priemus was scientific director of this programme, Rob Konings coordinated the programme. TRAIL Research School also had a coordinating role in the FTAM programme, which stimulated a multidisciplinary approach and enabled the linkage of scientific results to practical applications. We believe these aspects are also reflected very well in this book.

In addition, we wish to thank the participating authors for their contribution to this book, and the referees for their excellent reviews. Finally, we also highly appreciated the help of Kate Pearce and Alexandra O'Connell of Edward Elgar Publishing in guiding us through the various stages of the production process of the book.

Rob Konings
Hugo Priemus
Peter Nijkamp

1. The future of intermodal freight transport: an overview

Rob Konings, Hugo Priemus and Peter Nijkamp

1.1 INTRODUCTION

Generally speaking, freight is transported from door to door: sometimes it is taken from the place where the raw materials are found (mines, for example) to the processing plants, and sometimes from these plants to factories where the various raw materials and components are combined into industrial end products, which are then transported to the wholesalers, distribution centres and eventually to the final consumer in the shape of a company, an organization or a household.

It is often impossible to arrange just one modality for freight transport, making two or even three modalities necessary: intermodal freight transport. The market share of intermodal freight transport is relatively low and is not showing a spectacular increase. The share of road transport is very high in most countries. This may contribute to the flexibility of freight transport, but emissions (soot) and road congestion (where passenger and freight traffic use the same roads) are causing a growing problem. A larger share for inland shipping, short-sea shipping and rail transport would be an advantage, particularly where there are intense flows of goods. Many countries will need to modernize their rail transport rigorously and ensure the proper coordination of passenger and goods transport on the railway network. Dedicated freight rail links could be the solution in some cases.

Air transport and maritime transport are two fairly well-defined market segments in the international goods transport sector. Both supply chains must be properly connected to inland freight transport: inland waterways, roads and rail for maritime freight transport, and roads for air transport.

A breakthrough in intermodal freight transport is being hampered by numerous factors. There are problems with operations due to a lack of interconnectivity and interoperability. There are still wasted technological opportunities and perspectives for design and modelling. And, last but not least, there is a lack of interorganizational and international coordination, as a result of which the reliability, the speed and the costs of intermodal freight transport are suboptimal. This raises challenges for improving the implementation and public policies.

1.2 CONTENTS OF THE BOOK

In this book the challenges for successful development of intermodal freight transport are discussed. This theme is elaborated along three topics, which can be considered as main determinants for the performance of intermodal transport and its potential role as an alternative mode for road transport. The first chapters of the book are devoted to an overview of the present role of intermodal freight transport operations and elaborate on the structure of intermodal freight transport systems. They also outline future development paths to improve the performance of intermodal transport. The next chapters then go on to focus on some innovative approaches regarding the design of terminals and the modelling of intermodal networks.

Design and modelling tools are presented that can be used to analyse and support the performance of intermodal transport. The book closes with an analysis of the requirements to get promising intermodal innovations implemented and the policies needed to improve the competitiveness of intermodal transport. In particular the role of governments comes into play here. The book is structured according to these main lines and consists of three parts, each dealing with one of these topics. This structure can also be recognized in the subtitle of the book.

Part I: Intermodal Transport Operations

The current operations of intermodal freight transport are not the same in different parts of the world. State-of-the-art overviews are presented for the European Union, the United States and Japan. In addition, issues of hinterland network developments, bundling of freight flows and terminal handling quality are dealt with.

The first contribution in this part of the book, Chapter 2, presented by Johan Woxenius and Fredrik Bärthel, gives an overview of the structure and operations in the intermodal road–rail transport sector in the European Union. Their presentation is based on a system approach in which, successively, the system elements of actors, activities and resources are used as a framework to describe and analyse the structure of the intermodal transport sector. The argumentation is empirically supported by previous market studies of the authors covering in-depth interviews with key players involved in intermodal transport. The chapter starts with a description of the actors of the demand and supply side of intermodal road–rail transport. The role and activities of these actors are explained and typical differences in their role and position in a variety of European countries are discussed. The types of resources needed to offer intermodal road–rail transport services are elaborated. The way in which these resources are used are part of the operational principles of designing networks, that is, the production models for intermodal transport services (for example direct or shuttle train operations or hub-and-spoke operations). A major observation from this overview is that intermodal road–rail transport is a rather complex system, partly due to the involvement of many actors and different kinds of resources. Deregulation of the sector has changed the structure to the benefit of the sector and more changes can be expected according to Woxenius and Bärthel. However, many barriers for further growth of intermodal road–rail transport must still be overcome, for example, low infrastructural interoperability, missing infrastructural links and missing access to attractive time slots, lack of standardization of load units, lack of information systems and inefficient administrative procedures. The authors conclude that the future of road–rail transport will also strongly depend on developments affecting the competitiveness of road transport.

In Chapter 3 Latta Chatterjee and T.R. Lakshmanan discuss the origin, the development and prospects of intermodal transport in the United States. In their contribution the driving forces for intermodal transport are explicitly addressed. The authors argue that the interplay of broader forces of economic evaluation, technological changes, institutional and organizational developments, as well as specific and changing conditions of the transport system in the United States, have shaped the interest in intermodal transport. Globally organized production and a shift from supply-oriented (mass) manufacturing to high value-added custom-oriented manufacturing have changed logistic supply chains significantly. With its potential for integrating multiple modes, intermodal transport seems to offer a flexible response to the supply chain requirements in the global production and distribution system. Of course containerization has revolutionized intermodal transport, but other technological innovations in transport and communication have greatly enabled improved performances of intermodal transport as well. Deregulation of the US transport sector has also stimulated intermodal transport. These impacts are underpinned by an interpretative statistical overview of developments in freight transport, showing recent trends in intermodal transport in the United States. The chapter proceeds with an analysis of emerging developments in US intermodal transport in the context of observed and emerging technological, institutional and organizational factors. In addition, policy and strategic issues related to the future of intermodal transport are explored, attempting to identify the enabling role of the public sector. Chatterjee and Lakshmanan conclude that extending the role of intermodal transport would be desirable if the physical, organizational and information infrastructure structures across a network were integrated in an optimal way in order to reduce transaction costs and maximize operational efficiencies. This would translate into lower costs and an increase in the competitiveness of US firms in the global marketplace.

In Chapter 4 Eiichi Taniguchi and Toshinori Nemoto give an insight into the position of intermodal freight transport in Japan. Its role in the total transport system is very modest and examples of intermodal transport services are still rather rare. Indeed the potential benefits of intermodal transport are acknowledged, but according to the authors the exchange of modes in terminals is a relatively expensive operation, making intermodal transport only attractive for long distances. Moreover, as opposed to the rail network, the road network in Japan has been significantly improved and trucking companies have improved their transport services. As a result, road transport has become very cost-efficient and competitive with rail transport. The successful examples of intermodal transport discussed by Taniguchi and Nemoto reflect rather exceptional conditions. Improvement of the intermodal transport infrastructure, including in particular improvement of access routes to railway stations and seaports, are considered as the most crucial measures to stimulate intermodal transport.

In Chapter 5 Theo Notteboom zooms in on a very interesting and important market segment of intermodal transport, that is, hinterland transport of seaports. Transport of containers between the seaport and a place in the hinterland is in fact the most developed market for intermodal transport, and also definitely today the most dynamic market. Since market players in the maritime industry have identified inland logistics as one of the most promising areas still left in which to cut costs, to add value and to increase profitability, interest in landside operations has increased significantly. In their search for efficient inland services, shipping lines, transport operators, port authorities and shippers have come up with different network solutions leading to new dynamics in transport system development. The bundling of freight flows in a limited number of transport nodes proves to be one of the main driving forces in this development. Notteboom elaborates the role of freight bundling in designing intermodal services and uses these conceptual notions to discuss the hinterland network developments in intermodal rail and barge transport for the Hamburg–Le Havre port range.

In Chapter 6 Bart Wiegmans, Peter Nijkamp and Piet Rietveld deal with the terminals in the intermodal transport chain. They address the quality of services of container terminals as a competitive asset. Low container handling prices are a major competitive factor, but offering additional and high-quality services has gained importance in this very competitive business of container handling. Quantitative information on quality features of terminals is rather rare and therefore the authors suggest an approach to measure container terminal service quality and to determine critical performance conditions. The chapter starts with a definition of terminal service quality and presents the SERVQUAL model as a framework to analyse the terminal service quality. This SERVQUAL model comes from marketing theory and has been adapted to give an operational view on the judgement of service quality of container terminals by terminal operators. The service quality analysis is applied to maritime (deep-sea shipping) terminals and continental (barge and rail) terminals. Reliability is a critical performance condition for all types of terminals, but differences between the terminals exist. The authors conclude that the terminal quality measurement should be incorporated with methods to measure the performance in the total transport chain.

Part II: Design and Modelling

When in general situations are suboptimal, technology often is mobilized to solve current problems and create better solutions. This implies challenges for design and modelling. This second part presents an overview.

The contribution of Joan Rijsenbrij, Chapter 7, discusses the future strategies of container terminals in seaports to accommodate growing transport volumes. This discussion raises the question of what kind of investments in handling facilities and inland infrastructure are desirable in ports. Rijsenbrij elaborates this intriguing issue by postulating that the future scale of vessels and inland transport vehicles plays a major role. In reviewing the impact of scale developments he observes that vessel size development has had significant influence on the design of handling facilities, such as the cranes and the internal transport systems, but it has also affected the infrastructure of the ports, for example the port entrance. Rijsenbrij argues that further scale developments are likely, but these developments will also demand more dramatic changes in the terminal handling systems, both at the waterside and the landside. The profitability of these new investments however seems rather uncertain, provided that terminal clients demand both lower costs and higher service levels. Following the scale developments of vessels by large investments in terminals in order to remain attractive for shipping lines may result in underutilization and financial losses. On the other hand, if the scale developments are not anticipated the service level may be endangered, resulting in a loss of customers and financial losses as well. Rijsenbrij believes that the answer to this dilemma could be found in establishing more cooperative structures between the major participants in the door-to-door chain, where increasing the vessel size is no longer a completely unilateral decision of the shipping line.

In Chapter 8 Klaus-Peter Franke presents a technical solution for a new logistic concept of hinterland transport, where intermodal transport innovations in the seaport are combined with new developments in the hinterland. A key element of this concept is to use land in container ports more efficiently, because with increasing throughputs at terminals and vessels becoming bigger and bigger, storage in container ports is becoming more and more land-consuming, and has driven many container ports to their spatial limits. The main idea of this concept being launched in the United States is to split container ports into an Efficient Marine Terminal part ashore and an Intermodal Interface Centre inland, both connected by a dedicated railway line. In this chapter Franke shows how this idea, named the Agile Port System, could be elaborated from a technical perspective to improve the performance of this logistic system, in both the Efficient Marine Terminal and the Intermodal Interface Centre. As for the Efficient Marine Terminal, a technology is proposed that enables containers to be transhipped between vessel and freight trains without the need to start moving the quay cranes along the vessel for positioning purposes. The big advantage of this concept is that yard transfer vehicles are not required, saving substantial machinery and labour costs. With respect to the Intermodal Interface Centre, a container handling technology is presented that allows for the transhipment of containers between trains instead of shunting wagons. As a result dwell-time of wagons can be significantly reduced, the handling speed can be remarkably increased and the amount of land required is much lower compared to shunting yards. With the container handling equipment proposed in these systems being of proven technology, the author concludes that it offers a great opportunity to realize a challenging logistical solution for high-throughput marine terminals in crowded locations.

In Chapter 9 Ekki Kreutzberger elaborates a conceptual approach to identify promising intermodal rail and barge network operations. He observes that particularly in the 1990s there has been a strong emphasis on technical innovations to improve the performance of intermodal transport. Many ideas, such as new types of terminals, trains, barges and storage and transport systems, have been proposed, but most of them were not implemented. However, despite the slow pace of implementation, Kreutzberger argues and demonstrates that a more efficient load unit exchange can create important advantages for link operations in the network in such a way that it can improve the cost and quality of door-to-door intermodal operations.

The possible synergy between exchange and network operations is addressed and from this perspective the author emphasizes the need for a reorientation in the choice of bundling concepts by train and barge operators. This issue of bundling of freight is elaborated through the relation between network volumes, transport frequencies, scale of transport and network layout. A typology of bundling concepts and a mathematical formulation of the bundling effects are presented, and for rail transport also results of performance and cost calculations. One of the results is that, given one daily service on each transport relation, hub-and-spoke concepts have the lowest main modality costs for networks with medium-sized flows, line concepts and for networks for small flows. The network design logic presented in this chapter has a somewhat different approach than existing network design research. As a result the author ends with some recommendations focusing on methodological issues. A main suggestion is to strengthen the quantitative consistency between the entities of network volumes, transport frequencies and the scale of transport units in network design models and to let this relation be influenced by the choice of bundling concepts.

In Chapter 10 Arne Jensen develops a conceptual and methodological framework for the design and evaluation of intermodal freight transport systems. This theoretical-oriented framework can be considered as a generic toolbox, which can be used in a practical way. It assumes that any transport system has to compete for customers and therefore competitiveness plays a crucial role in this system design approach. The author introduces two notions to operationalize the competitiveness or viability of a new intermodal transport system. These are the concepts of significant, sustainable competitive advantage (SSCA) and market entry ability (MEA). The SSCA concept assumes that shippers evaluate transport performance in a multidimensional way and that cost, transport quality and market orientation are important performance dimensions. The MEA concept refers to ways to avoid or overcome entry and survival problems. Jensen demonstrates how these concepts can be applied in the system design process to specify the features of a new intermodal transport system that has promising market perspectives. This design approach seems not only applicable for new transport systems, but can also be used to modify existing systems. An original feature of this approach is that it actually integrates a methodology of transport system design and transport system evaluation. This means that if this framework is used properly, costly mistakes can be avoided in the design phase of transport system development.

In Chapter 11 Florian Schwarz sheds light on the issue of modelling intermodal freight transport. In the field of transport modelling intermodal freight network modelling is a relatively new research area, but due to a wide range of problems addressed by these models different modelling approaches exist. Schwarz argues that the choice of a model should be carefully based on the objective of the model and the actors' point of view, because many different actors are involved in intermodal transport: from policy decision makers, who set the legal framework for freight transport, to different actors organizing and operating intermodal transport chains, to shippers, that produce the demand for transport. Also the planning horizon of the model determines possible modelling approaches. In addition, the author emphasizes the role which different network structures can play in modelling. The chapter provides an overview of contemporary modelling approaches for intermodal freight networks, discussing the models that make use of geographic information systems in more detail. The rest of the chapter is used to present a new approach for modelling of intermodal transport networks for seaport hinterland container traffic, focusing on trimodal transport networks, combining barge, rail and road transport within the same transport chain. This modelling approach is based on using both geographic information about the available transport infrastructure for road, rail and inland navigation, and detailed information about necessary processes within intermodal transport chains.

Part III: Implementation and Policy

Many technological designs and models created on paper are never implemented. Apparently there are barriers for increasing the scope of intermodal freight transport. This third part deals with interconnectivity and interoperability as critical success factors, development strategies, information technology and policy challenges for innovations in intermodal innovations.

In Chapter 12 Bryan Stone reviews a number of important barriers to efficient intermodal transport. He emphasizes in particular two issues, which are inherent to the structure of an intermodal transport system and therefore can be considered as critical success factors, namely interconnectivity and interoperability. His chapter starts with a brief historical overview of the development process of transport and the critical conditions that enabled this new transport mode to take off in those early days. Of course maritime containerization has paved the way to intermodal transport as we know it today, but the container was, according to Stone, just one element of the new vision to integrate modes. Maclean, founder of Sealand in 1955, created interconnectivity and imposed interoperable equipment, although it was still in his own closed system. The author moves on to highlight the different types and causes of interconnectivity and interoperability problems, thereby also comparing the situations in Europe and the United States. As the liner shipping industry moved rapidly to intermodal operations in a short space of time, interoperability within the chosen system was achieved rapidly. As far as the integration of the land-based transport systems is concerned, their interconnectivity and interoperability have been and still are more problematic, particularly with regard to the railways in Europe. Stone believes that EU legislation should solve these problems, as unsolved interconnectivity and interoperability issues create additional burdens to efficient intermodal freight operations and restrict the competitiveness of intermodal transport with road transport.

Intermodal transport is a typical multi-actor business, in which many organizations with different interests, cultures and core activities are involved. Coordination of the processes of these organizations and their relationships is a key element for the performance of intermodal transport. In Chapter 13 Mariëlle den Hengst addresses this important issue of interorganizational coordination and discusses the opportunities of information technology to change and support interorganizational coordination. Information and communication technology enables organizations to decrease costs and increase capabilities, and thus to change their interorganizational coordination. The author starts with a theoretical framework on interorganizational coordination. Within this framework the direction in which interorganizational coordination will change due to the impact of information and communication technology (ICT) is indicated. The framework is used to design an ICT-based system to support interorganizational coordination. The model base basically consists of an algorithm to find a transport solution that matches a transport request, incorporating several criteria to indicate the degree to which the transport solution meets the requirements of the transport request. In addition, the algorithm and the information structure have been translated into a prototype to demonstrate the possibilities of ICT support to strategic coordination processes. Both the framework and the prototype have been applied to the container transport industry for evaluation.

In Chapter 14 Dimitrios Tsamboulas investigates ways and possible strategies to develop intermodal transport in Europe further and to increase its modal share. Tsamboulas summarizes the unsatisfactory current status of intermodal transport quality and limited use as a result of poor infrastructural inheritance, poor levels of interoperability, fragmentation of operational control, separation of operational control from responsibility and institutional arrangements that are unclear and continuously changing, due to their transitional nature. However, the intermodal transport environment as well as the policy framework within which European intermodal transport operates are gradually changing, and create opportunities for new products and markets in intermodal transport.

Five promising areas are being identified and discussed: the role of railways as traction providers, short-distance intermodal services, intermodal services for small shipments, integration of air transport into intermodal transport chains and new trends in short-sea shipping services. In addition, Tsamboulas addresses a number of general topics and related actions for intermodal transport development. Based on this overview of issues he formulates priority actions and a policy action plan. His conclusion is that the development of intermodal transport in Europe needs the combination of the top-down approach, for example European Commission policies and legislation, and the bottom-up approach, which is the identification of the needs of the intermodal transport market actors. Collaboration between all actors, including private and public bodies, is an important condition and point of departure for this development strategy.

In the final contribution to this book, Chapter 15, José Holguin-Veras, Robert Paaswell and Anthony Perl explore the role of government in fostering intermodal transport innovation and research. The authors highlight the factors that enable or constrain intermodal innovations in the American freight transportation sector. The institutional setting, the industry structure, and government–freight industry dynamics in transportation policy can influence these innovations. Once the workings of these factors have been highlighted, key challenges to intermodal innovation are identified and a set of possible approaches to overcoming them is considered. The conclusion assesses how these forces play out in other socio-economic environments. A major finding is that multiple implementation paths to innovation are possible. These policy recommendations to stimulate and implement intermodal innovations are not only applicable to the United States, but seem to have a much wider interest.

PART I

Intermodal transport operations

2. Intermodal road–rail transport in the European Union

Johan Woxenius and Fredrik Bärthel

2.1 INTRODUCTION

An intermodal freight transport system is characterized by the subsequent use of different traffic modes for moving goods stowed into an intermodal loading unit (ILU) from the consignor to the consignee. It involves a wide variety of activities, actors and resources, which implies a certain degree of technological as well as organizational complexity. Other features are the derived demand, dependency on surrounding activity systems and in Europe a typical lack of formal systems management as well as of objectives shared by all actors.

European intermodal road–rail freight transport (EIT) is regarded by many as the universal solution to a wide range of problems related to road freight transport as well as to the financial problems of national railway freight operations. The European Commission estimates that external effects from road transport in the EU cost €250 billion annually, of which half relates to congestion. As an example, Van Schijndel and Dinwoodie (2000) claim that 10 per cent of lorry operating time in the Netherlands is spent in congested conditions. Supporting words have been abundant and a truly wide range of political instruments have been used for promoting EIT but they have still not created a truly level playing field for competition with road transport. On the contrary, political promises that were not delivered have caused disillusion within the industry although initiatives like the Marco Polo Programme, the German road toll (the LKW Maut) and the French subsidy to forwarders using EIT are promising.

The high expectations of increased EIT flows, in particular from political actors, have not been fulfilled although the industry has shown substantial growth over a number of years. According to the European Commission (2002), EIT almost doubled from 33 to 64 billion metric tonnes-km between 1990 and 2000, accounting for 2.2 per cent of the total transport performance in the EU in the latter year. The transport markets that have been successfully penetrated are mostly related to Alpine crossings and transport between the main seaports and their hinterlands (Eurostat 2002).

There are many reasons for the unsatisfactory development (Bukold 1993 and 1996; Henstra and Woxenius 1999; Zapp 1999):

- time and cost handicap due to the transshipments;
- inferior frequency;
- lack of standardization of swap bodies;
- rigidity of government-owned railways;
- fear of internal competition with wagon-load transport within railways;
- inadequate long-term stable access to rail capacity at strategic times; and
- lack of realization of political promises.

In previous theoretical work (Woxenius 1994), the systems approach (Churchman 1979) and the actor approach (Gadde and Håkansson 1992) have been used to develop a three-element approach. The elements consist of actors, activities and resources, and they have been found useful as starting points for analyses of industrial structures with different purposes. This chapter deals with the whole transport chain although the focus is stronger on the core of EIT – terminal handling and rail haulage – and from the moment the ILU is filled to the moment it is emptied. The focus is also on the 'conventional' EIT industry with unaccompanied haulage of goods loaded in containers, swap bodies and semi-trailers offered to an open market. This limitation implies that ILUs are seen as part of the goods and not explicitly as a system resource. The focus is also restricted to transport chains including rail transport. Inland or short-sea shipping in combination with road transport are intermodal transport chains which are not being discussed.

The empirical foundation for the description and analysis of the market is a study carried out in 1994 (Woxenius 1994) and an update and revision in 2002 (Woxenius and Bärthel 2002). The study in 1994 was based upon 20 structured interviews with officials of EIT companies, forwarders, terminal companies and shippers as well as upon scientific literature, public statistics, annual reports and brochures. The update was based upon information from journals, Internet sites and interviews with industry representatives along with continuous coverage of the industry while addressing related research questions.

2.2 THE MARKET AND THE ACTORS

The EIT system may be described by its core activities: pre- and post-haulage by road (PPH), transshipment, rail haulage, coordination activities and, where applicable, sea transport. In addition, infrastructure and supporting activities such as lease of equipment, inspection, cleaning, mending and empty stacking of ILUs are needed for the system to work. Stuffing of goods in ILUs is performed by the shipper or by the forwarder if the goods are consolidated in its general cargo terminal and not included in the system model.

Although EIT by definition involves at least two traffic modes, the focus here is on the core of EIT, as shown in Figure 2.1, including rail haulage and transshipments. This is what distinguishes EIT from all-road transport and the road–sea combination. Most intermodal research implicitly takes this perspective, although studies on PPH by road have been published for instance by Morlok and Spasovic (1994), Niérat (1997) and Taylor et al. (2002).

The Demand Side of the Core of the EIT Market

The role of the shippers in the EIT system is largely determined by the size of their shipments. Shippers sending full ILUs (15–35 tonnes depending on type of ILU and country) obviously take an interest in the system, while customers sending general cargo typically do not know or care how their consignments are forwarded. Apart from stuffing and stripping and supplying the ILUs, the activities occasionally performed by shippers include transshipment at private sidings and PPH. Some large shippers arrange their own logistics, maintaining a forwarding role, and exceptionally, like IKEA, they coordinate the core of EIT.

The role of the forwarders, sometimes referred to as logistics service providers, is to act as an intermediary in the transaction of transport services between shippers and operators supplying physical transport and transshipment services. The definition of the market used here implies that

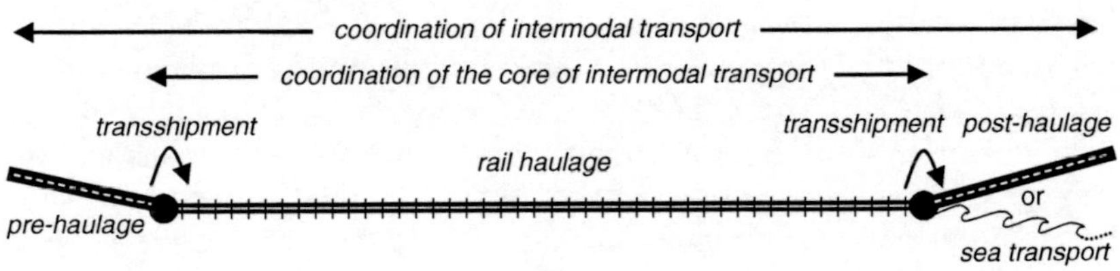

Figure 2.1 A system model focusing on activities in the intermodal chain

forwarders, mediating the specific demands from a multitude of shippers, can be called 'proxy customers' (Ohnell and Woxenius 2003) and are thus part of the demand side.

Traditionally forwarders perform activities such as physical and administrative consolidation of small consignments, documentation, warehousing and supplying ILUs. Ties to the hauliers have traditionally been very strong for the land transport segment, but increasingly they are traffic mode neutral. Many forwarders also operate lorries themselves and are thus both forwarders and hauliers. Exceptionally, like Hangartner (owned by German Railways, DB, since 2002), they operate intermodal terminals and coordinate the core of EIT.

Forwarders have a dominant position in the transport system, but their scale is often overestimated since they are wholesalers and they show large turnover figures, but figures of value added, number of employees or the balance sheet are not equivalent to, for instance, those of the railway companies. This is especially true for the much-hyped but still rather insignificant fourth-party logistics service providers or 'non-asset-based operators', such as Exel, GeoLogistics and Celexor, which take on a coordinating role only and subcontract all physical activities.

In EIT, forwarders act on different markets defined by size of consignments, geography or type of ILU. The traditional forwarders such as Schenker, DHL (mainly the former Danzas part) and Kühne and Nagel, have a history of close connections to road hauliers and use EIT as part of some regular services, as reserve capacity or on customers' request. These large forwarders attempt to offer all types of transport between all geographical areas. The wide range of transport on offer implies that the traditional forwarder covers the full-truckload, part-load and general cargo as well as parcel segments. Mergers and acquisitions to form players with larger geographical and service scope have created a new picture in which the German state maintains a very dominant position in Northern Europe.

Semi-trailer operators such as Euroute and GT Spedition usually own semi-trailers and buy the haulage services from small hauliers, short-sea shipping lines or intermodal operators. They have terminals for grouping shipments, however, on a smaller scale than the traditional forwarders since they primarily move part-loads and full loads. Geographically, they often specialize in transport between two countries and cooperate bilaterally with a similarly focused forwarder.

The business orientation of the swap body operators is to transport full loads directly between major industrial areas. The road haul costs of swap bodies is higher than for semi-trailers and they are less suitable for roll-on/roll-off shipping, which means that this segment is most tightly connected to EIT.

Container shipping lines and their shipping agencies have shown a particular interest in extending their control to port operations and hinterland transport. Consequently, Maersk-Sealand and P&O Nedlloyd are partners in intermodal train operators specializing in shuttles to and from the big ports.

It should be noted, though, that there are vast differences in the forwarding role between the national markets. In Germany, France and Sweden large traditional forwarders dominate, while Dutch forwarders, to a larger extent, have vehicles of their own, combining the forwarding and haulier roles. Italy and Spain have almost as many hauliers as lorries and lack a strong forwarding industry although the trend is to cooperate in different forms of alliances.

Beside information and communication technology (ICT) systems for controlling the flows, resources controlled by forwarders are mainly general cargo terminals and ILUs.

The size of hauliers varies widely between European countries. In Germany, Italy, Spain and Sweden the hauliers are of small or moderate size, while the French and Dutch road transport market is dominated by somewhat larger hauliers. In domestic transport, hauliers are often contracted for a long-distance haul and decide whether to subcontract an intermodal operator. In international EIT, hauliers have a role of supplying the forwarder with one local road haulage, while another haulier is contracted for the other haul. Hauliers can hence be placed both on the demand and the supply side of the market.

The resources of the hauliers vary according to their size. Some hauliers have specialized in hauling one type of ILU, while other larger companies possess vehicles for all types of transport. Other activities performed are supplying ILUs and, occasionally, operating terminals. With horizontal transshipment systems like the Swiss–Austrian Mobiler and the French Modalohr, the hauliers will become more important for the transshipment activity.

The Supply Side of the Core of the EIT Market

The supply side of the EIT market is traditionally divided between companies based upon rail and road transport respectively. Considering regulated monopolies and the historic scope of concessions, the borderlines between market segments have been drawn according to types of ILU and geographical markets (Bukold 1996). Due to transport policy deregulation in the EU, this practice is now diminishing (Aastrup 2002).

The classic role of the rail operators has been to sell rail haulage between intermodal transshipment terminals. They also operate terminals and supply rail wagons. In addition, the railway companies have owner interests in virtually all of the other actor categories needed for producing EIT services.

The intermodal operators are obviously of particular interest to this study. When the maritime or ISO container was introduced in the 1960s, the national railway companies founded container transport companies in order to offer complementary land transport. Intercontainer, later Intercontainer-Interfrigo (ICF), was founded for international transport and companies like Transfracht in Germany, Compagnie Nouvelle de Cadres (CNC) in France (founded in 1948 for moving smaller containers) and Italcontainer in Italy were founded for domestic transport. In Scandinavia, faced with less rigid transport regulations, the railways offer transport of all types of ILUs. The railways and the Norwegian intermodal operator CargoNet retail to shippers, while CargoNet's Swedish subsidiary Rail Combi wholesales the core of EIT.

ICF and the national container companies have their base in the transport of maritime containers to and from seaports, but they also offer transport of containers, swap bodies and to some extent semi-trailers between European inland terminals. Deregulation implies that the intermodal operators in the railway family are less restricted by national borders, and ICF now operates domestic trains, while container companies compete for border-crossing flows.

Forwarders and hauliers established their own national companies such as CEMAT (in 1953) in Italy, Trailstar (in 1964) in the Netherlands, TRW (in 1965) in Belgium, Novatrans (in 1966) in France, HUPAC (in 1967) in Switzerland and Kombiverkehr (in 1969) in Germany (Wenger 2001). The original purpose of these organizations was to organize the transport services for which the road-based transport companies had concessions. Now in the post-regulation days, they still coordinate the core of EIT, but due to the fact that most hauliers are small companies, their role as a strong counterpart to the railways in negotiations is more important. This goal is, however, rarely stated since the national railways usually hold at least a minority share of the companies. In the case of German Kombiverkehr, DB now owns 50 per cent of the company. Since 1970, the companies coordinate their international operations through the International Union of combined Road–Rail companies (UIRR). Earlier, the UIRR companies worked as pure intermediaries, but increasingly they carry the commercial risk of filling trains.

Many, not least the European Commission, entertain hopes that new intermodal operators will emerge onto the scene. However, high initial investments, large economies of scale, lack of clearly established market shares and the industry's currently low profitability keep new entrants out of the picture. Also the lack of long-term transport policies and the strong market position of the national railways discourage private investments. One exception has been that American companies have tried unsuccessfully to practise their domestic intermodal experiences in Europe. There are also some genuine new actors such as IKEA Rail, NeCoSS and Hafen und Güterverkehr Köln. The general trend, though, is that the already active European actors find new markets or extend their scope of services. The present actors have also formed alliances, such as Polzug, Metrans, Hansa Hungarian Container Express, TARES and European Rail Shuttle in order to get access to critical resources, knowledge or clearly established shipper contacts in line with the suggestions of Gifford and Stalebrink (2002).

In general, the new intermodal operators are found in the northern part of Europe and in particular in the large market for hinterland transport of maritime containers related to the ports of Hamburg, Bremerhaven, Rotterdam and Antwerp. The ports themselves have also demonstrated their interest in hinterland transport by rail. In the case of Germany, for instance, the port operator HHLA has bought 50 per cent of Transfracht from DB. These initiatives all aim at 'cherry-picking' EIT: they do not capture new market shares from road transport, but rather from existing intermodal services.

Most terminals are operated by actors that also maintain other roles, but increasingly by dedicated terminal operators. One category is container port operators such as PSA of Singapore, Hutchison of Hong Kong and American CSX World Terminals that build global networks. Another category is shipping lines that operate port terminals supporting their own shipping operations, but also as businesses in their own right in subsidiaries such as APM Terminals (Maersk), P&O Ports and Evergreen Ports. In line with the so-called dry-port concept, these port operators might expand to inland terminals on a large scale. Yet another category is local companies operating a single terminal, often with local authorities, rail or intermodal operators, hauliers and dominant shippers as co-owners.

So far most of the rolling stock has been supplied by the rail or intermodal operators, but there is a clear tendency towards avoiding large investments by using leasing companies offering engines and wagons. A clearer actor role concerning rail traction is also distinguishable with many small rail companies, often with a short-line origin. The actor analysis is presented in the actor version of Figure 2.2.

In more detail, the actors and their activities are better presented in a table. As an example, the Swedish intermodal operators are presented in Table 2.1.

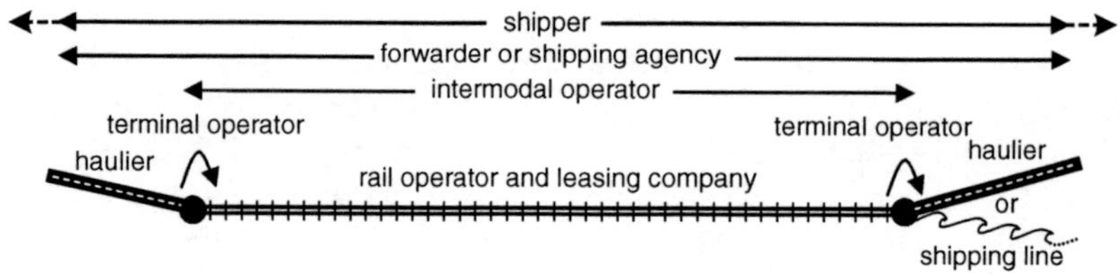

Figure 2.2 *A system model focusing on actors in the intermodal chain*

Table 2.1 *The Swedish intermodal operators and their activities*

Operator Activity	Green Cargo (GC) Shuttles	GC Light-combi	(GC) Recycling	Gothia Rail	Intercontainer Scandinavia	Rail Combi	Swe-Kombi	Vänerexpressen	IKEA Rail	TGOJ Trafik
PPH	D	D	*D*		SD/SI	*SD*		D	SI	
Transshipment	D	D	D		SD/SI	D/I	*SD/SI*	SD	I	
Terminal services		D	D			D/I				
Rail haulage	D	D	D		SD/SI		*SD/SI*	D	SI	D
Market to shippers	D	D	D		D/I			D	*I*	
Coordinate EIT		D	D	I	D/I				I	
Coord. EIT core	D	D	D		D/I	D/I	*D/I*	D	I	
Supply ILUs		D							I	
Supply rail wagons	D	D	D	I	D/I		*SD/SI*	D	I	D/I
Supply rail engines	D	D	D		SD/SI		*SD/SI*	D	SI	D/I
Launched, year	2002	1998	2000	1996	1993	1992	1990	1998	2001	
Closed, year		2001		2000			2003		2004	

Note: D: domestic, I: international, *italics*: exceptional cases, S: by subcontractor.

The Marketplace

The way EIT providers approach the shippers varies depending on whether the service is domestic or international and also on the history and strategies of the intermodal operators. ICF, CNC and CargoNet offer their services to shippers or intermediaries, while the UIRR companies, Transfracht, Italcontainer, Rail Combi and most of the new entrants strictly limit their services to forwarders, shipping agencies and hauliers. On demand, the former operators offer PPH, while the latter ones leave this to their customers. The railways often maintain a forwarding role and offer door-to-door EIT.

On the way to the shippers the services are bundled in different ways. The principles for this bundling are shown in Figure 2.3, where dotted lines indicate occasional supplier relations.

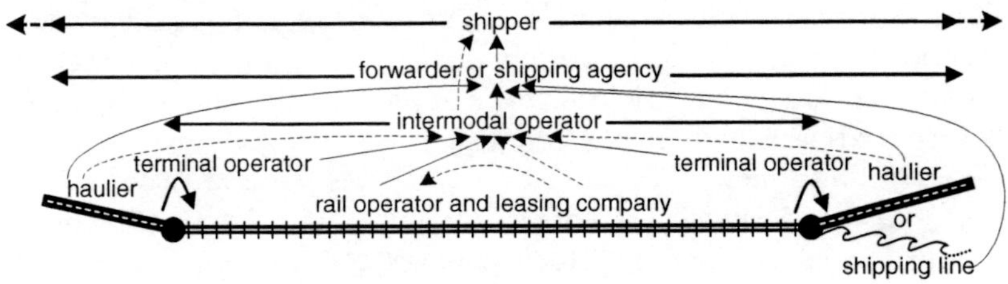

Figure 2.3 A system model focusing on actors with typical supplier relations in the intermodal chain

2.3 THE PRODUCTION SYSTEM

The physical components of the European EIT system definitely qualify as mature technology. Lorries are either semi-trailer tractors, flatbed container lorries or swap body lorries equipped with air suspension. Rail engines are of standard freight design, occasionally capable of multi-current power supply, while rail wagons are either pocket wagons for semi-trailers or flatbed wagons for containers and swap bodies. In addition, rail wagons for special applications, mainly horizontal transshipment, have been developed, but except for turntable wagons (for example ACTS), bimodal boggies for trailers (for example Wabash's RoadRailer as implemented by BTZ) and wagons for roll-on/roll-off (RoRo) loading (for example Modalohr), very few are in use. In case of sea transport a ship is obviously needed.

The vast majority of terminals base their operations on gantry cranes and reach stackers. Many suggestions for new intermodal transshipment technologies have been presented (for overviews and evaluations, see Ballis and Golias 2002; Bontekoning and Kreutzberger 1999; Woxenius 1997), but very few have been commercially implemented. Most new technologies aim at either small-scale and low-cost operations or large-scale, automated and fast applications. For the mid-range terminals, say 50 000–200 000 transshipments a year, conventional technologies are sufficient for the current use with transshipments during some hours in the morning and in the late afternoon.

Beside transshipment technologies, ICT systems attract most attention. Railways were among the really early users of computers, but mainly of mainframes controlling their own production and administration. Electronic data interchange connections with customers are of rather recent date. Efficient ICT systems are vital to forwarders controlling huge numbers of small consignments for many shippers, but less crucial to hauliers, rail and intermodal operators which can move a single container or some 80 boxes in a shuttle train for a limited number of customers. The resource analysis is presented in Figure 2.4.

In addition to these physical resources, operations clearly depend on a large number of skilled employees, organizational know-how, brands, developed procedures and legal agreements as well as permissions and train slots from authorities. Road and rail infrastructure is needed to accomplish EIT, but as this is supplied by government in exchange for user charges and shared with passenger and other freight operations, it is not treated as a resource.

About 100 of the 2000 European intermodal terminals correspond to 90 per cent of the total freight volumes (Nelldal et al. 2000) and the challenge is to offer services to smaller terminals. This underlines the importance of fast train-forming, marshalling and handling techniques to facilitate market coverage and a high average speed (for example Siegmann and Tänzler 1996). In order to combine economies of scale and frequency in the rail haul and a dense terminal network, the EIT industry uses a

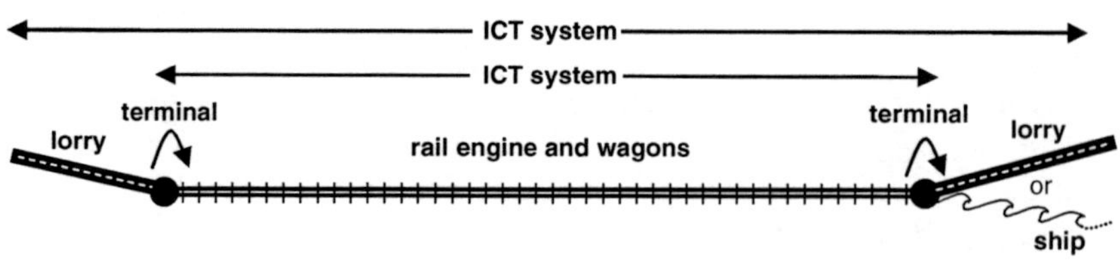

Figure 2.4 A system model focusing on resources in the intermodal chain

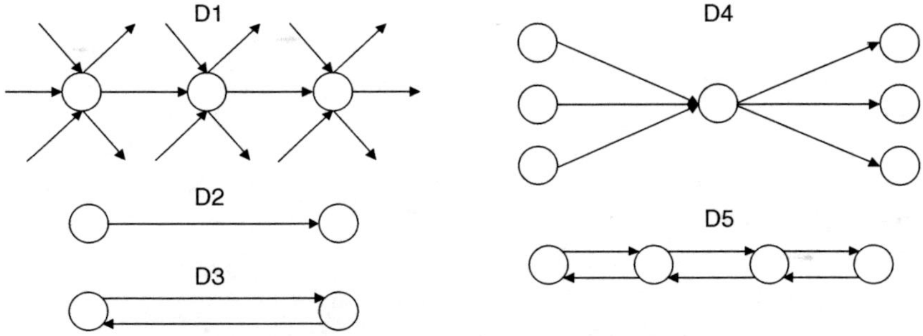

Figure 2.5 *Network designs for EIT: (D1) hierarchic network, (D2) direct connection, (D3) shuttle train, (D4) hub-and-spoke network and (D5) transport corridor*

number of operational principles when they design their networks. The design principles are schematically illustrated in Figure 2.5.

The deregulation of the European rail network has entailed a separation of the production systems for passenger and freight, in order to specialize and to avoid cross-subsidy. In the rail freight industry, the co-production of wagon-load and intermodal services has continuously decreased, due to the mono-functional rail terminals, the focus on full trains and diverging service requirements. The flexibility, earlier maintained through a combination of different wagon-load and intermodal services as well as a wide market coverage, are lost.

An operational design consisting of a hierarchic network (D1) forms the foundation in the conventional wagon-load network. The train sets are operated along routes with repeated shunting or marshalling operations. The trains stay at the terminals only briefly, requiring rapid handling or marshalling. The operator can choose among many different routes between the origin and destination terminal. The maximum degree of freedom is possible if the routes are dynamically allocated in real time as a function of actual demand.

Economies of scale are clearly present in rail transportation and since approximately 1990, EIT companies have abandoned their networks and focused on transport quality (primarily transport time and reliability), economies of scale and a high utilization rate for each train. Thereby the production philosophy has changed dramatically from conventional hierarchic networks towards a focus on shuttle trains or block trains between economic centres and ports.

The direct connection design (D2), aims at large flows transported directly between origin and destination terminals over relatively long distances. Direct connections require some 100 000 annual tonnes for daily departures, which limits this design to a small fraction of the total transport demand. The handling capacity requirements depend on how long the trains stay at the terminal and the conventional night-leap traffic reduces these requirements to a non-critical parameter.

The shuttle train design (D3) is a special application of D2 distinguished by the operation of fixed-formation train sets, operating specific origin–destination connections. This creates a base for reliable and cheap operations, since neither cost- and time-consuming shunting of wagons, nor sophisticated information systems, are needed. The timetable is not dependent on other transports and can easily be tailor-made for the customers, that is, there is a high degree of flexibility regarding time planning. EIT shuttles are used for: (1) transports of containers on high-volume connections between ports and their hinterland, for example the network operated by Transfracht and new entrants; (2) as infrastructure replacement, for example for rolling highway transit operations through the Alps and under the English Channel; and (3) as fixed-capacity trains in the railway networks, for example by CargoNet in Norway.

In the hub-and-spoke (H&S) design (D4) a centrally situated terminal is selected as hub and all transports pass through this terminal, where wagons are marshalled or ILUs transshipped between the trains. The advantage is good market coverage despite insufficient volumes for direct trains between the different origin and destination terminals. Rational marshalling or handling at the hub is crucial as it compensates for longer transport distances.

One application is CNC's network in France, in which Paris assumes the function as hub. The hub function, however, is not absolute since large parts of CNC's flows relate to the region of Paris. The transport network operated by ICF is based on two H&S networks, the Quality Net and the X-net, operated by block trains. The Quality Net is operated with 60 trains six days a week and connects 12 countries via a hub in Metz. The recently developed Cargo Express system in Switzerland, serving the market for high-value products over medium distances in co-production with wagonloads, is operated as a H&S system with fast day- and night-leaps through the Dänicken hub.

In the transport corridor design (D5), trains, sometimes called liner trains, make frequent stops along a corridor line and thus cover the intermediate markets and so enable PPH on shorter distances. Along the corridors, fixed train sets operate at a high frequency according to a tight and precise timetable. Transfer time must be kept at a minimum so as not to prolong the total transport time too much. Storage at the terminals is needed since road and rail operations must be detached. These trains are for dual transport markets – dispersed flows over long distances and dense flows over short distances – and by combining these markets, the service can attract enough flows for good resource utilization. Interconnected liner trains permit large areas to be covered at relatively low costs. The organization of such services, however, is difficult and needs to be tailored to the business. Corridor services could perhaps be considered as supplementary to the network of direct links, serving the less busy corridors. Empirically, the Swedish Light-combi concept shows that long distances, 650 km, can be covered during the night-leap including four intermediate stops (Bärthel and Woxenius 2003).

2.4 THE SIZE AND CHARACTER OF THE FREIGHT FLOWS

The transport performance in Europe increased from 1.4 trillion metric tonnes in 1970 to 3.1 trillion metric tonnes in 2000, that is, by 119 per cent, or 2.6 per cent per year (European Commission 2002). Fifty per cent of this transport work regards distances between 150 and 500 km and 20 per cent distances over 500 km. The market share of unimodal road transport, measured in metric tonnes, increased from 35 per cent in 1970 to 44 per cent in 2000 and also intra-European sea transport increased its market shares as shown in Figure 2.6. The transport performance of domestic sea transport, pipeline and rail transport and inland shipping was rather stable, implying significantly reduced market shares. In the case of rail transport, it decreased from 20 to 6 per cent.

The EIT flows have grown substantially and doubled in volume between 1990 and 2000 (European Commission 2002). Figure 2.7 shows the development between 1990 and 2002 for the largest operators in Europe. Notable are the large increase for the UIRR companies, the decreasing volumes for ICF and the large market share for the Swedish operator Rail Combi. Earlier estimates of the intermodal freight flows are often based on aggregated statistics of the UIRR companies and ICF. This was adequate until the beginning of the 1990s, but due to services by new intermodal operators and the railways themselves, for example the large flows of automobile parts to and from Spain, statistics must be dealt with in more detail.

Besides the price–quality ratio of competing transport modes, the competitiveness of EIT depends on geographical and demographical conditions. Conventional EIT, characterized by transshipment of unit loads by use of gantry cranes and reach stackers, full train night-leaps directly between terminals and services offered to shippers through intermediaries, is generally competitive at distances above 500 km (Van Klink and Van den

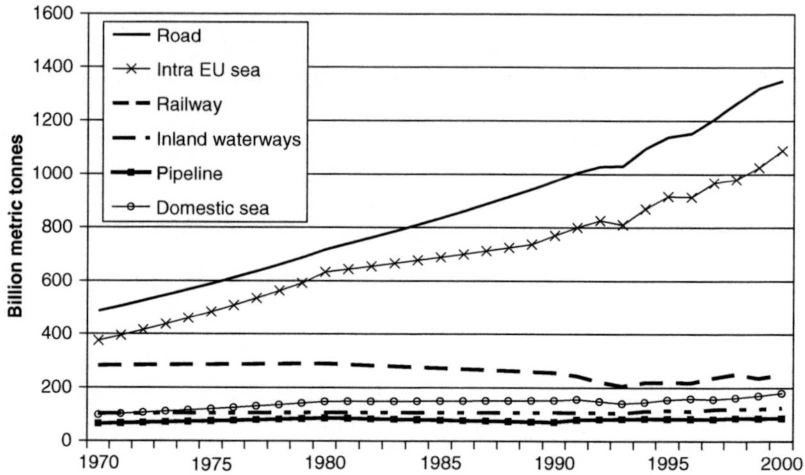

Source: Eurostat (2002).

Figure 2.6 Transport growth in the EU between 1970 and 2000 by transport mode (in billion metric tonnes)

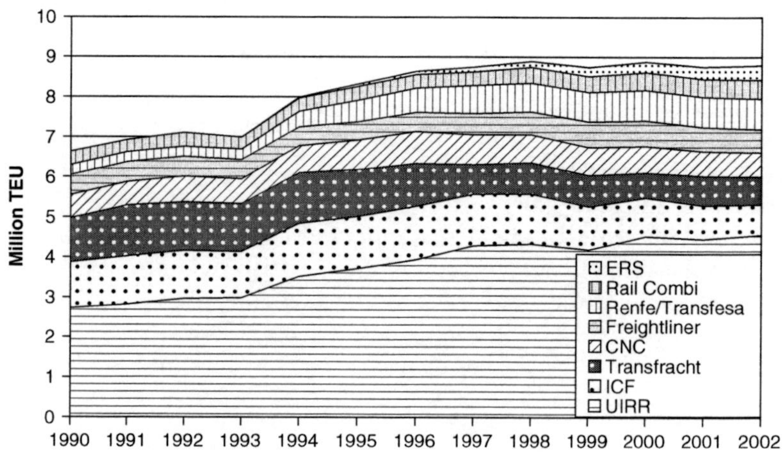

Note: Data from Italcontainer are not available.

Source: Intermodal transport operators.

Figure 2.7 Transported volumes (in TEU) of the major European intermodal transport operators, 1990–2002

Berg 1998). For container shuttles to and from ports, the distance is slightly shorter (Rutten 1998). The average distance for the largest EIT operator, ICF, was 784 km in 1991 and increased to 952 km in 2002. For domestic transport, the largest operator, Kombiverkehr, reported a break-even distance of 350 km in 1998. The average transport distance for the UIRR companies was 550 km domestically and 760 km internationally.

Germany holds a dominant position with almost half of Europe's domestic EIT, and even more so if EIT by inland waterways is included. In France domestic EIT operations are also substantial. Many countries, for example Belgium, the Netherlands and Denmark, are not large enough for competitive domestic EIT. Peripheral countries, like Italy, Spain, the UK and the Scandinavian countries, have rather substantial domestic networks with border crossings defined as gateways to other networks.

A few relations across the Alps dominate border-crossing EIT. Partly due to Swiss and Austrian regulation and tax policies, EIT has a large market share for the flows between Italy–Benelux and Italy–Germany, for example 50 per cent between Italy and Belgium. Other examples of large market shares for EIT are between Sweden and Italy with 60 per cent, Belgium and Spain with 30 per cent and Sweden and Belgium with 30 per cent (IQ 1998). A truly unexplored market is the triangle of France–Germany–Benelux, where the unimodal road flows are 100 times larger than the EIT flows (ibid.). The major EIT flows are presented in Figure 2.8.

It might be questioned whether this is a real network or some independent direct connections. Figure 2.8 also reveals the previous trend regarding the east–west corridors connecting the accession countries in Eastern Europe with the economic centres and ports in Western EU.

The general trend regarding types of ILUs transported by the UIRR reveals an increasing share of rolling highway and swap bodies at the expense of semi-trailers. Between 1995 and 2000 the number of swap bodies transported by the UIRR increased by 27 per cent to 1 367 000, compared to a decrease in semi-trailers of 32 per cent to 152 000 units. The use of semi-trailers is more common in France and Germany. In Germany, the shorter class C (7.15–7.82 m length) almost universally prevails, but elsewhere there is a clear trend towards an increasing share for Class A swap bodies of semi-trailer length.

2.5 SYNTHESIS AND OUTLOOK

Comparing the studies of 1994 and 2002, it is obvious that due to deregulation, changes have taken place in the EIT industry. Some 'cherry-pickers' have entered, some of them have left, while others maintain and develop

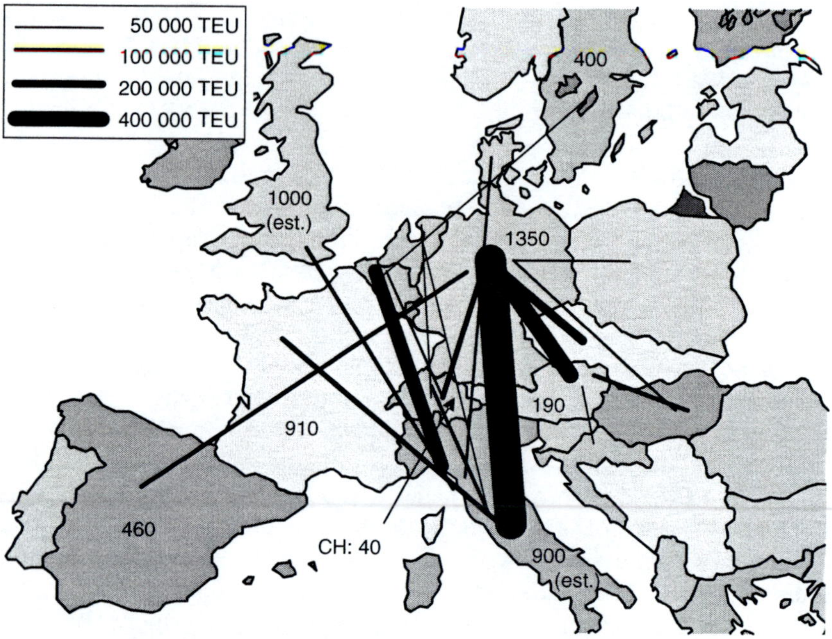

Source: Statistics from the operators and Eurostat (2002).

Figure 2.8 Major European intermodal transport flows in 1999 (flows exceeding 40 000 TEU/year), domestic flows (figures) and international bilateral flows (lines)

their position in the market. Above all, however, the large players have changed strategies, entered new markets or formed alliances which give much faster and more dramatic changes as well as a more scattered picture than in the monopoly days. In general, the new intermodal operators are found in the northern part of Europe and in particular in the large market for hinterland transport of maritime containers related to the large ports. The comparison reveals that the national railways have widened their scope, that less intermodal operators sell directly to shippers and that the forwarders' mediating role is strengthened.

Capital for intermodal equipment is found to be a major barrier for EIT operators (Golias and Yannis 1998). For a long time, rail wagons have been leased, but companies offering traction services, often with a short-line origin and leasing of locomotives, play a new and vital role in lowering the entry barriers for new entrants.

Moreover, a political discussion on whether terminals should be part of the infrastructure or of transport operations is initiated. This distinction

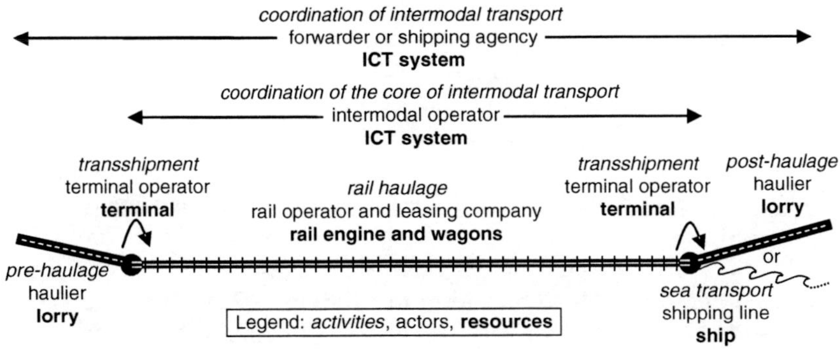

Figure 2.9 Results of a system analysis of the intermodal transport system applying the network approach

is crucial under the current EU regulatory framework, in which infrastructure is a government concern while operations should be open for competition. It might well end in a situation where the fixed terminal installations are supplied by public infrastructure providers at a marginal social cost, while the terminal operation is up for tender and commercially charged.

The statement that ICT is most essential to forwarders is in line with contemporary research by Patterson et al. (2003), who conclude that new ICT systems are more likely to be adopted by large and also by decentralized companies, rather than by small ones and hierarchies. It is then logical that the adaptation of ICT in the transportation sector is led by the large forwarders and neither by the small hailers nor by the hierarchic railways. Golob and Regan (2003) find that road transport companies operating large fleets are more likely to adapt ICT like EDI than, interestingly, those engaged in EIT.

Still, ICT systems are not unimportant to railways and hauliers. Applications making their own production and administrative processes more efficient, exchanging orders and billing information with the coordinating actors and supplying them with tracking and tracing data, are useful. Lack of tracking and tracing systems has often been argued to be the main competitive disadvantage for EIT, but just adding that capability will not solve all reliability issues. Tracking and tracing systems can only mitigate the consequences of reliability problems, not remove them.

The merger of Figures 2.1, 2.2 and 2.4 focusing on activities, actors and resources respectively results in the system model in Figure 2.9.

Concerning train operations, there is obviously no point in plying terminals when the train is already full with ILUs bound for a single terminal, but the question that arises is: how large are the flows needed for the shuttle train services and how are market coverage and train frequency affected? As a dedicated freight rail network emerges (European Commission 2001), 'night-leaps only' will be abandoned by sensible operators that do not allow trains to stand idle at terminals during the daytime. ICT improvements will facilitate flexible timetables for freight trains.

Attempts at lowering marginal costs by increasing train sizes are limited by the infrastructure, and increases must be matched against departure frequency and transshipment productivity gains (Ballis and Golias 2002). It is vital for the competitiveness of EIT that services with different characteristics can be co-produced (Trip and Bontekoning 2002) and the integration of different and flexible network designs can facilitate the utilization of economies of scale. For example, Liu et al. (2003) prove that hybrids of operating principles can save at least 10 per cent of the travel distance in consolidation networks, an issue also addressed by Houtman (2002).

Shippers usually argue that poor price and quality performance prevents them from using EIT (Ljungemyr 1995; Ludvigsen 1999), and that a substantial cost and/or quality leap, primarily regarding frequency and reliability, is necessary to improve the competitiveness of EIT (Konings and Kreutzberger 2001). The cost components obviously differ between the countries and companies, but the high proportion of fixed costs compared to unimodal lorry transport implies a break-even distance of 400–500 km. The PPH often constitutes 40 per cent of the total cost and the transshipment some additional 20 per cent (Persson 2003; Bergstrand 2001). The competitive disadvantages are particularly distinguished in border-crossing relations due to technical and organizational interoperability problems between the national rail systems. Substantial improvements have been achieved through the change towards shuttle and block train designs, but the most effective improvements have been obtained through an improved interorganizational cooperation between the European rail authorities (Vleugel et al. 2001; Hansson 2003).

From a supply-side perspective the main barriers for further growth of EIT are related to infrastructure, such as a lack of spatial coverage and terminals, insufficient infrastructural interoperability, some missing links and bad access to attractive slots. The lack of standardization of ILUs, information systems and administrative procedures are also hampering, as well as the remaining lack of competition for rail traction, despite EU efforts (Henstra and Woxenius 1999). The problems related to ILUs are acknowledged by the European Commission (2003) when proposing the European Intermodal Loading Unit, the EILU, combining the benefits of the ISO container with those of the swap body.

Demand for environment-friendly transport will affect the demand positively, but EIT cannot solely rely on its 'environmental friendliness' (IFEU and SGKV 2002). Once lorry engines can be made more energy-efficient and the discharge of emissions lessens, their currently superior operational efficiency might actually also make them superior from an environmental perspective. Moreover, on a local level, neighbours to intermodal terminals protest against the increased local traffic and related disturbances (Slack 1999). This implies that some present terminals have to operate during restricted hours and others have to be relocalized. New terminals will be built outside city centres or be designed for less noise emissions.

Nevertheless, the key to a prosperous EIT sector actually lies in the competing unimodal road transport sector. Governments clearly state that investments in roads to cope with increasing vehicle flows will not be realized, and road hauliers threatened by congestion will turn to the tracks to fulfil their promises for fast and reliable service.

REFERENCES

Aastrup, J. (2002), 'Networks producing intermodal transport', Doctor's dissertation, Department of Marketing, Copenhagen Business School.

Ballis, A. and J. Golias (2002), 'Comparative evaluation of existing and innovative rail–road freight transport terminals', *Transportation Research Part A: Policy and Practice*, **36** (7), pp. 593–611.

Bärthel, F. and J. Woxenius (2003), 'The Dalecarlian Girl: evaluation of the implementation of the light-combi concept', Alliance for Global Sustainability Annual Meeting, University of Tokyo, 24–27 March.

Bergstrand, J. (2001), interview, Vice-President, Celexor AB.

Bontekoning, Y.M. and E. Kreutzberger (1999), *Concepts of New-Generation Terminals and Terminal Nodes*, Delft: TRAIL Research School, Delft University Press.

Bukold, S. (1993), 'Marktzugangsbarrieren in einem semi-deregulierten Markt' (Market entry barriers in a semi-regulated market), *Internationales Verkehrswesen*, **45**, pp. 494–501 (in German).

Bukold, S. (1996), *Kombinierter Verkehr Schiene/Strasse in Europa – Eine vergleichende Studie zur Transformation von Gütertransportsystemen* (Combined road–rail transport in Europe: a comparative study on transformation of freight transport systems), Frankfurt am Main: Peter Lang Verlag (in German).

Churchman, C.W. (1979), *The Systems Approach*, 2nd edn, New York: Dell Publishing Co.

European Commission (2001), *White Paper. European Transport Policy for 2010: Time to Decide*, Luxemburg: Office for Official Publications of the European Communities.

European Commission (2002), *European Union: Energy and Transport in Figures*, Luxemburg: Office for Official Publications of the European Communities.

European Commission (2003), 'Proposal for a Directive by the European Parliament and the Council on Intermodal Loading Units', Brussels, 7 April.

Eurostat (2002), *EU Intermodal Freight Transport: Key Statistical Data 1992–99*, Luxemburg.

Gadde, L.-E. and H. Håkansson (1992), 'Analyzing change and stability in distribution channels: a network approach', in B. Axelsson and G. Easton (eds), *Industrial Networks: A New View of Reality*, London: Routledge, pp. 29–143.

Gifford, J.L. and O.J. Stalebrink (2002), 'Remaking transportation organizations for the 21st century: consortia and the value of organizational learning', *Transportation Research Part A: Policy and Practice*, **36** (7), pp. 645–57.

Golias, J. and G. Yannis (1998), 'Determinants of combined transport's market share', *Transport Logistics*, **1** (4), pp. 251–64.

Golob, T.F. and A.C. Regan (2003), 'Trucking industry adoption of information technology: a multivariate discrete choice model', *Transportation Research Part C: Emerging Technologies*, **10** (3), pp. 205–28.

Hansson, M. (2003), interview, Marketing Director, Green Cargo AB.

Henstra, D. and J. Woxenius (1999), *Intermodal Transport in Europe*, Report within the EU project TRILOG Europe, Delft: TNO Inro.

Houtman, J. (2002), 'The portfolio effect in hub-networks with stochastic cargo volumes, Integrationsaspekte des supply chain management', *Logistikmanagement*, **4** (4), pp. 61–70 (in German).

IFEU and SGKV (2002), 'Comparative analysis of energy need and CO_2 emissions of road transport and combined transport road/rail', IRU/BGL Energy and CO_2 Study, Geneva.

IQ (1998), 'Intermodal quality, quality of the networks', 4th FP project PL 95313.

Konings, J.W. and E. Kreutzberger (2001), *Towards a Quality Leap in Intermodal Freight Transport, Theoretical Notions and Practical Perspectives in Europe*, Delft: TRAIL Research School, Delft University Press.

Liu, J., C.-L. Li and C.-Y. Chan (2003), 'Mixed truck delivery systems with both hub-and-spoke and direct shipment', *Transport Research Part E: Logistics and Transportation Review*, **39** (4), pp. 325–39.

Ljungemyr, H. (1995), 'Vilka transportfaktorer har betydelse för kombitrafikens andel av godstransporterna? (Which factors influence the market share of intermodal transport?', VTI-meddelande, 773, Linköping (in Swedish).

Ludvigsen, J. (1999), 'Freight transport supply and demand conditions in the Nordic Countries: recent evidence', *Transportation Journal*, **39** (2), pp. 31–54.

Morlok, E.K. and L.N. Spasovic (1994), 'Redesigning rail–truck intermodal drayage operations for enhanced service and cost performance', *Journal of Transportation Research Forum*, **34** (1), pp. 16–31.

Nelldal, B.-L., G. Troche and J. Wajsman (2000), *Järnvägens möjligheter på den framtida godstransportmarknaden* (The possibilities of rail on the future freight transport market), Stockholm: Department of Traffic Planning, Royal Institute of Technology.

Niérat, P. (1997), 'Market area of rail–truck terminals: pertinence of the spatial theory', *Transportation Research Part A: Policy and Practice*, **31** (2), pp. 109–27.

Ohnell, S. and J. Woxenius (2003), 'An industry analysis of express freight from a European railway perspective', *International Journal of Physical Distribution and Logistics Management*, **33** (8), pp. 735–51.

Patterson, K.A., C.M. Grimm and T.M. Corsi (2003), 'Adopting techonologies for supply chain management', *Transport Research Part E: Logistics and Transportation Review*, **39** (2), pp. 95–121.

Persson, P-Å. (2003), interview, Production Manager, Rail Combi AB.

Rutten, B.C.M. (1998), 'The design of a terminal network for intermodal transport', *Transport Logistics*, **1** (4), pp. 279–98.

Siegmann, J. and R.U. Tänzler (1996), 'Linienzüge des Kombinierten Verkehr brauchen innovative Umschlagssysteme', in *Innovative Umschlagsysteme an der Schiene*, VDI Berichte 1274, Düsseldorf: VDI Verlag, pp. 33–40.

Slack, B. (1999), 'Satellite terminals: a local solution to hub congestion?' *Journal of Transport Geography*, **7** (4), pp. 241–6.

Taylor, G.D., F. Broadstreet, T.S. Meinert and J.S. Usher (2002), 'An analysis of intermodal ramp selection methods', *Transport Research Part E: Logistics and Transportation Review*, **38**, pp. 117–34.

Trip, J.J. and Y. Bontekoning (2002), 'Integration of small freight flows in the intermodal transport system', *Journal of Transport Geography*, **10** (102), pp. 221–9.

Van Klink, H.A. and G.C. Van den Berg (1998), 'Gateways and intermodalism', *Journal of Transport Geography*, **6** (1), pp. 1–9.

Van Schijndel, W.-J. and J. Dinwoodie (2000), 'Congestion and multimodal transport: a survey of cargo transport operators in the Netherlands', *Transport Policy*, **7** (4), pp. 231–41.

Vleugel, J., E. Kreutzberger and Y.M. Bontekoning (eds) (2001), *Concepts of Innovative Bundling Networks*, Delft: TRAIL Research School, Delft University Press.

Wenger, H. (2001), *UIRR 30 Jahre* (*UIRR 30 years*), Brussels: UIRR.

Woxenius, J. (1994), *Modelling European Combined Transport as an Industrial System*, Licentiate Thesis, Report 24, Göteborg: Department of Transportation and Logistics, Chalmers University of Technology.

Woxenius, J. (1997), *Inventory of Transshipment Technologies in Intermodal Transport*, Geneva: International Road Transport Union (IRU).

Woxenius, J. and F. Bärthel (2002), 'The organisation of the European intermodal road/rail freight transport industry', Delft: FTAM, 23–24 May.

Zapp, K. (1999), 'DB Cargo kontra Kombiverkehr?' *Internationales Verkehrswesen*, **51** (in German).

3. Intermodal freight transport in the United States

Lata Chatterjee and T.R. Lakshmanan

3.1 INTRODUCTION AND OVERVIEW

A variety of interrelated factors have converged in the last quarter of the twentieth century to alter, in significant and pervasive ways, the nature and scope of the US freight transportation enterprise – what is being transported, how it is transported, where from and where to (origins and destinations of goods). There have been major changes in the volume and composition of goods, which are moved over longer distances in both domestic and global markets; freight is moved more frequently in smaller shipments, and, on average, is of higher value than before (Figure 3.1). Major freight routes (domestically and globally) are evolving, in short order, in response to changes in the global economy and in the geography of emerging production centres (US DOT 2000).

A major factor underlying this transformation of freight transport is represented by the changes in the scale, in the composition, and in the structure of the American and global economies. The demand for transportation services has grown in response to the generally brisk performance of the US and global economies in this period. The US economy is becoming dominantly services-oriented, and shifting from mass manufacturing to high value-added custom manufacturing. The resulting combination of increasing information content and decreasing material intensity of goods changes the character and value of goods being moved. Further, the US and other Organisation for Economic Co-operation and Development (OECD) countries, in search of lower overall factor costs, have created global and regional free trade regimes, and globally organized production systems and value chains, which require speedy and timely movements of goods. These flows of goods are coordinated across national and global transport nodes and links in order to support the smooth functioning of the globalized economy.

Technological changes in the transport sector in the US have arrived in the form of the Interstate Highway System, the jet aircraft, the container and container ships, roll-on/roll-off vessels, and a variety of micro infrastructure

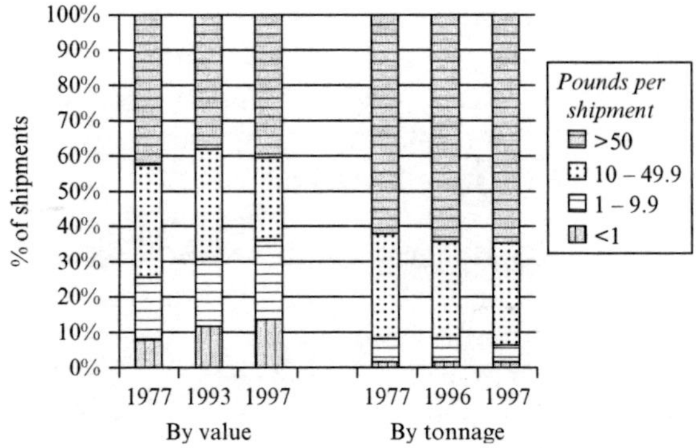

Source: US DOT (2000), pp. 2–55.

Figure 3.1 Freight shipments by value and tonnage: 1977, 1993 and 1997

to facilitate operations at seaports and airports. The use of information technology (IT) greatly enhances transport operator and system efficiency, offering not only speedier goods transport at declining costs but also the ability to 'integrate' goods supply chains regionally and globally, while maintaining lean inventories.

The third factor underlying the major changes in the freight system is the institutional and organizational restructuring of the transport system since the 1980s. Public policies to reform economic institutions by deregulating and privatizing the transport sector have stimulated technical innovations and enhanced productivity in that sector – in the process lowering costs and improving speed and reliability. At the same time, two organizational innovations – business logistical systems and intermodalism – provide major sources of change in the freight sector.

Business logistical systems, aimed at minimizing total logistical costs (transportation, warehousing and inventories, insurance, administration, and so on), are providing customers with a number of additional valuable services such as global time-definite delivery, lean inventories, strategic outsourcing of the distribution function, flexibility of destination choices, and so on. Such services from freight transport companies add value to the operations of their customers, thereby conferring strategic competitive advantages on customer US firms operating in the global economy.

Intermodalism is defined as the fully coordinated door-to-door efficient delivery of freight using two or more dissimilar modes of transport. While it has faced complex problems in the US with its history of mode-based development of infrastructure and public policies, three recent developments are, however, promoting intermodalism.

First, transport logistics goals are performance-based (for example minimizing time and cost, improving reliability), rather than modally based. The capacity to connect origins and destinations is vital, and individual modes can fill niches (for example low cost or high speed) in an intermodal framework. Consequently, improving logistical practices stimulates intermodalism. Second, the arrival of supporting technologies (for example containers) enables intermodalism. Third, the rising congestion in major US freight corridors, characterized by poor intermodal cooperation, is yet another stimulus to intermodal development.

The objective of this chapter is to describe the origin, development and prospects of intermodalism in the US. Section 3.2 traces the origin and evolution of intermodalism in the US, describing the interplay of broader forces of economic evolution, technological changes, institutional and organizational developments and the specific conditions of the US transport system and its adaptation. The next section outlines the recent trends in intermodalism in the US, offering an interpretive statistical portrait of developments. The chapter proceeds to an analysis of emerging developments in US intermodalism in the context of observed and emerging technological, institutional and organizational factors. Next, policy and strategic issues related to the future of intermodalism are explored, attempting to identify the public sector's enabling role. The final section concludes the chapter, sketching out future prospects for intermodalism.

3.2 EVOLUTION OF INTERMODAL TRANSPORT IN THE US

Definition and Elaboration

Intermodalism, as noted, is the fully coordinated door-to-door delivery of freight using two or more dissimilar modes of transport. Often the term 'seamless' is appended to this definition. This, in our view, is premature. It can be only a long-term goal as we are far from seamless transport. As noted below, there are many rigidities and inefficiencies in the system – a legacy of a freight system with a history of modal competition and mode-oriented infrastructure and other public policies. The current issue is how to bind the seams, that is, reduce transaction costs at transfer points. The aim of the ongoing institutional and technological innovations in intermodalism is to minimize these transaction costs.

At this juncture it may be useful to differentiate between two concepts – multimodalism and intermodalism – occasionally used interchangeably in the literature. Multimodalism is not a new phenomenon in the US or elsewhere. Cargo shipment using two or more dissimilar modes has existed for hundreds of years. From early times trade and passenger movement across water necessitated integration of land and water modes at sea and river ports. Railway terminals in the nineteenth century and airports or terminals of pipelines in the twentieth century also involved freight movement across multiple modes. As detailed in Table 3.1, integration of dissimilar modes always occurred when transport across two or more media – land, water and air – were involved in cargo and passenger movements. Multimodalism prevailed in the pre-1950 era (from pre-industrial times to 1950) with an increasing number of transport modes being linked with the use of new technologies identified in Table 3.1. In the pre-industrial era, cargo was transferred from ships and barges to wheeled vehicles on land, the process facilitated by the development of ports and locks. In the railroad period, the multimodal exchanges expanded beyond ship and road vehicles to include the railroad.

What distinguishes the post-1950 period from the earlier pattern? We can distinguish between the multimodal character of the pre-1950 era, the incipient and early stages of intermodality of the 1950–80 period, and the more robust intermodalism of the period after 1980. In the latter period, there is a revolution in the manner in which freight shipment is conceptualized. Not only are two or more modes involved, but the cargo moves in unitized form. Intermodalism is qualitatively different from multimodalism.

Intermodalism is desirable since inefficiencies in the freight sector impact upon the competitiveness of US firms in the transport and transport-using sectors. Intermodalism seeks to enhance the performance of the transportation system by increasing safety, reducing congestion and decreasing delays, thereby enabling more efficient freight and passenger trips (Hickling 1995). Greater efficiency translates into lower costs and an increase in the competitiveness of US firms in the global marketplace. The Intermodal Surface Transportation Act (ISTEA) emphasizes the importance of intermodalism and challenged the transportation authorities, at the federal, state and local levels in the US, to increase interconnectivity between the maritime, air and land transport modes, and thereby enhances the effectiveness of the total network.

It is widely recognized in the US, in both industry and policy circles, that cooperation between transport modes has the potential to reduce congestion, especially in major freight corridors. While congestion problems result from a variety of factors, the concentration of production and trade in a relatively small number of metropolitan gateway cities, the increased dominance of a few ports, and the intermodal competition for the same freight, adds to the congestion. The traditional attitude toward infrastructure investment, namely building one's way out of congestion, has not been helpful since

Forces Propelling Intermodalism

The major factor underlying the increasing demand for intermodalism is the globalization of the American economy. North America, Europe and other countries have built on the Bretton Woods system, the General Agreement on Tariffs and Trade (GATT) and the World Trade Organization (WTO) to create a global free trade regime, including regional Preferential Trading Areas such as the North American Free Trade Agreement (NAFTA), the EU and Mercosur. The industrialized countries, driven by the pressure to reduce overall factor costs in the competitive global economy, are using these open trading regimes to erect a globally distributed production system. There is increasing division of labour in the production processes as component activities are further disaggregated and spatially reallocated. This partition of the production process – the slicing of the 'production value chain' – across national borders leads to different stages of production being carried out across several countries. Raw materials and components may come from two different countries, with assembly in a third, and marketing from yet another country, in response to market signals from around the world. Since parts and components are 'sourced' internationally, they need to be transported cheaply, speedily and reliably at specific times required in the production process. The resulting supply chain – defined as a set of three or more organizations directly linked by one or more of the upstream and downstream flows of products, services, finances and information from a source to a customer – needs to be managed (DeWitt and Clinger 2000). Intermodal transportation, with the potential for integrating multiple modes, offers a flexible response to the supply chain requirements in the global production and distribution system. Integrating modes requires a systems approach and a high level of knowledge and competence in information, equipment and infrastructure, which together coordinate transport and supply chains.

Technological innovations in transport and information sectors in recent decades have made possible intermodal transportation and supply chains. These enabling and space-shrinking transport and information technologies (IT) are fundamentally transforming space–time relationships worldwide. Specifically, containerization has enabled interchange of goods between modes in a timely, cost-effective manner. US shipbuilding innovations in advanced containerships and roll-on/roll-off vessels, and companion inventions like double-stack trains, have revolutionized intermodal transport. The performance of transport vehicles and infrastructure is greatly increased by developments in the complementary IT. Information technologies, which represent a confluence of computer and communication technologies, are improving the responsiveness and efficiency of vehicles and their operators and making possible numerous transport innovations – in the process transforming both the technologies of transport and communications and the technologies of products and processes. Containers and cargoes are continually 'visible' in transit to shippers and carriers, as the use of intelligent transportation systems (ITS) and global positioning systems (GPS) increases.

Institutional and organizational reform in the transport sector has been the third force propelling intermodalism in the US. The deregulation of the US transport sector since 1978–80 has not only improved the performance of the various modes, but has also stimulated intermodalism. First, major changes occurred in the US in the conduct, performance and structure of airlines, trucking and railroads after deregulation: more competition among all modal carriers, lower prices, a wider set of service offerings, and new entry into most geographic and product markets. Carriers have been able to rationalize their networks, improve the efficiency of their operations, and set rates in line with competitive market conditions. There was a significant change in the cost structure of the railroad industry following deregulation, with productivity growing at well over 2 per cent a year (Bereskin 1996). Figure 3.2 shows the distinct progress of productivity in the various modes following deregulation.

The logistics system was a 'push' system in the pre-1980 era, when manufacturing, retailing and distribution were organized to support mass

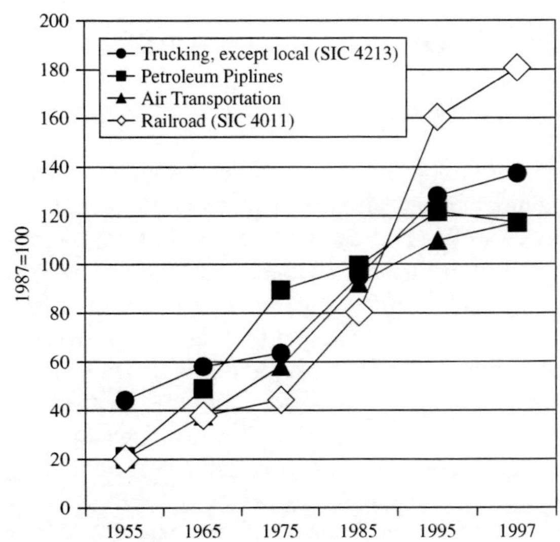

Source: US DOT (2000).

Figure 3.2 Productivity trends for transportation industries: 1955–97

production, warehousing and retailing. Centralized design, production, marketing and long production lines to achieve scale economies were the rule. Large costly inventories were kept to buffer against supply–demand variations. Transportation moved goods from supplier to manufacturer, to distributor, to retailer – each link managed and priced independently.

Today, it is increasingly a 'pull' logistical system, made possible by IT. Here customer demand is tracked daily or more often by suppliers, manufacturers, retailers and distributors. Orders and sales patterns pull goods through the supply chain. Production follows the order, leading to just-in-time (JIT) manufacturing and retail systems. The risk of over- or undershooting market needs, through large inventories, is reduced since the 'pull' system adjusts production and delivery to consumers' time trajectory of needs. The consequence of the 'pull' system is a restructuring of the freight transport sector. Taking advantage of the new IT capabilities of measuring, monitoring, communicating and controlling the supply chain, goods producers and retailers provide smaller, more frequent and longer-distance transport services in order to secure lower costs of labour and supplies. This approach requires the provision of integrated and intermodal transportation services which are timely, reliable, cost-effective and can be tracked from origin to destination. Hence the spurt in intermodalism.

3.3 PATTERNS OF INTERMODALISM IN THE US

Statistical Highlights of the US Freight Sector

The US freight services sector has witnessed significant quantitative and qualitative changes in recent decades. Between 1965 and 1998 total tonnage moved in the US rose from 4.54 billion tons to 6.21 billion tons (an increase of 37 per cent), while ton-miles rose more sharply from 1854 billion ton-miles to 3710 billion ton-miles (an increase of 100 per cent). As noted below, these aggregate changes reflect the interacting effects in this period of several broad economic processes, that is, increasing spatial integration and robust growth of the American economy, increasing shift to less material-intensive service sectors, and a variety of technological and organizational changes in the economy. The qualitative change since the 1980s, as noted above, is in the scope of the freight services being offered to transport-using firms in the form of greater speed and reliability, time-definite global delivery of goods and flexibility in destinations.

Since the 1960s, freight and passenger mobility has increased with the growth of the Gross Domestic Product (GDP). Passenger miles have grown

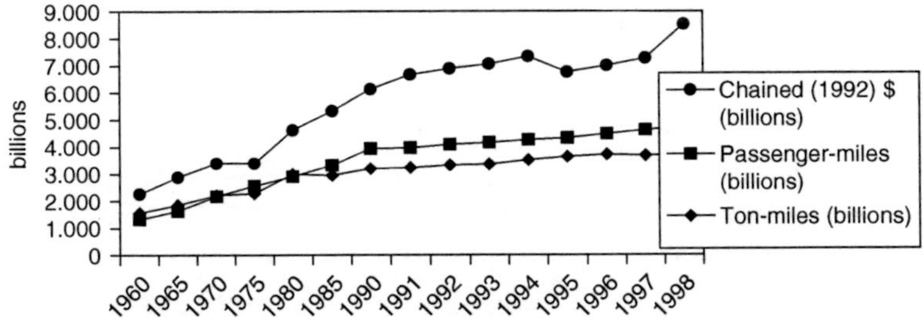

Source: National Transportation Statistics (2000), BTS, USDOT.

Figure 3.3 Growth of the economy and passenger and freight transport development, 1960–98

more rapidly, relative to freight, in the 1960–90 period, with an income elasticity over the entire period of close to 1 (0.94). Ton-miles of freight exhibit a slower relative growth with an income elasticity of 0.50. In the decades of the 1960s and 1970s, however, freight traffic growth kept pace with GDP growth, but has subsequently slackened (Figure 3.3).

In about the same period (1970–95), the growth in tonnage and ton-miles varied, however, by mode (Figure 3.4). Intercity trucking ton-miles grew by 124 per cent, while air freight ton-miles grew by 468 per cent.

The measure of freight intensity, relating freight levels to GDP, tell the same story more sharply. Tons per US dollar 1000 GDP (1992 prices) declined between 1965 and 1998 by 54 per cent from 1.58 to 0.73 tons. Ton-miles per US dollar GDP dropped between 1960 and 1998 by 36 per cent from 0.69 miles to 0.44 miles (Figure 3.5). Clearly, the economy shows a consistent trend towards lower intensity of freight use.

The measures of freight intensity (Figure 3.5) reflect the recent transformation of the US economy, with less and less of the GDP deriving from goods production. The oft-noted increasing shift in the US to a service economy over this period signifies a reduced resource and energy intensity and the consequent lower intensity of goods generation for movement. At the same time in this period, transport technology changes such as the introduction of containers, the Interstate System and jet aircraft continued to lower transport costs sharply. The common measure of shipping costs (the ratio of cost, insurance, freight, c.i.f. trade value – measured as cost to the importing country – to free on board, f.o.b. trade value – measured as it leaves the exporting country) declined from 9.5 per cent in 1950 to about 6 per cent in 1990 (Frankel 2000).

In the American economy, where the transition to knowledge-intensive sectors is advanced, the characterization of the freight sector in terms of

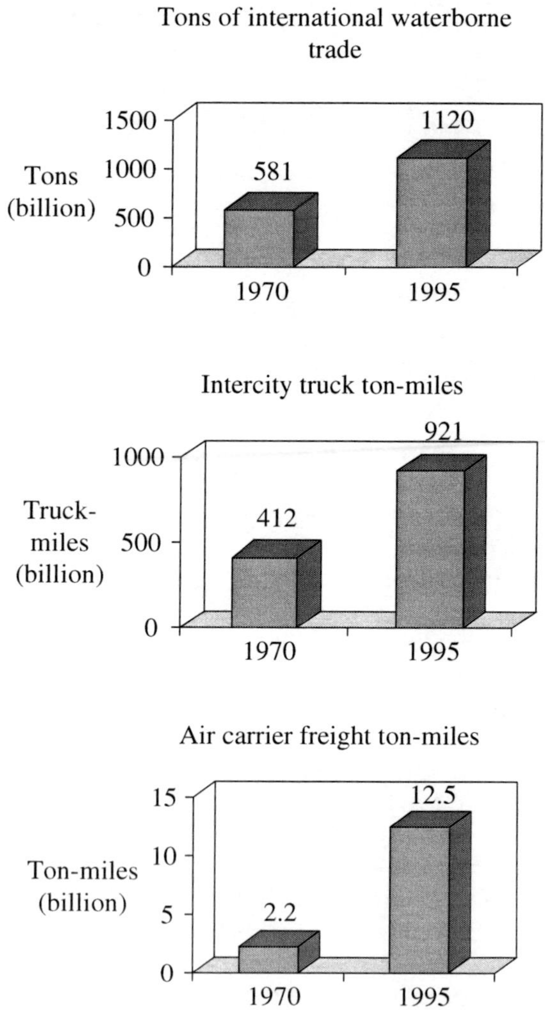

Figure 3.4 Growth of freight traffic by modes, 1970–95

tons and ton-miles is inadequate and somewhat misleading in view of the changes in the value and weight composition of goods. The Commodity Flow Surveys conducted by the US Department of Transportation (DOT) Bureau of Transportation Statistics (BTS) in 1993 and 1997 provide a rare measurement of freight by value (in addition to tons and ton-miles), and a richer view of some of the recent changes in the freight services industry (Lakshmanan and Anderson 2001).

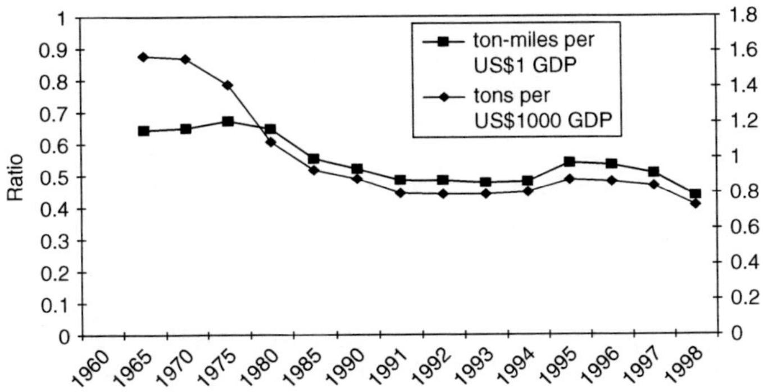

Source: National Transportation Statistics, BTS, USDOT.

Figure 3.5 US freight intensity 1960–98

Table 3.2 US freight by value, 1993, 1997

Indicator	1993	1997	% increase, 1993–97
GDP (billions) chained 1992 dollars	7054	7270	3.0
Freight (value)	6335	6944	9.6
Freight (value) / GDP	0.90	0.96	6.6

Source:
BTS Commodity Flow Survey, 1993–97.
Special Tabulations by Felix Amma-Tagoe, (2001).

Table 3.2 displays the freight moved measured in value terms in 1993 and 1997. The value of freight moved in the US in this period grew three times as fast as GDP. The value of freight to be moved for a dollar of GDP rose between 1993 and 1997 by 6 cents or 6.6 per cent. High value-added sectors increasingly contributed to freight movements and the growth in size of the economy.

Intermodal Freight Patterns

During this period of robust freight sector growth in the US, technological advances and organizational innovations led the move towards intermodal freight shipments. The intermodal container, which was first introduced in the US in 1956 for domestic ocean–truck services, has become a common denominator across modes, revolutionizing freight movement and ushering

Table 3.3 Estimate of total commercial freight activity in the United States by mode of transportation, 1997

Mode of transportation	Value ($ billions) 1997	Tons (millions)	Ton-miles (billions)
Overall total (CFS plus out-of-scope estimates)	8 556	14 800	3 951
Commodity Flow Survey data			
Mode			
Truck	4 982	7 701	1 024
Rail	320	1 550	1 023
Water	76	563	262
Air (includes truck and air)	229	4	6
Pipeline[1]	113	618	169
Intermodal			
Parcel, US Postal Service or courier	856	24	18
Truck and rail	76	54	56
Truck and water	8	33	35
Rail and water	2	79	78
Other multiple modes	4	26	19
Other and unknown modes	279	437	73
CFS subtotal, all modes	6 944	11 090	2 761

Notes:
These out-of-scope estimates were calculated by the Oak Ridge National Laboratory. The Bureau of Transportation Statistics, Commodity Flow Survey, US Department of Transportation, Washington, DC, May 2000.
1 The pipeline ton-miles shown here are not a Commodity Flow Survey (CFS) estimate. CFS data for pipelines exclude most shipments of crude oil. The ton-miles were estimated based on Association of Oil Pipelines data.

Source: US Department of Transportation, Bureau of Transportation Statistics, based on 1997 Commodity Flow Survey data plus additional estimates from the Oak Ridge National Laboratory.

in intermodalism. As the efficiency of containerized transport became evident, ports, railroads and motor carriers invested in container facilities. Associated developments, such as double-stack trains in the railroad and port sectors as well as the explosion of container traffic worldwide have stimulated intermodal transportation.

Table 3.3 highlights the modal composition of freight movements in the US in 1997 as gleaned from the Commodity Flow Survey of the US Bureau of Transportation Statistics. Trucks, accounting for 72 per cent of freight by value (69.4 per cent of tonnage, and 37.6 per cent of ton-miles), are the dominant mode. Growth in high-value trade in general, the growth of high-value trade with the US's NAFTA partners – Canada and Mexico – and the growing global market for time-sensitive, high-value goods account for this. Domestically, trucks carry domestically more freight than railroads when measured in value terms. While railroads account for about the same ton-miles, their share of value is under 6 per cent, and of tons 14 per cent. Railroads move low-value goods (coal, grain, and so on) over long distances (Lakshmanan 1998).

Intermodal transport – represented by parcel post, truck and rail, truck and water, rail and water, and other multiple modes not including truck and air – accounts for 13.62 per cent of total freight value and 7.4 per cent of total ton-miles. This share is higher than that of pipelines. However, in terms of tonnage moved, intermodal transport is very small, accounting for 0.02 per cent of total tonnage. Higher-value goods are transported longer distances intermodally. Within the intermodal category, parcel, postal or courier service clearly had the highest value in 1993 ($29 816/ton) while other intermodes, such as truck and rail had higher value per ton than unimodal transport – $690 for truck, $160 for rail, $134 for pipeline, $118 for water (Figure 3.6).

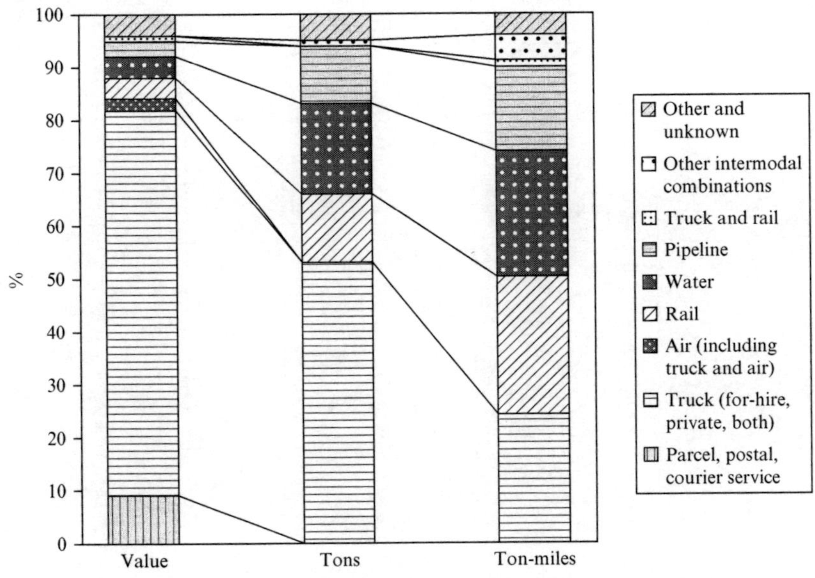

Source: Bureau of Transportation Statistics (BTS) (1996). US Department of Transportation, p. 16.

Figure 3.6 Value, tons and ton-miles of freight shipments by mode, 1993

	Air	Truck	Rail	Pipe	Barge	Ship
Air						
Truck	Express Containers, JIT shipments, comman-dation					
Rail	None	Domestic intermodal DST and TOFC				
Pipe	None	Petroleum gas	None			
Barge	None	Coal, grain, chemicals	Coal, grain, ore	Petroleum, chemicals		
Ship	Express Containers, JIT shipments	Inter-national containers automo-biles	Containers, grain Autos, chemicals	Petroleum, gasoline	Coal, petroleum, containers	

Note: JIT: just-in-time, DST: double-stack trains

Figure 3.7 Forms of freight intermodalism by commodities

In Figure 3.7 the forms of intermodalism by type of commodities are shown. There are cooperative relations between some modes, for example air–truck, rail–truck and ship–truck. Rail and truck cooperate with trailer on flatcar (TOFC) and chassis on flatcar (COFC) for long-distance hauls. Air–truck partnerships handle high-value shipments of express goods as noted above. On the other hand, several modes have virtually no interaction – some due to their inherent competitiveness such as air–rail or pipelines–rail, others due to lack of common infrastructure interfaces at terminals.

Intermodalism promotes greater efficiency through cost reductions and improved service quality as each mode has different cost or service advantages. Modes vary in their average haul distances due to these differential cost–benefit advantages. For instance, trucks provide door-to-door delivery and are most efficient for shorter hauls. Rail and water have the advantage of low–cost line haulage, in contrast to private trucks which operate at local levels. The US has the largest active rail network in the world, amounting to more than 128 000 miles. In terms of ton-miles railways still dominate the movement of heavier bulk commodities. Railways have the longest average haul distance among the land modes. Air and air–truck have advantages of speed and are valuable for express packages and just-in-time delivery as shown in Figure 3.7, which indicates the complementarities between the modes. Intermodal cooperation occurs more commonly for longer hauls of freight as it permits a combination of the cost savings advantage provided by each mode. Even though rail intermodalism has been doubling since 1990 the base is still relatively small (Muller 1999). The total intermodal shipments including rail–water, truck–water, rail–truck and truck–air are still minor and account for less than one-fifth of the volume of freight moved by rail alone.

3.5 TECHNICAL AND INSTITUTIONAL DEVELOPMENTS

Institutional and Organizational Factors

Intermodalism is economically viable only through reduction of transaction costs at points of connectivity. Interconnectivity along a transport network requires improvement of the links and nodes. The nodes – the air and ocean ports, railway and truck terminals – pose the greatest challenges as interconnectivity occurs at these locations. Prior legacy has left physical infrastructures lacking spatial connectivity between terminals of the various modes, and lack of sufficient space to retrofit the urban form to accommodate to intermodalism. For instance, container ports require vast spaces for assembling and moving thousands of containers. Often these ports are located proximately to congested metropolitan areas that impede the flow of trains and trucks at the gateways. Some of these problems are being addressed through infrastructure investments, others involve adoption of technological innovations in information and cargo handling. Institutional changes such as greater cooperation between public and private sectors and evolution of new forms of business enterprises such as third- and fourth-party logistics firms are also working to relieve congestion and increase interconnectivity between modes.

As noted earlier, except for parcel, package and courier service, intermodalism is still in its early stages of development. Intermodalism implies freight transfers between modes and intermodalism will not be adopted if these transfers involve high human, time and monetary costs. In this section we discuss selected facilitative technologies and institutional factors that are reducing these transaction costs.

The ability to move cargo smoothly at the water–land and air–land boundaries is a necessary precondition for successful adoption of intermodal delivery schedules. A number of new enterprises have been created to facilitate goods movement and transfer and thereby reduce transaction costs at these boundaries. These enterprises have developed two classes of adaptive responses. First, the total task has been segmented by specialized firms whose personnel perform selected functions and through their expertise and contacts are important in saving time and improving connectivity and system reliability. Second, these enterprises utilize Internet and communications technologies in the creation of associations and cooperative ventures between firms with a common interest.

The following types of firms are important for outsourcing and intermodal coordination:

- Freight forwarders are responsible for the transportation of goods from origin to destination including the assumption of liability for loss or damage of cargo. They contract with motor, rail, water carriers and shippers for procuring freight to consolidate intermodal shipments and also provide intermodal bills of lading.
- Container leasing companies allow carriers to lease containers, and slightly less than 50 per cent of the world's land–ocean container fleet is owned by them. In 1997, ten of the largest leasing companies owned 90 per cent of the world's leased containers and 80 per cent of all leased TEUs (twenty-foot equivalent units) are owned by American companies. These firms provide flexibility to carriers in times of high demand. Containers are a multi-million dollar fixed investment, where

usage is subject to business and trade cycle fluctuations. Consequently, ownership of containers is highly concentrated – two US companies, Transamerica Leasing and Genstar Container Corporation, control 45 per cent of the worldwide rental fleet of TEUs due to their worldwide facilities and container availability, which allows them to capture scale economies.

- Consolidators take LTL (less-than-truckload) loads and consolidate them into trailer or boxcar loads. Also they break down truckload shipments and distribute them to warehouses by geographic area or location of hub. The consolidators could be truckers, warehouse operators or customs brokers.
- Customs brokers are important for JIT shipments. As authorized agents of shippers for dealing with the US Customs they currently handle 90 per cent of all goods entering the US. They are important for time savings by providing highly specialized expertise in documentation of cargo entry, bills of lading, entry manifests, making invoices and paying customs duty which they later recover from the importer.
- Logistical firms: third- and fourth-party logistical firms specialize in the provision of logistical services on contract, having been spurred by the changing relationship between shippers, carriers and intermediaries following transport deregulation. These firms provide for-hire services to client firms which need to outsource functions such as inventory and order management, selection of carriers and warehouses, negotiation of transport rates and management of logistical information services. Currently, 50 per cent of Fortune 500 companies have contracts with third-party firms with business amounting to $46 million in 1999 (Bradley, Gooley and Cooke 2000). Physical and human capital asset considerations such as adequate fleet size and composition, and in-house availability of personnel skilled in a rapidly changing environment of logistical innovations, are fueling the rapid growth of logistical firms.

Technological Factors

Intermodalism had its start in technological improvements such as containerization. However, the rapid growth of container transportation was made feasible by related technological improvements through the rationalization of cargo-handling equipment. For instance, gantry cranes discharge containers between the ship and pier at an average of 30 containers per hour and double-handling equipment on a single gantry can increase the rate to 40 containers per hour. Such rapid offloading of containers requires technological developments in ground container moving and stacking equipment such as corn stackers. These types of equipment permit better utilization of space in container terminals and more rapid interface during load transfers between modes. On-dock railways with roll-on and roll-off transfers on flatcars allow speedier transfers between sea, rail and road. Intermodalism also requires standardization of containers compatible with two or more modes. For instance air–truck intermodalism requires smaller-sized containers and can be contrasted with larger containers for ocean–rail–truck. These are only a few of the numerous innovations in physical technologies which have facilitated intermodalism (Hagler Bailly 1999).

Information technologies provide a different function and have been critical for intermodalism as efficient and timely transport of freight across a variety of modes requires a plethora of information on the type, size, composition, origin, destination and the location during transit of these containers. Innovations such as automated electronic identification (AEI) and GPS have been crucial for intermodalism. To provide greater accuracy, the US DOT is implementing the DGPS (differential GPS) to increase accuracy in predictability, to provide finer area coverage (US DOT 2000). Automatic vehicle location (AVL) technologies are used for tracking mobile assets such as vessels, vehicles, containers and so on.

A wide variety of innovations are grouped under the rubric of intelligent transportation systems (ITS). Intermodalism would not have been possible without these advances in information processing and communications technologies. ITS has increased system capacity, permitted better coordination between modes, reduced transit times and increased overall productivity of the network (Proper 2003). For instance, intelligent grade crossings reduce accidents at modal interfaces, that is, road and rail. The US DOT has played a key role in the development of a national ITS architecture and standard definition.

The interaction between the physical and information technologies has fuelled the institutional and organizational development discussed above. These organization innovations can monitor the freight movement, adjust and control the timing of shipments, and so on. Moreover, the recent explosion of IT and data management software for the transport sector allows the acquisition of capability at lower and lower costs.

3.6 PUBLIC POLICY ISSUES

There is an important role for the public sector in facilitating intermodalism. The type and nature of the public role in intermodalism derives from the fact that intermodalism is a quasi-public good that in some aspects reflects market failure. Even though there are system-wide external benefits from investments in intermodalism, there will be an underprovision due to market failure, leading to congestion along major corridors, and at terminals such as airports and seaports. In addition to the standard public-good attributes of transportation infrastructure such as non-excludability and pervasive externalities, additional problems arise from the fact that each mode views itself as a private good. The legacy of modal competition in the overall transportation system and transportation network reflects this attitude as each mode made investment and management decisions to maximize its individual private interests. As noted earlier, landside congestion of containers or truck queues at access gateways arose because the port authorities were interested in unloading and offloading containers to maximize turnaround times for ships, that is, servicing their major client. Indeed, the efficiency of a port is still measured by the standard indicator of 'idle' time spent by a freighter at the port, instead of measuring throughput such as time spent by containers at ports. The latter is an intermodal indicator in contrast to the former which is a modal indicator. Each mode in optimizing its own welfare in terms of service provision as a private good can only lead to suboptimal transportation conditions in the country, as noted by the US government in its legislative mandate. Hence, here is the attribution of an important role for the public sector.

It is important to recognize that the roots of intermodal cooperation lie in private sector activities, starting with the container revolution. The lag has occurred in the requisite infrastructure provision. The federal government has recognized the importance of fostering and speeding up the market-driven forces for intermodalism, as the poor coordination between modes posed serious constraints to national productivity (Krebs 1994). As early as 1988, the Subcouncil on Public Infrastructure drew attention to the importance of intermodalism for increasing national competitiveness; concerns that are reflected in the ISTEA (1991) and TEA 21 (1998) legislations. The ISTEA created the Office of Intermodalism, which was a valuable first step in recognition of the important role of the public sector. The ISTEA also set standards for a National Intermodal Transportation System and prioritized the need for a more integrated system (National Research Council 1993). However, much more needs to be accomplished by the public sector to improve the efficiency and effectiveness of the total transport system in the US (Gwilliam 1998). We briefly highlight some classes of enabling interventions.

What is the role of public policy if we recognize the public-good character of intermodalism? That role includes: (1) coordination, planning, location and design of intermodal facilities; (2) infrastructure provision through direct investment in grants and loans, and indirectly through loan guarantees and insurance mechanisms; (3) improving safety and security issues through regulation and enforcement; and (4) facilitating information flows. We have discussed these aspects in the body of the chapter. Here we discuss only the logic for these types of interventions.

The public role in planning and design guidance is necessary due to the fundamental lack of coordination between the numerous agents supplying and using the transport infrastructure at points of modal contact. For example, any change in the existing situation implies differential costs and benefits to the various modal users, and rearrangement of positive and negative externalities. The public sector can shape the physical environment through analysis provided by planning agencies and consultants, provide incentives and enforce regulations. In addition, the public sector can use the powers of eminent domain (compulsory purchase or expropriation) to secure land for terminals on both brownfield and greenfield sites. In cases of heavily built-up land, as around Long Beach, the government can provide planning alternatives such as the Alameda Corridor. The ISTEA and TEA 21 have resulted in greater attention being paid to efficient movement of goods to and from aircraft in truck and aircraft operations. As several state transportation agencies such as the Oregon Department of Transportation (ODOT) and the Massachusetts Department of Transportation have demonstrated, the public sector can play an important role in providing the framework for discussion, brokering interactions among various stakeholders toward a common goal, and analysing and planning the spatial organization in a regional context. This role is critical as there are relatively few locations where most of the bottlenecks and congestion occurs – predominantly around metropolitan areas with imperfectly articulated networks of associations that include public, private and civil society sectors.

The public sector needs to channel economic resources in order to support the need for massive demand for finance and to overcome the potential of underinvestment. This role is a direct extension of the logic for public expenditure decisions in funding construction through tax revenues, raising capital through bonds or underwriting private investment through risk insurance. The expenditure of funds can minimize or mitigate the stasis and resistance to change found in intermodal decision making. The US DOT (1998, p. 62) notes that expanded public–private partnerships will be required to fund costly projects. The total cost for the Alameda Corridor is projected to be $100 million per mile.

Safety and security of cargo at terminals becomes an increasing problem with the relaxation of the regulatory and enforcement role of the public sector. Indeed cargo crime at intermodal points of transfer has become a major activity of organized crime. Theft of containers has become relatively easy due to their mobility, and yet a single container of a high-value good can be valued at millions of dollars. Enforcement is an important role for the government. In addition there are environmental and traffic safety issues. There is an important role for the public sector in incorporating safety enhancement standards into the physical design of intermodal terminals, along with technology to monitor theft with a greater focus on prevention rather than after-the-fact mitigation.

Much of the information technology which brings about data connectivity and operational cohesion in the transportation industry has been fostered by the transportation companies. Each mode has invested significantly in electronic communication. However, intermodalism involves the interchange of information across the industry actors and there are serious problems arising from poor communication interfaces between and within modes. There are numerous vendors producing customized software and there is a public role in standardizing and making uniform standards for intermodal shipments of cargo. The Transportation Data Coordinating Committee (TDCC) began to address the standardization and coordination needs as early as 1968. Electronic Data Interchange (EDI) standards were developed by the American National Standards Institute (ANSI) in 1983 for the electronic exchange of data between and within a large variety of organizations such as public sector agencies, firms and port authorities. However, there are different standards that are not compatible in software. Cumbersome translation software is routinely used, which becomes a problem for intermodalism (Norris and Haines 1996). For example, Muller (1999, p. 285) notes that only a fraction of the 2000 licensed forwarders in ocean shipping have adopted information and process standardized procedures. The majority use customized software which is a handicap to intermodal interactions even as it increases firm and modal efficiencies. The public sector has an important role to play in developing and sponsoring the use of protocols such as the Montreal Protocol for handling waybills. There is an increased need for integrating information technology with infrastructure and the development of multinational standards and requirements (US DOT 1998). The Intermodal Association of North America (IANA) provides a forum for such discussions.

Since the 1980s, transportation has moved from a highly regulated industry to a situation where competitive market forces are guiding the development of the industry. While this has increased modal efficiencies through a diversity of technological applications, the proliferation of alternatives poses constraints for intermodalism. It is in the areas of coordination, guidance and ensuring safety, that is, where externalities are most prevalent, that there is a critical role for the public sector.

BIBLIOGRAPHY

Aylward, A. (1996), *Intelligent Transportation System and Intermodal Freight Transportation*, Washington, DC: FHWA, USDOT.

Bereskin, C.G. (1996), 'Econometric estimation of the effects of deregulation on railway productivity growth', *Transportation Journal*, **35** (4), pp. 34–43.

Bradley, P., T. Gooley and J. Cooke (2000), 'Major motor carriers merge logistics business', *Logistics Management and Distribution Report*, **39** (4), p. 26.

Bureau of Transportation Statistics (BTS) (1996), *Transportation Statistics Annual Report*, Washington, DC: US DOT

Bureau of Transportation Statistics (BTS) (2000), *National Transportation Statistics*, Washington, DC: US DOT.

DeWitt, W. and J. Clinger (2000), 'Intermodal freight transportation', in *Transportation in the New Millennium*, Washington, DC: Transportation Research Board.

Frankel, J. (2000), 'Globalization of the economy', NBER Working Paper No. W7858.

Gwilliam, K. (1998), 'Multimodal transport networks and logistics: the changing role of government', *Public Policy Issues in Global Freight Logistics*, Washington, DC: FHWA, US DOT.

Hagler Bailly, Inc. (1999), 'The market for emerging technology applications in transportation: market analysis and forecast', in *The Changing Face of Transportation*, Washington, DC: Bureau of Transportation Studies, US DOT, Chapter 6.

Hickling, L. (1995), *Measuring The Relationship between Freight Transportation and Industry Productivity*, NCHRP Report 2-17(4), Final Report, Washington, DC: Transportation Research Board.

Krebs, R.D. (1994), *Toward A National Intermodal Transportation System*, Final Report, Washington, DC: National Commission on Intermodal Transportation.

Lakshmanan, T.R. (1998), 'Transportation in knowledge society', in M.J. Beckmann, B. Johansson, F. Snickars and A.R. Thord (eds), *Knowledge and Networks in a Dynamic Economy*, New York: Springer Verlag, pp. 391–418.

Lakshmanan, T.R. and W. Anderson (2001), 'A White Paper on 'transportation infrastructure, freight services sector, and economic growth', prepared for the US Department of Transportation, Federal Highway Administration.

Meyer, M.D. (1996), National Conference on Intermodalism, 'Making the case, making it happen', Transportation Research Board, 7–9 December, New Orleans, pp. 1–7.

Muller, G. (1999), *Intermodal Freight Transportation*, Virginia, VA: Eno Transportation Foundation.

National Research Council (1993), *ISTEA and Intermodal Planning: Concept, Practice and Vision*, Special Report 240, Washington, DC: Transportation Research Board.

Norris, B. and M. Haines (1996), *Implications for Intermodal Freight Movements for Infrastructure Access, Capacity and Productivity*, Washington, DC: FHWA, US DOT.

Proper, A. (2003), *Intelligent Transportation System Benefits and Costs*, FHWA Report OP-03-075, Washington, DC.
US DOT (1998), *US Freight Economy in Motion*, Publication No FHWA-PL-98-034.
US DOT (2000), *The Changing Face of Transportation*, BTS00-007, Washington, DC: Bureau of Transportation Statistics.

4. Intermodal freight transport in urban areas in Japan

Eiichi Taniguchi and Toshinori Nemoto

4.1 INTRODUCTION

Intermodal transport indicates the use of at least two different modes of transport in an integrated manner in a door-to-door transport chain (OECD 2002). Intermodal transport is similar to multimodal transport but puts more emphasis on connectivity of different transport modes.

For domestic freight transport in Japan, intermodal transport has often been discussed in relation to the use of railways and roads as well as coastal shipping and roads. Using aeroplanes for freight transport is not a dominant phenomenon in Japan. Table 4.1 shows the modal split in terms of ton-kilometre for Japanese domestic freight transport. Roads and coastal shipping were major freight transport modes in the 1980s and 1990s. Railways used to be dominant for inland freight transport in the 1950s and 1960s and declined to only 4 per cent in 1999. The main reason for the decline of the railways is that the road network including motorways has been dramatically improved and trucking companies have provided faster and better services with lower costs than railways. Specifically, trucks are used for urban pickup and delivery of goods.

Intermodal transport using railways and coastal shipping for intercity goods movement is normally connected with urban distribution using pickup and delivery trucks. Therefore, 'road and rail' or 'road and ship' are of major concern in intermodal transport in Japan. As production and consumption points – the starting and arrival points of freight transport – are mainly located in urban areas, the supply chain of goods in general includes urban collection and distribution. Along with the trend that economic activities have been carried out in broader areas and internationally, there has been an increasing need for efficient intermodal freight transport using railways and coastal shipping for intercity goods movement combined with urban collection and distribution by pickup and delivery trucks.

Taniguchi et al. (2001) and Taniguchi and Thompson (2002) proposed innovative solutions for city logistics for efficient and environmentally

Table 4.1 Modal share of domestic freight transport in ton-kilometre in Japan (in %), 1950–99

Year	Road	Coastal shipping	Railway	Air
1950	8.4	39.4	52.3	0.0
1955	11.7	35.5	52.9	0.0
1960	14.9	45.8	39.2	0.0
1965	26.0	43.3	30.7	0.0
1970	38.9	43.1	18.1	0.0
1975	36.0	50.9	13.1	0.0
1980	40.7	50.6	8.6	0.1
1985	47.4	47.4	5.1	0.1
1990	50.1	44.7	5.0	0.1
1995	52.7	42.6	4.5	0.2
1999	54.8	41.0	4.0	0.2

Source: Ministry of Transport, Transport Policy Bureau, Information and Research Department (1998).

friendly urban freight transport systems. They include cooperative freight transport systems, application of advanced information systems, and Intelligent Transport Systems (ITS)-based vehicle routing and scheduling planning. These measures can enhance intermodal freight transport systems by improving access to intermodal freight terminals by trucks in urban areas (see also OECD 2003).

For international freight transport in Japan the intermodal freight transport systems are very important in terms of the connectivity at seaports of maritime transport and road transport using containers. The seamless and efficient intermodal freight transport systems often allow international maritime containers of 40 ft to be carried directly to their destination in the hinterlands of seaports. In most cases large trailers transport these maritime containers on the roads in urban areas and they sometimes generate negative impacts on the environment as well as crashes. Therefore, good management schemes of maritime container transport in urban areas are required including recommended truck routes and the banning of large trucks in residential areas.

4.2 CHARACTERISTICS OF INTERMODAL FREIGHT TRANSPORT

Railways and coastal shipping can provide environment-friendly freight transport systems with lower costs compared with trucks under some conditions. Specifically, for long-distance freight transport, for example over 500 km, railways and coastal shipping can be successful in providing faster service at lower costs. Emissions of CO_2 by railways are much lower than emissions by trucks. For example, Japan Railway Freight Company estimated that CO_2 emissions for transporting goods of 100 tons for 1000 km by truck amount to 35 tons. In contrast, CO_2 emissions for transporting the same amount of goods by railways (980 km) plus trucks (20 km) amount to 2.66 tons, which is only 7.6 per cent of trucks.

Intermodal freight transport by 'road and rail' or 'road and ship' has great potential to decrease the negative environmental impact in terms of CO_2 and other hazardous gas emissions. However, intermodal freight transport inevitably requires mode changes at connecting points or intermodal terminals. It requires huge investment for constructing and maintaining intermodal terminals, and transshipment at intermodal terminals involves time and costs. The functions and efficiency of these terminals are crucial for successful operations of intermodal freight transport.

Figure 4.1 shows an example of costs for intermodal freight transport by road and rail. The cost for railways per ton-kilometre is generally lower than that for roads. Therefore, the inclination of the line representing railways between intermodal terminals in Figure 4.1 is smaller than that for roads only. But at intermodal freight terminals, loading and unloading costs will be incurred. As a result, the total cost for intermodal freight transport will be higher than the cost for road-only transport over shorter distances than the critical distance, d_c in Figure 4.1. For transport over longer distances than the critical distance, d_c, intermodal freight transport will be preferable in terms of costs. If new technology for transshipment of goods allows loading and unloading costs at intermodal freight terminals to be reduced, the critical distance, d_c, will become shorter to ensure intermodal freight transport is more widely acceptable. The critical distance is defined as the distance where the costs for the road-only freight transport and those for intermodal (road and rail) freight transport including terminal costs are the same.

We assume that cost per distance for roads only, and the road part of intermodal transport, is the same. This assumption may not be realistic. In reality cost per distance for pre- and end-delivery by road for intermodal transport is higher than that for road-only transport, since the transport distance is shorter for pre- and end-delivery by road for intermodal transport. However, in that case, the explanation in the previous section still holds, if the distance of rail transport is long enough and total cost for intermodal transport is lower than that for road-only transport in the long-distance transport region.

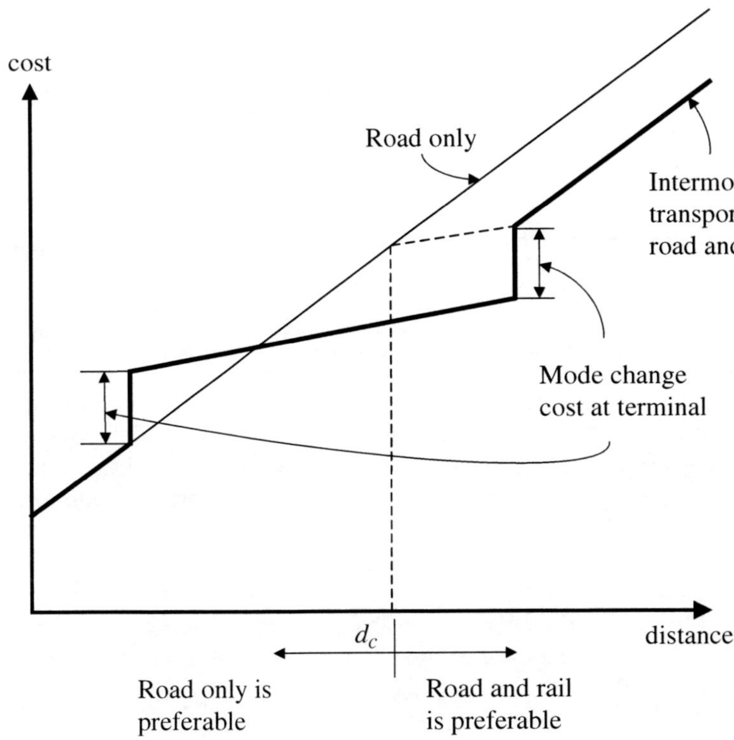

Figure 4.1 *Costs for intermodal freight transport*

4.3 EXAMPLES OF INTERMODAL FREIGHT TRANSPORT

Transporting Waste Materials by Railways

Kawasaki City, located south-west of Tokyo, initiated the transportation of waste materials using railways in 1995. There was a need to transport waste materials, which are generated in the northern part of the city with its increasing population, to the Ukishima waste-disposal centre at the southern coastal area of the city, which has a larger capacity to process waste (900 tons/day). Fortunately there existed a railway line connecting the northern and southern areas of the city and a freight railway station was located near the Ukishima waste-disposal centre. Kawasaki City planned the intermodal freight transport of waste materials using rail, although the distance between the railway stations was only 23 km. Trucks are used for

Table 4.2 Amount of transported waste materials in Kawasaki City, 1999

Item	Capacity of container (ton)	Number of containers per day	Owner of container
General house garbage	10	19	Kawasaki City
Large house garbage	5	20	Kawasaki City
Incinerated ash	10	20	Kawasaki City
Cans	5	10	Freight carrier
Bottles	5	10	Japan Railway Freight

collecting waste material from many generation points to the starting railway station and delivering waste material from the ending railway station to the waste-disposal centre. This system carries general house garbage, large house garbage, incinerated ash, cans and bottles in containers. Table 4.2 shows the amount of waste materials transported in 1999. A specific container was developed for general house garbage, large house garbage, incinerated ash and cans.

The incinerated ash was transported by trucks before intermodal systems were introduced. Under the intermodal system, the number of trucks used for carrying incinerated ash was reduced to seven from 14 with the trucking system. This led to a substantial reduction in hazardous gas emissions.

Intermodal freight transport systems are competitive in general for long-distance transport over 500 km. However, in the Kawasaki case the distance by rail is only 23 km. The reasons for the success of this case are: (1) the railways have a line to the ideal location for the project; (2) they could receive subsidies for the initial investment in the system during the first year of the project from the Ministry of Environment, because it could decrease negative environmental impacts; (3) Japan Railway Freight Company was eager to increase the operation rate of its freight stations.

The Kawasaki case is a successful intermodal freight transport solution over a short distance. It may not be possible for other cities, unless the above-mentioned good conditions are given. In particular a certain amount of demand is required for railway transport, and concentrated disposal of waste materials is needed.

Inland River Shipping

Inland river shipping used to be the dominant mode for freight transport in urban areas before railways became popular in the nineteenth century in Japan. Inland river shipping has declined with the development of railways and roads. At the moment just a small amount of oil, gravel and waste materials are carried by barges and small tankers. The number of freight vessels observed at the mouth of the Arakawa River, Tokyo, was only 56 (including 29 tankers) and that at the mouth of the Sumidagawa River, Tokyo, was 219 (including 49 tankers) in 1997. The total fleet including leisure and tourist boats is only 119 at the Arakawa River and 304 at the Sumidagawa River. Therefore, the use of barges and tankers in inland rivers in Tokyo is very limited. The situation is similar in other cities in Japan.

An example is the transport of gasoline by small tankers from Kawasaki City, Kanagawa Prefecture to Wako City, Saitama Prefecture via the Arakawa River. Wako City is located 31 km upstream from the mouth of the Arakawa River. The capacity of a tanker is about 500 kilolitres. Tankers leave the oil refinery of Kawasaki City at 3 a.m. and arrive at a quay in Wako City at 7–8 a.m. The gasoline is carried to an inventory centre from the quay by pipeline and then distributed by tank lorries to gas stations in Saitama Prefecture and the northern part of Tokyo. Costs for transporting gasoline by tankers are low enough to give a good reason for a slightly lower price of gasoline in Saitama Prefecture.

Another example is that Tokyo Metropolitan Government is transporting waste materials by barges from five waste material collection points via the Arakawa River and its branch rivers. Two types of transport by bulk and containers are applied.

Inland shipping has received attention in terms of alleviating road congestion, reducing negative impacts on the environment and being an alternative mode in emergency of disaster. However, there are several issues to be solved, as listed below:

1. Whether or not to be competitive in terms of total costs including transshipment at quay in rivers.
2. The need to improve river space suitable for shipping by maintaining the depth of water, the clearance under bridges, the width at lock.
3. The need to improve reliability of barge transport due to natural conditions including typhoon and flood.
4. The need to improve quay and storage facilities.

Although we have these problems, from an environmental point of view it may be preferable to transport waste materials and construction materials by inland shipping rather than by road transport. We need to consider inland shipping as an option for urban freight transport. Moreover, inland shipping can be an alternative mode to road in emergencies, such as cases of strong earthquakes. Therefore it is necessary to build loading and unloading facilities along rivers for emergency cases.

4.4 METHOD FOR THE PROMOTION OF INTERMODAL FREIGHT TRANSPORT

The Foundation for Promoting Personal Mobility and Ecological Transportation (1999) conducted a questionnaire survey of 3000 shippers in Japan (receiving answers from 10.1 per cent of them) on the promotion of intermodal freight transport using railways and coastal shipping. The results indicated some important shortcomings regarding both modes of intermodal freight transport:

- The travel time is longer than that for roads.
- Carrying methods and lot size are not always suitable.
- Not always appropriate railways or sea routes.
- Poor access routes to railway stations and seaports.

Improving the access route to railway stations and seaports is essential for promoting intermodal freight transport. If we can reduce door-to-door travel times by improving the access route to intermodal terminals, it is possible to shift more goods from trucks to intermodal systems. It is interesting that not many shippers pointed out that the price is higher than for trucks. We can recognize that travel times are more important than costs for promoting intermodal freight transport. Therefore, if customers set very strict time windows for trucks to arrive to collect or deliver goods, it is very important for freight carriers to focus on reducing total travel times in applying intermodal freight transport.

For the promotion of intermodal freight transport, it is necessary to improve infrastructure and information systems. Regarding infrastructure, roads, railways, seaports and airports have been planned separately and there are not enough terminals for mode change. However, in 1997, national government adopted major policy measures for intermodal freight transport. For example, the 'connectivity index' was taken as a performance index, which measures the level of easiness of access to seaports and airports. The connectivity index, for example, indicates the percentage in terms of number of seaports to which a vehicle can access from the nearest interchange of motorways within ten minutes.

Improvement of information systems is important for the promotion of intermodal freight transport. For example, an electronic manufacturing company in Osaka improved information systems for transporting their products by trucks from their factory to a railway freight station. As a result, three containers of 5 tons can be carried together, while previously each container was carried separately. This improvement is actually due to the cooperation of the production and transport sections of the company, which was achieved through the improvement of information systems between both sections. This company enjoys a substantial reduction of transport costs using intermodal (road and rail) systems. It carried about 7 per cent of its products by intermodal systems in 2002 and is trying to increase the percentage up to 15 per cent.

Intermodal freight transport systems will become more important and will often provide solutions for reducing the negative impacts of freight transport on the environment in the near future. The reasons are that intermodal freight transport systems can fully utilize the existing infrastructure of roads, railways, seaports and so on with minimum costs, and that they can successfully apply advanced information systems to improve freight transport systems. These innovative ideas are beneficial in solving complicated freight transport problems, taking into consideration the balance between efficiency and the environment which is required for sustainable freight transport systems.

REFERENCES

Foundation for Promoting Personal Mobility and Ecological Transport (1999), *Report on Modal Shift Model Projects* (in Japanese), Tokyo: Foundation for Promoting Personal Mobility and Ecological Transportation.

Ministry of Transport, Transport Policy Bureau, Information and Research Department (1998), *National Transportation Statistics Handbook*, and additional information from the home page of the Ministry of Land, Infrastructure and Transport, which is the reformed Ministry.

OECD (2002), *Benchmarking Intermodal Freight Transport*, Paris: OECD.

OECD (2003), *Delivering the Goods: 21st Century Challenges to Urban Goods Transport*, Paris: OECD.

Taniguchi, E. and R.G. Thompson (eds) (2002), *Innovations in Freight Transport*, Southampton: WIT Press.

Taniguchi, E., R.G. Thompson, T. Yamada and R. Van Duin (2001), *City Logistics: Network Modelling and Intelligent Transport Systems*, Oxford: Pergamon.

5. Bundling of freight flows and hinterland network developments

Theo Notteboom

5.1 INTRODUCTION

In the pre-container era boxes were shipped from the inland production centre to the nearest port and shipping lines designed routes to cover all ports within a coastal range, resulting in captive hinterlands and limited inter-port competition. Containerization and innovations to the inland transport systems led to a time–space convergence and made market players reconfigure and synchronize liner service schedules and associated hinterland networks. As a result, captive hinterlands have quickly been replaced by intensified competition between ports, with cargo moving more flexibly from any inland location to any suitable port that interests an ocean carrier or shipper. Containerization and intermodality have strengthened the symbiotic relationship between foreland and hinterland in the sense that a true foreland–hinterland continuum has come into existence.

In a shipping industry already dominated by large vessels, mergers and acquisitions and strategic alliances, the potential cost savings at sea still left are getting smaller and the pressure to find cost savings elsewhere is growing. Market players in the maritime industry have identified inland logistics as one of the most vital areas still left to cut costs, to add value and to increase profitability. This has triggered an upsurge in the interest for landside segments of the transportation market. In their search for efficient inland services, shipping lines, transport operators, port authorities and shippers have come up with network solutions leading to new dynamics in transport system development. The bundling of freight flows in a limited number of transport nodes proves to be one of the main driving forces in this development.

This chapter discusses intermodal network development with particular reference to bundling systems. The first two sections approach the topic from a conceptual point of view, whereas a third part seeks to apply some of the concepts to the intermodal situation in the Hamburg–Le Havre port system.

5.2 BUNDLING OF FREIGHT FLOWS

The Design of a Container Liner Service

There are three key decisions for service planners to make: the service frequency (including the fixed days and hours of the week for departure and arrival), the loading capacity of the transport equipment used and the number of stops at intermediate terminals (if any). These elements are highly interrelated.

Before an operator can start with the actual design of a regular container service, he has to assess the market to be served and the distribution of service demand. The variables to consider include the number and dispersion of final destinations, the density of cargo flows to and from these inland destinations and the existence of trade imbalances. The service planner needs concise information on the cargo availability and related volatility on the intended route as this will have a crucial impact on the possibilities with respect to unit capacities deployed, service frequency offered and the number of intermediate stops along the route. A container service has more chances of survival if a substantial part of the necessary cargo volume is guaranteed by a large customer (for example a shipper or a shipping line). There is no such thing as an ideal service configuration that could be recommended for all origin–destination relations. Each situation warrants a separate study to determine the configuration that will provide the services best suited to market needs.

Service frequency

In deep-sea liner shipping, shippers typically demand a weekly call at each and every port of call in the rotation. Service frequencies in hinterland transportation largely depend on the route considered, but typically range between one and six departures per week. The marginal utility to shippers of an additional departure sharply declines once a daily service is offered. Consequently, not many routes exist with shuttle services running at ten departures per week or more. In the case of such high frequencies, operators are doing so primarily to deal with huge container volumes (for example container exchanges and repositioning between major load centre ports), not to please the shippers.

Loading capacity

The optimal size of the vehicle depends on cargo availability, shippers' needs for transit time, or other service elements and choices made with respect to the two other key variables. Container service operators have to make a trade-off between frequency and volume on the trunk lines: smaller unit capacities allow meeting shippers' demand for high frequencies and lower transit times, while larger units allow operators to benefit from economies of modal size. In liner shipping, the biggest vessels are deployed on the longest routes to benefit the most from economies of scale at sea; see for example Cullinane and Khanna (1999). The relation between vehicle capacity and transport distance is less straightforward when dealing with inland transport services. One of the reasons is that physical and operational restrictions in hinterland networks put an upper limit on unit capacity. Typical examples are draft conditions and bridge heights along a river system, or the maximum rail track length in an inland rail terminal (that is, typically 600 to 750 m in Europe and 2000 to 2500 m in the US and Canada).

The relationship between service frequency, loading capacity and annual transport volume for regular inland services is depicted in Figure 5.1. The cross-hatched areas referring to double-stack shuttles, rail shuttles and inland services by barge will be explained later in this chapter.

Stops at intermediate terminals

This decision variable in liner service design relates to a choice between a direct service between loading point and discharging point, or an indirect service calling at one or more intermediate terminals for reasons of bundling.

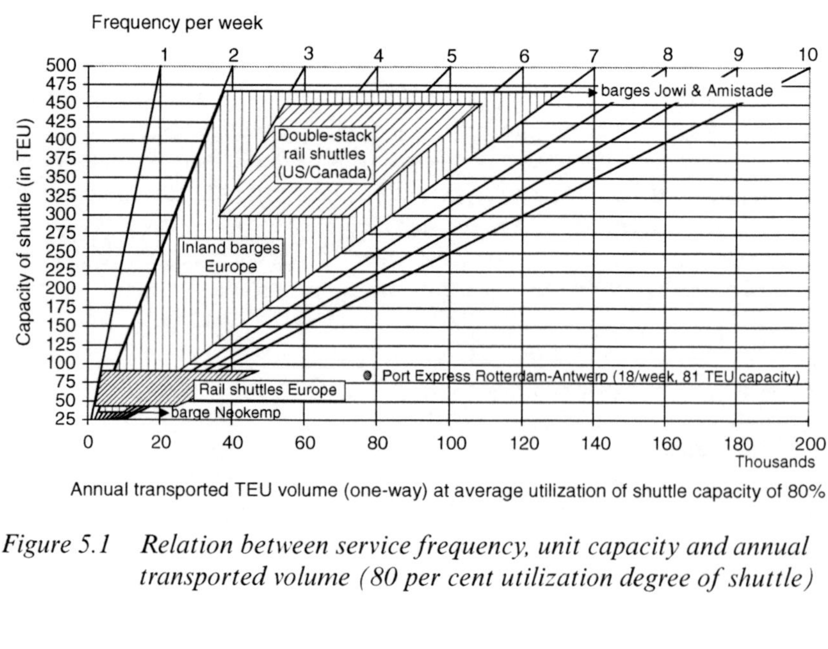

Figure 5.1 Relation between service frequency, unit capacity and annual transported volume (80 per cent utilization degree of shuttle)

Basic Concepts of Bundling

Bundling is one of the key driving forces of container service network dynamics. The bundling of cargo typically involves several layers, starting with the consolidation of parcels onto a pallet and going up to the bundling of a large number of containers onto a trunk line at sea or in the hinterland. In this chapter the focus is on the upper level of bundling activities involving a large number of boxes grouped as one batch on a vessel, train or barge.

Figure 5.2 depicts four types of complex bundling networks that can be used as an alternative to direct point-to-point container services. Networks B up to E rely on en route bundling in intermediate or transfer terminals. In liner shipping, rail transport and inland shipping, these types are often combined to form multilayer networks.

The advantages of complex bundling are higher load factors and/or the use of larger transport units in terms of TEU (twenty-foot equivalent unit) capacity and/or higher frequencies and/or more destinations served. The main disadvantages of complex bundling networks are the need for extra container handling at intermediate terminals (higher transit time, increased risk of damage), longer transport distances and a higher dependency on service quality. These elements incur additional costs which could counterbalance the cost advantages linked to higher load factors or the use of larger unit capacities.

Complex bundling networks strongly rely on the speed and cost-effectiveness of the transfers at intermediate terminals. Appropriate handling equipment needs to be in place, which is financially justified only where there is sufficient traffic. In rail, automated container transfers offer possibilities as an alternative to the practice of shunting container trains. Bontekoning (2000) illustrates that lo-lo hub terminals (load-on/load-off) can even outperform marshalling yards when it comes to efficiency and speed. One way to guarantee higher volumes is by providing a broader range of services and modes and by mixing local traffic with transit traffic. Another way is by directing cargo of different ports to one and the same inland hub. The duplication of hub terminals, each operated by other market players, is only feasible in places with sufficient cargo volumes.

Longer transport distances combined with time lost at intermediate terminals result in longer transport time compared to direct shuttles. However, bundling networks often go hand in hand with higher frequencies per individual route. These higher frequencies could eventually make the bundling option more attractive when it comes to transit times and time costs to the cargo. Figure 5.3 underlines this statement by using two hypothetical situations: a direct shuttle service from a seaport to an inland destination (that

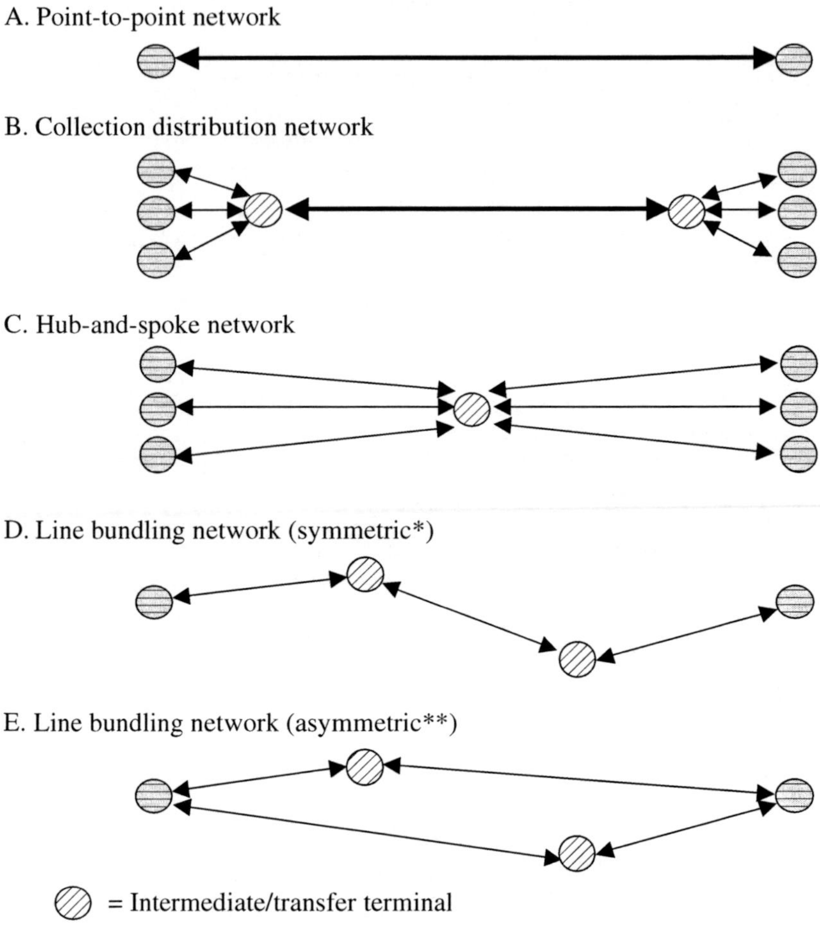

Notes: * outbound voyage and return voyage feature the same intermediate terminals
** return shuttle calls at other terminals

Figure 5.2 Basic bundling concepts

is end terminal) on the basis of two departures per week (dotted lines in Figure 5.3) and an indirect shuttle via an intermediate terminal on the basis of six departures per week (bold lines in Figure 5.3). Total transit time for the latter option equals about two days compared to one day for the direct shuttle. These transit times only take account of transport time and time in intermediate terminals. However, the dwell-time at the deep-sea terminal (that is, time between the discharge of the deep-sea container vessel and the departure of the inland service) needs to be integrated in the equation as

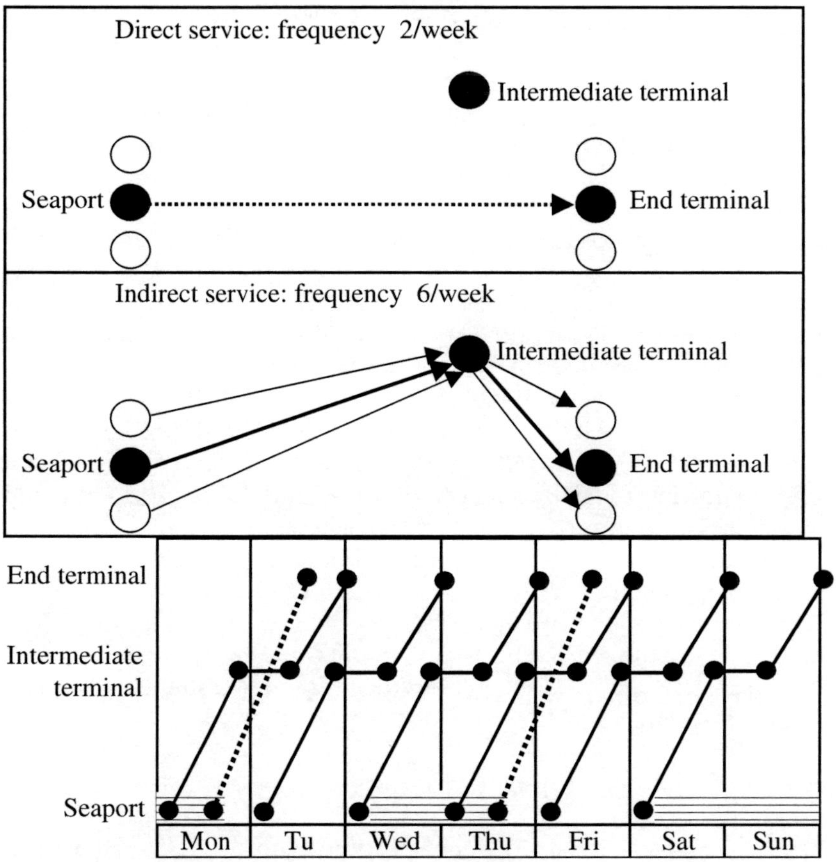

Figure 5.3 Direct versus indirect inland services

well. If a deep-sea liner service schedule is badly synchronized to the hinterland service schedule, then dwell-time – even for time-sensitive cargo – can be rather elevated. As such, the direct shuttle option offers the shortest delivery time only if the container arrives during the hatched time intervals. For example, a container which is ready for inland transport on Wednesday afternoon is better off with a direct shuttle service. For a container discharged from a deep-sea vessel on Friday at dawn, the indirect shuttle option provides the shortest transit time to the inland destination.

This example demonstrates that the competitiveness of direct shuttles with a low frequency largely depends on the ability of the operator to coordinate departure and arrival times with deep-sea operations and the normal working hours of firms. There also exist some time constraints caused by typical use of infrastructure, for example train path availability for freight trains (which in Europe is rather low during the day because of slots dedicated to passenger trains) and lock operating hours (for example the locks on the Flemish waterway system do not operate on Sunday).

If an operator opts for a line bundling network a decision has to be taken with respect to the number of intermediate stops. Limiting the number of stops at intermediate terminals shortens round trip times and increases the number of round trips per year, thereby maximizing revenue and minimizing the equipment required for that specific service. This is a combined result of several effects: (1) lower total (inland) port time and inland port charges on the round trip; (2) a smaller number of units needed to run a service; and (3) a smaller total round trip length as possible diversion distances to intermediate terminals are avoided.

More intermediate stops can lead to lower pre- and end-haul costs. These costs typically are very significant in intermodal transport. Moreover, it might be possible to realize a higher utilization rate of the transport equipment by having more calls per round trip. Hence, the vicinity of an inland terminal could convince shippers to opt for intermodal transport.

In shipping and in barge transport, the addition of an extra intermediate terminal in a round trip might generate additional costs for more complicated vessel stowage and rehandles. In rail transport the inclusion of an additional intermediate terminal leads to more complex shunting of wagon groups or container repositioning.

Network Design and Shippers' Requirements

Operators typically aim for cost minimization of their intermodal network operations. As such, transport operators are tempted to design only the bundling networks they find convenient to offer, but at the same time they have to provide the services their customers want in terms of frequency, direct accessibility and connectivity. Moreover, operators have to offer regular schedules with service characteristics that do not alter too frequently.

Shippers' preferences are driven by the minimization of generalized costs. These costs include all costs of freight movements, costs of loading and unloading and transfer, handling operations at groupage points, capital costs of the goods and depreciation during transport, costs related to damage and inventory costs to the consignee. Shippers also show a keen interest in the qualitative performance of the whole transport chain in terms of reliability, availability and compatibility. Hence, inefficiencies at this level will generate indirect logistics costs (for example production losses caused by late deliveries). Operators have to take account of the wider logistics perspective of the shippers.

The tension between routing and demand is important. The network planners may direct flows along paths that are optimal for the system, with the lowest cost for the entire network being achieved by indirect routing via hub terminals (ports or inland centres) and the amalgamation of flows. However, the more efficient the network from the operator's point of view, the less convenient that network could be for shippers' needs. Time, cost or reliability concerns of the shipper could make an operator with indirect routes less competitive, thereby opening the possibilities for other operators to fill gaps in the market. The optimal service schedule as such is a function not only of operator-specific operational factors, but also of shippers' needs (for transit time and other service elements) and of shippers' willingness to pay for a better service. It is clear that the spatial development of bundling networks largely depends on the balance of power between shippers and operators.

The Impact of Human Behaviour on Network Design

Human behaviour might impede operators from achieving an optimal network configuration. Incorrect or incomplete information results in bounded rationality in operators' network design, leading to suboptimal decisions. Shippers sometimes impose bounded rational behaviour on transport operators, for example where a shipper asks to call at a specific port or to use a specific land transport mode. Secondly, opportunistic behaviour of economic actors or informal commitments to individuals or companies might lead to non-cost-minimizing behaviour. Thirdly, carriers might stick to a specific network design as they assume that the mental efforts (inertia) and transactions costs linked to changes in network design will not outweigh the extra costs of the current non-optimal solution.

Behavioural aspects are surely having an influence on network design by shipping lines and transport operators, but the exact measurement of these impacts remains a challenge that is not tackled in this chapter.

The Spatial Concentration of Cargo in Port Systems and in the Hinterland

The feasibility of bundling systems in hinterland container traffic partly depends on the level of cargo concentration in the port system and on the dispersion level of maritime cargo volumes in the hinterland (Figure 5.4).

Much literature discusses the spatial development of seaport systems in relation to maritime and hinterland networks. The model of Taaffe et al. (1963) suggests an increasing level of port concentration as certain hinterland routes develop to a greater extent than others in association with the increased importance of particular urban centres. The geographical system

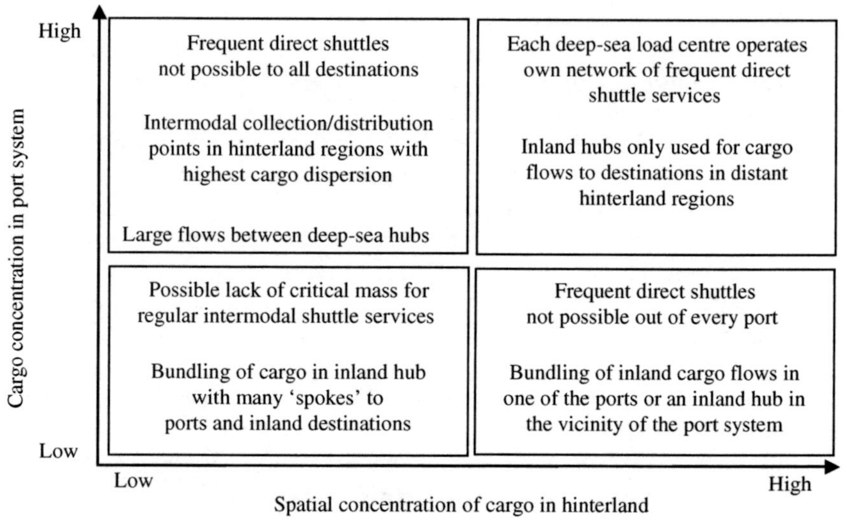

Figure 5.4 Inland service configuration as a function of the level of cargo concentration in port systems and in the hinterland

would evolve from an initial pattern of scattered, poorly connected ports along the coastline to a main network consisting of corridors between gateway ports and major hinterland centres. The models of Barke (1986) and Hayuth (1981) are quite similar, though they have introduced a process of port system deconcentration. In the meantime, some authors have introduced modifications to the above models in order to reflect the uniqueness of some port regions (see for example Wang 1998). Empirical research has demonstrated that some port systems and port ranges are getting more spatially concentrated while others are evolving to a more evenly distributed system, see for example Kuby and Reid (1992), Notteboom (1997) and Lago et al. (2001). Cargo concentration at the level of an entire container port system is clearly something else than concentration of cargo at the level of the liner networks of individual carriers, simply because not all carriers will choose the same load centres in their liner service networks (Cullinane and Khanna 1999, p. 133). Shipping lines often use port equalization systems to ensure that shippers are compensated for possible cost disadvantages linked to the bundling of cargo in just a few ports of call. The carriers will equalize charges for inland transport from points in the hinterland to a range of designated base ports which it serves (Gilman 1997). With the severe pressure on ocean freight rates of recent years, the limited shipping revenue of major sea carriers makes it increasingly difficult to sustain the existing port equalization systems.

Experts generally agree on the fact that a certain level of traffic concentration in a limited number of seaports is required in order to allow a virtuous cycle of modal shifts from road haulage to high-volume transport modes. Most big ports are witnessing a virtuous cycle: the availability of cargo makes it possible to build an extensive network of intermodal hinterland services and this in itself attracts even more cargo (partly triggered by economies of scale and density). But even port systems with a low degree of concentration have embraced intermodal transport as maritime container traffic has increased sufficiently in the last decades to allow the operation of frequent inland shuttles to destinations in the immediate hinterland. As such, a low level of cargo concentration in a port system can still be beneficial to the development of intermodal services if it goes hand in hand with substantial cargo volumes per load centre or if inland hubs are in place where outgoing container flows of the individual seaports can be bundled.

There is no general rule available to determine the critical mass that a port needs to set up a network of direct shuttles to the hinterland. Much will depend on the spatial dispersion of cargo in the service area of the port. A port that only serves a dense local economic cluster will typically have less difficulties in developing a regular inland service than a port handling containers for a large number of final destinations dispersed over a vast hinterland. Empirical evidence demonstrates that a load centre with a large local cargo base will sooner or later be tempted to increase the inland penetration of its intermodal hinterland network so as to increase its capture area. From that moment on, the existing dense network of direct shuttles to nearby destinations might be complemented by indirect inland services to more distant destinations built around one or more inland hubs. Extensive cargo concentration on a few trunk lines opens possibilities to economies of scale in inland shuttles (through the deployment of longer trains or larger inland barges) but even more likely to higher frequencies.

Extreme forms of cargo bundling in seaports and inland centres could decrease the efficiency of transport systems because shipments would be significantly delayed, although having low transport costs. Hence, the current development and expansion of intermodal transportation relies on the synchronization of different geographical scales. But when the synchronization level increases, the sea–land network as a whole becomes more unstable (Rodrigue 1999).

Bundling Concepts in Port Areas

The formation of shuttles in large seaports requires the grouping of containers within the port area. Two alternative systems exist in this respect (Figure 5.5): either the vehicle (that is, barge or train combination) calls at various

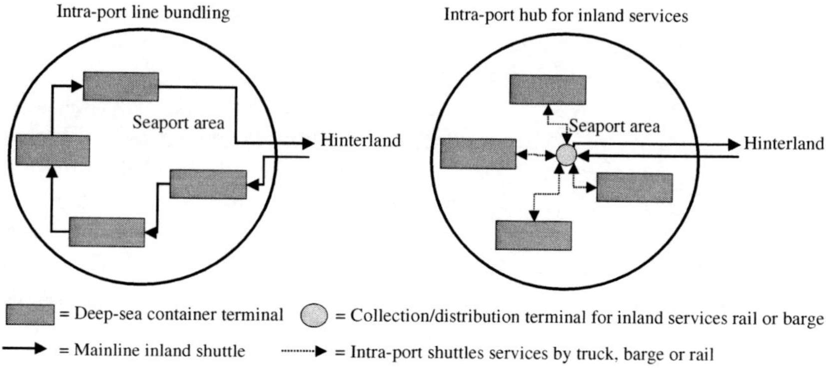

Figure 5.5 Container bundling concepts in multi-terminal container ports

deep-sea container terminals in order to fill the available capacity, or all containers bound for a specific inland shuttle are brought to one or two central transshipment points through a network of separate intra-port services by truck, barge or rail. In the first option, barges and trains consume time while collecting hinterland cargo. Study results with respect to barge operations in the port of Rotterdam revealed that in 1997 container barges spent some 28 hours in the port on average. In this time span the number of calls at terminals in the port area amounted to eight, with 16 moves per call on average (Konings 2002). The use of one or two central loading and discharging points in the port area dramatically reduces port time for barge and train combinations, but incurs extra costs related to the operation of inter-terminal container transfers and extra container handlings. The desired configuration is highly dependent on the spatial layout of the port area (as compared to inter-terminal distances), operational characteristics of terminals, berths and transport equipment, and the decision of who will have to bear the costs of inter-terminal transfers (shipping line, terminal operator or any other party).

5.3 INLAND SERVICE CONFIGURATION AND BUNDLING IN THE HAMBURG–LE HAVRE RANGE

Introduction

This section seeks to apply some of the above concepts to one specific port range in Europe, that is, the Hamburg–Le Havre range (H-LH range) consisting of Antwerp, Zeebrugge, Ghent and Ostend in Belgium (B), Le

Table 5.1 *Cargo throughput ('000 TEU) and concentration in H-LH range*

	1975	1980	1985	1990	1995	2000	2002	2004	2005
Rotterdam (NL)	1 079	1 901	2 655	3 666	4 787	6 275	6 515	8 281	9 287
Hamburg (D)	326	783	1 159	1 969	2 890	4 248	5 374	7 003	8 087
Antwerp (B)	297	724	1 243	1 549	2 329	4 082	4 777	6 064	6 488
Bremen/ Bremerhaven (D)	405	703	986	1 163	1 518	2 752	2 982	3 469	3 736
Le Havre (F)	232	507	566	858	970	1 465	1 720	2 150	2 100
Zeebrugge (B)	151	181	218	334	528	965	959	1 197	1 408
Dunkirk (F)	38	63	71	71	71	149	161	200	205
Rouen (F)	14	98	135	93	120	146	144	139	161
Amsterdam (NL)	32	72	79	69	91	53	45	52	66
Flushing (NL)	28	83	35	26	6	3	9	27	39
Cuxhaven (D)	0	0	0	3	16	24	27	36	35
Ghent (B)	10	10	10	10	6	10	21	35	31
Ostend (B)	0	0	0	0	0	0	9	15	9
Wilhelmshaven (D)	0	0	0	0	6	29	41	43	3
Emden (D)	0	0	0	0	0	57	69	1	0
Total	2 612	5 125	7 158	9 811	13 338	20 257	22 856	28 713	31 655

Source: Based on data provided by the respective port authorities and Containerisation International Online: www.ci-online.co.uk.

Havre, Dunkirk and Rouen in France (F), Rotterdam, Amsterdam and Zeeland seaports in the Netherlands (NL) and Hamburg, Bremerhaven, Cuxhaven, Emden and Wilhelmshaven in Germany (D). The results presented here are not transferable to other port ranges in the world as each port system has its distinctive characteristics with respect to the spatial configuration of ports and hinterlands, the strategies of shipping lines and transport operators, and the policy outlines of local, regional, national and supranational public authorities.

With a total maritime container throughput of 31.7 million TEU handled along a shoreline of merely 500 nautical miles, the H-LH range ranks among the busiest container regions in the world. The C4 index, that is, the joint market share of the four biggest container ports, amounts to an elevated 87 per cent. The Gini concentration ratio remained rather stable since the 1980s at around 0.7, pointing to a considerable inequality in size among the ports considered.

Most mainline operators running deep-sea liner services to and from the Hamburg–Le Havre range stick to line bundling itineraries with calls scheduled in each of the main markets, that is, three to five regional load centres per loop, of which one call is at a load centre in the UK. Maritime hub-and-spoke networks and related feeder connections in Northern Europe have not developed to the level at which some observers have predicted. Sea–sea transshipment volumes in the H-LH range do not exceed 40 per cent of any port's throughput. Consequently, the competitiveness of the load centres in the range is largely determined by the ports' capabilities in dealing with container flows to the immediate and more distant hinterland regions.

Competition for hinterland cargo is fierce. Antwerp, a centrally located port in the range, competes heavily with Rotterdam for local and European hinterland cargo, with Le Havre for French cargo, and with Bremen and Hamburg for traffic to and from Germany, the Alpine region, northern Italy and Central and Eastern Europe (Figure 5.6). Major hinterland overlap regions characterized by intense port rivalry are the Rhine axis (the German Ruhr Area in particular), northern France, northern Italy and the

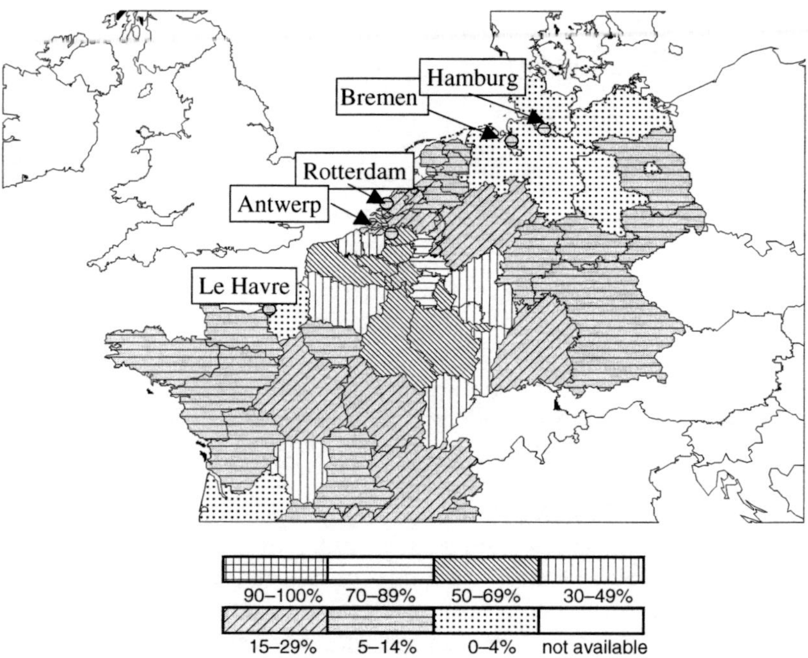

Notes: Market shares are based on total hinterland container flows of Le Havre, Antwerp, Rotterdam, Bremen/Bremerhaven and Hamburg.

Figure 5.6 The market share of Antwerp in hinterland traffic to/from the Benelux countries, France and Germany (basis = container flows in TEU)

Table 5.2 Modal split in the hinterland transport of containers

	Rail			Road			Barge		
	1998	2001	2003	1998	2001	2003	1998	2001	2003
Rotterdam	14.5%	13.0%	10.0%	51.3%	48.7%	50.0%	34.2%	39.0%	40.0%
Antwerp	7.8%	8.8%	9.5%	64.5%	61.3%	59.5%	27.7%	29.9%	31.0%
Le Havre	14.3%	11.4%	12.4%	84.6%	85.3%	82.8%	1.3%	3.1%	4.8%
Zeebrugge	34.4%	41.9%	40.2%	50.6%	48.8%	55.1%	15.1%	9.2%	4.7%
Dunkirk	9.0%	13.5%	20.5%	90.0%	82.5%	76.7%	1.0%	4.0%	2.7%
Hamburg	29.7%	28.7%	28.7%	70.1%	69.9%	69.8%	0.2%	1.4%	1.7%
Bremerhaven	33.1%	36.0%	30.6%	65.0%	62.0%	67.3%	1.9%	2.0%	2.0%

Source: Based on data port authorities and Ocean Shipping Consultants.

east–west corridors from the Benelux ports to the hinterland. Captive hinterlands are rare in the H-LH range.

The German ports have developed a strong orientation on rail shuttles, whereas Antwerp and Rotterdam heavily rely on barges to reach water-linked hinterland regions (Table 5.2). Most ports have achieved a considerable modal shift in hinterland container transport, but rail and inland navigation still have not reached their maximum potential. Trucking remains the most important transport mode in all ports, especially in cargo volumes destined for France and to inland destinations outside the large economic centres.

The modal split figures include container exchanges between the load centres. For example, many carriers have limited the number of port calls in the Benelux to just one port per loop (Notteboom and Winkelmans 1999). Large landside container interchanges between Rotterdam and Antwerp on the one hand (that is, 740 000 TEU by barge and 110 000 TEU by rail in 2001) and between Zeebrugge and Antwerp on the other (that is, 153 000 TEU by rail in 2001) are the result.

Carrier haulage on the European continent is still relatively low compared to North America and many parts of the Far East. The share of carrier haulage in 2005 was about 30 per cent on average, but large differences can be observed among routes and regions (MDS Transmodal 1998). A few carriers have succeeded in attaining a high level of carrier haulage (cf. Maersk Line). Other carriers with less experience or interest in European inland transport control less than 10 per cent of inland container movements. The high level of merchant haulage on some traffic relations can make it more difficult for operators when setting up new hinterland services, as it typically demands more effort to bundle cargo that is dispersed over a large number of cargo-controlling shippers.

Container Bundling in Rail Networks

Inland transport costs in North America have been squeezed through the introduction of the double-stack technology in combination with the minibridge concept (see for example Slack 1994). The breakthrough of the double-stack technology came in 1984 when APL started a scheduled rail service between Los Angeles and Chicago. Thuong (1989) demonstrated that operating costs of double-stack trains are up to 60 per cent lower than traditional COFC and TOFC technologies (container on flatcar and trailer on flatcar). Carey (1987) suggested a reduction of 30 per cent. Double-stack trains have a large unit capacity (see Figure 5.1) and typically bridge distances of more than 1000 km.

In Europe, rail logistics are highly complex. A geographically, politically and economically fragmented Europe prevented the realization of greater intermodal scale and scope economies (Charlier and Ridolfi 1994). In recent years, initiatives have emerged that should lead to real pan-European rail services on a one-stop shop basis. For instance, the Eurogate group has developed the Hannibal project, a north–south rail corridor that connects the intermodal services of subsidiary Sogemar in Italy to the shuttle network of boxXpress.de in Germany (Alberghini 2002).

The backbone of rail services out of the load centres in the H-LH range is formed by direct shuttle trains that offer uninterrupted services between a port and one point of destination at a fixed time schedule and a fixed composition of wagons (typically around 70 to 80 TEU capacity). These shuttle trains can only be exploited in a profitable way on a number of high-density traffic corridors such as the Rhine axis and the transalpine route. At present, intermodal transport accounts for some 10 per cent of transalpine traffic between Italy and France and some 20 per cent in Germany and Italy. On some tracks, such as the Cologne–Milan corridor, the figure is as high as 40 per cent. The profitability of a lot of individual direct shuttle trains, even to the immediate hinterland of the Northern European load centre ports, remains insecure. As a result, a new direct shuttle service is often terminated within a time span of less than one year, simply because cargo availability is low or highly fluctuating. Some carriers and rail operators have resolved the problems related to the fluctuating volumes and the numerous final destinations by bundling container flows in centrally located nodes in the more immediate hinterland. Hence, it is much easier to fill a mixed block train containing cargo for various destinations to a nearby inland hub than to run a direct dedicated shuttle train to a final destination in the distant hinterland. Moreover, the services offered by the master hubs allow for increasing the frequency of the scheduled services between load centres and distant destinations. In the 1990s numerous intermodal railway networks of the

B-or C-type emerged (see Figure 5.2), thereby allowing higher service frequencies and the inclusion of smaller container ports in the network. The nodes within these networks were connected by frequent block and shuttle trains with capacities for a single train combination ranging from 40 up to 90 TEU. Shuttle trains from the main ports carrying containers for many destinations arrived in the hub on a regular basis. The wagon groups were exchanged between trains at Metz and were combined to form new single-destination shuttle trains heading for the distant hinterland of the Rhine–Scheldt delta ports.

Some examples were the Qualitynet of Intercontainer-Interfrigo (ICF) with Metz-Sablon in the north-east of France as master hub linking up the Rhine–Scheldt delta ports with the rest of Western Europe, the North European Network (NEN) with master hub Dry Port Muizen, and Combi 24, an extensive intermodal shuttle train network covering the whole of France via the inland hub of Paris and with extensions to Benelux ports.

Once a hub-and-spoke network is installed, it is hard for the associated rail operator to shift back to a system of direct shuttle trains. The conversion of one rail service out of the hub-and-spoke network to a direct service decreases total cargo volume in the network and as such might negatively affect the profitability and operational efficiency within the bundling system.

In the new millennium, European rail liberalization has partly contributed to a decline of many of the hub-and-spoke networks. New railway operators often engage in cherry-picking by introducing competing direct shuttle trains on a spoke of an established hub-and-spoke network of a competitor. This organizational dimension in the rail industry has a clear spatial impact: it creates a negative affect on cargo volumes on the spoke and might lead to a collapse of the whole hub-and-spoke system. For example, both ICF's Qualitynet and IFB's North European Network (NEN) stopped operations in 2004. The rail operators involved shifted operations to a system of direct shuttle trains out of the main load centres. A further decline of hub-and-spoke rail networks in Europe could seriously affect the future growth potential of smaller and new ports as they would remain confronted with the vicious circle effect.

Most ports in the H-LH now rely on a blend of direct shuttles, inter-port shuttles (for example DeltaExpress and PortExpress between Antwerp and Rotterdam, and Railbarge on the Antwerp–Zeebrugge link) and block trains. The Antwerp situation is depicted in Figure 5.7. Rotterdam and Antwerp each have between 150 and 200 intermodal rail departures per week. Le Havre features only a limited number of direct shuttles via the joint-venture Le Havre Shuttles (LHS), but is well connected to CNC's hub-and-spoke network assembled around a central node near Paris.

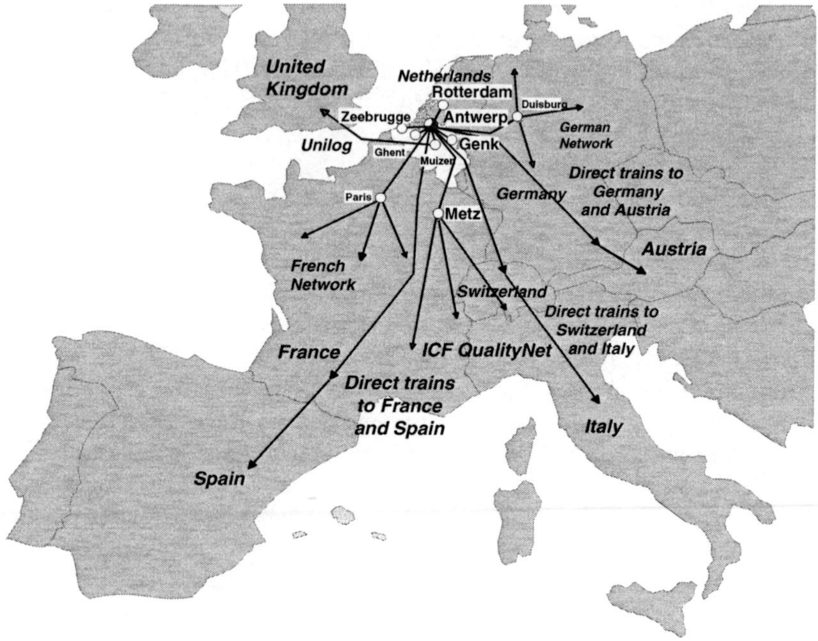

Figure 5.7 Antwerp's rail network for containerized cargo

Hamburg's rail connections outperform all other ports in numbers (that is, more than 200 international and 250 national shuttle and block train services per week) and in traffic volumes by rail (that is, nearly 1 million TEU in 2003). German container terminal operators are directly involved in intermodal rail transport. HHLA has a stake in Metrans, Polzug and HHCE (Hamburg Hungaria Container Express) and formed Hanse Express with DB. Eurogate Intermodal formed boxXpress.de together with ERS (European Rail Shuttle) and KEP Logistik. BoxXpress.de organizes shuttle trains to and from German ports completely independently of DB Cargo. Furthermore, Eurogate has a controlling interest in the Italian rail operator Sogemar (through Contship Italia). The German case is quite unique in the H-LH range.

A number of shipping lines have joined forces to develop intermodal shuttles, especially on routes where the existing rail products lack a good price–quality relation. A good example of carrier cooperation in the rail sector is European Rail Shuttle (ERS), controlled by the Maersk group. ERS operates shuttle trains mainly out of the port of Rotterdam to inland destinations in the Benelux countries, Germany, Poland, Italy, the Czech

Republic, Hungary and Slovakia. Starting at three shuttles a week in 1994, ERS now offers more than 200 shuttles a week. Sea carriers typically buy capacity from the different national railway companies. As such, the quality of service to the customer is partly determined by the performance of the national railway companies. Sea carriers often complain about the elevated traction cost and the long preparations and negotiations with the national railway companies needed to install fast direct rail services. The existing rail operators often complain about cherry-picking practices exerted by newcomers in the market.

Most European rail terminals are owned and operated by the multimodal subsidiaries of the national railway companies. For instance, IFB operates the rail terminals in the seaports of Antwerp, Zeebrugge and Dunkirk, the rail hub Dry Port Muizen and numerous other terminals in Belgium. Conliner owns an extensive network of rail terminals in Germany. Some stevedoring companies have interests in rail terminals (for example ECT runs a rail terminal in Venlo). The fact that most rail operators act as both rail terminal operator and long-haul carrier implies a more or less rational approach to rail system design and the balancing of rail capacity and traffic demand.

Smaller container ports in the Hamburg-Le Havre range tend to seek connection to the extensive hinterland networks of the large load centres by installing shuttle services either to rail platforms in the big container ports or to master rail hubs in the hinterland.

Bundling in the European Barging Network for Container Transportation

Barge container transport in Europe has its origins in transport between Antwerp, Rotterdam and the Rhine basin, and since the mid-1990s it has also developed greatly along the north–south axis between the Benelux countries and northern France. Antwerp and Rotterdam together handle about 95 per cent of total European container transport by barge. Volumes on the Rhine have increased from 200 000 TEU in 1985 to some 1.5 million TEU in 2004, leading to higher frequencies and bigger vessels. The fact that barge traffic is primarily concentrated in only two maritime load centres (Antwerp and Rotterdam) makes it easier to benefit from economies of scale in barge services.

The development of the basic volume for barge transport only started to bring large-scale initiatives on the lower Rhine from 1985 onwards. In order to raise the level of service and prevent destructive competition, the existing barge carriers started to operate joint liner services on the different navigation areas of the Rhine (lower Rhine, middle Rhine and upper Rhine), through operational collaboration agreements (for example

Table 5.3 Typical vessels in the barge fleet of Combined Container Service

	Length	Beam	Max capacity	Max layers	TEU wide	TEU long	Draft
Amistade/Jowi	135.5 m	16.84 m	470 TEU	5	6 TEU	17 TEU	3.6 m
Azolla/Cunera/ Noordkaap/							3.09 m
Saros/Skyline/Victor	110 m	11.45 m	208 TEU	4	4 TEU	13 TEU	3.6 m
Theodorus-Johan	105 m	11.40 m	192 TEU	4	4 TEU	12 TEU	3.52 m
Neokemp	63 m	7.00 m	32 TEU	2	2 TEU	8 TEU	2.8 m

Source: CCS Tariff Information System.

Fahrgemeinschaft Oberrhein on the upper Rhine). These agreements still exist today, although some barge operators such as CCS started services independently from the consortium members.

River systems typically have a tree-like structure with limited or no lateral connections between the different 'branches'. Moreover, the vessel capacity that can be deployed (and consequently the service network that can be used) is restricted and not homogeneous due to varying draft limitations and other physical conditions in various parts of the river system. These elements favour the use of (symmetric) line bundling systems. At present the liner service networks offered on the Rhine are mainly of the line bundling type with each rotation calling at three to eight terminals per navigation area. The inland vessels used on the Rhine have capacities ranging from 90 to 208 TEU, although some bigger units and push convoys can be spotted occasionally (Table 5.3). The average frequencies of barge services on the Rotterdam–Rhine connection increased from four in 1994 to at least a daily service in 2006 Rotterdam has a strong position for barge traffic from and to the lower Rhine and middle Rhine, whereas Antwerp and Rotterdam are equally strong on the upper Rhine.

In the past few years, barge container transport has been characterized by a number of radical structural changes in liner network design.

First, after a period of decentralization in the Rhine basin, the large container carriers are following a strategy aimed at concentrating river freight volumes in just a handful of freight terminals. This rationalization in the number of Rhine terminals served (in particular on the lower and middle Rhine) opens up the possibility of larger barges being introduced. Exceptional examples are the sister ships *Jowi* and *Amistade*, fully cellular motorized barges with a slot capacity of 398 TEU (on the basis of four boxes high) which are used on the CCS services between Antwerp–Rotterdam and the Rhine.

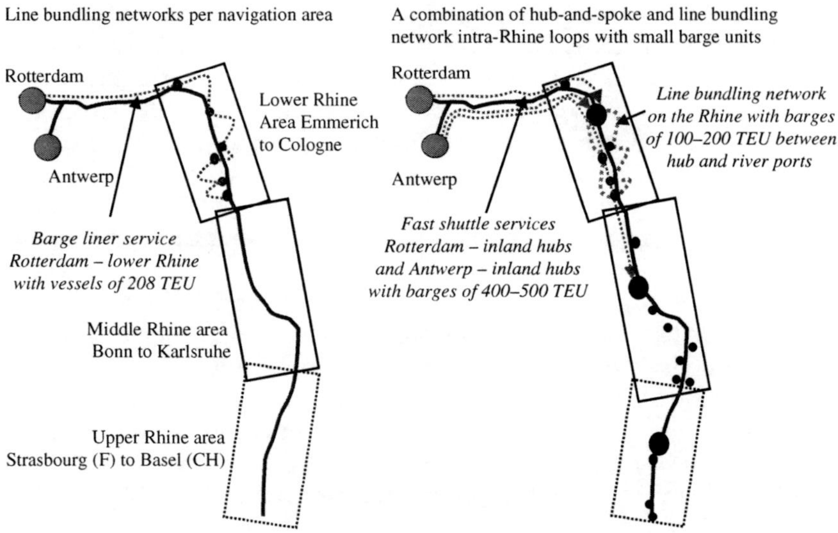

Figure 5.8 An alternative to line bundling networks on the Rhine

Second, although at present there still are no genuine hub-and-spoke structures for barge container transport on the Rhine, the market is tending towards large inland waterway hubs from where the containers can be further distributed by feeder barges, rail and/or road transport. This would add to the pure line bundling networks per navigation area that are currently in use. The Duisburg–Düsseldorf region and the middle Rhine between Mannheim and Wörth are suitable locations for setting up such hubs as part of waterway-based hub-and-spoke networks. Duisburg is generally considered as a superhub, as the port is home to two container terminals: the DeCeTe terminal (partly owned by ECT of Rotterdam) and the Duisburg Intermodal Terminal (owned by DP World and Rhenus each with 37.5 per cent and Duisport with the remaining 25 per cent). Duisburg has a number of direct shuttle services to the Benelux ports (for example Duisburg Express using ships of 268 TEU) and is now developing feeder services to other Rhine terminals (for example the three-times-weekly service to Hamm near Dortmund). At present, the barging industry shows some scepticism as regards extensive hub-and-spoke networks on the Rhine. Nonetheless, it is likely that in the near future new types of bundling systems will be introduced. Figure 5.8 depicts a possible alternative network design.

Third, despite the spatial concentration of freight at the carrier level, the number of terminals in the Rhine basin is steadily increasing. This is the result of new terminal operators arriving on the market (for example DP World in Duisburg) and of new terminals appearing along the Rhine and its tributaries (for example Aschaffenburg, Krefeld and Mannheim Container Terminal).

Fourth, the growing realization of the potential offered by barge container shipping has led to a wave of investment in new terminals over the past few years, in northern France, the Netherlands and Belgium. The Benelux countries and northern France now have more than 35 container terminals, about as many as in the Rhine basin. In 1991 there was still no terminal network on the north–south axis (only two terminals), while the Rhine basin already had 24 container terminals. Outside the Rhine basin, much smaller barges are used, not only because of the limited width of many waterways (for example the Leie and upper Scheldt), but also because of the conviction that smaller units offer greater flexibility and shorter port turnaround times. The next step is to establish a network of liner services connecting the various terminals outside the Rhine basin on a line bundling basis. It is expected that domestic and short-distance networks for container transport by inland barges will emerge in the years to come.

And finally, a number of inland terminals are increasingly concentrating on the complementarity between rail and barge transport. The German inland terminals are emphasizing the trimodal character of the facilities offered, seeking connections to the KLV (Kombinierten Ladungsverkehr) network operated by Deutsche Bahn. Emmerich, Neuss, Mainz, Mannheim, Cologne, Duisburg and Dortmund are some of the inland ports trying to combine their leading role in barge transport with a hub function in international intermodal rail networks. However, in most of them there is still no combined barge–rail transport to speak of: the transit volumes between barge and rail on most of the Rhine terminals (except for Ludwigshafen, Cologne and in particular Duisburg) are still very low. The rail–barge combination requires an advanced synchronization of services as well as the coupling of networks which differ substantially in basic design, that is, line bundling in inland shipping versus direct shuttles and hub-and-spoke systems in rail.

The bulk of the barge services are controlled by independent barge operators. They have always shown a keen interest in the exploitation of inland terminals. About two-thirds of all terminals in the Rhine basin are operated by inland barge operators or the logistics mother company of a barge operator. The remaining terminals are operated or owned by stevedoring companies of seaports, inland port authorities (for example Port Autonome de Strasbourg) or logistics service providers. Stevedoring companies and forwarders have understood that inland terminals can strengthen their position in the market. In many cases, inland terminals serve as extended gates for deep-sea terminals.

5.4 CONCLUSIONS

The performance of seaports is strongly entwined with the development and performance of hinterland networks. Load centres are only as competitive as the inland and relay links that connect to them. This chapter has substantiated the importance of cargo bundling systems as one of the main drivers of hinterland transport system dynamics.

In liner shipping the limits to economies of scale and density have been reached. In the hinterland routing of containers, hub-based indirect shuttle networks have complemented direct rail shuttles. In inland navigation, line bundling services are very common, but might be replaced in the future by a combination of direct shuttles to inland hubs and local line bundling networks. The reorganization and reconfiguration of rail and barge shuttle services to the hinterland is a powerful economic stimulus for actors to redefine their role in landside operations.

There is no such thing as an ideal service configuration that could be recommended for all ports on all origin–destination relations. Each situation warrants a separate study to determine the configuration that will provide the services best suited to market needs. The optimal network design is a function not only of carrier-specific operational factors, but also of shippers' needs (for transit time and other service elements) and of shippers' willingness to pay for a better service. As such, the future spatial development of inland service networks will largely depend on the balance of power between carriers and shippers.

REFERENCES

Alberghini, G. (2002), 'The potential benefits of a European intermodal network for the transport of maritime containers', presentation, ITMMAPS Conference, Antwerp, 18–20 April.

Barke, M. (1986), *Transport and Trade*, Edinburgh: Oliver & Boyd.

Bontekoning, Y. (2000), *A Jump Forward in Intermodal Freight Transport: Are Hub Terminals an Alternative for Shunting?*, Delft: Trail Research School.

Carey, B. (1987), 'How it stacks up in Chicago', *American Shipper*, **29**, p. 39.

Charlier, J. and G. Ridolfi (1994), 'Intermodal transportation in Europe: of modes, corridors and nodes', *Maritime Policy and Management*, **21** (3), pp. 237–50.

Cullinane, K. and M. Khanna (1999), 'Economics of Scale in large container ships', *Journal of Transport Economics and Policy*, **33** (2), pp. 185–208.

Gilman, S. (1997), 'Multimodal rate making and the structure of container networks', in *Essays in Memory of Professor B.N. Metaxas*, Piraeus: University of Piraeus, pp. 327–35.

Hayuth, Y. (1981), 'Containerization and the load center concept', *Economic Geography*, **57** (2), pp. 160–76.

Konings, R. (2002), 'Network design to improve the performance of intermodal barge transport: a case-study for the Rhine river', International Congress on Freight Transport Automation and Multimodality, Delft, 23–24 May.

Kuby, M. and N. Reid (1992), 'Technological change and the concentration of the US General Cargo Port System: 1970–1988', *Economic Geography*, **68** (3), pp. 272–89.

Lago, A., M. Malchow and A. Kanafani (2001), 'An analysis of carriers' schedules and the impact on port selection', *Proceedings of the IAME 2001 Conference*, Hong Kong: Hong Kong Polytechnic University, pp. 123–37.

MDS Transmodal (1998), *The European Container Freight Market: Containers Inland*, Chester: MDS Transmodal.

Notteboom, T. (1997), 'Concentration and load centre development in the European container port system', *Journal of Transport Geography*, **5** (2), pp. 99–115.

Notteboom, T. and W. Winkelmans (1999), 'The load centre ports in the Rhine–Scheldt delta area: complements or substitutes in container liner shipping?' *Proceedings IAME Conference 'Liner Shipping: What's Next?'*, Halifax: International Association of Maritime Economists.

Rodrigue, J.-P. (1999), 'Globalization and the synchronization of transport terminals', *Journal of Transport Geography*, 7, pp. 255–61.

Slack, B. (1994), 'Domestic containerisation and the load centre concept', *Maritime Policy and Management*, **21**, pp. 229–36.

Taaffe, E.J., R.L. Morrill and P.R. Gould (1963), 'Transport expansion in underdeveloped countries: a comparative analysis', *Geographical Review*, **53**, pp. 503–29.

Thuong, L.T. (1989), 'From piggy-back to double-stack intermodalism', *Maritime Policy and Management*, **16** (1), pp. 69–81.

Wang, J.J. (1998), 'A container load center with a developing hinterland: a case study of Hong Kong', *Journal of Transport Geography*, **6** (3), pp. 187–201.

6. Container terminal handling quality

Bart Wiegmans, Peter Nijkamp and Piet Rietveld

6.1 INTRODUCTION

In the container terminal handling market, quality is important in attracting and retaining customers. In Europe, container carriers do have choices between different container ports that can meet their demand. For the terminal operator, this results in increasing importance of quality of services and the need to know the needs of (potential) customers. A favourable network position and well-organized processes are no longer sufficient to attract container volumes. Meeting customer needs and delivering high quality (speed, reliability, and so on) for low costs are critical factors. Currently, adoptions of innovative handling systems to improve operations (and thus quality) have not been signalled in the European container terminal market (Bontekoning 2002). This might be due to the fact that these systems are not cheap and their added value is not recognized by terminal operators so far.

Transport research in the EU (Intermodal Quality 1997; European Commission 1997; TERMINET 1998) shows the following important quality elements concerning transport: time, reliability, flexibility, qualification, accessibility, control, handling price, frequency, speed, long-term planning, management, and safety and security. Dedicated quantitative information on container terminal handling quality is hard to find in the literature. Container terminals are monitoring their quality levels (mainly internal processes), but the results are not made public. Therefore, a more general literature survey forms the main input for this chapter combined with 14 interviews with terminal operators.

The aim of this chapter is to offer an approach for measuring container terminal service quality and to determine critical performance conditions. For this purpose, the well-known SERVQUAL model is used. This model has been adapted to container terminals and presents an 'operational' view on the judgement of service quality of container terminals by terminal operators (Parasuraman et al. 1991). The focus is on container terminals, because the terminal is an important link in the total intermodal transport chain (change of transport mode, collection, distribution, and so on). In the next section characteristics of services are explored and adapted to the container terminal market. Next the service quality of maritime terminals and continental terminals is analysed. The chapter ends with conclusions.

6.2 THEORY ON SERVICE QUALITY AND CONTAINER TERMINALS

Service Production Process

In the service process, usually the front office of a service organization interacts directly with customers. This direct interaction is conceded to be 'the moment of truth' for the service organization. The conventional service triangle consists of three actors (de Vries et al. 1994):

1. the service organization (back office);
2. its contact personnel (front office);
3. its customers.

The production process of a service can be based on a customer-orientation, a competitor-orientation or a market-orientation. In a customer-orientation, the main objective of the producer of the service may be to fulfil customer needs. He can strive to provide a better price–quality service than his competitor (competitor-orientation), or he can provide his service as both customer- and competitor-oriented (market-oriented) (Narver and Slater 1990; Slater and Narver 1994a and 1994b; Slater and Narver 1995). A relatively newly distinguished orientation is process-oriented. In this case, the service is seen as part of the whole supply chain and there is an extensive exchange of information between actors in the supply chain in order to be able to perform all services smoothly. This seems a suitable approach for terminal services, because they form part of an integrated transport chain.

The terminal service buying process can be divided into three activities:

1. pre-purchase phase (problem definition, information collection and evaluation of alternatives);
2. consumption of the terminal service;
3. post-purchase phase (evaluation of the terminal service).

In the pre-purchase phase, the actors are the terminal operator and the terminal customer. Usually, the terminal–customer personnel, the terminal personnel and the terminal operator consume the terminal service. The terminal customer and his personnel evaluate the service. Generally, the customer's management does not have an obligation to be present in person. The service delivered to the terminal customers is quite homogeneous and there is no need for participation of the terminal customer's management in the service production process. Furthermore, the customer service is intangible, there is no need for simultaneous production and consumption, and the (objective) terminal transit time is highly important. However, as long as the needed terminal transit time fits in the total transport solution it does not need to be fast but it needs to be on time.

Costs of Service Quality

Achieving quality services costs money. A useful concept in analysing the cost of terminal service quality may be that of value density, that is, value per unit weight. The value density reflects the relative importance of the container in transit and inventory in the logistics system (Magee et al. 1985). In any business, this suggests that it might be preferable to stock low-value items rather than high-value items. The terminal operator can also use this knowledge: the higher the value of the container the operator is handling, the more important reliability and speed become. Generally, costs of service quality comprise (de Vries et al. 1994):

1. prevention costs, for example training programmes;
2. inspection costs, for example costs of quality tests;
3. internal repair costs, for example costs to repair errors before the service reaches the customer;
4. external repair costs, for example costs to repair errors after the service has reached the customer;
5. lost sales, these do not result in direct costs, but may well represent the highest damage to a company delivering poor service quality.

Delivering good-quality services only requires inspection costs and prevention costs, whereas in the case of poor service quality, costs also consist of internal and external repair costs and lost sales. The total container handling service costs should always be placed in the perspective of the total transport channel costs. The terminal handling costs depend – besides the desired quality level – on container characteristics (value of freight), size of shipment (volume), weight, handling difficulty, density, buying of additional terminal services, and transport distance to and from the terminal. Therefore, more tailor-made handling services might 'produce' more satisfied customers and justify higher prices.

Terminal Actors in the Service Process and Quality

The terminal customer provides the terminal operator with requirements concerning the desired terminal service. In particular, flexibility requirements have been growing in importance during recent years (Kuipers 1999). This requires improvements from terminal operators in order to meet the service demands of their customers. In this respect, much is expected from new-generation terminals in the Continental terminal market (Bontekoning and Kreutzberger 2001). These types of terminals are expected to improve the cost and quality performance of terminal operations (Konings and Kreutzberger 2001). However, so far, no new-generation terminals have been built. In Figure 6.1, the main elements influencing, and following from, terminal service quality are depicted. The terminal customer consists of two elements: the management (back office), and the employees (front office) who are present when the service is produced at the container terminal. The terminal operator also consists of two sub-elements: front office and back office. This results in four groups that may have different expectations and observations about terminal service quality. This means that both the terminal customer's front and back office must judge the quality of the terminal service. An additional complicating factor is that for the terminal operator the inclusion of the total supply chain in the quality delivery is extremely important, because it is the channel, not the terminal operator, that actually delivers the products and services to the final customers.

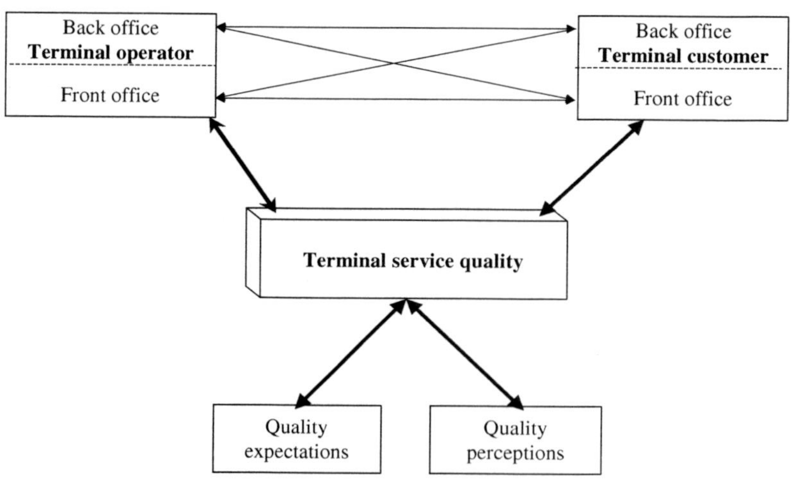

Source: Based on de Vries et al. (1994).

Figure 6.1 Terminal service quality environment

Without channel coordination, it may be even harder to achieve an adequate terminal service performance level.

If the focus is placed on terminal customers of both maritime and continental terminals, four main customer groups can be distinguished:

1. container carriers (deep-sea shipping companies);
2. transport companies (rail, road, barge and short-sea transport companies);
3. importers/exporters (intermediaries, such as stevedores, ship brokers, shipping agents and forwarders);
4. shippers/consignees (companies that send and receive the freight).

The main customer groups must be identified in order to be able to determine the weight that must be placed on the judgements of the different groups. The services that are provided can be grouped according to type of customers, importance of different sales categories, type of container (process) or transport mode (network). Usually, terminal operators are not entirely clear about their customers, and therefore offer a broad package of services for the sake of risk-spreading and widening the operating base (that is many potential customers).

Measurement of Service Quality

Service quality can, in general, be measured on three aspects: search, experience and credence attributes. Search attributes are quality features that can be identified by the customer before the purchase of a certain service. Experience attributes are features that can only be disclosed during or directly after the consumption of a certain service. Finally, credence attributes are features that cannot be identified by customers, neither before nor after the consumption of the service.

Bowersox et al. (1986) view handling as one of the most costly aspects of logistic channel performance, and thus the objective is to reduce handling operations in the logistic chain to an absolute minimum. This creates an extra dimension concerning quality: there is a tendency to minimize terminal handling, stressing the importance of quality even more. The distinction between services is necessary in order to be able to determine which services are important or should be important to the terminal operator. At a container terminal the following main activities can be found:

1. ship-oriented services: discharging the ship, loading the ship, direct transshipment, warehousing and storage of container, and container groupage;
2. yard-oriented services;

3. other terminal services: manufacturing; renting, leasing and selling services; collection and distribution of containers; physical transport of containers; container monitoring; and other services.

SERVQUAL to Measure Container Terminal Service Quality

The SERVQUAL model is used as a framework to analyse the terminal service quality. In the SERVQUAL model of Parasuraman et al. (1985), the difference between customer expectations and observations (valuations or judgements) is measured. If the expectation of the customer is greater than his observation, there is a lack of quality. Quality is delivered when the observation is equal to the expectation. More quality is delivered if the observation of the customer is greater than his expectation. The expectations must be carefully dealt with, as expectations can be low (which is the case in the container terminal market). In this respect, it is better to focus on the aspirations of customers rather than on expectations. In the terminal interviews dealt with later in this chapter, the expectations of terminal operators about terminal customers expectations have been used as a proxy for the important quality elements for terminal services. The 'general' objectives of terminal operators may be stated as cost minimization and profit maximization, capacity-oriented and realizing political goals (for example concerning the environment, enhancement of status and role). The terminal operator should translate the customers' quality expectations into performance statements and define 'target' quality levels. The set of SERVQUAL quality questions served as input for the interviews. It has not been possible to interview terminal customers in this chapter. Testing the SERVQUAL model with terminal customers is thus an important item for further research. This would make it possible to compare the terminal operators' expectations with terminal customer judgements of service quality.

6.3 MARITIME CONTAINER TERMINAL SERVICE QUALITY

Maritime Quality Judgement History

In general, container terminal services have no extensive history concerning quality measurement. Some research has been carried out on quality aspects in the broader field of transport mode comparison and also in the field of logistics. In that field, it has been shown that, in the past, average delivery time was the most important customer service element determining

Table 6.1 Customer service elements and customer satisfaction

Customer service elements	Correlation coefficient[1]
Average delivery time	0.76
Delivery time availability	0.72
Order status information	0.67
Rush service	0.59
Order methods	0.56
Action on complaints	0.56
Accuracy in filling orders	0.46
Returns policy	0.44
Billing procedure	0.39

Note: [1] Correlation between service element and customer satisfaction.

Source: Perreault and Russ (1976).

customer satisfaction (see also Table 6.1). This table indicates the importance of different quality aspects to customers. It not only applies to transport or logistics companies, but also to terminal operators. If time, availability of service and information are important to customers, these service elements are automatically important to terminal operators as well. Their solutions must fit these requirements in order to be competitive.

Characteristics of Maritime Terminal Services

For the maritime terminal operator, ship services are the most important. All services are offered (ship, yard and other), but the handling service is of prime importance. The container carriers are the main customers and the central focus is on the quality of service that they receive. Maritime terminals are open 24 hours a day, 365 days a year. The average transit time for a container is between 48 and 96 hours through a maritime terminal. According to terminal operators, in the service production process, the reliability of the service is most important for their customers. Compared with the results from Perreault and Russ (1976), 'average delivery time', 'time availability' and 'rush service', have decreased in importance, while 'reliability' (for example accuracy, action on complaints) has increased in importance. See Table 6.2 for an overview of the terminal interview results.

Relative Importance of Maritime Handling Quality Conditions

The importance of maritime container terminal quality – according to terminal operators – has been tested on five quality dimensions. These

Table 6.2 Service characteristics in the maritime terminal market

Variable	Characteristic
Kind of services	Ship, yard, other
Average container terminal transit time	48–96 hours
Operating hours	24/7, all year
Critical performance condition	Reliability

Source: Terminal interviews, 2002.

Table 6.3 Quality importance according to maritime terminal operators

Variable	Share (%)
Tangibles	20
Reliability	30
Responsiveness	15
Assurance	20
Empathy	15

Source: Terminal interviews, 2002.

dimensions are: tangibles – the appearance of the physical facilities; reliability – the ability to provide the promised service; responsiveness – the willingness to help customers; assurance – the knowledge of the personnel; and empathy – the caring for terminal customers. The interviewed terminal operators were asked to divide 100 points between the five items (see Table 6.3 for an overview) in order to define relative importance of quality conditions.

The interviews show that 'reliability' is of main importance to maritime terminal operators. The main finding for maritime container terminals is that all quality variables are important, but 'reliability' is the most important one.

Maritime Terminal Services and Quality Conditions

Several characteristics of the maritime container terminal service were tested in the interviews. According to terminal operators, maritime terminal customers expect excellent service, therefore quality costs are concentrated at the beginning of the internal service production process. Costs are made in order to prevent internal quality defects. Terminal performances measured by the maritime operators are crane performance, container damage, straddle carriers performance, and that of other transport modes (besides deep-sea). The percentage of containers that is not handled according to customer requirements is far less than 1 per cent, and the conflicts over false handlings are solved to the maximum extent possible. However, maritime terminal customers are also interested in channel performance, suggesting that terminal operators might start measuring channel performance in addition to internal performance. The attitude of maritime terminals should improve from a production-oriented (internal process) to a more customer- and process-oriented attitude. The maritime terminal operators conclude that better-educated personnel, shorter container terminal transit time, better handling performance, and quality measurement may improve the container handling service. However, these items are just facilitators to help the terminal customers with a good transport channel performance.

Conclusion about Maritime Terminals

Several characteristics of maritime terminals have been identified. Ship services are the most important to maritime terminals, but related services (yard and other) are offered as well. Container carriers are the main customers and are served 24/7, 365 days per year with an average container transit time through the terminal of 48–96 hours. In the 1990s, the importance of speed and time relatively decreased in favour of reliability of the service. According to past transport research, average delivery time was judged to be of main importance. The interviews have proven that this has changed for the container terminal sector in Europe. As transport services are, in general, price-inelastic, container handling price reductions will not generate a dramatically increased demand for container handling. However, the market is very competitive on a port-by-port basis. Quality levels must meet high standards set by the container carriers. Costs incurred by better quality performance cannot be recovered through higher rates. Therefore, the relatively most critical performance condition for their customers – according to maritime container terminal operators – in terms of quality is 'reliability'. It has not been possible to produce a table with the scores of maritime terminals, concerning the adapted SERVQUAL model, because the response on this part of the questionnaire was insufficient.

However, several tools to improve maritime container terminal services can be developed, based on this research. Current terminal performances measured by operators are crane performance, container damage, straddle carrier performance, and that of other transport modes (besides deep-sea). The maritime operators conclude that better-educated personnel, shorter container terminal transit time, better handling performance, and quality measurement may help improve the container handling service. Handling speed, information and communication are quoted as important tools to improve the quality performance of maritime container terminals. However, faster handling is not important as long as the terminal service fits the total transport solution. Information and communication is what counts in order to improve the terminal operator attitude, the channel perspective and performance, and the flexibility.

The attitude of maritime terminals should improve from a production-oriented (internal process) to a more customer-oriented attitude. Internal processes are important, but the transport channel of the customer – which the terminal service forms part of – counts. Measuring 'total' container channel performance, through an increased number of terminal performance measures, might help to improve the reliability of container terminals. Most maritime container terminals measure performance on the basis of their terminal; container carriers are interested in channel performance: is container X reliably transported from point A to B in the agreed time-frame? Internal terminal performance measures must therefore be extended with external terminal performance measures. These external performance measures measure the container carriers' on-time performance. A performance improvement for maritime terminals might be 'flexibility'. Deep-sea ship arrivals are no easy planning task, as weather influences and other problematic developments make the terminal operator's task more difficult. Through strict contracts, all risks of delays and terminal berth congestion are passed onto the terminal operator. This makes 'flexibility' a critical performance condition in order to optimally service the terminal customer.

6.4 CONTINENTAL CONTAINER TERMINAL SERVICE QUALITY

Continental Quality Judgement History

Research into Continental terminal services has no extensive history. Research has been carried out on quality aspects in a broader perspective (logistics). In the annual report of RENFE (1998) there is a short section on quality measurement concerning intermodal freight transport including the use of Continental rail terminals (see Figure 6.2 and 6.3 for the main results).

This quality judgement by customers concerns rail services in Spain, including the use of Continental container terminals. Figure 6.2 shows that, according to clients, 'compliance with terms' and 'quality–price relationships' are the most important quality aspects. 'Compliance with terms' may also be stated as 'reliability'. Figure 6.3 shows that the most important

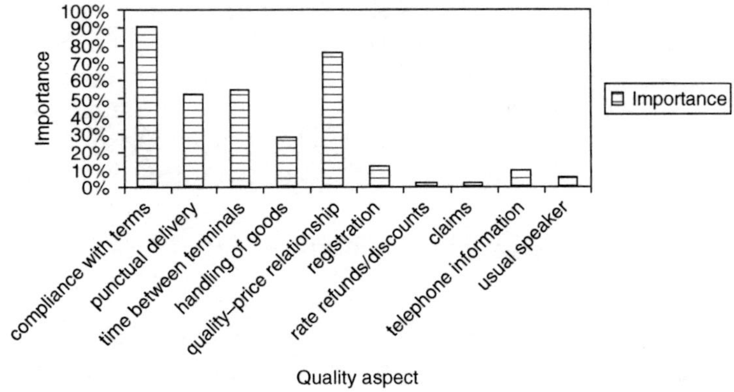

Note: 'Usual speaker' refers to usual contact person.

Source: RENFE (1998).

Figure 6.2 Customer judgement of rail service quality conditions

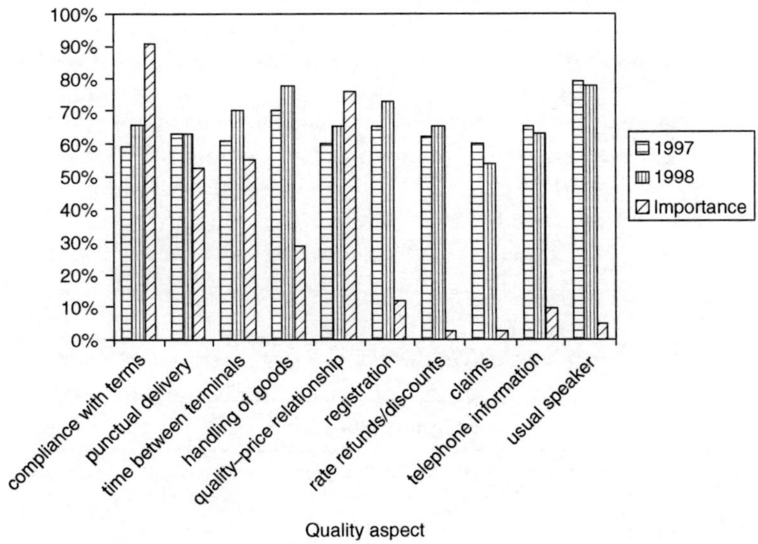

Source: RENFE (1998).

Figure 6.3 Importance of quality elements and corresponding judgements

quality aspects ('compliance with terms' and 'quality–price relationship') are not those customers are most satisfied by. The differences between the quality aspects are quite large and especially the most important quality aspects must perform better. In general, it is more important for operators to perform better in aspects that are more important to customers. Below, the interviews with the Dutch container terminals will be discussed.

Characteristics of Continental Terminal Services

Most Continental terminal operators who were interviewed (11 in the Netherlands) have large customer bases, and most of the customers are located close to the terminal. The operating hours for barge terminals show a mixed picture, ranging from 05.00 Monday to 12.00 Saturday every week to 24/7, 365 days a year. The average container terminal transit time for barge terminals is 48 hours and for rail terminals 73 hours. In the service production process, reliability of the service is most important (see Table 6.4 for an overview of the interview results).

Relative Importance of Continental Handling Quality Conditions

Table 6.5 shows that 'reliability' is of relatively main importance to both barge and rail terminal operators. Several characteristics of the container terminal service were tested in the interviews. The percentage of containers that is not handled according to customer requirements is less than 1 per cent for rail terminals, and the conflicts over these false handlings are solved where possible. For barge terminals, the false handlings are between 1 and 3 per cent, with one terminal reaching almost 10 per cent (interviews with terminal operators in 2002). Terminal performance measured by the barge

Table 6.4 Service characteristics in the Continental terminal market

Variable	Characteristics: barge	Characteristics: rail
Kind of services	Barge, yard, other	Rail, yard, other
Average container terminal transit time	48 hours	73 hours
Operating hours	Most 24/7, all year	05.00 Mon.-12.00 Sat
Critical performance conditions	Reliability	Reliability

Note: Most terminals are open 24/7, all year, with few (mainly rail) exceptions.

Source: Terminal interviews, 2002.

Table 6.5 Quality importance in the Continental container terminal market

Variable	Barge	Rail
Tangibles	13	9
Reliability	25	55
Responsiveness	22	13
Assurance	20	12
Empathy	21	11

Source: Terminal interviews, 2002.

operators concern barge on-time performance, and customer pre- and end-haulage on-time performance. Rail terminals measure the on-time performance of trains (departures) and trucks (percentage handled within 30 minutes).

Continental Terminal Services and Quality Conditions

The main finding for Continental barge container terminals is that the differences between the quality variables are not large. This means that all quality variables are relatively important, and 'reliability' is the most important one. According to Continental rail terminals, customers are strongly focused on 'reliability' and relatively less on the other quality aspects. This might be due to the great chance of disruption in the rail transport chain. According to terminal operators, barge and rail terminal customers expect 'reliability', 'good price' and 'added value'.

Conclusion about Continental Terminals

Characteristics of Continental terminal service were revealed in the interviews. Most operators have large customer bases, and most of the customers are located close to the terminal. The operating hours differ from terminal to terminal. The average container terminal transit time for barge terminals is 48 hours and for rail terminals 73 hours. The percentage of containers that is not handled according to customer requirements is less than 1 per cent for rail terminals and for barge terminals the false handlings are between 1 and 3 per cent. According to terminal operators, barge and rail terminal customers expect 'reliability', 'good price' and 'added value'. 'Reliability' is a critical performance condition for Continental terminal operators, especially for rail terminals, due to the great likelihood of disruption of the system flow, in the rail part of the transport chain. Barge

Table 6.6 Quality judgements of Continental container terminals

Quality dimension	Barge terminals	Rail terminals	Difference: barge–rail
1. Tangibles: equipment	5	5	=
2. Tangibles: facilities	5	5	=
3. Tangibles: clothes	5	5	=
4. Tangibles: promotion	4	5	−1
5. Reliability: promise	7	7	=
6. Reliability: solve	7	7	=
7. Reliability: 1st time	7	7	=
8. Reliability: on-time	7	7	=
9. Reliability: mistakes	7	6	+1
10. Responsiveness: tell	7	6	+1
11. Responsiveness: adequate	7	7	=
12. Responsiveness: always	7	7	=
13. Responsiveness: busy	6	6	=
14. Assurance: behaviour	6	7	−1
15. Assurance: safe	7	6	+1
16. Assurance: careful	6	6	=
17. Assurance: knowledge	7	6	+1
18. Empathy: individual	7	6	+1
19. Empathy: open	5	6	−1
20. Empathy: personal	5	5	=
21. Empathy: customer	7	6	+1
22. Empathy: needs	7	7	=

Note: The quality dimensions on the left-hand side correspond with the extensive described numbers in Table 6.1

Source: Terminal interviews, 2002.

terminals, in order to determine their own quality, but also in order to determine the total channel performance, monitor the start and the end of the trip of a container. The differences between the quality judgements (see Table 6.6) are not large. According to terminal operators, this means that all quality variables are relatively important to their customers, and 'reliability' is relatively important. Better-educated personnel, shorter container terminal transit time, better handling performance, and quality measurement may enable an improvement in the container handling service. Quality improvements must come down into cost reductions as price increases seem difficult. This is even more complicated as the investment costs for improved quality are concentrated at the terminal, while most advantages occur in the networks (Trip and Kreutzberger 2002).

Tools to improve the Continental terminal service can be developed based on this chapter. To make the Continental container terminal – and the transport service it forms part of – more competitive it is necessary to offer a total service package, increase the already broad customer base, and have increased quality checks. Single-mode transport is the reference point on which the terminal operators base their price. They must ideally meet the single-mode road transport price, or even better, be cheaper. A tool for improvement for Continental terminal operators is to offer a 'total service assortment'. The total service, including pre- and end-haulage (logistics solution) is important, not only the container handling. The competitive position of Continental (mainly barge) terminals is stronger than that of maritime and rail terminals. A large customer base and a broad service package offers opportunities to make money. This already good competitive position must be retained and enlarged where opportunities exist. Some terminals measure quality performance, and others do not. It is not possible to recover the extra quality control costs through higher prices. Individualized attention and caring for customers may be as good as making the effort to measure quality performance. Due to the limited scale of Continental barge and rail terminals, it is often possible to work without a professional quality performance measurement system. However, if the container terminal grows larger, an automated system to monitor quality performance might be implemented.

6.5 CONCLUSIONS AND FURTHER RESEARCH

Conclusion for Maritime Terminals

Critical internal performance improvement characteristics for terminal operators are information and communication about transport channel performance. In past transport research, average delivery time was judged to be of main importance. According to terminal operators, 'reliability', in terms of meeting container carriers' demand, is thus a critical performance condition for maritime container terminals. Measuring 'total' container channel performance, through an increased number of terminal performance measures, might help to improve the reliability of container terminals. Most maritime container terminals measure performance on the basis of their terminal. Container carriers are interested in channel performance: is container X reliably transported from point A to B in the agreed timeframe? Internal terminal performance measures must therefore be extended with external terminal performance measures. These external performance measures measure the container carriers' on-time performance. An external performance improvement characteristic might be 'flexibility'. Through strict contracts, all risks of delays and terminal berth congestion are passed onto the terminal operator. This makes 'flexibility' a critical performance condition.

Conclusion for Continental Terminals

A critical performance condition for Continental terminal operators is to offer a 'total service assortment'. The total service, including pre- and end-haulage (logistics solution) is important, not the container handling only. The competitive position of Continental (mainly barge) terminals is stronger than that of maritime and rail terminals. A large customer base and a broad service package offers opportunities to make money. 'Reliability' is a critical performance condition for Continental terminal operators, especially for rail terminals, due to the great likelihood of disruption of the system flow, in the rail part of the transport chain. Barge terminals, in order to determine their own quality, but also in order to determine the total channel performance, monitor the start and the end of the trip of a container. The interviews indicated that the main group of barge terminals may be further advanced in measuring transport channel performance than maritime and rail terminals. It is not possible to recover the extra quality control costs through higher prices. Individualized attention and caring for customers may be as good as making the effort to measure quality performance. Due to the limited scale of Continental barge and rail terminals, it is often possible to work without a professional quality performance measurement system. However, if the container terminal grows larger, an automated system to monitor quality performance might be implemented.

Further Research

The container terminal is very important in the transport chain and must thus meet the transport channel requirements. Terminal quality measurement should then be focused on the channel performance, besides the internal processes that must be good. Where possible, future quality research might incorporate the transport channel perspective. Several customer groups are involved in terminal services, this might require different services with different quality requirements. These customer requirements must be analysed in future research and confronted with the terminal operators' judgements.

REFERENCES

Bontekoning, Y.M. (2002), *Towards New-Generation Terminal Operations: Identifying Implementation Obstacles*, Delft: Delft University Press.

Bontekoning, Y.M. and E. Kreutzberger (2001), *New-Generation Terminals*, Delft: TRAIL.

Bowersox, D.J., D.J. Closs and O.K. Helferich (1986), *Logistical Management*, New York: Macmillan Publishing Company.

European Commission (1997), *Intermodal Quality and Performance Indicators*, Deliverable 1, INRETS.

Intermodal Quality (1997), *The Quality of Terminals, Executive Summary*, Intermodal quality and performance indicators, Brussels.

Konings, J.W. and E. Kreutzberger (2001), *Towards a Quality Leap in Intermodal Freight Transport*, Delft: TRAIL.

Kuipers, B. (1999), *Flexibiliteit in de Rotterdamse Havenregio*, Delft: Uitgeverij Eburon.

Magee, J.F., W.C. Copacino and D.B. Rosenfield (1985), *Modern Logistics Management Integrating Marketing, Manufacturing, and Physical Distribution*, New York: John Wiley & Sons.

Narver, J.C. and S.F. Slater (1990), 'The effect of a market orientation on business profitability', *Journal of Marketing*, **54**, October, pp. 20–35.

Parasuraman, A., V.A. Zeithaml and L.L. Berry (1985), 'A conceptual model of service quality and its implications for future research', *Journal of Marketing*, **49**, pp. 41–50.

Parasuraman, A., V.A. Zeithaml and L.L. Berry (1991), 'Refinement and reassessment of the SERVQUAL-scale', *Journal of Retailing*, **67**, pp. 420–50.

Perreault Jr, W.D and F.A. Russ (1976), 'Physical distribution service in industrial purchase decisions', *Journal of Marketing*, **40**, p. 8.

RENFE (1998), *Annual Report*, Madrid: RENFE.

Slater, S.F. and J.C. Narver (1994a), 'Does competitive environment moderate the market orientation-performance relationship?' *Journal of Marketing*, **58**, pp. 46–55.

Slater, S.F. and J.C. Narver (1994b), 'Market orientation, customer value, and superior performance', *Business Horizons*, **37**, pp. 22–8.

Slater, S.F. and J.C. Narver (1995), 'Market orientation and the learning organisation', *Journal of Marketing*, **59**, July, pp. 63–74.

TERMINET (1998), *Indicators and Criteria for New-generation Bundling, Terminals and Terminal Nodes*, Delft: Delft University of Technology.

Trip, J.J. and E. Kreutzberger (2002), *Complex Bundling Networks and New-generation Terminals: A Synthesis*, Delft: Delft University Press.

Vries Jr, W. de, H. Kasper and P.J.C. van Helsdingen (1994), *Dienstenmarketing*, Houten: Educatieve Partners Nederland BV.

PART II

Design and modelling

7. Container handling in mainports: a dilemma about future scales

Joan Rijsenbrij

7.1 INTRODUCTION

The ongoing expansion of world population, and the further economic development of almost every country, maintain increasing cargo flows all around the world. This globalization, along with the growing demands from consumers and the economies of scale, are essential drivers in container shipping and related container terminal operations and land transportation.

Today containerization has expanded to a global door-to-door transportation system with efficient 6000–8000 TEU (twenty-foot equivalent unit) vessels, large high-tech terminals, intermodal, inland transportation and computerized online information systems. Shippers and consignees are increasingly demanding better performance, such as flexibility for last-minute changes, a rapid response with fast deliveries and a perfect fit in their logistics chains. However, reliability and low costs are the major issues in door-to-door containerized transportation. Shipping lines have conquered the pressure on rates with the application of economies of scale to their container vessels; ports and terminals followed with enlarged facilities with improved productivity, and inland transportation responded both with economies of scale (barge and rail transportation) and more efficient planning (trucking) to avoid empty-leg operations.

In the late nineties, this drive for economies of scale has encouraged many mergers and takeovers among shipping lines, terminal operators and logistics service providers. But, nevertheless, severe competition and the inability to control capacity have resulted in tremendous price erosions, leaving a broad awareness to look for cost reduction. The pure shipping costs have already been decreased considerably and therefore the focus on cost reduction is more and more directed towards terminal operations. At the same time, the introduction of large container vessels and the scrapping of older (small) container vessels has made shipping lines demand enlarged berth productivity and more flexibility to handle operational peaks.

It is expected that volumes in container shipping will continue to grow, despite some lower growth rates during 2002. From 2000 to 2010 the worldwide annual growth in container shipping could range from 5–7 per cent per annum, thus showing a doubling in the next 10–15 years.

The growing volumes, the increased vessel sizes and the demand for increased performance at lower cost will encourage the realization of new, larger and faster container terminals. Currently many ports all over the world are projecting new facilities (for example Shanghai, Pusan, Tanjung Pelepas, Norfolk, Algeciras, Southampton, Rotterdam, Bremerhaven, Wilhelmshaven and Le Havre) and all decision-making bodies are confronted with some major questions: how to design and construct the quay wall, with what type of container cranes to handle the future vessels, which gate systems to handle the inland flows in a secure way and what type of automation to adopt to assure cost-effective handling in the future.

So, terminal operators, port authorities, governments and inland transportation companies are challenged to expand and improve their handling facilities and inland infrastructure and at the same time to provide a better performance with even lower cost. Unfortunately they are faced with one dilemma: what future scales can be expected, both for vessel sizes and inland transport vehicles?

The (too) long preparation times for new facilities and infrastructure and the long lifetime of the dominant assets in ports (access channels, quay walls, terminals, road and rail systems) require action today in order to be ready for tomorrow, with ongoing globalization and a projected world population of 9 billion people by 2050.

7.2 TRENDS AFFECTING MAINPORT DEVELOPMENTS

The development of mainports will be highly influenced by the trends in global container logistics and the future demands of shippers, which continuously monitor the service levels and cost-effectiveness of their worldwide supply chain. The following trends can be recognized:

- Container shipping volumes will continue to increase in the near future. Yearly growth figures of 5–7 per cent are projected for the coming years and that will create demands for more terminal capacity both in handling (waterside and landside) and storage; some terminals will be confronted with double-digit growth figures. Especially in the Far East (China, Korea, India, Vietnam and so on), considerable growth is expected.

- Shipping will maintain the application of economies of scale, resulting in larger vessels, larger numbers of cargo per call (both for mainline and feeder vessels) and enlarged peak demands. This necessitates larger stack capacities and special attention for special cargo like reefer-containers and break-bulk cargo. The increased volumes and larger yard areas put high demands on internal transportation, where many more movements must be processed over the existing infrastructure.
- Shippers and consignees are requiring better services from the shipping lines. This will increasingly result in service level agreements between shipping lines and terminal operators. Guaranteed service times for the delivery and receival of containers, guaranteed flows to be handled and sufficient flexibility in case of peak demands must be offered by the operator. Non-performance will result in penalties, either collected by the shipping line or by the land transportation companies. Railway companies and barge operators will demand time slots in order to maintain (tight) turnaround schedules.
- The formation of alliances and still more mergers will decrease the number of global players (shipping lines, shippers, logistics providers). However, the remaining parties will try to improve their buying power. Power play between the major carriers and shippers will continue; the fast-expanding global logistics service providers will become new players in this area.
- An increasing number of shipping lines are opting for dedicated facilities including marine terminals, intermodal terminals and inland depots. This may result in varying conditions for receivals and deliveries, gate handling, documentation, inspection and so on. Shipping lines will attain more commercial interest in all major worldwide mainports.
- Privatization (or financing with public money) will be further encouraged; however, the private sector shows some reluctance due to the limited profitability of port investments.
- The continuing demand for port facilities and the awareness of the scarcity and value of land for many applications (industry, housing, infrastructure, leisure and nature) will cause an increasing scarcity of land for port operations (terminals). This will result in growing demands among terminal operators for better area utilization, affecting stacking systems and landside services. In this respect the development of satellite terminals will contribute to a better utilization of mainport facilities. The dwell-time of containers at deep-sea ports can be reduced and diverted to the inland satellite terminals. All kinds of secondary services (Container Freight Stations (CFS),

depots, repair, Value Added Logistics (VAL) services, security checking) can be shifted to those inland terminals as well, and that will benefit the utilization of high-cost facilities in deep-sea ports.

- Society is asking for more control over imported cargo entering the country. All kinds of inspections are required, such as X-rays (to detect drugs, illegal immigrants, illegal shipments), visual inspection (to check quantities, packing, control of due taxes) and even product tests (veterinary checks, bacteriological tests and so on). All such activities require additional transportation (mostly to the edges of a terminal), sometimes planned but often at random.
- All major ports will further improve their Electronic Data Interchange (EDI)-based port community information systems. Web applications will be further developed allowing for online information and tracking and tracing of shipments. The planning of terminal and inland transportation operations will be further supported with more pre-information and real-time data sharing.
- A growing reluctance against trucking (fuel consumption, air pollution, noise pollution and scarcity of drivers for long-haul operations) will encourage a further shift to rail, barging and coastal shipping. Such modes require capacity for internal transportation, either in small (one-by-one) quantities or in large blocks for last-minute handling.
- For the expansion of existing container terminals and for the planning and construction of new port facilities, the environmental issues will increasingly determine the selection of location and the possible speed of realization of such new facilities. Noise and emissions reduction, avoidance of visual hindrance and the preservation of nature and wildlife are the most prominent issues.
- Safety and sound working conditions will become an increasingly important topic for port operations. The still increasing amounts of hazardous cargo will get more attention from public regulatory bodies. Labour unions will rightly ask for safe working conditions and some participation in the daily decision-making processes.
- The last but certainly not the least trend is the strong drive for further cost control. For many years the transportation industry has not been very profitable (it is a buyers' market) and despite the annually increasing volumes and the economies of scale it is expected that the near future will not show any improvement. So, cost control will remain a major issue and probably will be diverted from the ocean leg towards terminals and inland transportation.

The above trends will influence the container operations in mainports. The dilemma for terminal operators, port authorities and port planners is the question about future scale, the uncertainty about the size of future hub-and-spoke systems, and the concentration of shipping lines in a few large mainports.

7.3 THE IMPACT OF INCREASED SCALE

The continuing growth in container shipments and the competitive climate with the focus on service improvements and lower costs has fuelled the drive for economies of scale. Scale developments can be clearly recognized in the following areas:

1. Sizes of transport vehicles, such as seagoing vessels, barges, trains and road trucks.
2. Sizes of terminals, both in throughput (that is, terminal dimensions) and service performance.
3. The magnitude of information exchange and process control.

Waterborne transport has shown the largest scale developments (Figure 7.1). Seagoing vessels carry twentyfold more cargo than 50 years ago; motor barges and push-barge systems have only grown two to five times. The developments in rail transportation capacity have been limited with the exception of the USA, where the introduction of double-stack trains (with train lengths up to 3 km) supported a modal shift towards rail transport. Road trucks as well have showed little development with respect to cargo-carrying capacity. Only a few countries allow three-TEU trucks (the USA, Sweden). However, there is a tendency to accept three- and four-TEU trucks on the roads under some specific conditions (Canada).

Figure 7.1 Scale developments in general cargo vessels (1946–96)

Over the years the terminal handling capacity (throughput, normally measured in containers or TEUs moved over the quay wall) has increased from a few hundred thousand moves to about 5 million moves per terminal at present. However, the majority of terminals were sized for a capacity between 0.5 and 2 million moves (0.75 million – 3 million TEU). Scale developments are seen in the terminal area (up to 200 ha) and the quay wall designs. Equipment as well has been designed larger (loads almost doubled, due to twin-lift operation) and especially quay cranes have been enlarged with load moments rising from 600 ton-metres in the 1960s towards 6000 ton-metres nowadays. The handling and storage systems have been enlarged tremendously. The control over the internal container movements to carry hundreds of boxes per hour at the right time and to the right place (scheduling, sequencing), has enlarged the labour organizations and their management systems up to the limits of human capabilities. Some terminals have already been divided into several smaller units which can be better managed. The first automated handling systems have been installed, which boosted the scales in planning and control systems.

Scale developments in container transport would not have been possible without the impressive developments in information and communication technology (ICT). Worldwide connections between information databases, many Internet applications and a variety of identification techniques have supported a large-scale development towards continuous tracking and tracing of containers. This allows last-minute decisions in trade transactions, scheduling of vessels and vehicles and terminal handling. Today's availability of high-capacity computer systems standardizes EDI messages, and effective planning and management information software is a prerequisite for further increases in the scale of container logistics (Saanen et al. 2000).

Vessel size developments have been dominant by far in the design of handling facilities for mainports, a reason to review the impact of vessel sizes in more detail.

Vessel Size Developments

The considerable lifetimes of container cranes (25 years), terminal quay walls (50 years or more) and port entrances and breakwaters (100 years) require long-term projection when it comes to the impact of future vessel sizes and shipping lines' demands on the design of terminal quay walls and cranes.

Reviewing some recent publications on vessel size developments and considering vessel size developments in adjacent shipping activities (for example bulk materials) leads to the conclusion that 200 000–250 000 DWT

Table 7.1 Characteristics of future type container vessels

Vessel characteristics	Type I	Type II
Vessel capacity (TEU)	12 500	18 000
Length overall (m)	375–395	400
Approximate deadweight (tons)	160 000	240 000
Beam (m)	55	65
Draught (m)	15–16	18–20
Speed (knots)	25	26
Containers across on deck	22	26
Tiers under deck	10–11	11–13
Tiers on deck	7	8

container vessels should certainly be considered as a feasible size for a ULCV (ultra-large container vessel). However, speculation about the most likely size will probably continue and that explains why it is recommended to use a range of characteristics for tomorrow's container vessels (see Table 7.1).

From these data the following requirements may be put to ports and terminals in the future:

- minimum channel depth 20–23 metres;
- a turning basin of 600–750 m diameter;
- sufficient fendering and mooring facilities;
- call size (lifts per call) 6000–10 000 lifts, preferable to be handled in 24 hours;
- outreach for handling equipment about 70 metres from fenderface;
- lifting height (under the spreader) above water level 47–55 m, depending on the ratio 8 ft 6 ins high/9 ft 6 ins high containers.

The arrival of vessel type I (12 500 TEU) is a fact; the application of the much larger type II may take another 10 years. The introduction of such large vessels does not only depend on technical demands (strength, available diesel engine, propeller dimensions). Scale benefits are not dramatic when going from 8000 TEU towards 12 500 and 18 000 TEU, although the savings in fuel consumption per slot may become of more interest. Other factors will influence the selection of vessel size as well:

- risk of investing in vessel sizes with a limited area of application;
- a further concentration of container traffic in a few mainports causing more complexity in logistics;

- reluctance from shippers to further concentration in the shipping industry;
- the arrival of new ports close to the existing ones, stopping a further growth in mainport sizes (see port planning in Korea, Japan, PR of China, US West Coast, North-West Europe);
- the tremendous investments in port facilities required for 18 000 TEU vessels, including the environmental constraints related to dredging of entrance channels and port basins.

In September 2006, the first 12 500 TEU class vessel was introduced (see Figure 7.2). The *Emma-Maersk* (officially 11 000 TEU, but unofficially 13 600 TEU) is the first of eight Maersk vessels for a Europe–Far East service. It remains to be seen whether this type of vessel or even further enlarged vessels will come into use in the next decade. In general it should be questioned whether such large vessels will really contribute to a cost benefit for the whole transport chain.

Figure 7.2 Ultra-large container vessel Emma Maersk, 156 000 DWT

Port and Terminal Developments

The possible future vessel characteristics and related handling operations will put high demands upon infrastructure and superstructure of ports and terminals. The long lead time of expansion programmes and the increasing shortages of land and connecting infrastructure necessitates planning well in advance, and making area reservations for such possible developments. The rapid introduction of post-Panamax container vessels (see Figure 7.3) has shown that many ports and terminals were insufficiently prepared to accommodate these large vessels and their related operations. Only through very costly modifications could many ports and terminals compensate for their lag in providing facilities.

For long-term planning, ports should consider the following demands of ultra-large container vessels:

- The access channel should provide sufficient keel clearance, so 20–23 m water depth will be required. Such a deep channel may influence sediment depositing which could include additional (expensive) regular dredging.
- A large turning basin will be required and powerful tugboats to assist manoeuvring. Obviously, due to the required short stay in port,

Figure 7.3 Large post-Panamax container vessel

pilotage must be available 24 hours a day; a helicopter service for pilots will be helpful.
- The mooring will require an increased fender system and even upgraded bollards (maybe 100 tons per bollard) could be required.
- A redesigned quay wall will be necessary, not only because of the increased forces from mooring, the larger quay cranes and the increased water depth (approximately 20 metres), but also to withstand the forces from enlarged power installed for bow and aft thrusters.
- There must be sufficient facilities to provide 10–15 000 tons of bunker oil within 20 hours during berthing of the vessel.
- Due to the time pressure from such vessels there must be sufficient (spacious) access to the vessel for maintenance and supply activities.

If terminals want to prepare themselves for services for the ULCVs, they should meet the following demands:

- The berth productivity should be in the range of 275–375 lifts per berth hour. A 24-hour stay in port may generate 8000 lifts that must be handled in about 22 effective operating hours. Working with six quay cranes, this will require a sustainable net productivity of 60–65 lifts per crane hour and that can only be realized if the technical crane productivity is 100 lifts/hour (undisturbed cycle).
- There will be increased transshipment activities asking for more internal movements in the terminal (repositioning in stack, transportation to adjacent dedicated terminals), and more last-minute decisions.
- The vessel stowage planning systems must be further improved due to the large amount of boxes to be handled and the complex operations connecting feeder, barge and rail services, arriving just-in-time (or even late).
- Enlarged stack capacity will be required to absorb the high volume of discharged containers and some spare capacity in case of vessel clashing. Unforeseen delays in vessel arrival schedules (due to bad weather, vessel breakdown or whatever) will affect the storage capacity. Special attention should be given to the space required for specials like reefer-containers, hazardous cargo, over-height (OH) and over-wide (OW) containers and break-bulk cargo.
- Lashing will remain necessary if hatch-coverless vessels continue to be rare species. The handling of SATLs (semi-automatic twist locks) will require special attention and could easily become a major bottleneck in performance improvements and automation of waterside operations.

- The probably increasing peak demands may require more flexible work rosters and the availability of stand-by (part-time) employees in case of sudden changes.
- There will come an increased need for efficient inland satellite terminals, operationally connected to the major seaside terminal and provided with all kinds of secondary services (depot, repair, CFS, VAL and so on) and even the possibility to store cargo in bonded areas.

A weekly vessel call with 6000–8000 lifts/call will result in 300 000–400 000 lifts (450 000–600 000 TEU) per year and that is only a one-day-per-week operation (that is, costly underutilization). The terminal's economics ask for much more cargo and so the larger vessels will probably encourage (partly) dedicated terminals with an annual handling capacity of about 5 million TEU (compared to the 2 million TEU/annum operations of today).

Requirements for Container Cranes

One important component has not been mentioned: the container handling cranes at the terminal quayside. The two most important influences of the vessel scale development on the design of cranes are the increased dimensions in order to handle the containers of the vessel and the required increased handling capacity, which should be at least doubled.

The majority of mainport terminals are in the process of preparing themselves for the type I future vessel (12 500 TEU) by just 'beefing-up' the crane characteristics. Recently purchased container handling cranes have the following characteristics:

- Outreach 60–65 m from centre waterside (WS) rail.
- Back reach 15–25 m from centre landside (LS) rail.
- Rail gauge 25–35 m centre to centre WS/LS rail.
- Lifting height above quay level 40–44 m.
- Lifting capacity up to 100 tons.
- Lifting speed full load up to 100 m/min.
- Lifting speed low load up to 200 m/min.
- Trolley travel speed up to 325 m/min.

However, these specifications will not fulfil the demands from vessels of type II (15 000 up to 18 000 TEU). Future demands may increase with the following specifications:

- Outreach 70–80 m from centre waterside rail.
- Lifting height above quay level up to 50 m.

- Lifting capacity up to 125 tons (twin-lift, tandem-lift).
- Effective handling capacity 60–70 containers/hour, which asks for a technical handling capacity of at least 100 containers/hour.

Related to this impressive upscaling, some aspects should be recognized:

- The enlarged cranes may require at least double the amount of power supply (redundant).
- The increased height of the crane structure and the enlarged structural dimensions (Van de Bos and Rijsenbrij 2002) will increase the total wind load, but at the same time the crane base will remain almost the same as the vessel hatch spacing is still designed for 40–45 ft containers and so the preferred maximum crane width will remain 25–28 m (resulting in a stability base of 16–18 m). Corner loads may well increase towards 800 tons.
- The increased corner loads (and resulting wheel loads) and wind loads will require much stronger quay wall designs, real heavy-duty rail tracks and appropriate provisions for parking the cranes during storms or hurricanes.
- Larger crane dimensions and no changes in trolley travel and main hoist speed will result in larger cycle times for increased vessel sizes, due to the longer trolley travel and hoist and lowering distances. The number of handlings for a complete unloading or loading of one vessel bay will increase from 300 lifts (Panamax vessel) to more than 800 lifts (ULCVs); however the technical crane productivity will decrease from about 60 cycles to only 48 cycles (that is, lifts) per hour (Luttekes and Rijsenbrij 2002).
- To compensate for the longer crane cycle times, single trolley cranes are provided with increased drive speeds, to compensate for the longer trolley travel or hoist distance. In order to minimize the additional requirements for horsepower it is recommended to optimize maximum speeds and maximum acceleration rates. An example is shown in Figure 7.4.
- Another means to increase the effective crane productivity is the use of twin-lift operations, which will result in a design load of about 75 metric tons (on the hoist cables). Further increases can be obtained by the application of tandem-lift allowing the handling of two 40 ft containers (and even four 20 ft containers). Figure 7.5 shows the result of a research project of Stinis and Delft University of Technology, based on a split head block and two long-twin spreaders.

It is doubtful whether beefed-up single trolley cranes will ever realize a sustained average operational productivity of 45 moves/hr. Surely, the

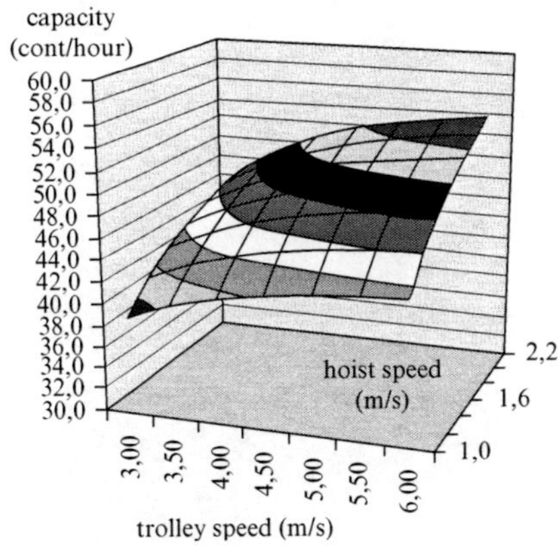

Figure 7.4 Optimization of speeds (Stinis/TUD)

Figure 7.5 Tandem lift spreader

application of twin-lift, tandem-lift and dual cycling (that is, combined discharge and load operation) will increase this figure to 60–75 boxes/hour. However, only a part of the vessel handling volume can be operated with these special handling techniques.

A quantum leap in crane productivity will ask for new crane concepts. The first steps in this direction have been made through the introduction of second-trolley systems (at ECT Rotterdam in 1979), a height-adjustable main girder and the application of separate waterside and landside handling with a buffer in between for SATL handling and smoothing stochastics (see Figure 7.6).

Figure 7.6 Separated crane functions, including a buffer (CTA Hamburg)

More effective will be the use of special conveying provisions in the crane, but still within the existing portal structures (Tax 1989).

Some concepts go even further: a crane structure adapted to innovative new functionality to satisfy the need for 100 lifts/hour technical handling capacity (see Figure 7.7).

The Carrier Crane is another recent development using two waterside trolleys (rope-driven) which position containers onto moving carriers. In addition, traversing motions in the trolley avoid crane gantry travel for small positioning displacements and to handle 20 ft containers in 40 ft cells (see Figure 7.8). The carriers provide a buffer function integrated into the crane cycle and the landside trolley can even be designed for a double-hoist capability.

In fact these types of cranes must be considered as the combination of two cranes in one stable structure. The operational performance can be 75 moves/hour and even higher when using twin-lifts. The quiet and controlled way of operation will result in a steady flow of containers, being an advantage for the connecting transport system to the stacking yard.

The arrival of much larger container vessels (type I or even type II) will require a doubling of the net average productivity and that is impossible with the single trolley cranes presently in use.

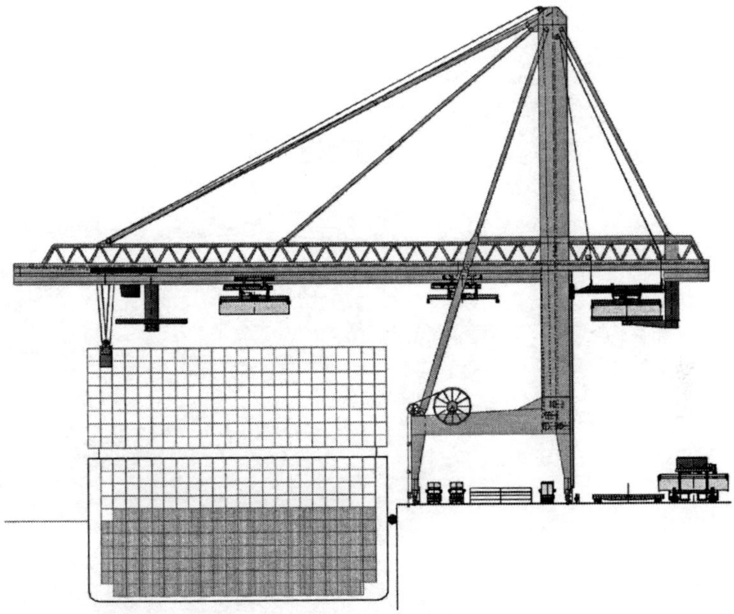

Figure 7.7 Gottwald Port Technology RCE Jumbo Crane

The above consequences of increased scales have not yet been fully evaluated. A substantial increase in container vessel capacity will have a tremendous impact on the required investments in ports and terminals and could well result in higher operating costs for the overall transportation chain.

7.4 DEVELOPMENTS IN TERMINAL HANDLING SYSTEMS

The introduction of post-Panamax vessels (4500–8000 TEU) took place in a very short period of time (between 1989 and 1996) and within five years around 50 ports and their terminals had to realize large investments, not only in quay walls, cranes, handling systems and terminal area, but also in the connecting infrastructure. A considerable number of cranes had to be replaced or extensively modified to cope with the new demands from these post-Panamax vessels. Ports and terminals had to absorb a lot of extra costs related to early replacement, well before the end of the technical lifetime of the existing assets.

On top of that the larger volumes asked for more handling capacity and an increased performance at both the waterside and landside. In addition

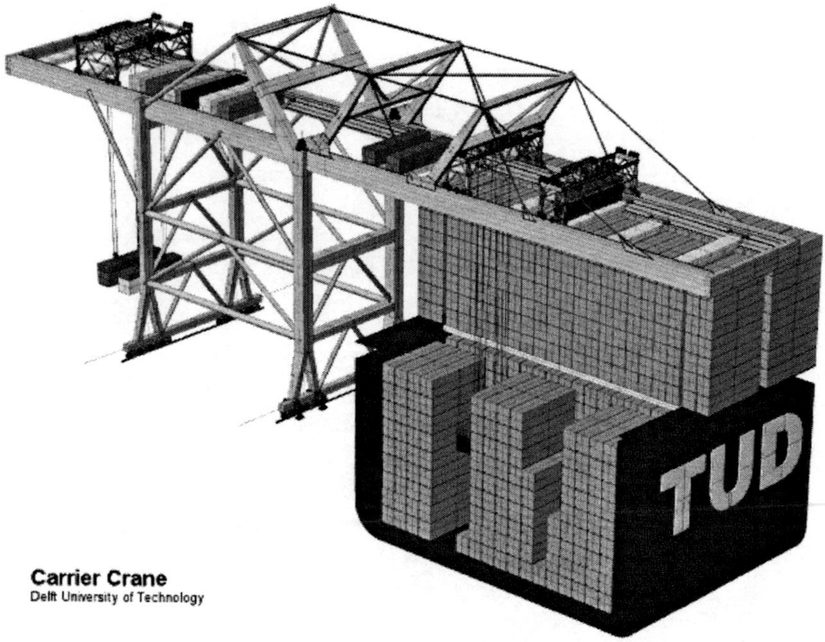

Figure 7.8 Carrier Crane designed for 100 lifts/hr

all the partners in the transport chain expected cost reductions as a basic driver from the introduced economies of scale in liner services. Many terminals struggle with the balance between performance and cost. Moreover, the dominance of waterside operations diminished and nowadays there is much more focus on landside operations.

The introduction of large scales has resulted in various developments in terminal handling systems for waterside and landside operations.

Waterside Operations

Here the larger vessels have caused larger peaks in hourly handling capacities (moves per hour over the entire quay wall) and the following developments can be recognized.

The longer transportation distances between quay cranes and enlarged stack areas (more stochastic) and the increased quay crane handling productivity has resulted in a demand for more transport capacity connected to the cranes (Rijsenbrij 1979). In some mainports five to seven terminal tractors per crane are required and that is an expensive operation. Some terminals use straddle carriers for the transport (and stacking) between quay crane and stack and for those operations dynamic order control systems were introduced. In these order-planning systems the transport equipment is directed to cranes based on algorithms referring to crane demand, minimized transportation distance, minimized waiting and so on. Basically the order processing is focused on a guaranteed waterside performance with minimized costs.

It is expected that such control systems for the pooling of equipment will be further developed to attain better equipment (and manning) utilization.

The increased stacking height at the vessel decks made labour unions and safety boards decide to reject container-lashing activities on board. The introduction of semi-automated twist locks (SATLs) indeed supported safer handling. However, it also caused extra complexity in the waterside handling process, including additional labour. This SATL handling and the related handling of storage bins will remain a major hindrance to further productivity improvement of waterside operations.

Stacking operations will be further focused on improved area utilization, easy response to last-minute changes, and cost-effectiveness. Pioneering terminals like ECT Rotterdam, HIT (Hong Kong), Thamesport (UK) and PSA Singapore started the introduction of rail-mounted gantry cranes (RMGs) and overhead bridge cranes (OBCs) and this trend will certainly continue. Rail-mounted cranes (RMGs and OBCs) can be automated with proven technology and can be electrically powered (to avoid pollution). A proper load control (sway control) and reliable automated positioning are essential requirements for these cranes. Present and future technology can fulfil these requirements and thus this type of equipment is attractive for increased stacking demands. The higher initial investments can be compensated for by their longer lifetime and automation potential.

Automation is becoming an attractive approach in the design of handling systems to control the increased scales at reduced costs. Since ECT started its robotization project at the Delta Terminal in 1988 a number of terminals have implemented robotized yards (Rijsenbrij 1996). However, only ECT Delta Terminal (commissioned in 1993) and Container Terminal Altenwerder (commissioned in 2002) operate a completely automated system for both the waterside transportation and stacking of containers (see Figure 7.9 and Figure 7.10). The experience with automated guided vehicles (AGVs) and automated stacking cranes (ASCs) is promising for further developments in this field. Some terminals and manufacturers concentrate on the automation of straddle carriers and shuttle carriers. However, straddle carriers are less attractive for high-density stacking (necessary for increased throughputs) and automated shuttle carriers still have to prove the same reliability as shown by AGVs today. The development of

Figure 7.9 Automated container handling ECT Rotterdam, 1993

Figure 7.10 Automated container handling CTA Hamburg, 2002

control software is a major issue for automated operations and here the support from simulation models will become a valuable tool in the design of efficient control algorithms that can cope with the dynamics of terminal handling operations.

Further scale developments will definitely change the terminal handling systems towards more automation and an increased application of control software and communication technology.

Landside Operations

Services to the landside terminal connections are getting more attention. The truckers' turnaround time and the maintenance of schedules for barges and trains are becoming more important when volumes are growing and inland transportation costs must be controlled.

Mainport terminals are confronted with a variety of influences beyond their control, such as:

- liaison activities from agents, brokers, shipping lines and so on;
- the average dwell-time of containers: often more than four days for full containers and even 14 days for empty containers;
- stochastic arrival patterns (especially for trucking);
- insufficient (or no) information on connecting modes, expected delivery date;
- daily peaks caused by priorities in rail networks and trucking patterns;
- late arrivals and last-minute changes;
- a short closing time (for export cargo) and a demand to deliver containers 1–2 hours after landing the box at the terminal;
- many non-standard containers (reefers, OH, OW, odd-size);
- Customs regulations and directives for hazardous cargo;
- security checks for containers, which might contain illegal cargo.

Nevertheless the operator should deliver an agreed service level and that boils down to three major issues: sufficient storage capacity in the yard, a flexible handling capacity to support landside operations and a proper gate complex.

The selected landside terminal handling system and its characteristic average cycle times and cycle time distribution for the handling equipment determine the service level offered to landside operations. The application of RMGs and OBCs requires a proper balancing between stack sizes and numbers of cranes per stack. When using straddle carriers or reach stackers it enables the operator to put in more equipment under peak conditions (which may occur daily, for example in the afternoon), but the equipment and operators to drive it must be available.

For larger operations it is recommended to create simulations for these landside operations in order to determine the required amount of equipment and to analyse influences from interference of waterside priorities, filling degree in the stack, stacking equipment characteristics (speeds, acceleration or deceleration) and stack layout. For manually operated stacking systems it should be noticed that in general the performance per stacking machine decreases when more machines are working in the same area. The service times from stacking equipment are influenced by the number and locations of interchange areas. Here the advantage of many interchange areas (close to the location of the stacked container) results in more connecting infrastructure and that may cause unacceptable extra cost (or sometimes the land is not available). A final selection for a stacking system should be based on a total cost approach and a quantitative definition of the required service levels.

Some developments in landside operations are focused on a faster processing of large volumes per hour and with less labour involved. The following ones are of interest.

Gate Operations with Increased Automation

Especially for terminals dominated by trucking at the landside (the US East Coast, the Far East, the Mediterranean) gate handling is of growing importance. Gate design includes sufficient parking and traffic lanes, a controlled processing time in gate lanes, exception handling of truckers with incomplete documentation, the integration of Customs and security activities, and dedicated lanes for special functionality (empty containers (MTs) and trucks without chassis (Bob Tails)).

It is well known from queuing theory that the demand for waiting (parking) is largely determined by the processing time in a lane. The gate process comprises: container identification (ID) (ID number, type-size code, CSC plate), checking of the container weight (a questionable activity due to many uncertainties), checking of tractor and chassis licence plate, seal checking and trucker's identification. Security is a major item in the gate process. The terminal's liability requires a 100 per cent certainty that the right container is picked up by the right trucker. In many places the driver is identified by checking his face and driver's licence (meanwhile respecting his privacy) or by checking some unique characteristics like hand shape or iris. When truck drivers have to come to an office before entering the gate this security check can be centralized, and after checking the presented documentation, the truck driver may receive a unique

Figure 7.11 Automated gate at Maher Terminals USA

process ID card (magnetic or chip), which can be used as a process trigger during the entire receival or delivery process through the gate and in the terminals.

The application of tag readers, digital cameras and sensors has been initiated to automate gate processing (Maher Terminals, PSA, ECT, Hessenatie, see Figure 7.11).

Some terminals have already reduced their gate processing time to less than 30 seconds. Further progress can be obtained when the shipping world decides on more standardization for tags at the containers (ID number, type-size code, operator) and electronic seals. The radio-frequency identification (RFID) technology looks promising for these types of identity checks.

Automated Handling of the Truck Interface

The existing automation of stacking cranes and some trials with automated straddle carriers promise a further automation of landside pickup and deliveries to road trucks. Remote control is already used (Thamesport, PSA) and further applications are under development. In such applications one operator will be able to control (remotely) four or even more stacking cranes, and this is an interesting cost saving.

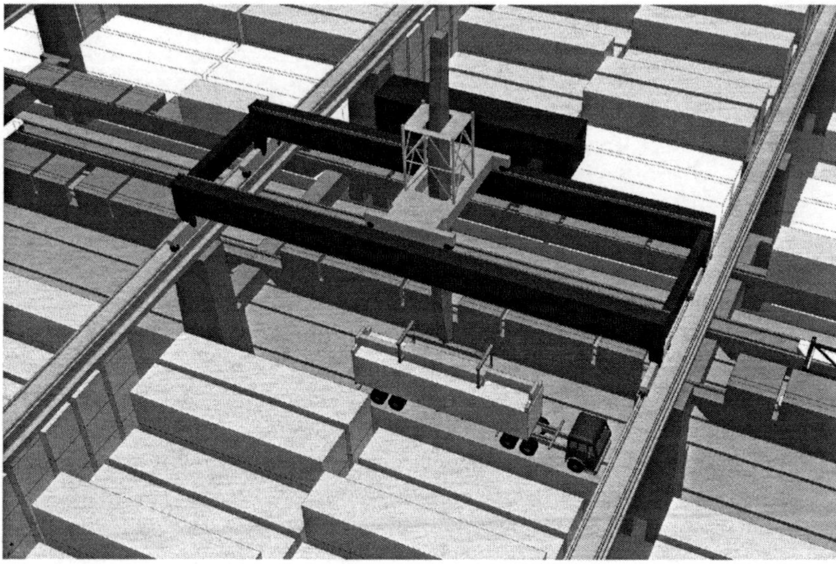

Source: Gottwald Port Technology.

Figure 7.12 Automated handling at landside interface

The next step could be to include the truck driver himself in the process of lowering a container onto his chassis or connecting a spreader to his container. The simplicity of today's crane control features and maybe some training could eventually result in a truck driver-operated crane. The first applications are already in use for internal movement tractors.

Automation of the landside handling will not be limited to large-scale operations. Some manufacturers have developed downscaled automated stacking systems, which will be attractive for medium-sized and small terminals with high labour cost (see Figure 7.12).

Partnership Between Trucking and Terminals

A further cooperation between large trucking companies and terminals will allow for a better exchange of information and the announcement of an estimated time of arrival in advance. In this respect gates for public traffic control and/or road pricing stations could be used to process data from truckers to the terminals in advance.

Another challenge is to integrate the logistics from shippers and truckers in the landside stack planning. There are some examples in the industry where truckers plan their next day's workload based on the consignee's demands and on the terminal stack layout and this helps to prevent false moves.

Gate Process Redesign with Reduced Inspection Activities

Shipping lines are increasingly aware of the tremendous costs related to the frequent inspection of equipment (container, chassis). Equal to developments in the rent-a-car business, the future might bring less physical inspections. Digital imaging from containers and storing such images over a two-month period should be sufficient to have proof in case of severe damage (under liability clauses).

Cooperation with Satellite Terminals

The increased inland container flows have supported the introduction of daily shuttles (by barge and/or rail). A partnership between deep-sea terminals and some major inland satellite terminals will allow the movement of containers directly after discharging or one day before loading. This will improve the dwell-time at the deep-sea terminals, will decrease transportation cost (through high utilization of transportation equipment) and will give better service to truckers (faster turnaround) and shippers (who can order the delivery of containers at shorter notice and with a better predicted time of arrival at their plant). The full benefit of satellite terminals for the improvement of landside operations can only be obtained when there is a strong operational coordination and a 100 per cent information exchange between deep-sea and satellite terminals.

Train Shuttles, Every Hour on the Hour

The tendency to shift towards rail transportation will probably continue. Larger volumes require more trains which must fulfil proper train scheduling. Train shuttles between mainport terminals, satellite terminals and other inland destinations can be run efficiently when the train is operated as a fixed set of wagons with minimal requirements to container weight and so on (to ease the planning of trains). Increasingly, shipping lines, terminals and logistic service providers operate such shuttles and a further privatized rail network will support better and faster rail services.

Obviously the above-mentioned trends, developments and influences will be affected by increasing volumes and peak demands. Mainports are in the process of reconsidering their service products, but the uncertainty about the future scales in operations hamper their decision-making.

7.5 THE DILEMMA

Since 1995, the rapid introduction of much larger container vessels forced ports and terminals to invest in new facilities, although the old ones were still in good shape and not fully depreciated at all. And again, a new wave of investments will be required to accommodate container vessels of 12 500 TEU capacity, now introduced to the market.

At the waterside, access channels, water depth before the quay wall, quay wall strength, container cranes and handling system must be enlarged or increased, but will there be sufficient volume and revenue for a sound payback period?

On the landside, gate systems must be improved, the arrival of three-TEU or four-TEU trucks need redesigned interchange areas, and the larger and more frequently arriving shuttle trains ask for larger shunting yards and on-dock rail facilities with more handling capacity. Again, where is the profit from these investments?

That is the dilemma for ports and terminals. Their long-term continuation requires a profitable operation but the competition between shipping lines, terminal operators, shippers and consignees, and inland transportation companies is increasingly asking for more services with eroding margins. Basically, ports and terminals can follow two alternatives: a service-driven or a cost-driven approach.

Service-Driven Approach

In this philosophy the focus is on berth performance, fast turnaround times and maximum flexibility, regardless of the size of vessels, trains, or barges and the stochastic nature of arrival patterns and port capacity demands. Vessel arrival and truck arrival are the most difficult to cope with. The ability of peak handling will result in underutilized (costly) handling capacity. Last-minute changes, fluctuations in flow density and frequent delays in arrivals will cause extra costs for the operator. Service guarantees, fixed time slots, guaranteed hourly productivities under all circumstances and related penalties for non-performance will result in a surplus of available capacity and thus increased costs.

Cost-Driven Approach

Observations using activity-based costing have revealed that ports and terminals should strive for a sound cost–service ratio at both waterside and landside. In this case the terminal operator is looking for predictability, a spread of the workload over the day and a 100 per cent quality of information to

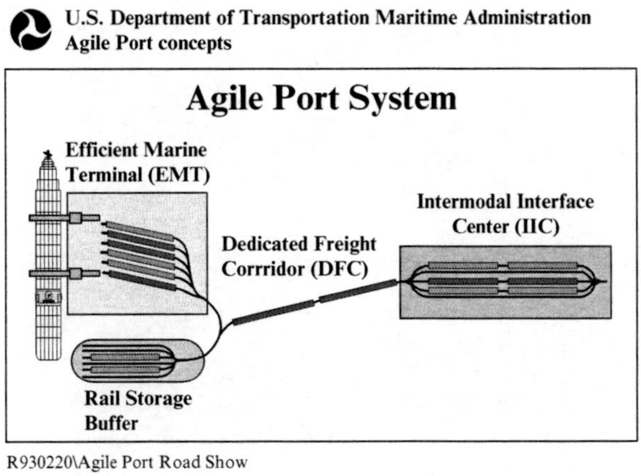

Sources: Vickerman (1999); Avery (2000a)

Figure 8.3 The Agile Port System: splitting marine container ports into two parts

- load and unload trucks which serve the region nearby, inland at the IIC.

8.3 ADDING EFFICIENCY TO REDUCED LAND REQUIREMENTS: THE EFFICIENT MARINE TERMINAL

The Efficient Marine Terminal as proposed by the US consortium operates like a conventional marine terminal, but features a rail interface instead of a conventional yard. Vessels are unloaded at the EMT and yard vehicles transport containers in much the same way as they are carried now (Figure 8.4), but the containers are then loaded directly onto trains in the yard. Some buffer storage would be provided in a separate area, but most of the containers would leave the terminal directly. The main idea behind the logistical concept of the EMT is to load and unload large vessels on a reduced area of land with minimal impact on the inland public traffic system and the environment (Avery 2000a).

In addition, the EMT concept developed by Noell Crane Systems is targeted on maximizing port productivity by transshipping boxes directly from vessel to trains and vice versa at the quay.

The proposed solution (Figure 8.5) features a combination of improved semi-automated ship-to-shore cranes (STS), semi-automated cantilevered

Figure 8.4 Straddle carrier on duty at the container terminal at Hessenatie NV, Antwerp, Belgium

rail-mounted gantry cranes (RMG) and a box mover based on rail-mounted automated shuttle cars driven by linear motor technology (LMTT), to be described in detail further below.

Drawing on its experience of the innovative quay cranes with lashing platform (Figure 8.6) in Hamburg (HHLA), the test site for gantry crane automation in Würzburg, and the LMTT pilot installations in Hamburg (Eurokai) and Würzburg, Noell improved the original EMT concept by incorporating the following features:

- Single trolley ship-to-shore cranes able to unload containers to a platform in the quayside portal, where the twist locks from deck containers can be removed.
- A conveyor to move containers from the lashing position on the platform to a second position underneath a RMG cantilever, which could be extended to provide additional buffer-space. The idea of

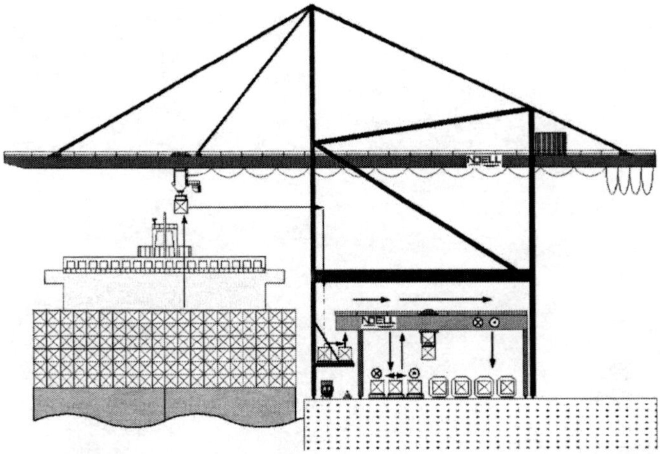

Figure 8.5 Noell design of the Efficient Marine Terminal: Direct handling of containers between vessel and trains

integrating a conveyor into a quay crane as a dynamic buffer for containers is not new. It was realized years ago by Matson Terminal, Los Angeles.

- RMGs that operate under the portal of the ship-to-shore cranes, covering for example four rail lanes and a three-lane wide box mover.
- Two extra service lanes under the lashing platform of the STS.

The big advantage of this concept is that yard transfer vehicles are not required, saving a great deal of machinery and labour, which, it should be remembered, is not particularly cheap in the Western world. When serving the vessel, one duty of the RMG would be to take containers from the platforms and place them on the linear motor-based transfer system or the rail cars on the shortest possible way and vice versa. The linear motor lanes could serve additional RMG loading and unloading along the trains as well as a buffer stack where this is required. The linear motor system would allow boxes being out of sequence to be held aside and shuffled without interrupting the ship-to-shore import–export cycle. Five to eight RMGs could service five ship-to-shore cranes between them (Avery 2000a).

Figure 8.6 Lashing platform of one of the double trolley quay cranes at terminal Burchardkai, HHLA, Hamburg, Germany

8.4 BUNDLING OF RAIL-BOUND CONTAINER FLOWS INLAND: INNOVATIVE HUB TECHNOLOGY

Intermodal Interface Center

The Intermodal Interface Center as proposed by the US consortium operates like a conventional rail terminal, performing either rail transshipment (without using an efficient sorting facility) or train/truck transfer (Figure 8.7).

In addition, the IIC concept proposed by Noell Crane Systems is targeted on maximizing node productivity by featuring a combination of

Figure 8.7 *Rail-mounted gantry crane serving trains and hustlers at the APL terminal in Los Angeles*

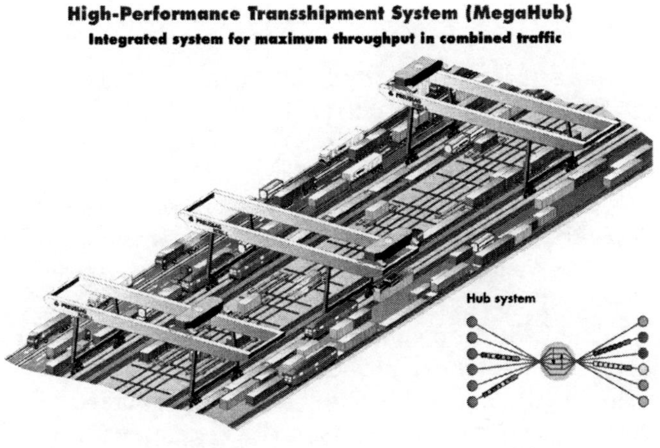

Figure 8.8 *Intermodal Interface Center (MegaHub): transshipment instead of shunting*

semi-automated cantilevered rail-mounted gantry cranes and again a box mover as it is to be used in the EMT. This innovative MegaHub technology, as it is known, was elaborated on behalf of Deutsche Bahn (German Railways) for bundling Continental container flows (Franke 1997) and the plan is to implement this technology near Hanover (Lehrte) in Germany (Figure 8.8).

MegaHub

The MegaHub production system for container trains has been developed for the transportation of container volumes that are currently considered too small to make it cost-effective for direct train carriage (Avery 2000b). The benefits of this system to the railway network have been described in the EU research project TERMINET (TERMINET Consortium 2000b).

Initially all containers are loaded onto the train, including those not scheduled for the train's particular destination. These are then offloaded once the train has stopped at the MegaHub and loads from other trains intended for the first train's specific destination are loaded on. The containers have to be loaded in groups according to destination, but shunting is not necessary.

Different proposals for the design of a MegaHub have been made in response to a design contest arranged by Deutsche Bahn in 1995 (Kortschak 1997; Fabel and Sarres 1997). The winner of the contest in technical and economical terms was the Noell MegaHub concept. Even though many years have passed, no technical alternative has been proposed since then.

At the MegaHub the actual transfer is undertaken on a surface covering an area as small as 730 m $\times$ 80 m, at a rate of up to ten ITU (intermodal transport units, either a container or swap body) per minute between dedicated trains. The storage capacity is a maximum of 270 ITU, but can be enlarged. Each transfer is carried out using electrically powered and semi-automated cantilevered yard gantry cranes (Figure 8.9) which span the transfer area and are able to lift to and from road vehicles, railway wagons, shuttle cars and the storage area.

The first MegaHub in Lehrte is planned to consist (in its initial state) of three semi-automated gantry cranes and about 12 fully automated shuttle cars controlled by an overall computer system. The transfer by crane is best done while the crane is travelling over very short distances. Long-distance travel is carried out by linear motor-driven shuttle cars, which can move along or across the sorting area (this is on one level only).

The outstanding feature of the MegaHub system is the modular construction using classic transfer technology. Put another way, if a very high performance level is not required, fewer gantry cranes and shuttle cars may be used. It is even possible to first store boxes flat at the location where, later, the runway for the pallets can be installed. For higher performance requirements it is possible to add extra cranes and to integrate the pallet system. The modular concept stands for economy even though the transport figures should not be too high when introducing this technology.

Figure 8.9 *Cantilevered rail-mounted gantry crane at the intermodal terminal in Basel/Weil, Germany*

In January 2000, the results of a feasibility study (TERMINET Consortium 2000a) for the MegaHub concept, which formed part of the EC-funded TERMINET project (TERMINET Consortium 2000b) were presented to an expert hearing arranged by the German Social Democratic Party at the new Reichstagsgebäude in Berlin (Franke 2000). The focus was on the MegaHub's main advantages: using transshipment to eliminate shunting, increasing handling speed and minimizing land area and cost per transfer.

When shunting is eliminated, generally the handling speed is increased remarkably (Figure 8.10). Handling six trains of 40 wagons with 64 Intermodal Transport Units (ITU) on each train takes five hours and 20 minutes using a shunting yard. By using a MegaHub with ten gantry cranes and 40 shuttle cars this can be reduced to just one hour and ten minutes. In the case of the shunting yard of Metz-Sablon, where most container trains of the ICF Quality Net service are shunted, this enables the number of ITU handled to be increased from 1120 per day (the maximum capacity of the existing shunting yard) to 2500 (the maximum capacity of the MegaHub using six gantry cranes and 15 pallet wagons).

The high performance of a MegaHub with up to ten gantry cranes and up to 45 pallets running together has been proven by simulation in two

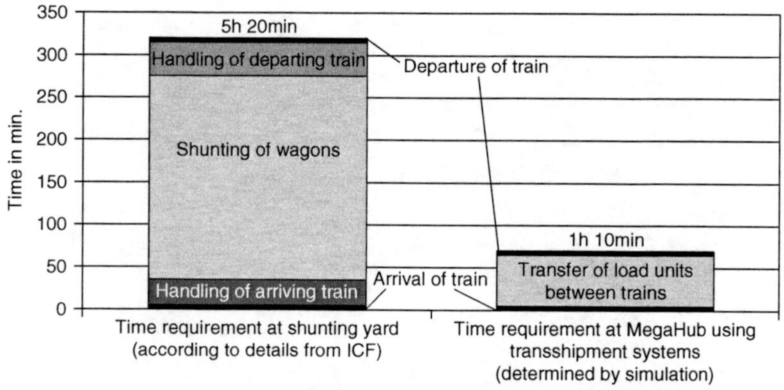

Figure 8.10 Minimum time spent by load units in the shunting yard or transshipment yard

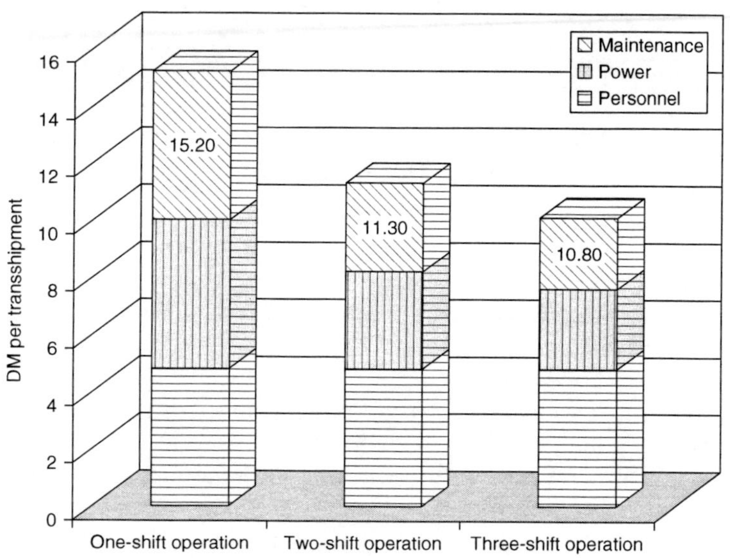

Note: Remark: 290000 T/a equal to 500 wagons or 800 ITU/shift

Figure 8.11 Case study MegaHub Metz: operating costs

independent doctoral theses: Dr Peter Meyer's at the University of Hanover (Meyer 1999) and that of Dr Knut Alicke at the University of Karlsruhe (Alicke 1999).

The cost savings are equally impressive (Figure 8.11). In the case of Metz the operational cost per move range from €5.50 (three shifts, 870 000 visits per year) to €7.75 (one shift, 290 000 visits per year) with minimum personnel required. By comparison, the cost of handling 700 wagons per day (1.6 ITU per wagon) in the existing shunting yard at Metz in France is estimated to be €20 per ITU.

As far as total costs are concerned, a MegaHub in Lehrte (ten gantry cranes, 40 pallet wagons) able to handle 3600 wagons carrying 5760 ITU per day is estimated to require an investment of €105 million, of which €60 million is for superstructure. The cost of shunting infrastructure to handle the same throughput at the Munich Nord One facility was €250 million.

Aside from the impressive cost savings, perhaps the MegaHub's greatest advantage for the future is the minimal amount of land required. Taking the Lehrte–Munich Nord example again, the Munich site needs 130 ha on which to handle 3600 wagons per day, compared with just 10 ha for a MegaHub.

8.5 HIGH-CAPACITY BOX MOVER FOR COLLECTION AND DISTRIBUTION ALONG THE TRAINS

Part of the Efficient Marine Terminal as well as of the Intermodal Interface Center (MegaHub) is a horizontal transport system for the sorting of boxes along the trains featuring linear motor-based transfer technology. Due to heavy obstruction, there would be no efficient container handling possible without such a horizontal transport system when loading and unloading trains by several gantry cranes using the same track.

Linear Motor-Based Transfer Technology (LMTT)

Generally the fully automated horizontal transport system consists of a system of tracks running parallel and at right angles to one another. Fully automatic shuttle cars are conducted lengthwise and crosswise along these tracks (Figure 8.12). What makes the system so attractive for applications in container terminals (Franke 2000) is the wagon's ability to turn at right angles by moving the wheels by 90° instead of turning the whole wagon.

The shuttle cars are rail-mounted and bi-directional (straight ahead and sideways). They comprise a base frame and a loading platform that is capable of carrying loads up to 41 tonnes, which may well be increased to 54 tonnes for twin-lift operation. They are also equipped with double wheel sets that can be rotated 90° for the carrying and guiding functions. In addition, permanent magnet strips have been installed for the transmission of the driving power (Figure 8.13). The units for drive (linear motors) and

Figure 8.12 LMTT pallet wagon propelled by electromagnetic force

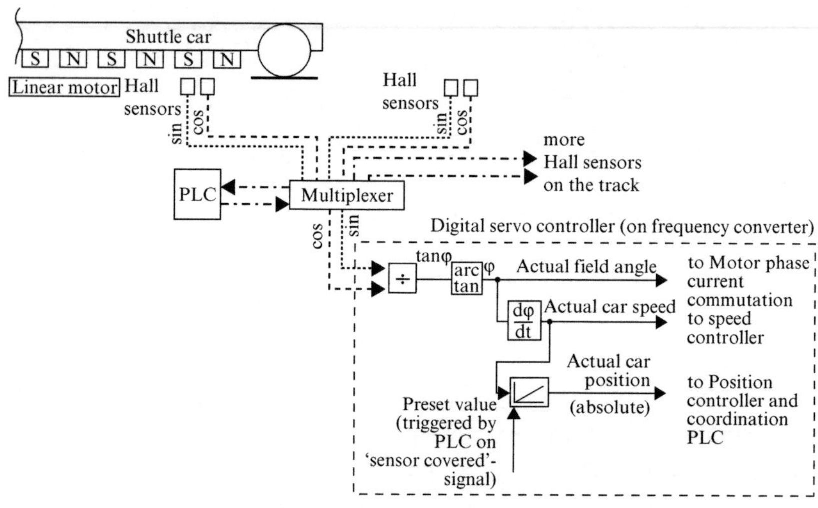

Figure 8.13 LMTT – Position detection system

position detection are integrated into the runway. The control system is stationary.

The runway may consist of ordinary UIC 60 rails, mounted on steel twin sleepers. To make it possible to turn the wheel sets (of the shuttle cars), a circular steel surface with transverse guides has been fitted at the crossing points, that is, the intersections of the longitudinal and transverse travelling rails (Figure 8.12).

A major advantage is that the chassis does not need an engine, brakes, gears, a Programmable Logic Control (PLC) or sensors. The shuttle cars are driven by means of contact-free linear synchronous motors, which are distributed over the track according to the requirement of driving force. They act on the magnets located on the underside of the shuttle cars. It is possible to set a variable speed by means of a mobile electromagnetic field, generated using a frequency converter. A contact-free actual position detection system (Hall sensors) is integrated into the runway and responds to the individual magnets located on the shuttle cars. This enables the absolute position of the shuttle car to be determined and supplies the input values required to ensure that the linear drives are supplied with power and switched over in the correct order.

The shuttle cars move at 3 m/s with an acceleration of 0.3 m/s^2 and can be positioned with an accuracy of +/− 3 mm. With so few moving parts, maintenance costs are kept to an absolute minimum and no fossil fuel is required (Bauer 1998).

The linear motor-driven transfer technology was initially developed with funding from the German Ministry of Research, BMB+F (Consortium 1997). Between 1995 and 1998, test and demonstration plants (on a scale of 1:1) were set up at the Port of Hamburg, Eurokai (Wölper and Huth 1997), at the headquarters of Noell Crane Systems GmbH in Würzburg (both in Germany) and on the plant grounds of Noell Crane Systems (China) Ltd. in Xiamen.

Simulation of the Box Mover Based on LMTT

Each EMT (Figure 8.5) and MegaHub (Figures 8.8, 8.14), features two runways for longitudinal travel in parallel to the trains: one runway for each direction, plus one transfer lane between with access from both runways by a 'sidewards step' of a shuttle car. The transfer lane is also used for parking and loading and unloading of the shuttle cars by the gantry cranes. Each of these box movers is no wider than 13 m and about 700 m long.

Of course it is of high importance to know how many shuttle cars are necessary to fulfil given transport requirements and whether there might be deadlocks or not.

The modelling of the box mover as well as the simulation was done by using a version of SCUSY (Simulation von Containerumschlag-Systemen) software, which was developed by the ISL (Institut für Seeverkehrswirtschaft und Logistik) in Bremerhaven. This software was upgraded by adding an LMTT software module. This version of SCUSY enables the programmer to design the layout of the horizontal transport system easily by choosing from a software library of standardized runway modules (uni- or bi-directional,

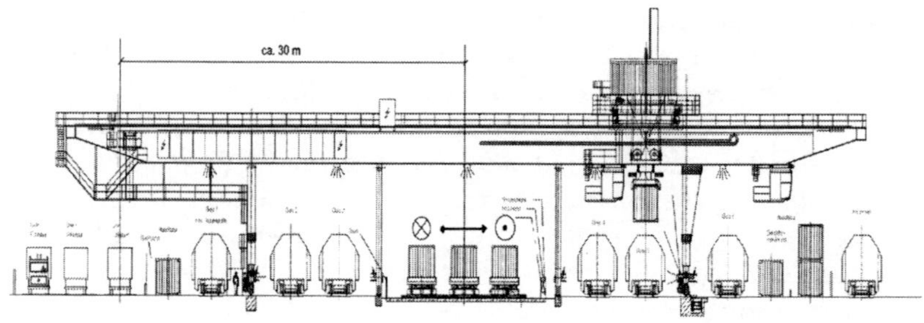

Figure 8.14 MegaHub application of box mover

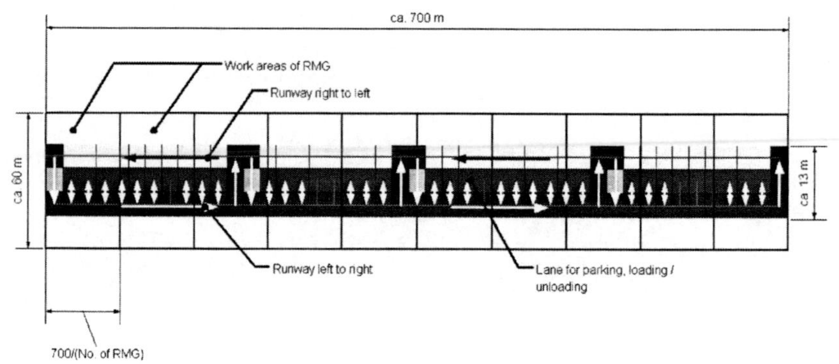

Figure 8.15 Layout of box mover based on LMTT (MegaHub)

longitudinal or transverse, crossings) which may be further specified to a certain extent. It is important to say that the LMTT software module features traffic regulations at crossings as well as distance regulations between vehicles following each other, while taking into consideration realistic kinematics and time requirements for positioning of the vehicles.

The simulation (duration = 100 min) was based on the following assumptions:

- Transshipment of boxes between six trains, each of them being 700 m long.
- Random distribution of boxes between trains.
- Sequential entry and exit of trains are unconsidered.
- Layout of the box mover (700 m × 13 m) as described above (Figure 8.15).
- Access to loading or unloading position by shuttle cars only from one of the two runways possible (no trespassing).

While rethinking networks, network design actors are aware of the performances which are achievable by current or innovative physical means. During the last 20 years, especially in the 1990s of the twentieth century, many designers of intermodal transport networks[2] were faced with or were involved in the development of new options, namely innovative node exchange concepts, like innovative terminals and vehicles. The innovative concepts were different from their predecessors. In fact they were so different, that they could be called new-generation concepts (NG concepts), like NG terminals, other NG node concepts, or NG vehicles. And for the bundling of flows they promised a substantial reduction of the impedance of load unit exchange. The number of presented NG concepts was large, and so was the number of innovative networks in which the NG concepts were to play a role. The whole resembled an innovation wave.

In the meantime many innovation initiatives have been stopped. The high level of expectations has been tempered. But the core issue, namely to enlarge the range of bundling options on the basis of innovated node exchange operations, which have a substantially increased quality–cost ratio, remains extremely relevant. The enlargement of bundling options would allow the finding of appropriate intermodal solutions for more situations, hence increasing intermodal competitiveness. The challenge is to identify promising directions of intermodal network development.

This chapter is devoted to that challenge. It compares alternative bundling concepts for different situations, hereby assuming the presence of advanced exchange operations at exchange nodes, especially intermediate exchange nodes. Section 9.2 explains the principles of bundling and discusses the (dis)advantages of direct and so-called complex bundling. The terms are explained in the section. Section 9.3 gives an overview of the innovation wave and of the state-of-the-art of innovation and it briefly evaluates the reasons for innovation progress and stagnation. Section 9.4 elaborates the principles and (dis)advantages of bundling choices, which were the subject of section 9.2, hereby providing a framework for quantitative comparisons. The framework is used in section 9.5 (nodes) and 9.6 (networks). In section 9.6 alternative bundling networks are compared on the basis of operational costs of the main modality network. The section's focus is rail transport. Section 9.7 compares the chapter's approach with that of other network design research. In section 9.8, the conclusions of the chapter's analyses are drawn.

9.2 THE PRINCIPLE AND (DIS)ADVANTAGES OF COMPLEX BUNDLING

The Principles of Bundling

For many transport connections, flow sizes are not sufficient to provide a direct service from the begin to the end terminal (BE), unless a small vehicle scale and/or low frequency are acceptable. Small vehicle scale means that the vehicle size is small and/or the vehicle's loading degree is low. Such a situation is shown on the left side of Figure 9.1: the two transport services, one from A to B, the other from C to D, in this example both have an unsatisfactory loading degree.[3] The figure refers to the main mode (for example rail or barge) only.

In such a situation complex bundling may be an outcome (right side of Figure 9.1). This is the process of transporting goods which belong to different flows (different begin and end terminals;[4] or different origins and destinations[5]) in common transport and/or load units during common parts of their routes, in order to achieve one or more of the following advantages, despite the small flow size:

1. an increase in economies of scale in terms of higher loading degrees (transport units or load units) and/or larger transport units (top right side of Figure 9.1);[6]
2. an increase in the transport frequency (bottom right side of Figure 9.1);[7]
3. an increase in the number of E terminals from each B terminal. This means that the number of destinations to be reached from each origin becomes larger. In other words, the service areas can be enlarged and/or intensified (right side of Figure 9.1).

Further potential advantages are the possibilities to reduce the length of pre- and post-haulage (PPH) and to equalize terminal peak and valley performance requirements. This potential advantage is not visible in Figure 9.1.

The meaning of these advantages is as follows. Economies of scale (1) allow a reduction in the operational costs per load unit. More precisely, larger vehicles, like longer trains, let the traction costs per load unit decline. Higher loading degrees lead to a reduction in all train costs per load unit. Higher transport frequencies (2) imply shorter waiting times for load units at a begin terminal. Interest costs for freight in circulation and other time costs of shippers can be reduced. Next, the number of required load units in circulation and hence the costs of (empty) load units per unit are likely to shrink. More E terminals from each B terminal (3) lead to more demand

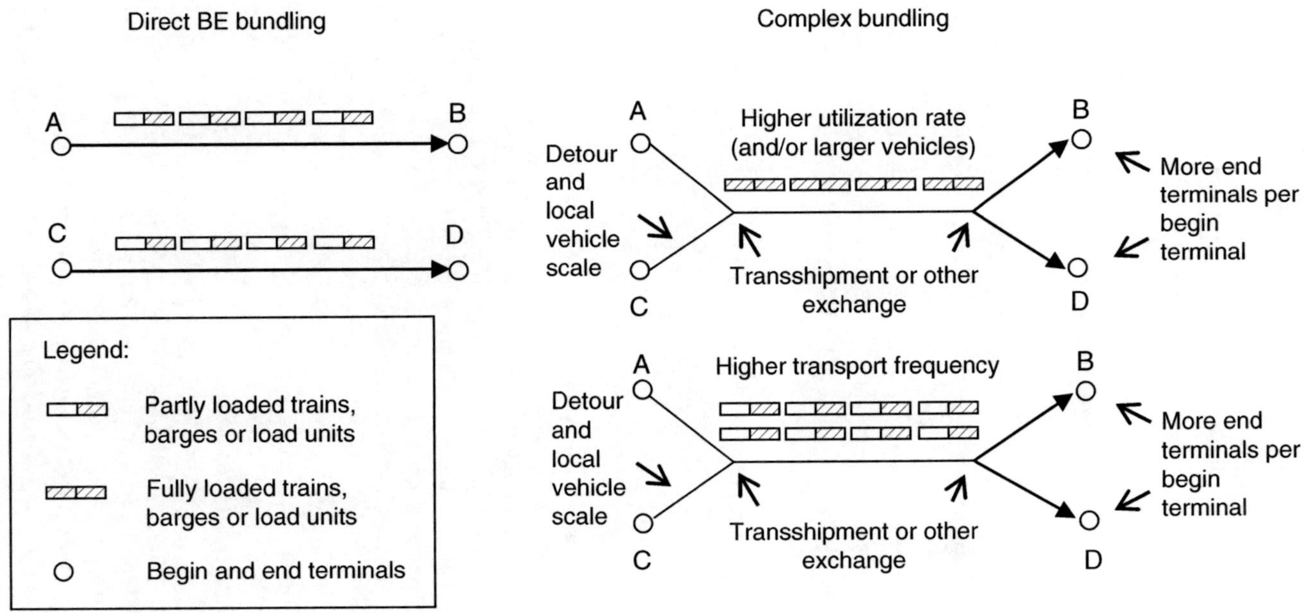

Figure 9.1 Principle and impacts of complex bundling (main mode only)

and income on the one side. The related reduction of PPH distances contributes to the reduction of one of the most costly parts of any intermodal transport chain, the PPH costs.

However, complex bundling has some disadvantages as well:

- It causes additional handling at intermediate nodes, such as the exchange of load units between trains or barges:
  - by means of transshipment;
  - by means of reassembling train wagons or wagon groups of different trains at shunting yards or sidings, or push units of different push barges. This additional handling of course costs time and money and is likely to reduce the door-to-door reliability of the transport chain;
- It causes detours of routes for most transport services. The transport distances most likely are larger than in cases of direct terminal–terminal services. The additional distance increases time and distance costs;
- The local branches have a restricted vehicle scale, making this part of the network expensive. This is the case if the local networks have the same frequency as the trunk networks, which should be the case. Otherwise the higher frequencies of the trunk network have no function.

Whether direct or complex bundling is a better response to the transport demand, depends on the balance between the above-mentioned advantages (loading degrees, economies of scale on the links, transport frequencies, number of destinations) and disadvantages (additional node costs, detour costs). And this balance in turn depends on the size of the network volume. If the volumes are large enough to run direct services at the required frequency and scale levels, direct bundling clearly deserves priority. The bundling advantages are present, and the bundling disadvantages can be avoided. However, flow sizes are often smaller than required to load a full-length train. Often complex bundling will then be appropriate, because the advantage of vehicle scale and/or higher frequencies will most often overrule the disadvantages of additional intermediate node costs, detours and local network costs. This would especially be the case, given NG means for the advanced exchange of load units at intermediate exchange nodes.

There are different types of complex bundling networks (Figure 9.2), namely the hub-and-spoke network (HS network), the trunk collection and distribution network (TCD network), the trunk-feeder network (TF network) and the line network (L network), as well as combinations of these and/or hierarchical versions. Each type differs by:

GEM (NG terminals) or the NG terminal 'Goed aan boord', design commissioned by the Dutch Ministry of Transport.
- Different NG concepts for ro-ro traffic for the barge sector, amongst which were Rollerbarge for the barge sector (Netherlands) and some NG terminals and NG vessels, initiated by Volvo (for example the concept of TTS Drobak).

The performances of these concepts have been analysed in numerous research projects, amongst which are:

- European or national research projects such as Cargo 2000 (Brunn 1991), SIMET (1995), HaCon et al. (1995), IRIS/OSIRIS (Möller 1998), IMPULSE (1999) and TERMINET (2000); also Bontekoning and Kreutzberger (2001b). They have investigated the suitability of different NG terminal concepts for different exchange types and/or the network performance of networks with NG terminals. TERMINET (2000) also analysed the performance of certain shunting yards and compared these with those of rail–rail terminals.
- The UIC research project Modular Freight Train System (Bürkl 2001a), which investigated the performances of operations with robotized trains, Cargo Sprinters and trains with innovative wagons in mixed bundling networks.[11]
- SAIL (TFK et al. 2000) researched NG transport systems for semi-trailers.
- InHoTrA (Seidelmann and Frindik 2003) researched terminals and systems for the horizontal transshipment of load units.

Many of these research projects compare the performances of competing NG concepts.

Realized Implementation of NG Concepts

The realization of NG concepts is very restricted, quite contrary to the enthusiasm of their initiators or inventors. The most relevant intermodal examples in Europe are:

- The (robotized and non robotized) internal transport systems of ocean harbours, like Rotterdam Maasvlakte, Felixstowe and Hamburg. They have connection and sorting tasks.
- The robotized stack of Rotterdam Maasvlakte, with a storage and sorting function.

- The rail terminal in Rotterdam Maasvlakte. It has a BE terminal function, but the operational design and technical means could be of interest for hinterland bundling terminals as well.
- The main hub-terminal in the harbour of Antwerp. It functions as an H, CD and a BE terminal. The rail–rail exchange is substantial, and distinguishes this terminal from many gateway terminals in Europe. Rail tracks and wagons provide in-terminal internal transport between different crane segments. This is less innovative and powerful than the internal transport systems of Noell and Commutor, but simpler to realize.
- A small number of rail systems with horizontal transshipment. An important example is Cargo Domino, the domestic intermodal rail network in Switzerland. It employs load units, rail wagons and trucks with sliding techniques. Another example – for bulk transport – is ACTS;
- A small number of ro-ro rail systems. Most spectacular is the ModalOhr concept operated by French operators for a restricted network. Ro-ro systems, also cheaper and less powerful concepts, are on the border of functioning in niche or mainstream markets.
- The classic national railway companies have partly modernized their shunting yards. Some of the modernization is spectacular, such as the robotization of wagon pushing in the train-forming part of the yard (the Netherlands, Switzerland).

Other projects have not been started, or have been ended after a pilot stage. The CargoSprinter pilots, including some complex bundling operations, have been stopped.

The hopes of producers or potential clients (KombiVerkehr) to realise the rail megahub terminal at Lehrte near Hanover on the basis of the Noell concept, have recently been buried.

On the other side, the interest in NG terminals has not completely ended. ÖBB built a pilot NG terminal in Vienna in 2003. The evaluation of its feasibility was planned to be finished by 2005.

In the barge sector, the most important implementations of NG concepts relate to vehicles (barges), not nodes. Most important intermodal products are the cellular guided 300 and 400 TEU (twenty-foot equivalent units) barges and the 30 TEU large Neokempenaars. Both supply-driven innovations have an impact for bundling:

- The large barge means that complex bundling becomes more and more important. This feature is not new, as L networks already dominate the barge sector. But the new interest in HS or TCD networks

(Denis 2000) can be explained by this background. One may expect that existing terminals, optionally with minor adjustments, will fulfil all exchange functions.
- The small barge means that complex bundling becomes unnecessary. Transport efficiency is mainly realized by fast round-trip speed (short terminal times due to small barge size).

Reasons for the slow speed of implementation, or the reluctance to implement any NG concepts at all, have not yet been entirely clarified. The spectrum covers the following points:

- The classic railways as DB Cargo/Railion were busy to heavily invest into shunting yards and were afraid to underutilize these, in case intermodal traffic was separated from non-intermodal traffic, then using (terminal) hubs; even if the shunting performances were worse for intermodal transport than terminal performances. In this regard the railways had a contradictive agenda.
- If it is of interest to bundle relatively small intermodal and non-intermodal flows (as some large European railway companies think), the shunting yard or siding allows this to be done, while the intermodal terminal does not. However, it could be reasonable to have two points of view for different markets, one of which focuses on exclusive intermodal operations, for which NG concepts are still reasonable.
- The value an NG concept adds to the performance of the network has not always been sufficiently elaborated on. Some terminals, like those of Krupp, were originally developed for L networks, later adjusted to the requirements of hub exchange. But this adjustment was never really convincing.
- Many concepts focused on high performance rather than low costs. This was likely to create a double disadvantage:
  - The technological state-of-the-art was less developed than the concepts required. This was especially the case for robotization. On the other hand, some deep-sea harbours are fully devoted to this challenge.
  - The fast exchange would only be required for certain connections. For other connections which do not need any operational acceleration the fast terminals only generate higher node exchange costs.
- Many concepts focused too one-sidedly on technical solutions, neglecting the potential of operational optimization without major technical changes. Take hub exchange: an important ingredient of innovative bundling concepts is the simplification of hub exchange

by restricting direct exchange to small exchange batches instead of continuing to allow large ones. The advantages can already be realized to a large extent at shunting yards.

One could easily conclude that the whole innovation wave was planned to be realized in a far too short a period. The ideas of the inventors were far ahead of their time. One could alternatively conclude that the innovation wave was too high-tech minded, as simpler solutions are more appropriate. But recent network developments oppose to such conclusions, at least in the rail sector.

Non-Technical Network Innovations

As far as the realised network innovation is concerned, technical innovation hardly played a role. Most important non-technical innovations were:

- The introduction of dedicated intermodal networks, in other words the splitting of intermodal and non-intermodal networks. The main advantage was the possibility to abolish local collection and distribution rail transport for intermodal transport, as load units did not need to be set on the train at the location of a shipper, but could make use of terminals. These had a service area, which was sufficiently large to load complete trains. Since the 1990s a comparable development is also taking place for non-intermodal transport: the so-called rail ports have a comparable function as terminals for non-intermodal flows. It is worth considering whether the emerging rail port networks would allow the reintroduction of mixed intermodal and non-intermodal trains for corridors with small flows.
- The streamlining of wagonload networks to networks which operate complete trains with a minimum of intermediate exchange nodes. Complete trains have a 'full' length between their BE terminals, but change the train composition (and to some degree also the length) during the journey, by dropping and picking up wagon (group)s at intermediate exchange nodes (shunting yards or emplacements).
- Re-promoting rail-friendly locations of sorting and distribution centres. These are located near to intermodal terminals. Optionally the centres are part of dedicated partial-load rail service networks. Good examples which illustrate the intention, are the Bahntrans network, which the German railways proposed in the 1990s, and comparable networks thereafter

There are examples of innovative networks which at their beginning had to decide whether they would apply NG concepts or not. One is the PNIF rail network of CNC and SNCF, created in the early 1990s. It is clearly an example of network innovation: a national hub-and-spoke network for maritime flows, centred around the Paris hub. The maritime flows were too small to transport them in BE networks. The PNIF network was also a dedicated intermodal network, allowing complete trains to run between all BE terminals. Finally, the PNIF network was the subject of the above-mentioned Commutor project, in which an NG megahub terminal was to fulfil the hub function. But after an evaluation of performance, SNCF decided to use an existing shunting yard as the PNIF hub instead of an NG terminal.

9.4 QUANTITATIVE ELABORATION OF THE BUNDLING LOGIC: VOLUMES, SCALE AND FREQUENCIES

There is a clear relation between network volumes, transport frequency and size of transport unit (the scale effect) in so-called directed[12] and separated networks.[13] Two of these variables can be kept constant, showing the effects for the third entity. We refer to the term 'bundling triangle' (Figure 9.3).

The bundling triangle relation is elaborated in Figure 9.3. Three different directions of elaboration are presented. In the frequency approach, the frequency varies; in the volume approach, the network volume varies; and in the scale approach the size (scale) of the transport unit and/or its loading degree varies. The three approaches could be defined as, respectively, frequency- or scale-increasing or volume-reducing network design strategies.

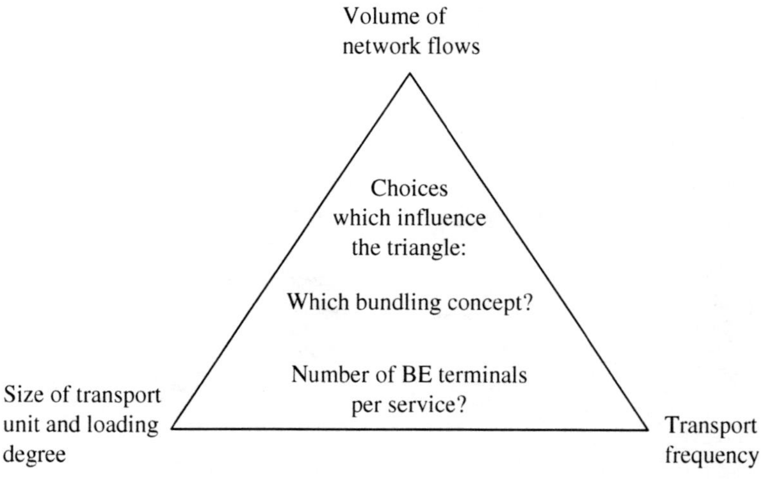

Figure 9.3 The triangle of quantities for designing bundling concepts

The frequency in Figure 9.4 is expressed by the number of arrows from each B terminal to each E terminal. The network volume is shown by the total number of arrows in each network. The (relative) size of the transport unit is represented by the size of the rectangles beneath each network.

The triangle is influenced by the number of BE terminals. In Figure 9.3, which has two BE terminals per service area, the quantitative relation of BE networks, HS networks and the other networks is 1:2:4 (service frequency and vehicle scale) or 4:2:1 (network volume). This means that:

1. in the frequency approach the number of departures from each B to each E terminal in the above-mentioned groups of networks is 1:2:4;
2. in the volume approach the required network volume in the above-mentioned groups of networks is 4:2:1;
3. in the scale approach the size of transport units in the above-mentioned groups of networks is 1:2:4.

With three BE terminals per service area the relation is 1:3:9, with four it is 1:4:16 and so on. The quantitative relation, conceptually shown in Figure 9.4, is mathematically expressed in equations (9.1)–(9.6).

The quality–cost advantages of best solutions in these three approaches are: (1) the reduction of waiting times for freight and empty load units in circulation at B or L terminals; (2) the capability of serving areas with relative small flows; or (3) the reduction of operational costs per load unit. The approaches can be mixed, resulting in less extreme, but therefore multiple advantages.

The potential cost–quality advantages of complex bundling is also illustrated by Figure 9.4, as far as the comparison of a BE network with an HS network is concerned.[14] It is evident that any set of (bundling) networks could be compared in a similar way. The additional operational costs at hubs plus the detour costs of an HS network must be compensated for by:

- (in the frequency approach) a cost reduction caused by less waiting of freight and load units (without their freight) at the B terminals (and L terminals). The time reduction implies lower interest costs for shippers;
- (in the volume approach) the reduction of external costs due to higher market shares of intermodal networks;
- (in the scale approach) the reduction of main modality costs as a result of higher loading degrees and/or larger transport units (upper left of Figure 9.4).

As time cost (reduction)s are relative low in many situations, the frequency approach will often lead to the lowest quality–cost improvements.

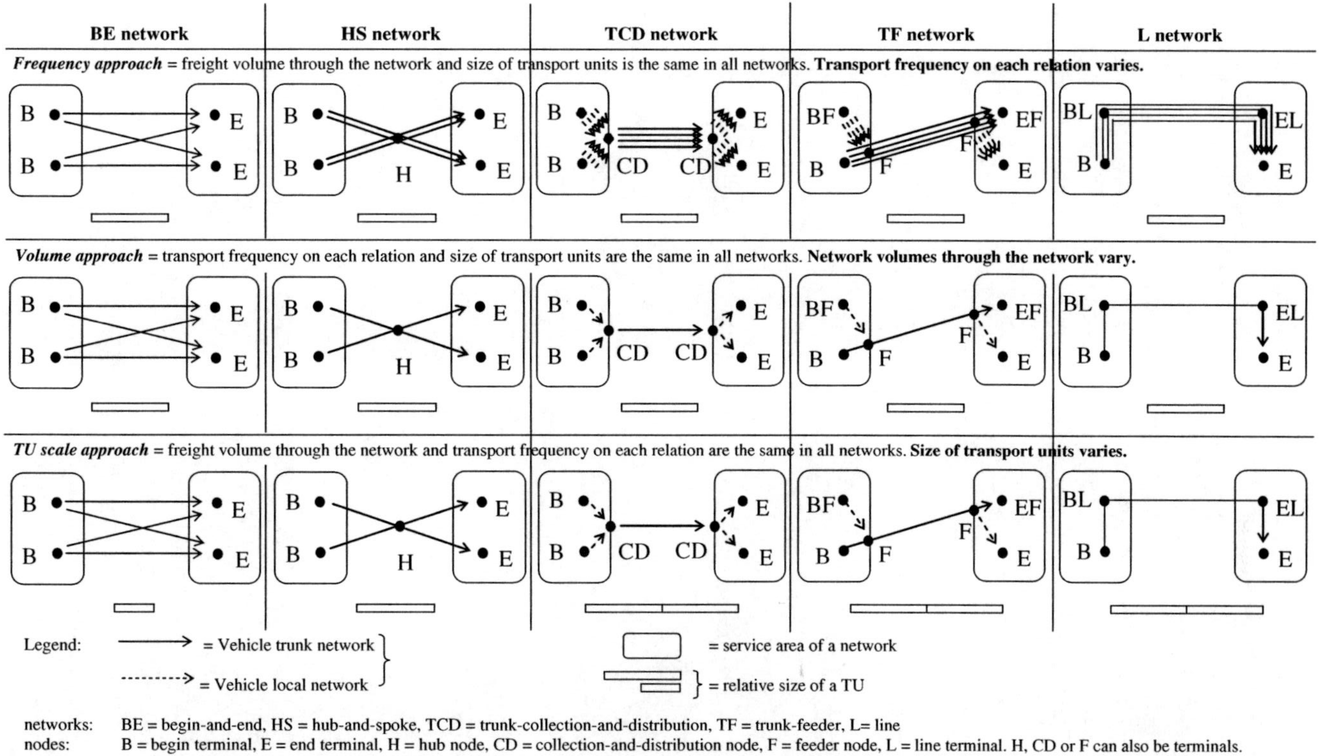

Figure 9.4 Frequencies, transport volumes and scale of transport units per bundling concept in different approaches

The quality–cost improvements in the framework of the scale approach are likely to be the largest. The weight of cost–quality improvements in the volume approach very much depends on the valuation of sustainability: how high are external costs? Some reports (for example EC 2002) suggest that these are substantial. Other researchers (for example IFEU and SGKV 2002) conclude that the external costs are restricted. The range of research results has currently made the European Commissioner more hesitant to make actors in the transport field pay for external costs (Simons 2002).

In the scale approach, the length of a train[15] in directed and separated networks can be calculated as:

$$L_{BE} = \frac{V^* l}{N_{be}^2 {}^* D^* F_{be} {}^* Lo_{be}} \tag{9.1}$$

$$L_C = L_{BE} {}^* B \tag{9.2}$$

subject to:

$$V = \sum_b \sum_e \begin{bmatrix} v_{beBERai} \cdot x_{beBERai} + v_{beHSRai} \cdot x_{beHSRai} + v_{beTCDRai} \cdot x_{beTCDRai} + \\ v_{beTFRai} \cdot x_{beTFRai} + v_{beLRai} \cdot x_{beLRai} \end{bmatrix} \tag{9.3}$$

$$x_{beBERai}, x_{beHSRai}, x_{beTCDRai}, x_{beTFRai}, x_{beLRai} \in \{0,1\} \tag{9.4}$$

$$x_{beUNIRo} + x_{beBERai} + x_{beHSRai} + x_{beTCDRai} + x_{beTFRai} + x_{beLRai} = 1 \tag{9.5}$$

$$L_{BE} \leq L_{BE}\, max \tag{9.6}$$

in which:

L_{BE} = length of train (in metres) in BE network
L_c = length of train (in metres) in a complex bundling network
V = transport volume on rail network (in number of load units) per time unit (for example year) per direction
v_{be} = volume of rail flow between b and e (= B terminal, E terminal) per time unit (for example year)
l = length of a train (in metres) per load unit
N_{be} = number of BE terminals in the region of origins
D = number of working days per time unit (for example year)

F_{be}	= daily departures from each B terminal to each E terminal in a BE network = frequency in a BE network. In the volume or scale approach this frequency is valid for any bundling network
Lo	= loading degree of a train (%)
$L_{BE} max$	= maximal length of (bundling) train (in metres)
B	= factor bundling concept = $\begin{cases} N \text{ for HS network} \\ N^2 \text{ for TCD, TF or L network} \end{cases}$
$v_{beBERai}$	= rail flow between b and e (= resp. B or E terminal) in a BE network
$v_{beHSRai}$	= rail flow between b and e (= resp. B or E terminal) in an HS network
$v_{beTCDRai}$	= rail flow between b and e (= resp. B or E terminal) in a TCD network
$v_{beTFRai}$	= rail flow between b and e (= resp. B or E terminal) in a TF network
v_{beLRai}	= rail flow between b and e (= resp. B or E terminal) in an L network

Equations (9.1) and (9.2) determine the length of trains in respectively a BE network or complex bundling network, if all flows of the envisaged service areas are served by only one bundling network (Equations 9.3, 9.4 and 9.5) and if the networks are directed and separated ones. Equation (9.2) expresses the impacts of complex bundling.

The result of the Equations (9.1) and (9.2) is an unlimited positive value. Beyond the maximal train length (restraint of Equation 9.6; in Europe for example 600 m or 700 m, in the future in some countries maybe 1000 m or more)[16] the scale approach cannot lead to further cost reductions. If network volumes keep on growing, further advantages can be achieved by increasing the service frequency.

The intention of the length restriction is illustrated in Table 9.1. Given the network conditions and choices of columns 1 to 3, the train lengths per bundling concept are mentioned in columns 4 to 8. A train length of 1 is – from the cost point of view – a maximal and best solution.

The maximum train length is an important technical restriction, as it implies – from the point of view of economies of scale – that there is no best bundling type in general, but only one in relation to certain network volumes and network design attributes like frequency. In the first row of Table 9.1 the HS network has the best train length. In the third row this is the TCD, TF and L network, in the second row the BE network.

Figure 9.5 is another way to express the outcome of equations (9.1) and (9.2). The figure shows train lengths in directed and separated networks with

Table 9.1 Length of trains per transport landscape and bundling concept in examples (in factors of a 600 m long train, which in this table is considered to be a maximum; loading degree 80 per cent; directed and separated networks)

Transport landscape and network characteristics				Length of trains in the trunk network (1 = whole train)				
Row number	1	2	3	5	6	7	8	9
	Annual network transport volume in two directions	Number of BE terminals per service area	Rail frequency per relation, direction and working day	BE network	HS network	TCD network	TF network	L network
	V	N_{be}	F_{be}	L_{BE}	L_{HS}	L_{TCD}	L_{TF}	L_L
1	100 000	2	2	0.5	[1]	2	2	2
2	100 000	2	1	[1]	2	4	4	4
3	50 000	2	2	0.25	0.5	[1]	[1]	[1]
4	50 000	2	1	0.5	[1]	2	2	2
5	100 000	4	2	0.13	0.5	2	2	2
6	100 000	4	1	0.25	[1]	4	4	4
7	50 000	4	2	0.5	0.25	[1]	[1]	[1]
8	50 000	4	1	0.13	0.5	2	2	2

Note: □ = favourable bundling network, as far as economies of scale on the trunk network are concerned.

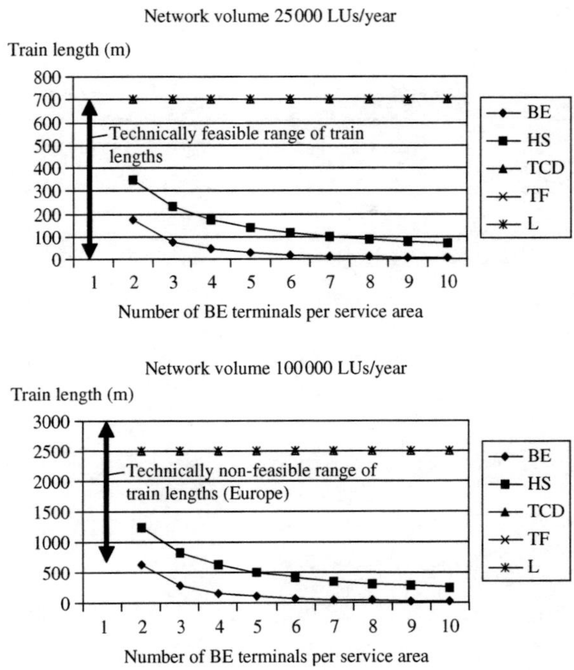

Figure 9.5 Length of trains, dependent on choice of bundling concept and number of BE terminals per service area (TCD, TF and L networks have same values) (directed, separated and fully interconnected networks, loading trains degree = 80%, frequency = 1/working day;)

one departure from each B to each E terminal per working day. Given a network volume of about 28000 load units/year TCD, TF or L networks have the best train lengths. If the network volume is 100 000 load units/year, a BE network has the best train lengths in case of two BE terminals per service area, an HS network has the best lengths in case of three or more BE terminals per service area. The constant train length for the TCD, TF or L network is due to the fact that these networks always have the same number of trunk connections, namely 1, no matter how many BE terminals are involved.

Table 9.2 elaborates the triangle of bundling quantities (Equations 9.1–9.6) for a larger range of network transport volumes and of number of BE terminals per network. The table is based on the idea that there is a daily train departure from each B terminal to each E terminal (five departures per week) and that the maximal train length is 700 m.

Table 9.2 Train lengths (in number of 700 m long trains) indifferent bundling concepts with different network volumes. Frequency = 1 per working day (DS networks)

Bundling concept	Annual network volume (LUs per direction	Number of BE terminals								
		2	3	4	5	6	7	8	9	10
		Number of trains per direction								
BE network	250 000	7.1	3.2	1.8	1.1	**0.8**	0.6	0.4	0.4	0.3
BE network	225 000	6.4	2.9	1.6	**1.0**	**0.7**	0.5	0.4	0.3	0.3
BE network	200 000	5.7	2.5	1.4	**0.9**	0.6	0.5	0.4	0.3	0.2
BE network	175 000	5.0	2.2	1.3	**0.8**	0.6	0.4	0.3	0.2	0.2
BE network	150 000	4.3	1.9	1.1	**0.7**	0.5	0.3	0.3	0.2	0.2
BE network	137 500	3.9	1.7	**1.0**	0.6	0.4	0.3	0.2	0.2	0.2
BE network	125 000	3.6	1.6	**0.9**	0.6	0.4	0.3	0.2	0.2	0.1
BE network	112 500	3.2	1.4	**0.8**	0.5	0.4	0.3	0.2	0.2	0.1
BE network	100 000	2.9	1.3	**0.7**	0.5	0.3	0.2	0.2	0.1	0.1
BE network	87 500	2.5	1.1	0.6	0.4	0.3	0.2	0.2	0.1	0.1
HS network	87 500	5.0	3.3	2.5	2.0	1.7	1.4	1.3	1.1	**1.0**
BE network	75 000	2.1	**1.0**	0.5	0.3	0.2	0.2	0.1	0.1	0.1
HS network	75 000	4.3	2.9	2.1	1.7	1.4	1.2	1.1	**1.0**	**0.9**
BE network	62 500	1.8	**0.8**	0.4	0.3	0.2	0.1	0.1	0.1	0.1
HS network	62 500	3.6	2.4	1.8	1.4	1.2	**1.0**	**0.9**	**0.8**	**0.7**
BE network	50 000	1.4	0.6	0.4	0.2	0.2	0.1	0.1	0.1	0.1
HS network	50 000	2.9	1.9	1.4	1.1	**1.0**	**0.8**	**0.7**	0.6	0.6
BE network	37 500	1.1	0.5	0.3	0.2	0.1	0.1	0.1	0.1	0.0
HS network	37 500	2.1	1.4	1.1	**0.9**	**0.7**	0.6	0.5	0.5	0.4
BE network	25 000	**0.7**	0.3	0.2	0.1	0.1	0.1	0.0	0.0	0.0
HS network	25 000	1.4	**1.0**	**0.7**	0.6	0.5	0.4	0.4	0.3	0.3
HS network	12 500	**0.7**	0.5	0.4	0.3	0.2	0.2	0.2	0.2	0.1
L, TCD or TF network	12 500	1.4	1.4	1.4	1.4	1.4	1.4	1.4	1.4	1.4
L, TCD or TF network	6 250	**0.7**	**0.7**	**0.7**	**0.7**	**0.7**	**0.7**	**0.7**	**0.7**	**0.7**

Note: □ = favourable bundling network, as far as economies of scale on the trunk network are concerned.

The following conclusions can be drawn from Table 9.2. In networks with transport frequencies of one per day, BE networks are promising for annual network flows of 50 000 load units per direction or more, because in this range BE trains can have full lengths. For the same reason the number of BE terminals per service area should not exceed six. Rail HS networks seem to be most interesting in network volumes between 25 000 and 175 000 load units. The range of suitable number of BE terminals per service area is larger. TCD, TF and L networks are most suitable for small network flows, which is about 13 000 load units per year.

Figure 9.6 summarizes the information of Table 9.2. It shows the areas in which the bundling concepts allow to operate long trains, given two BE terminals per service area and a frequency of 1 or 2. The figure shows the best areas in terms of network volumes for bundling concepts: best in the sense of allowing to operate long trains. Above or to the right of the best areas trains exceed the maximal lengths, downwards or to the left of the best areas trains become rather (or too) short.

The length of trains is nothing more than a first indication for the selection of best networks. Whether they really are the best also depends on node and distance performances, in other words on the integral costs and performances of nodes and links (sections 4 and 5).

9.5 EXCHANGE NODES

A major result of case studies on NG terminals in the European research project Terminet was that the exchange costs are about €20 to €50 per load unit, dependent on the chosen terminal concept and – more importantly – dependent on the utilization rate of the terminal (Franke et al. 2000). With utilization rates to be expected in practice, the range will rather be one of €30 to €50 per transshipment. These amounts are not very different from those of conventional terminals or shunting yards. The major difference is the performance in terms of handling time. This time reduction supports complex bundling, hence the increase of train or barge scale. And it potentially contributes to the acceleration of round-trip speeds. Both advantages can be incorporated in the calculation of network performance costs.

The performances and costs of another exchange-orientated NG concept, namely innovative transport units in rail networks, have been analysed in the European (UIC) research project Modular Freight Train System (Bürkl 2001a). The project investigated the effects of different modular trains, including the Cargo Sprinter, in a multilayer TF and L network. The exchange costs per load unit were estimated to be €20. Networks with some of the innovative train types were shown to be more

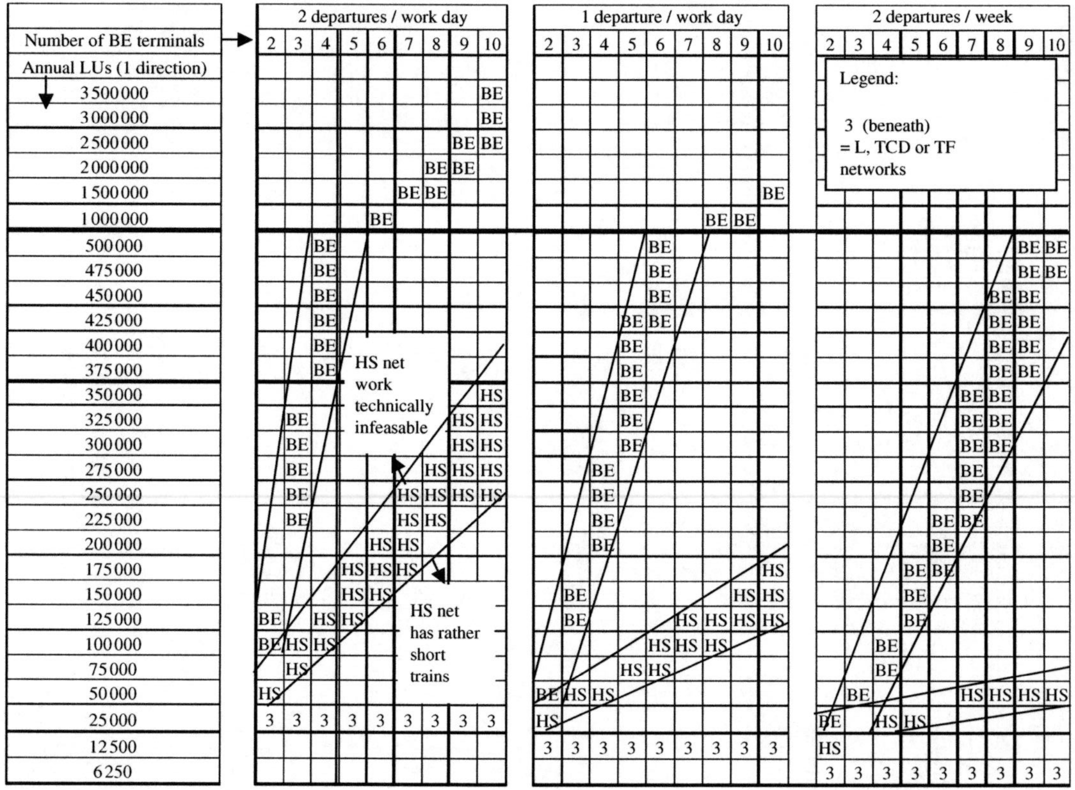

Figure 9.6 Volume-dependent best rail bundling networks (DS; trains have 700m loading degrees of 70% or more)

Table 9.3 The total costs of load unit exchange at intermediate terminals in different bundling networks (in euros per load unit)*

	Networks with 2 B terminals and 2 E terminals		Networks with 4 B terminals and 4 E terminals	
	High utilization rate	Average utilization rate	High utilization rate	Average utilization rate
BE network	n.a.	n.a.	n.a.	n.a.
HS network	10	15–25	15	25–40
TCD network	40	60–100	40	60–100
L network	0	0	5	5
TF network	20	30–50	30	45–75

Note: * Rounded off to a manifold of 5.

efficient than conventional trains with shunting yard operations.

The costs of load unit exchange at intermediate NG terminals are shown in Table 9.3 for different bundling networks, hereby taking account of the number of intermediate terminals, the amount of exchange at intermediate terminals, and the time costs of freight in circulation. The result is that the intermediate exchange will cost €2 to €100 per load unit. The values in L networks refer to time costs only, as L networks have the same number of rail–road terminals as BE networks.

9.6 INTEGRAL COSTS

Main Mode

This section indicates best intermodal rail bundling networks on the basis of main mode costs and performances. The cost calculations are carried out for the transport landscapes and network layouts described in Table 9.4. Network comparisons are restricted to networks with two BE terminals at each side of the network and in this sense rather indicative a than. representative. Rail–rail node exchange is assumed to take take a relatively short time. This may require NG terminals or vehicles.

The main mode costs consist of train costs, node exchange costs and time (that is, interest) costs of freight in circulation. Once the bundling triangle decisions have been taken, a large part of the input for the different cost modules is known (Figure 9.7). Other important input network decisions refer to the round-trip design of trains.

Table 9.4 Transport landscape and train length values for cost calculations

Network volume (2 directions)	Two BE terminals per service area	Length of trains, frequency
25 000 LUs	• BE network	156 m, 1
	• HS network	313 m, 1
	• TCD, L, TF network	625 m, 1
50 000 LUs	• BE network	313 m, 1
	• HS network	625 m, 1
	• TCD, L, TF network	625 m, 2
100 000 LUs	• BE network	625 m, 1
	• HS network	625 m, 2
	• TCD, L, TF network	625 m, 4

Notes:

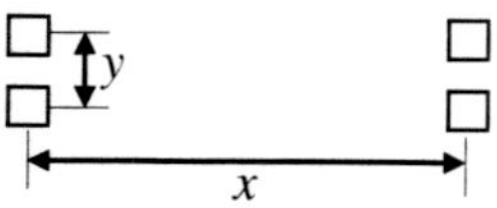

x = 1200 km, 900 km, 600 km, 300 km.
y = 80 km.
Number of BE terminals = 2 per services area.
Σy therefore = 80 km.

The cost results for networks with two BE terminals are shown in Table 9.5a (network lengths = 1200 km; costs per chain activity and total) and Table 9.5b (total costs with different network lengths). The average link speed is assumed to be 80 or 30 km/hour. The first value is typical for many national or other day-A-A or day-A-B connections. But for A-C distances (such as 1200 km) passenger priorities and border obstacles imply average link speeds of down to 30 km/hour.

Given this input, L networks have the lowest costs for rail networks with small volumes, HS networks the best values for rail networks with volumes around 50 000 load units per year, BE networks best values for rail networks of 100 000 load units per year. With other parameters, like other frequencies, node or rail costs, or distances, the results will differ.

These results confirm the outcome of the length-of-train-analysis. This is neither a coincidence nor necessarily the case. In the networks with 25 000 load units a year there will – as distances grow beyond 1200 km – be a point where the TCD networks generate larger net savings than line - networks. The distance may grow not only because of an increasing x, but also or instead by an increasing y and/or growing number of BE terminals.

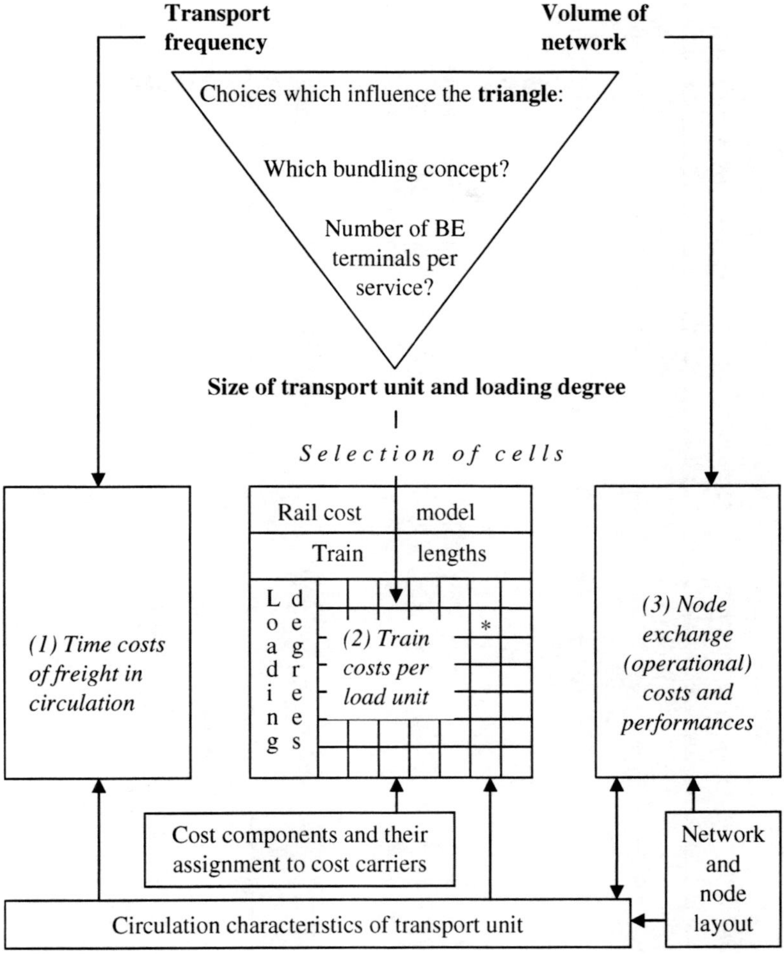

Note: * = example: costs per load unit, if train length is 600 m, and loading degree of train is 90 per cent.

Figure 9.7 *Network costs (= 1 + 2 + 3) and performances of main modality*

It is also interesting that – for the given transport landscapes – a TF network leads to larger net cost reductions than a TCD network. This is mainly due to the fact that only a part of the load units are exchanged at the F nodes. Some load units are not exchanged at any F node. At CD nodes all load units of the network are exchanged. This advantage is larger than the disadvantage of longer local branches.

Table 9.5a Cost differences per load unit (euro; preliminary results) in alternative networks (BE network is reference)

	25 000 LUs				50 000 LUs				100 000 LUs			
	Train length (m)	Costs trunk links	Costs intermediate terminals*	Costs local links**	Train length (m)***	Costs trunk links	Costs intermediate terminals	Costs local links	Train length	Costs trunk links	Costs intermediate terminals	Costs local links
BE network	155				315				625			
HS network	315	−375	+(15 to 25)		625	−150	+(15 to 25)		625–2	In all models: Additional link and node		
TCD network	625	−525	+(60 to 100)	+(70 to 125)	625–2	−150	+(60 to 100)	+ (70 to 125)	625-4	costs are higher than interest savings by shorter waiting times at		
L network	625	−480			625–2	−105			625-4	B terminals, which are the		
TF network	625	−525	+ (30 to 50)	+(45 to 75)	625–2	−150	+(30 to 50)	+ (45 to 75)	625-4	result of higher frequencies.		

Notes: $x = 1200$ km, 2 BE terminals per service area, $y = 80$ km and $\Sigma y = 80$ km (networks are separated and fully interconnected; values are rounded off to 5, except frequencies).

* The range is caused by utilization rate, choice of technical concept and fraction of load units of a train being exchanged.

** The range is caused by the choice of train lengths (half or full) and transport cycles per day (1 or 3). The choices imply that the local train only serves one trunk train (most expensive) or – given two BE terminals – six trunk trains.

*** 625-2 = train length is 625 m, if frequency is 2 departures/day. 625 = train length is 625 m, if frequency is 1.

Table 9.5b *Net cost differences per load unit summarized (sum of columns in Table 9.5a; euro; preliminary results)*

	25 000 LUs				50 000 LUs				100 000 LUs			
x = (km)	1200	900	600	300	1200	900	600	300	1200	900	600	300
BE network									**0**	**0**	**0**	**0**
HS network	−(350 to 360)*	−(285 to 295)	−(190 to 200)	−(90 to 100)	−(125 to **135**	− (85 to **95**)	−(50 to **60**)	−(15 to **25**)	Higher costs	Higher costs	Higher costs	Higher costs
TCD network	−(305 to 395)	−(200 to 290)	−(70 to 160)	+ 70 to − 20	−20 to +70	+ (110 to 20)	+ (175 to 55)	+ (225 to 130)				
L network	**−480**	**−380**	**−250**	**−135**	−105	−70	−35	+ 0				
TF network	−(405 to 450)	−(300 to 350)	−(170 to 220)	−(30 to 80)	−(60 to 75)	+ 10 to −35	+ 45 to −0	+ (85 to 35)				

Notes: Networks with 2 BE terminals per service area, $y = 80$ km and $\Sigma y = 80$ km (networks are separated and fully interconnected; values are rounded off to 5).

Best results in **bold** characters.

* This expression means that the HS network in the mentioned situations generates net cost reductions, compared to a BE network, of about €250–260 per load unit.

Pre- and Post-Haulage

The calculations of section 6.1 did not include any PPH costs. Integrating them will change some conclusions about the position of some main modality networks. On the other side, the PPH costs are influenced by the choices for the main modality network, for instance the number of BE terminals in a service area. The smaller the service areas and the shorter the PPH routes are, the lower the costs may be. On the other hand, a larger flow is likely to promote the ability to equalize flow peaks and valleys and to achieve more stable and higher average loading degrees and utilization rates of local trucks.

9.7 COST FUNCTIONS AND ECONOMIES OF SCALE IN NETWORK DESIGN IN RELATION TO THE BUNDLING TRIANGLE

The bundling triangle as the basis of cost functions is not in line with cost function perceptions in numerous network design studies. The following features are widespread, both in strategic (for example facility location) or tactical (for example service network) studies. (Generalized) costs are assigned to links. Their derivation misses clarity or is hardly appropriate. The impact of changing flow sizes on costs may be absent (Rutten 1995), not necessarily route-specific, or not explicitly consistently modelled in interaction with frequency (for example the Nodus model in TERMINET 1998; O'Kelly 1986; Mayer 2002). The guarantee of consistency of the triangle entities by constraints is not apparently part of the standard (service or location) network model repertoire.

In this regard economies of scale deserve special attention. Two main directions can be distinguished:

- The correction for scale effects by means of cost discount factors at the level of transport services. An example is O'Kelly (1986, p. 95), who applies 'proportionality-factors' for inter-hub services. The inter-hub services have larger flows than the services between the ends of the network and a hub. They are therefore expected to employ larger vehicles, which have lower transport unit costs. The proportionality factors are to reflect such reduction of transport unit costs, in other words to display economies of scale. The size of the factor in relation to frequency, vehicle size and flow sizes is not modelled explicitly or at all.
- The introduction of transport volume-dependent cost functions: the volume-dependent increase of transport costs declines with increasing transport volumes. Mayer (2002) shows the intention (left of Figure 9.8)

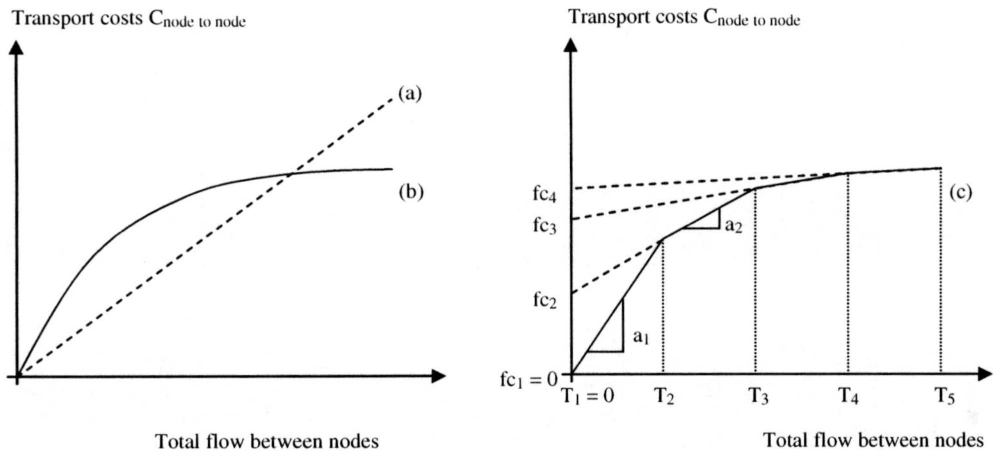

Legend (a) = volume-independent costs progression (b) = volume-dependent costs progression
(c) = partial linear approximation of non-linear costs
fc = volume-dependent constants
a = scale factor T = transport volumes

Source: Based on Mayer (2002) p. 162 (left) and p. 164 (right).

Figure 9.8 Degression of transport costs with volume-independent and -dependent scale factors

and a simplified version (right of Figure 9.8) of such an approach. In both cases the central factor of scale economies is the transport volume of a route or network, not vehicle scale as in the bundling triangle approach. The evidence or a (route or network) transport volume-dependent cost function is not clear.

A major reason for simplification of cost functions is the attempt of model makers to reduce model complexity. The result is a lot of effort invested to find appropriate optimization or comparison models or algorithms, but in return the model makers will accept cost functions which do not guarantee the consistency of volumes, vehicle sizes, frequencies and bundling choices, or which simplify scale-effects in a non-appropriate manner.

Much research suffers from the absence of an elaborated bundling typology. The term 'HS network' is often used for a number of complex bundling network types. For instance, many studies do not distinguish between different types of bundling networks with unimodal node exchange. They are all called HS networks. In a graph a double HS network looks very similar to a one-layer TCD network. But the first has an exchange between transport units of a comparable size, which – in the scale approach – implies the same scale effects on all branches. In the second network the CD branches of the local network have feeder characteristics, smaller transport units and therefore no or restricted scale effects.

9.8 CONCLUSIONS

Triangle Approach

When designing a freight service bundling network in response to a certain network volume, the scale approach will sort the most important (dis)advantages, namely operational costs. The frequency approach only leads to significant cost differences if the transport frequencies are very low, like one departure a week from each B terminal to each E terminal. But even then the cost effects of different waiting times are much smaller than those of different train lengths.

As far as the scale approach is concerned, the calculations, which include node and distance performances, will often confirm the assumptions about promising networks on the basis of length of trains only.

The presented cost analysis allows us to differentiate between TCD, TF and L networks. With respect to length of train, the three are alike, as Tables 9.2 and 9.3 have shown. But when also taking account of distances, times and node costs, these networks will certainly show differences.

Best Networks

The chapter has evaluated the differences in operational costs of intermodal freight transport in different bundling concepts for different distance classes. The results are preliminary, because the rail cost model is still provisional. Also, only one link performance has been taken into account. But with this in mind, and given the parameters used, L networks lead to the lowest rail costs for networks with small flows, HS networks for networks with about 50 000 load units a year, and BE networks for networks with 100 000 load units a year. The results refer to distances between 300 km and 1200 km. With other parameters, for instance another frequency, the results may differ. The expectation is that TCD and TF networks become of interest in the case of a larger number of BE terminals, rather from the quality than from the cost point of view. The reason is that they allow for collecting and distributing load units more simultaneously than L networks. TCD and TF bundling could also be cost-competitive in networks with longer trunk distances or asymmetric networks (with local network parts only on one side of the network).

These results will not yet permit us to draw conclusions about the feasibility of intermodal rail operations, but they do suggest that certain directions in which to expand the business are more promising than others. The results are roughly in line with rail practice. Common perceptions about break-even distances between intermodal rail and unimodal road transport may need some adjustments.

Pre- and Post-Haulage

The accounts of section 9.6 did not include any PPH costs. Integrating them will change some conclusions about the position of some main mode networks. Pre- and post-haulage costs are influenced by the choices for the main mode network, for instance the number of BE terminals in a service area. The smaller the service areas and shorter the pre- and post-haulage routes are, the lower the costs may be. On the other hand, a larger flow is likely to promote the ability to equalize flow peaks and valleys and to achieve more stable and higher average loading degrees and utilization rates of local trucks.

Network Design Research

From the point of view of the network design logic which has been presented in this chapter, network design research could be improved on the following areas. Network models should guarantee the internal consistency of the triangle entities, namely network volume, transport frequency, scale of transport units (and loading degree) and number of BE terminals. Secondly, models should introduce more explicitly an elaborated bundling typology and let the quantitative relation between the triangle entities be influenced by the choice of bundling concepts. As a consequence of such improvements the methods to incorporate economies of scale would be adjusted.

Such conclusions may be difficult to harmonize with the necessity to restrict the complexity of network models. On the other hand, applying models which solve problems on the basis of too-simplified operational assumptions is not very satisfying.

NOTES

* I would like to thank Piet Bovy, Professor at the Faculty for Civil Engineering and Geo Sciences of the Delft University of Technology, and Hugo Priemus, Professor of System Innovation Spatial Development and Dean of the Faculty Technology, Policy and Management, Delft University of Technology, for their critical and supporting remarks.

1. For example a barge, train or only its locomotives or wagons.
2. This chapter defines the term 'intermodal transport' as the unimodal or multimodal transport of load units, like containers, swap bodies or trailers, in contrast with United Nations (2001), which does not include unimodal transport. Any modality can be involved, as long as load units are involved. The term 'intermodal transport' is a synonym for 'combined transport', which is very common in the rail sector and also promoted by ECMT (1998). Actually, combined transport is a most appropriate term, as it focuses on the central attribute of this type of transport, namely a technique. In contrast to intermodal transport, the term 'combined transport' avoids confusion with the term 'multimodal transport'. The latter could also refer to non-combined transport, as with the bulk transport of coal and iron ore in barge–rail chains.
3. In this example the transport units have a loading degree of 50 per cent.
4. From now on, BE terminals.
5. Origin or destination nodes (respectively, origins and destinations) are locations with activities which generate a demand for transport. Examples are factories, non-transport storage facilities (like trade storage or logistic storage) or consumer nodes (like supermarkets or other shops).
6. In this example the loading degree is 100 per cent. Instead the size of the transport unit could be enlarged.
7. In this example the transport units have a double frequency.
8. Single wagons or wagon groups.
9. More precisely, an NG terminal has equipment and a layout which is designed to be an effective and efficient response to new types of load unit exchange or existing exchange types with higher performance requirements, like unimodal exchange (rail–rail, barge–barge), fast multimodal exchange (rail–road, barge–road), or cheap small-volume exchange. New crane types, handling devices, electrical catenaries for the powering of locomotives, and storage systems could be a result. Synergy between different terminal modules (for example transshipment, storage and internal transport) is of great importance. Therefore advanced internal sorting and transport systems or the (partial) robotization of operations may be part of some concepts. The whole terminal node including sidings has a low space demand, preferably a low energy consumption, and definitely a favourable quality–cost ratio. Summarizing, an NG terminal will have new functional qualities. Even though nothing more than an instrument to achieve the

projected performances, its technical means are often striking and are likely to draw some attention.

10. According to Tuchschmid also the use of (robotized) AGVs serving Tuchschmid-specific stack facilities represented proven technology.
11. The results of certain train type combinations are very promising (Bürkl 2001b). Unfortunately the major publication is not public.
12. In a directed network (for example a directional HS network) all services are directed to certain directions, opposite to an all-directional (for example HS) network (see Kreutzberger 1999).
13. In a separated network any multimodal terminal (B or L terminal) has – for a certain train or barge – either a loading or an unloading function. In the opposite, the diffuse networks, the above-mentioned terminal types load and unload load units to the same train or barge.
14. As both networks of Figure 9.4 have the same number of BE terminals, the costs of BE terminals and pre- and post-haulage can be excluded from the comparison. Both would have to be included whenever the best bundling concept is also to be compared with unimodal road transport.
15. The equations are a rail-specific version of the generic formulation, in order to support the understanding of Tables 9.1 and 9.2 and of Figure 9.4.
16. As possibly in France (Kerckaert 2001). In Switzerland tests have been conducted 'on a line section closed for passenger traffic in the vicinity of Solothurn with trains 750 . . . 1000 and 1500 metres in length'. In Switzerland long trains hold most promise for use in combined transport (Vogel 2000, p. 24). Tests with 1000 m trains have also been carried out in the Netherlands. The new research and development project LIIIFT is devoted to the implementation of 1000 m trains in the Rotterdam–Antwerp–Paris corridor. In the real world intermodal freight trains with lengths of 400 m and 500 m are no exception, also not from and to large ocean harbours.

REFERENCES

Bontekoning, Y.M. and E.D. Kreutzberger (2001a), *Concepts of New-generation Terminals and Terminal Nodes*, TRAIL, DUP Science, Delft. The report is based on the research carried out in the European research project TERMINET in 1998.

Bontekoning, Y.M. and E.D. Kreutzberger (2001b), *New-generation Terminals. A Performance Evaluation Study*, TRAIL, DUP Science, Delft. The report is based on the research carried out in the European research project TERMINET (co-financed by the European Community) carried out in 1998.

Brunn, E. (1991), 'Cargo 2000. Ein neues Behälter-Transportsystem für Teilladungen', *Die Bundesbahn*, **6**, pp. 695–701.

Bürkl, M. (2001a), 'Modular freight train system', *World Congress on Railway Research (WCRR)*, Conference Proceedings, Köln, Munich and Cologne: Deutsche Bahn AG and CGM.

Bürkl, M. (2001b), Interview, 11 December, Minden.

Denis, J. (2000), 'Capacity to spare: Europe's waterways in the intermodal network', *Intermodal Conference Papers 2000*, Geneva/London: Informa.

EC (2002), *Voorstel voor een verordening van het Europese parlement en de Raad betreffend de toekenning van communautaire financiële bijstand om de milieuprestaties van het vrachtvervoersysteem te verbeteren, COM 200254 definitief*, Brussels.

ECMT (1998), *Report on the Current State of Combined Transport in Europe*, Paris.

Franke, K.P., M. Vogtmann, D. Erni and Y. Bontekoning (2000), 'Terminal cost model', OTB, Delft University of Technology, Delft.

HaCon, Deutsche Bahn, DUSS, IVE (1995), 'Analyse und Bewertung der mittel- bis langfristigen Perspektiven einer Schienenvernetzung von KV-Umschlagbahnhöfen unter Berücksichtigung neuer Ansätze für die Produktionsgestaltung im Rahmen eines zentralen Hub-and-Spoke-Systems für den Kombinierten Verkehr', Endbericht, in charge of: Der Bundesminister für Verkehr, FE-Vorhaben 90433/94, Bonn.

IFEU and SGKV (2002), *Comparative Analysis of Energy Consumption and CO2 Emissions of Road Transport and Combined Transport Road/Rail*, in: charge of IRU and BGL, Geneva and Frankfurt am Main.

IMPULSE (1999), *IMPULSE Final Conference Documentation*, Brussels.

Jahnke, B. (1995), 'Innovative Systeme für den Schienengüterverkehr', *ETR* **4** (April), pp. 233–40.

Kerckaert, L. (2001), Interview, 30 May, by E. Kreutzberger.

Kreutzberger, E.D. (1999), *Promising innovative intermodal networks with new-generation terminals* (D7, WP 4.2 en 4.3), European (EC) research project TERMINET, OTB (TU Delft), Delft and Brussels.

Mayer, G. (2002), *Strategische Logistikplaning von Hub&Spoke-Systemen*, Darmstadt: DUV, Gabler Edition Wissenschaft.

Möller, K. (1998), 'Multimodal transport chains in freight traffic: innovations and experiences with the seaport hinterland traffic as an example', *RailTec 1998 Conference Proceedings*, Dortmund, www.railtec.nrw.de.

O'Kelly, M.E. (1986), 'The location of interacting hub facilities', *Transportation Science*, **20** (2), pp. 92–106.

O'Kelly, M.E. and J. Miller (1994), 'The hub network design problem: a review and synthesis', *Journal of Transportation Geography*, **2** (1), pp. 31–40.

Rutten, B.J.C.M. (1995) 'On medium distance intermodal rail transport', PhD research, Faculty of Mechanical Engineering, TU Delft, DUP, Delft.

Seidelmann, C. and R. Frindik (eds) (2003), *InHoTrA (Interoperable Intermodal Horizontal Transshipment). Final Management Report*, European research project (5th FP), Frankfurt/M., Brussels.

SIMET (1995), *Economic and Technical Research of Transfer of Goods: Design and Evaluation of Rapid Transfer. Future Optimum Terminals for Intermodal Transport*, Brussels.

Simons, J. (2002), 'De Palacio twijfelt terecht over doorberekening externe kosten', *Nieuwsblad Transport Weekend*, 9 August, p. 7.

TERMINET (1998), 'GIS-presentation of innovative bundling concepts' (D3), European (EC) research project, FUCAM, Mons, Delft and Brussels.

TERMINET (2000), 'Performance analyses 5 new-generation terminal case studies' (D10). TERMINET project, European (EC) research project, OTB/TU Delft, Brussels and Delft.

TFK, Kombiverkehr, Kombiwagon, Kögel & Cattanea, Duss & IMA (2000), SAIL (Semitrailers in Advanced Intermodal Logistics). Analysis of the State of the Ar, (D1), Bremen and Brussels.

United Nations (2001), 'Terminology on combined transport', New York and Geneva.

Vogel, H. (2000), 'Longer freight trains: possibilities and limitations', *Rail International* (Schienen der Welt), pp. 22–7.

Woxenius, J. (1997), *Inventory of transshipment technologies in intermodal transport*, IRU, Göteborg.

10. Designing intermodal transport systems: a conceptual and methodological framework

Arne Jensen

10.1 INTRODUCTION

In this chapter, the term 'conceptual framework' is looked upon as a scientific toolbox to be used by the researcher for designing intermodal transport systems for freight. As in other scientific contexts, the framework developed here consists of concepts, relationships between concepts, and some conditions for the existence of relationships. However, the framework also contains some methodological suggestions for intermodal transport system design and how to apply the concepts in this context. In this methodological sense, the framework is also somewhat normative. The word 'researcher' should not be taken too literally. The academic researcher as well as the advanced practitioner belongs to the target group for this chapter. It draws heavily on research reported in Jensen (1990), but the framework developed here has been generalized, modified and updated to suit the present purpose.

The System Designer

The intended user of the framework is assumed to be responsible for designing an intermodal transport system for freight that is able to enter a competitive market and survive there. This implies that the framework suggested here is demand oriented. It regards shippers' preferences as important determinants for transport system development.

Let us use the term 'system designer' for the person or group of persons having this responsibility. The system designer may represent a company, a group of companies, a government authority, or simply the research interest of the scientific community. It is assumed that the intended end result of this use of the framework is a model of a system for intermodal transport for a particular segment of the real world.

The principal for the system designer's research may be either real, as in practice, or hypothetical. The latter may be the case in scientific research. In any case, it is necessary for the system designer to try to define whose interests the intermodal transport system is expected to promote. This has an immediate relevance for the emphasis given to various performance measures of the system and also for other factors influencing system design. The real or hypothetical principal may belong to groups such as public opinion moulders, politicians, governments, public administrators, transport companies of various kinds, and shippers and their customers. The goals of the target principal should be reflected in the priorities that the system designer gives to performance measures such as costs, environmental impact and quality of the transport service.

Research Task and Research Design

It is assumed here that the appearance of a new intermodal transport system in the freight market of interest will not create any new demand for transportation. It is also assumed that the capacity of the existing transport system is sufficient to satisfy existing and expected demand. Our system designer is thus given the task of designing an intermodal transport system capable of entering the market and capturing a share of that market either in terms of existing demand or in terms of expected future demand. The market share aimed at may be a given from the start or it may be a variable to be determined in the design process. In any case, the system designer is confronted with a competitive situation with at least one competitor. These assumptions are important for system design.

The research design proposed here for developing and evaluating a transport system is the normative case study. In general terms, it can be described as follows (based on Jensen 1990, p. 29):

> We have a new transport system, say Sn, that is intended to replace partially or completely an existing transport system, say Se. The existing transport system is presumed to operate in a known reality R, which can be observed in its essential dimensions. Select a subset Rs of R for closer study. Rs can be said to comprise the case in the normative case study. Rs must now be described with regards to its essential variables such as customers, spatial conditions, goods flows, market structure, competition etc., depending on the nature of the problem. It must also be described with regard to the existing system Se. These descriptions form a model of Rs. This model is then used as a tool in the studies. If the research aims at developing a new transport system Sn, Sn is developed on the basis of, among other things, the observed properties of Rs, inclusive of the existing transport system Se. In the model of Rs, Sn now replaces Se. This gives a normative model, by which is meant a model which indicates how reality – the case – should be arranged. If, instead, the research assignment deals with the evaluation of the

new transport system Sn, then Sn is applied in the model of Rs, after which Sn is evaluated given Rs conditions.

In evaluation studies, simulation and/or mathematical methods can be used for manipulating the model of *Rs*. These methods, and especially their combination (see Jensen et al. 2001) are recommended here for predicting the performance of *Sn*.

10.2 DEFINITIONS AND SYSTEM COMPONENTS

Intermodal transport is defined here as the movement of goods in a load unit between a point of origin and a point of destination, where the load unit is tranferred at least once from one mode of transport to another between these two points. Between the points of origin and destination the load unit is neither loaded nor unloaded. Load units will usually be maritime containers, continental containers, swap bodies and semi-trailers of various sizes. A common example of intermodal transport is intermodal road–rail transport using swap bodies where goods are collected from shippers by truck, transferred from truck to train at a load unit terminal, back to truck at the receiving terminal, and from there distributed to receivers.

Central to the definition of intermodal transport is the requirement to use at least two different modes between origin and destination. However, it is up to the user of this conceptual framework to define the concept of 'mode'. As far as applicability is concerned, this framework may also be useful in cases where only transport units from the same mode, but of very different sizes, operate on different links separated by terminals in a transport chain. Line-based trucking could be one example where big trucks are used for the main haul and small trucks for pickup and delivery of load units. Another example could be big container ships cooperating with small feeder container ships.

Following the definition of the concept of intermodal transport given in this chapter, an intermodal transport may be a door-to-door transport from the shipper to the final receiver if the goods stay on the load unit in between. However, it may also be a subset of a door-to-door transport chain. In this case, the point of origin may represent a point where a road haulier finally consolidates the load unit with small shipments after a collection trip, and the point of destination may represent a first breaking point followed by a distribution trip to the remaining receivers.

To some users, the meaning of the term 'intermodality' is any cooperation between different modes in a transport chain, whereas others stipulate the use of load units in intermodality concepts. The latter is the view taken

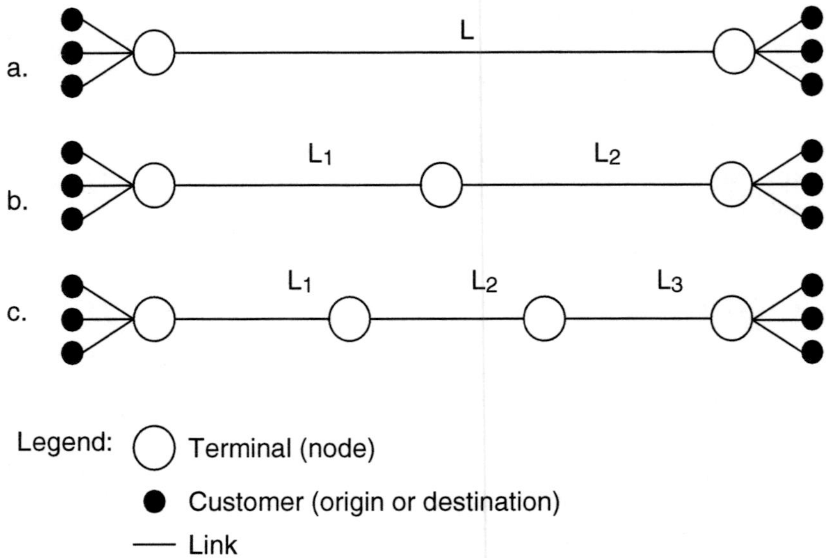

Figure 10.1 Intermodal transport chains

here. According to the definition developed here, intermodal transport is conceptually identical to combined transport. According to the former view, combined transport is a subset of intermodal transport.

Intermodal transport takes place in an infrastructure network of links and nodes. Transport units with motive power (trucks, trains, deep-sea vessels, short-sea vessels, barges and aeroplanes) move the load units along the links between nodes (terminals). If using a direct link between two terminals is inefficient, load units may be transferred between or within modes at intermediate terminals. Figure 10.1 shows that any move of a load unit in the network between origin and destination involves a chain of links and nodes.

All the different origin-to-destination transport chains making it up define an intermodal transport system or network. In these chains, it is useful to distinguish between boundary links having customer contact and line haul links in the interior of the network. In Figure 10.1a, L is a line haul link between two sets of boundary links. In Figure 10.1b there are two line haul links, L_1 and L_2. In Figure 10.1c, finally, there are three line haul links L_1, L_2 and L_3. The corresponding subsystems will be called boundary systems and line haul systems. Normally, transport units operating on line haul links have much higher loading capacity than those operating on boundary links. In extreme cases, a chain may consist of boundary links only, for example when the origin or destination represents a very high transport volume. Then one of the boundary links will function as a line haul link at the same time. In certain strategic analyses another concept, here designated 'extended intermodal transport system', is useful. It consists of all transport chains between shippers and final receivers of shipments in the market that are entirely or partly covered by the new intermodal system being analysed.

The first part of a journey of a load unit in a chain is a subset of a consolidation process in the boundary subsystem where load units are consolidated through a node to transport units with higher loading capacity. Transport units having the maximum loading capacity such as trains or deep-sea vessels operate the line haul link(s) of a chain. This link also, normally, extends over the longest distance, that is, the main haul. Having passed this link, the load unit becomes involved in a distribution process that includes at least one link. The main haul will normally be either by ship or by train. Ship is usually combined with train, barge or truck, or two of these, and train as the main haul is combined with truck. Load units may be transferred between links either at intermodal terminals or at intramodal terminals where load units on vehicle or vessel components without motive power are transferred between links. Depending on the combination of transport units, terminals and load units used, the systems will be rather different in practice.

10.3 SYSTEM DESIGN CONCEPTS FOR COMPETITIVENESS

Objectives of Intermodal System Design

It is assumed that the system designer has two main objectives:

- To design an intermodal transport system that has a significant, sustainable competitive advantage (SSCA).
- To design an intermodal transport system with good market entry ability (MEA).

SSCA refers to a unique combination of properties that allows the system to provide an output with a cost–service ratio that is preferred by customers over the closest competing alternatives. 'Significant' means that the difference is big enough and 'sustainable' that it will last for a sufficient period of time. Analytically, a negative SSCA outcome is defined here to represent a disadvantage. SSCA and MEA are not independent properties. An SSCA may facilitate a quick and easy entry into the market if there are sufficiently low entry barriers such as in competitive markets. However, if entry barriers are moderate or severe, as they may be in oligopolistic markets, an SSCA may not be enough to capture a sufficient market share fast enough for a system before financial difficulties occur. The result could be that a superior system might suffer severe capital losses and perhaps have to leave the market.

Intermodal transport systems are complex, capital-intensive projects. They require large task-specific investments in assets having a long life, assets that may have limited alternative uses. There is a risk that the system owners will incur sunk costs if they have to leave the market. Therefore, it is essential that the system designer understands the relationship between the sustainability of the SSCA of the proposed system on one hand and the risk of sunk cost on the other. This relationship is influenced by elements related to transport policy, competition, system component design and contracting between system actors, to mention a few. The need for sustainability increases with the size and probability of incurring sunk costs. Sustainability must be created by fundamental properties of the intermodal transport system that are difficult to meet or copy by competitors, at least in the medium run. Theoretically, the time horizon should be related to the pay-off time of major investments that may become sunk costs.

Significant, Sustainable Competitive Advantage (SSCA)

Several strategies may make intermodal transport competitive. However, applied to intermodal transport system design, an SSCA strategy seems to involve three general sub-strategies (for general treatments see Alderson 1957; Porter 1980; Faulkner and Bowman 1992) that are more important than others:

- Cost advantage strategy.
- Differentiation strategy.
- Focus strategy.

Possible strategy elements supporting the three strategies are shown in Table 10.1.

Cost advantage can be created in several ways, as seen in Table 10.1. Some are related to the capital assets of the system and others to the ways these are operated. The various factors in the table shall not be perceived as independent. Economies of scale and scope are related to resource utilization of infrastructure and transport units. These economies tend to increase with increasing demand, so high and stable demand is important for realizing cost advantage. Economies of network can be created by

Table 10.1 Possible strategy elements of cost advantage, differentiation and focus strategies in transportation

Cost advantage	Differentiation	Focus
Economies of scale	Transport quality:	Spatial segmentation
Economies of scope	• transit time	Customer segmentation
Economies of network	• frequency	Narrow product line
Standardization	• reliability	Unique specialization
Loading factors	• goods comfort	
Resource utilization	• security	
Choice of technology	• controllability	
R & D	• flexibility	
Automation of handling and traffic	• detachability • expandability	
Experience	Environmental impact:	
Terminal location	• emissions	
Round-trip timing	• other pollution	
Subsidies	• noise	
	• accidents	
	• land use	
	• energy use	
	• congestion	
	Marketing channels	
	• traditional	
	• Internet	

improved utilization of transport units and labour in networks by coordinating activities over different links. Loading factors are related to the resource utilization of load units. In the monetary dimension, all these 'economies' reduce unit costs by increasing output for given levels of common and fixed costs in various parts of the system. Standardization reduces investment needs in transport units, handling equipment and load units in two ways. One is by reducing their prices from suppliers owing to simplifications and scale economies in manufacturing. The other is by reducing their number, since standardization will improve their resource utilization in transportation. Another effect of standardization is lower maintenance costs. Subsidies (including positive non-monetary special provisions) will tend to reduce business economic costs[1]. Their socio-economic cost effect may be either positive or negative depending on the circumstances.

A differentiation strategy in economic and marketing theory describes how sellers can provide value to customers by making their product or service offerings different from those of their competitors. Central to the differentiation concept is how the output is perceived and evaluated by the buyers and by regulatory forces influencing output or its production. The buyers will in most cases be shippers, but may, by way of exception, be regulatory public bodies. In the latter case, the goal for a differentiation strategy must be to satisfy both.

The most obvious service differentiation of intermodal transport is quality differentiation. Most of the nine quality dimensions mentioned in Table 10.1 are well known. The term 'controllability' refers to the transparency of the freight flow to the customers regarding their own shipments. The availability of positioning and communication systems determines the transparency of the flow. Detachability refers to what extent shippers at points of origin and receivers at points of destination can release handling resources and administrative activities from the departure and arrival times of load units. Expandability is the ability to integrate the use of load units into the pre- and post-transport processes for logistics or manufacturing purposes, for example to move mini-containers into factories instead of unloading their content at loading docks.

The table includes environmental impact, that is, negative externalities, as a differentiation concept because it is a property that is regulated in various ways by society. It is also becoming increasingly important to the marketing departments of shippers' companies (Reinhardt 1999; Roy and Vézina 2001). The contemporary trend in transport policy is an ambition to convert environmental impacts to economic decision problems for the actors in the market by internalizing external environmental costs to business economic costs. Environmental impact is a property related to the entire system as such, and the system designer cannot neglect it.

The differentiation, cost advantage and focus strategies will of course always exist in combination. Emphasis may be on either differentiation or cost advantage or both. Since they are interrelated, emphasizing both tends to result in average profiles for both strategies. This result can be difficult to market to customers. The role of the focus strategy in transport is to strengthen the cost advantage–differentiation combination by offering the output to a set of selected spatial and customer segments in the market in order to maximize the SSCA. This has implications for intermodal system design.

As an illustration of the role of the focus strategy, let us assume that existing transport in a region can be improved by introducing a new intermodal transport system. For simplicity, assume that the impact from the intermodal system on the performance of the existing transport system can be neglected. Then it might be relevant to measure how the intermodal system could improve the performance of the goods flows

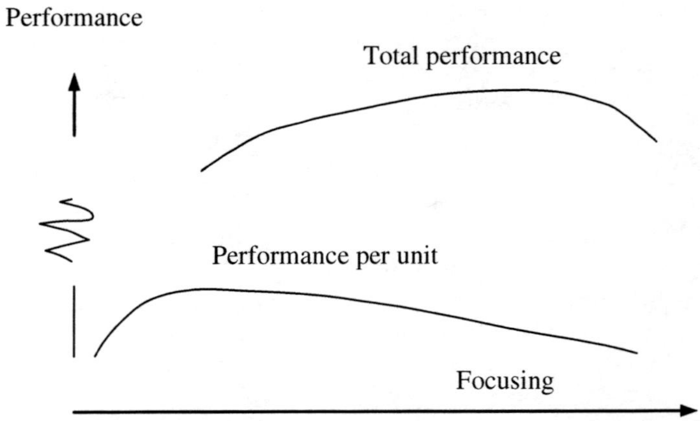

Figure 10.2 *Total performance and performance per unit as a function of level of focusing (increasing focusing here corresponds to increasing size of customer districts around terminals)*

conquered from the existing transport system. The role of focusing can be illustrated by comparing improvement in total performance with improvement per unit of output. Performance per unit of output can be represented by reduction in cost or emissions per unit, for example per tonne of goods or per load unit. Total performance improvement in turn could be represented by the reduction in total cost or emissions. Figure 10.2 illustrates performance as a function of spatial focusing along the horizontal axis in terms of increasing size of collection and distribution areas around end terminals following a well-defined rule for including spatial segments. In this context, the question for the system designer could be whether the objective is to design for an optimal niche market or an optimal mass market.

Market Entry Ability (MEA)

Some of the most important factors determining an intermodal transport system's ability to enter the market are designated integrability and communicability.

The concept of integrability represents the intermodal system's ability to prevent or reduce the difficulties it will meet when trying to enter the market. Such difficulties may be caused by the existing entry barriers or by turf-defending measures that the existing actors may invent in order to protect their market shares during a newcomer's first time in the market. A new transport system is said to be integrable if it is designed to reduce entry barriers and competitors' turf defence by absorbing critical components, if necessary, from the systems it is planned to gain major market shares from. As an example, a railway company may be able to integrate existing road hauliers into a new intermodal system for pickup and delivery activities instead of using its own trucks from a subsidiary company. Generally speaking, by 'critical components' are meant relevant interorganizational relationships and production resources. The most critical relationship may be the existence of strong ties between carriers in the existing transport system and the shippers, but ties between carriers producing the transport service in the existing system may also be critical. Production resources referred to in this context are mainly transport units, terminals and personnel. The need of integrability increases with:

- Increase in strength of ties between shippers and carriers in existing transport systems.
- Increased financial strength and increased ability of existing transport systems to take responsive action.
- Remaining life and lack of alternative uses of the existing transport systems' investments, which is related to increasing risks of sunk costs.

An intermodal transport system is said here to be communicable if it can be given a profile that facilitates potential buyers to compare its value to them with the value of the closest alternative. The image of this profile may be created both in direct communication with the buyers or indirectly by interpersonal or interorganizational processes. Creating this profile is not only a marketing issue; it is also related to intermodal system design. In order for a customer to change transport supplier or solution, the change must lead to significantly improved performance. For many shippers, the cost of transportation is only a small part of the total product cost, and the energy they are prepared to devote to transport decision problems is limited. If a forwarder or logistics service provider is the customer, he will also require a significant improvement in performance with controllable risk in order to accept a new system. Therefore the difference must be distinct and significant. If there are, say, three performance dimensions that are important to customers, then the system will be communicable if performance is better in all three and significantly so in at least one. The system is also communicable if it performs significantly better in one or two and is perceived as equal in the remaining ones. However, if it is superior in one dimension and inferior in another, the profile will lose in communicability. The conclusion is that a system designer must also consider the communicability of the SSCA of the system.

10.4 SYSTEM DESIGN PROCESS

External Conditions for Intermodal System Design

Early in the design process it is necessary to make a thorough external analysis in order to discover strategic factors that must be considered in shaping the new system's SSCA and MEA. The aim of the external analysis is to specify requirements for system design expressed in terms of SSCA and MEA. The most important factors in this context are those related to competitors, customers and the society's transport policy. With regard to competition, it will in most cases be sufficient to analyse the existing system representing the closest and most important competition and to use this as a reference alternative with which to compare the new system. The customer analysis, where shippers' quality needs and quality sensitivity are analysed, is a fundamental demand analysis, since the aim of the system designer is to develop a system that is able to gain market share in a competitive market. It is strategically important to analyse the effect of the new system on the performance of the door-to-door transport chains in which it is planned to operate, also in cases where the boundary of the new system does not include links to shippers and final receivers. If this analysis of the extended intermodal system is neglected (see section 10.2), critical shipper or carrier conditions outside the boundary system may not be discovered, such as required timings of departures and arrivals or track-and-trace capabilities.

Figure 10.3 shows relationships between external determinants and the various strategy elements of the SSCA and MEA of a new system. The strength of the requirements represented by these relationships will depend on the focus strategy assumed. That is, the system designer can adjust the focus strategy to discover various combinations of elements of MEA and SSCA in much the same way as the biologist adjusts his microscope to discover hidden relationships. The end result of the external analysis are sets of specifications of requirements, say *R1*, *R2*, *R3* . . . . Each set, say *Rj* for focus level *j*, contains SSCA requirements and MEA requirements. The SSCA requirements indicate what the intermodal transport system must fulfil in the various dimensions of the SSCA concept. In any dimension, these requirements must be expressed in relation to the performance of the competing reference alternative in terms of 'significantly better performance', 'the same performance' or 'inferior performance'. The specification *Rj* also contains MEA requirements or guidelines related to the communicability and integrability of the system corresponding to *Rj*. One or more specifications of requirements may be chosen as bases for further system development. In this choice, the system designer will also take various absolute constraints into

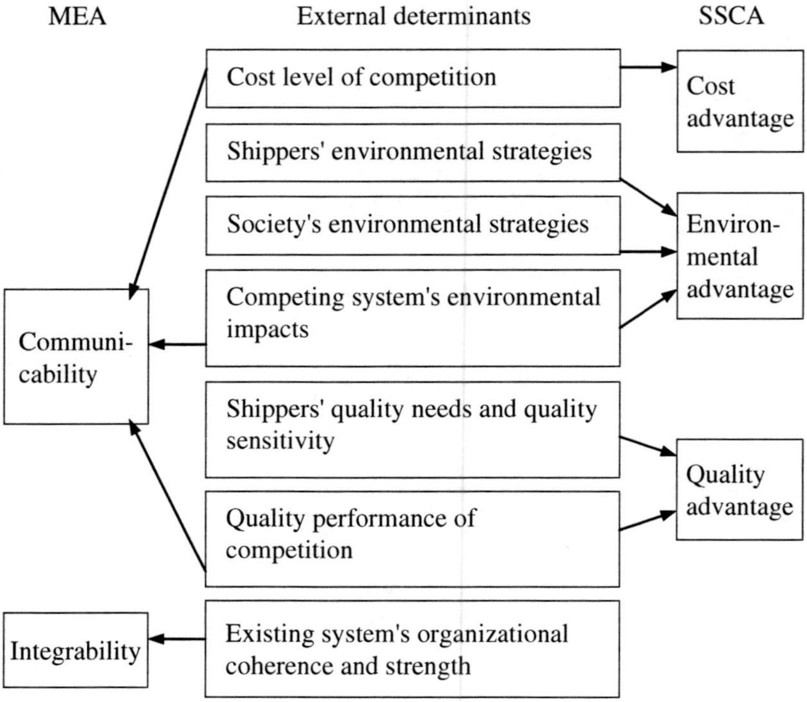

Figure 10.3 Relationships between external determinants and elements of MEA and SSCA of new system

consideration such as available technologies and resources for investment to the extent that these are known at this preliminary stage.

Relationships Between Intermodal System Design and Performance

Using the specification of requirements from the external analysis, the system designer is assumed to manipulate design components under his control to design an intermodal transport system fulfilling the performance objectives. Theory can give some guidance on main relationships between various design components and performance in terms of SSCA and MEA. Figure 10.4 shows some generalized main relationships. These will be commented upon below.

The choice of intermodal technology involves, among other things, a specification of the main types of load units, the main types of transport units, and the main types of terminal handling equipment to be used in the system.

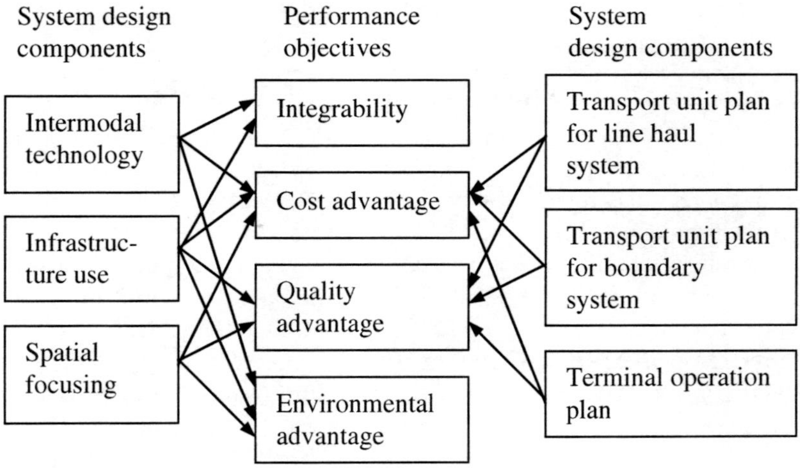

Figure 10.4 Main relationships between system design components and performance objectives

The choice of infrastructure use concerns the utilization in space and time of the infrastructure network. Fixed terminal assets are considered to belong to infrastructure. When links and nodes in the network have been chosen, the task is to investigate whether there are restrictions for the utilization of the network as regards time, load unit weight and profile, type of transport unit and so on.

The transport unit plans for the line haul system specify distance, transit time and capacity for transport units moving between terminals in transport chains. The plans are fundamental to the calculation of costs of transport capital such as ships, locomotives, railway wagons, trucks and handling equipment, and also to the calculation of operational costs such as labour and energy costs. The plans allow calculation of costs of infrastructure use. The transport unit plan for the boundary system has the same role for the system's interface with consignors and consignees. The plans for transport unit and terminal operations together influence transport chain quality.

The spatial focusing determines the areas within which goods are collected and distributed around end terminals of chains. It decides, among other things, the potential demand for the system and thus also the base for economies of scale and scope. The shape of areas and the spatial distribution of demand around terminals are determinants of the system's environmental advantage.

Design and Evaluation Process

The system designer's goal is to develop an intermodal transport system able to enter the market and survive there by attracting sufficient demand. Two conceptual instruments for analysing entry and survival problems suggested here are the SSCA and MEA concepts. SSCA contains the concepts representing potential competitive advantages: cost advantage, quality advantage and environmental advantage. A thorough demand analysis covering shipper and consignee conditions is a necessary first step in developing a new transport system with sufficient SSCA. The determination of an advantage also implies comparison with the most important competing system, here called the reference alternative. Therefore, the final choice of design of the intermodal transport system involves a design and evaluation process where various designs of the new system are compared with the reference alternative along selected performance dimensions in order to estimate whether the new system can attract the demand needed. Jensen (1990, p. 56) suggests an iterative method for this process until a satisfactory solution is reached.

The model in Figure 10.5 provides a normative picture of the organization of the design and evaluation process. It deals with some fundamental strategic issues of intermodal system design.

The first step (A) in the process in Figure 10.5 is the formulation of performance requirements (cost advantage, quality advantage, environmental advantage, integrability and communicability) based on an external analysis. It stipulates what performance dimensions to give priority to, and how to distribute the advantages across dimensions. The most important base for this analysis is the demand from the shippers of the competing transport system (the reference system).

The next step (B) involves selecting a system design from a large set of possible designs determined by the number of feasible combinations in practice of intermodal technologies, infrastructure uses, transport unit plans for line haul and boundary links, and terminal operation plans. Some of the performance requirements will be formulated as restrictions in step A. These restrictions will limit the number of alternatives that have to be studied.

Step D affects the cost advantage, quality advantage and environmental advantage of the system. For example, in the cost dimension, there is a complicated trade-off between lower unit costs due to economies of scale in the line haul system and higher unit costs in the boundary system for creating the goods volumes necessary for utilizing scale economies. Similar arguments can be applied to the environmental dimension. Step D uses a choice function predicting how customers will choose between the new and the reference system based on the performance for individual customers. In these analyses steps D–H may be interacting simultaneously. In step H the

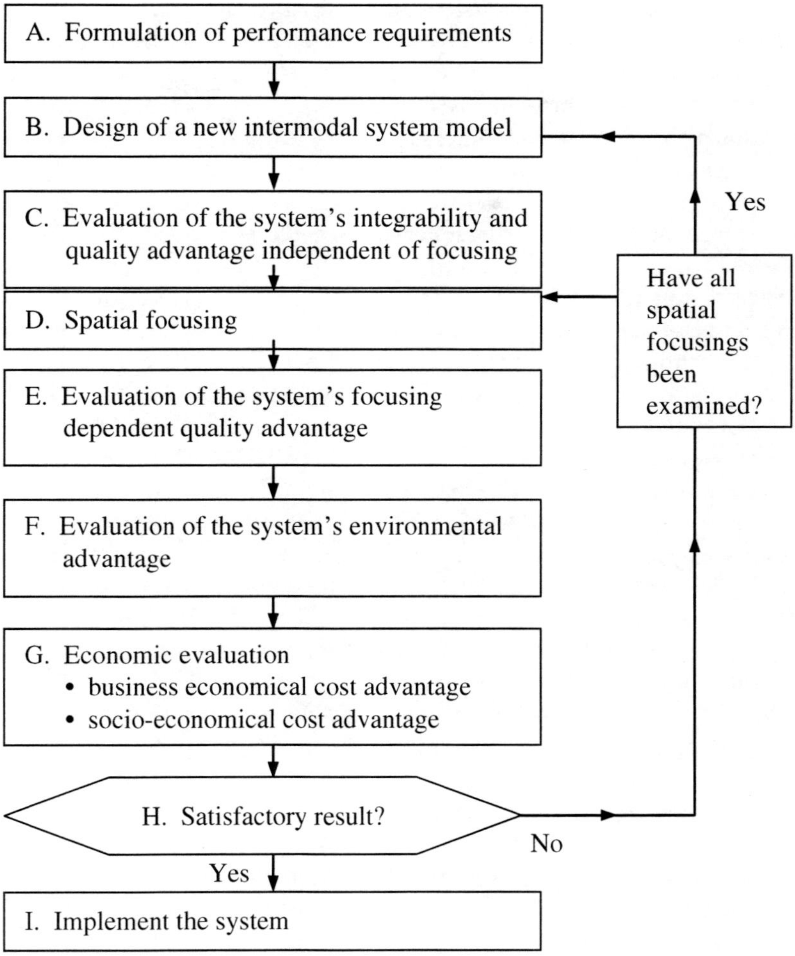

Figure 10.5 Intermodal transport system design and evaluation process

question is whether total gains within the given focusing will allow realization of the new system and fulfil the goals, possibly after some redistribution of gains among customers.

10.5 EVALUATING THE SSCA: SOME ASPECTS

In this early phase of research, a reasonable objective is to evaluate the SSCA of the proposed system assuming a steady state condition. One important problem is to conclude whether freight customers of the reference system having different choice criteria will choose the new intermodal system if given the opportunity. For a given customer, this is assumed to be the case if the new intermodal system will perform better in the performance dimensions than the reference alternative for that customer. The question is: when is it better?

The Problem of Multidimensional Performance Objectives

The evaluation approach developed here involves a door-to-door comparison between the new system *Sn* and the reference alternative *Se* along the most important performance dimensions. Effects outside system boundaries on other systems are assumed to be negligible. Let *P1*, *P2*, *P3*, . . ., represent outcomes for goods flows in performance dimensions 1, 2, 3, . . . and so on, and $\Delta P1$, $\Delta P2$, $\Delta P3$, . . ., differences in outcomes for goods flows between the new system and the reference system. Then the degree of SSCA will be a function of ΔPi, $i = 1, 2, 3, \ldots$. Analytically, the degree of SSCA of the new system will be a variable that has to be defined for individual goods flows between pairs of spatial coordinates, for example in an O/D-matrix containing all flows between origins (O) and destinations (D). Such flows can represent flows between pairs of customers, customer segments or spatial demand segments.

The new system's SSCA for a given goods flow may be more or less interpretable depending on the outcomes of ΔPi. If ΔPi, $i = 1, 2, 3 \ldots$, all represent some advantages and some ties[2] (or some disadvantages and some ties) for the new system, and interpretation is easy. However, if ΔPi represents both advantages and disadvantages, interpretation becomes more problematic. Should the advantages belong to the most important dimensions and the disadvantages to the less important ones, such an allocation could be interpretable.

If this is not the case, a general method suggested by Miller and Starr (1963, p. 162) can be used to create a rank order between the two systems consistent with the preferences of the decision maker (assumed to be associated with the goods flow of concern, for example the shipper). To use this method, it is necessary to rate the relative importance of the different performance dimensions to the decision maker, for example by the constant sum method (see Churchill 1995, p. 482). Let the relative importance be given by the positive numbers *a*, *b*, *c*, . . . and so on, where increasing value represents increasing importance. If the outcomes of the two systems in the *P*-dimensions are given by *Pe1*, *Pe2*, *Pe3*, . . . for *Se*, and *Pn1*, *Pn2*, *Pn3*, . . . for *Sn*, then the products of the powers for both systems $P(Sn) = (Pn1)^a\,(Pn2)^b\,(Pn3)^c \ldots$, and $P(Se) =$

$(Pe1)^a$ $(Pe2)^b$ $(Pe3)^c$ . . . represent composite performance indices. If $P(Sn)/P(Se) < 1$, then the new system *Sn* has the preferred composite performance (assuming that increasing *P*-values represent decreasing preference). This method is invariant to the unit of measurement used in the various dimensions. It assumes that the *P*-dimensions are measured along ratio scales.

Another approach that may solve the evaluation problem is to design the transport system so that the evaluation can be simplified. The method is to identify performance dimensions where the new system appears to be able to perform better than the reference system, and also the dimensions where the reference system is strong. In the latter dimensions, restrictions for system performance are placed on the design of the new system, and the creation of competitive advantage will have to be allocated to the former dimensions.

Such a design strategy could be that the new system must be at least as good as the reference alternative in some dimensions and significantly better in others. The guiding imperative for the system designer could be formulated as 'equal in quality and significantly lower in cost' or 'equal in quality and significantly lower in cost and environmental impact'. Such formulations also tend to maximize communicability to customers and principals.

Comments on the Performance Categories

The business economic cost is the fundamental cost dimension. The calculation implies simply to sum and compare the costs of the actors in *Sn* and *Se* assuming that payment flows between actors in *Sn* can be arranged to assure system cooperation. Strategic information may be extracted by grouping costs into infrastructure costs, flow capacity costs from transport units and handling equipment, and goods flow costs from utilizing the given flow capacity. Costs should also be allocated to links and nodes and to different actors.

From a strategic perspective, it gives additional insight to consider also the socio-economic cost dimension. If *Sn* has a business economic cost advantage, but a disadvantage in terms of socio-economic costs, a strategic risk is that government policy will internalize some of the external costs of transportation. This could turn the business economic cost advantage into a disadvantage. The opposite situation could represent a strategic opportunity, that is, if *Sn* has a business economic cost disadvantage but a socio-economic advantage. This situation may be changed either by internalization of external costs affecting *Se* harder than *Sn* or by giving subsidies to *Sn*.

There are several transport quality dimensions. However, in comparing *Sn* and *Se* some outcomes will be the same, and some dimensions may be of minor importance. This normally leaves transit time, frequency and reliability as candidates for further consideration. Transit time will depend on the spatial focusing and technological design of the system, frequency on the operational design, and reliability on both technological and operational matters. A viable approach is first to build outcomes of all four into the system by technological and operational design, and then to manipulate transit time by focusing.

The degree of environmental advantage for *Sn* depends on the location of the infrastructure network, technological designs, operational designs and spatial focusing on customers compared with those of *Se*. Some environmental advantages are possible to control to a certain extent at a cost by the technological design of transport units (for example air pollution other than carbon dioxide). Others are more dependent on the freight tonne-kilometres and transport unit-kilometres necessary to move the goods from origins to destinations (for example carbon dioxide). The recommendation here is to try to estimate air emissions in physical measures for both systems and to calculate the differences between *Sn* and *Se*. This can be done in the simulation study described earlier in this chapter. The remaining environmental dimensions will probably be evaluated on ad hoc bases both quantitatively and qualitatively. At least, congestion and accidents should be included in the socio-economic cost evaluation because they involve rather crude measurements and are events occurring in interaction between *Sn*, *Se* and surrounding systems.

10.6 CONCLUSION

This chapter develops a conceptual and methodological framework for the design and evaluation of intermodal freight transport systems. It has been written with the conviction that a young area of research such as intermodal freight transport research has to be generalized conceptually and methodologically without loosing its bonds to the specific area of application. It assumes that any transport system will have to compete for customers within the framework given by national and supranational transport policy. Therefore design aspects of competitiveness have been of prime concern in writing this chapter. The conceptual means for this, which also represent a unique feature of this chapter, are the concepts of significant, sustainable competitive advantage (SSCA) and market entry ability (MEA). The applicability of these concepts is not constrained to the development of new transport systems. They have relevance for modifying existing transport systems as well. Another unique feature of this chapter is the suggested integration between transport system design and transport system evaluation. If done properly, costly mistakes or foregone opportunities can be avoided in the design phase of transport system development.

NOTES

1. The term 'business economic cost' is used in this chapter as identical with 'private cost'.
2. A tie is said to exist if two values are equal.

REFERENCES

Alderson, W. (1957), *Marketing Behaviour and Executive Action*, Homewood, IL: Irwin.

Churchill, G.A. (1995), *Marketing Research*, Orlando, FL: Dryden Press.

Faulkner, D. and C. Bowman (1992), 'Generic strategies and congruent organisational structures: some suggestions', *European Management Journal*, **10** (4), pp. 494–9.

Jensen, A. (1990), *Combined Transport: Systems, Economics, and Strategies*, Stockholm: KFB.

Jensen, A., L. Brigelius and J. Flodén (2001), 'Strategic simulation of combined transport in a competitive market: a two-step model', presented at WCTR 2001, Seoul, published in *The 9th WCTR Selected Proceedings*, Oxford: Elsevier.

Miller, D.W. and M.K. Starr (1963), *Executive Decisions and Operations Research*, Englewood Cliffs, NJ: Prentice-Hall.

Porter, M.E. (1980), *Competitive Strategy*, New York: Free Press.

Reinhardt, F. (1999), 'Bringing the environment down to earth', *Harvard Business Review*, July–Aug, pp. 149–57.

Roy, M.-J. and R. Vézina (2001), 'Environmental performance as a basis for competitive strategy: opportunities and threats', *Corporate Environmental Strategy*, **8** (4), pp. 339–47.

11. Intermodal freight network modelling

Florian Schwarz

11.1 INTRODUCTION

Intermodal transport is expected to play a major role in European freight transport. In the past, however, most of the expectations of freight volumes to be handled by intermodal transport have been far too optimistic. For future research on intermodal transport networks two major tasks arise from this experience:

- Development of models that accurately describe intermodal transport networks and their possible influence on the modal split.
- Analysis and optimization of intermodal transport networks in order to achieve a more competitive intermodal transport system.

Both tasks require the modelling of intermodal freight networks. In this chapter, after a short introduction into intermodal transport modelling, some modelling approaches for intermodal freight networks are described, with special attention paid to models that make use of geographic information systems (GIS). Then a new approach for the modelling of intermodal transport networks for seaport hinterland container traffic is presented. The goal of this chapter is the investigation of new trimodal transport networks, combining barge, rail and road transport within the same transport chain. The modelling approach for this chapter is based on using both geographic information about the available transport infrastructure for road, rail and inland navigation, and detailed information about necessary processes within intermodal transport chains.

11.2 INTERMODAL TRANSPORT MODELLING

Intermodal freight transport is defined as 'the movement of goods in one and the same loading unit or road vehicle which uses successively two or more modes of transport without handling of the goods themselves in changing modes' (UN/ECE 2001). For an efficient transshipment between the modes the goods are unitized in loading units, for example containers or swap bodies. The set of processes forming intermodal transport is referred to as a transport chain, defined as 'the sequence of technical and organisational related processes, in which passengers or goods are moved from an origin to a destination' (DIN 1984).

'The advantages of intermodal transport are based on the cooperation of the transport modes road and rail [also barge], combining their system-specific strengths into an independent transport system:

- Efficient and environmentally-friendly transport of large transport volumes over long distances on the main axes of the railway network.
- High flexibility of trucks for the road-based pre-haulage from the shipper to the terminal and the end-haulage from the terminal to the receiver.' (Buchholz et al. 1998)

This definition clearly states one major prerequisite for efficient and competitive intermodal transport: the existence of large freight volumes and/or long transport distances. For transport relations that do not fulfil at least one of these requirements, only intermodal transport networks with bundling of freight volume, at least for some parts of the transport chain, can provide competitive transport offers. For the bundling of freight in intermodal transport networks some basic structures are possible,[1] that have been identified within the TERMINET project (Kreutzberger 2002; Trip and Kreutzberger 2002). These basic bundling principles have to be incorporated in some way into intermodal freight transport models.

In general, transport planning models for both passenger and freight transport have a relatively common structure (European Commission 1996), based on the phases:

1. Production and attraction: estimation of freight volume for each zone.
2. Distribution: origin–destination matrix of transport flows.
3. Mode choice: decision by which mode and means transport takes place.
4. Traffic conversion: conversion of transport volume from tons to vehicle trips; especially important for freight transport modelling.
5. Assignment: networks are loaded with the trip matrices.
6. Calibration and validation: comparison with observed traffic to validate the model results.

The actual approach for the modelling of intermodal transport networks, however, depends on the actual objective of the investigation. First of all, the planning horizon of the model determines possible approaches.

At least three levels of transport planning can be distinguished (Crainic 2000):

- Strategic planning (long term).
- Tactical planning (medium term).
- Operational planning (short term).

Within the tactical planning level Crainic (2000) distinguishes further between 'frequency and dynamic service network design models. The former typically addresses strategic/tactical planning issues . . . Typical issues addressed by such models concern questions such as: What type of service to offer? How often over the planning horizon to offer it? What traffic itineraries to operate? What are the appropriate terminal workloads and policies?' These issues are addressed by the new modelling approach discussed later on, which is to be classified as a strategic/tactical planning model.

Macharis and Bontekoning (2002), who performed an extensive literature survey to provide an overview of the use of operations research (OR) techniques in intermodal freight research, classify these studies additionally by the type of operator and their tasks, distinguishing:

- Drayage operators: planning and scheduling of trucks for pre- and end-haulage.
- Terminal operators: transshipment operation between the modes.
- Network operators: infrastructure planning and organization of rail or barge transport.
- Intermodal operators: users of intermodal infrastructure and services, route selection for a shipment through the whole intermodal network.

This classification, however, does not provide a complete picture of the type of actors possibly involved in intermodal transport. In the group of intermodal operators, a further distinction seems necessary, as the tasks described for intermodal operators can be performed by different actors:

- 'Real' intermodal operators like the German Kombiverkehr or the Swiss Hupac, that organize intermodal networks but usually buy the actual transport services from railway undertakings.
- Logistics service providers or forwarding agents, that determine the type of transport mode to be used and in some cases operate their own intermodal network.[2]

- Shipping companies, that for container traffic to or from the seaports often determine the transport mode to be used[3] and in some cases operate their own intermodal network.[4]

A group of actors that were not in the interest of the study by Macharis and Bontekoning, but nevertheless have a major influence on intermodal transport networks, are policy makers. From a regional level, for example concerning decisions about terminal locations, to a European level, for example regarding major infrastructure projects as well as taxation issues and charges for infrastructure use, the decisions taken by policy makers set the conditions for the planning and operation of intermodal networks. Hence, a multitude of freight transport models have been developed to describe intermodal networks and estimate the consequences of policy decisions on the modal split. An overview of available strategic transport models is presented in the APAS[5] study on transport strategic modelling (European Commission 1996), that identified 43 models for freight transport. A more recent overview of freight modelling is presented in a study by Marcial Echenique & Partners Ltd (ME&P) and others (Study team ME&P and others 2002), commissioned by the UK Department of Transport. This study identifies 78 freight models at the international, national, regional and urban levels. One of the models mentioned as state-of-the-art is the STREAMS model, developed on behalf of the European Commission for a European-wide transport flow forecast for 2020 (STREAMS 2000). The STREAMS structure includes both passenger and freight traffic, and incorporates all modes (road, rail, inland waterways, shipping, air, pipelines). The network presentation is link-based, where links represent either physical connections or transfer links between the modes.

However, from a logistics point of view, these policy-oriented models are often not detailed enough regarding the actual costs, capacities and frequencies of transport services. The STREAMS model for example distinguishes only two cost functions for freight transport by rail: bulk rail and unitized rail. However, both the bundling principles in networks and the actual transport means used within each mode highly influence the resulting transport costs and times. For actors directly involved in intermodal network planning at a strategic/tactical level more detailed models are therefore necessary.

The study by Macharis and Bontekoning identified a number of models using OR techniques for the different actors involved in intermodal transport. Still, one conclusion of the study is that 'the number of studies that integrate decisions of more than one operator and/or more time horizons are very limited'. Thus 'multi-actor, multi-stakeholder decisions support tools will have to be developed in order to capture the intermodal practise better' (Macharis and Bontekoning 2002).

For the scope of the modelling approach described hereafter studies on strategic and tactical planning for network operators and intermodal operators are of relevance. First of all it has to be noted, that within this group no model for intermodal operators was found by Macharis and Bontekoning. The models for tactical planning presented by Newman and Yano (2000) and Nozick and Morlok (1997) provide solutions for resource allocation for a planning horizon from one week to one month. These modelling approaches are not applicable for the strategic/tactical planning of new trimodal transport offers, where for example the traffic itineraries to operate have to be decided.

Janic et al. (1999) present a set of 20 evaluation criteria for intermodal network performance, that may also be used for strategic/tactical planning. These criteria were used for the assessment of innovative bundling networks, using the simple additive weighting (SAW) multicriteria analysis. Costs of different network concepts, however, were not included in the analysis.

Models for Strategic Planning for Network Operators

In this subsection, strategic models for network operators are presented that on the one hand use GIS technology and on the other hand allow for different transport means within one mode.

One of the first software tools that enabled the graphical analysis of multimodal transport networks was STAN ('Strategic Planning of Freight Transportation: STAN, an Interactive Graphic System') (Crainic and Florian 1990), which consists of several modules. The network editor of STAN is used to describe the underlying multimodal network, consisting of nodes and links. The flows are described specifying modes and products. A mode is defined as 'a means of transportation that has its own characteristics, such as vehicle type and capacity, as well as a specific cost function'. Parallel links between nodes are allowed, given that one link can be used by one mode only. In the study presented in Crainic and Florian (1990), ten modes were defined, five for rail, one for road, one for ports and three for navigation (inland, coastal and ocean). Unit cost functions associated with links and transfers are managed with the help of the function editor. The most general assignment procedure provided by STAN is a multimode, multiproduct assignment method, which minimizes the total cost of shipping the products considered, from origins to destinations, via the permitted modes.

A further development of this concept of 'virtual links' is incorporated in NODUS, a GIS-based software tool developed at the Facultés Universitaires Catholiques de Mons, Transport and Mobility Group

(Jourquin et al. 1999; Jourquin and Beuthe 2001). An important contribution was the development of a structured notation and automatic generation of the virtual links, making it possible to deal rather easily with very large networks. For this purpose, other than in STAN, a strict separation is maintained between transport modes (for example rail, inland navigation) and transport means (for example a train set, consisting of a specific locomotive and a number of specific wagons, or a type of barge). Also processes, which normally do not appear in a geographic representation, for example loading and unloading, are represented in NODUS. One of four different cost functions for moving, transit, transshipment, and loading and unloading is automatically associated with each virtual link. Minimizing the total generalized costs is possible by applying a shortest-path algorithm. It is supposed that all the costs are proportional to the total quantity transported. Further, 'the assumption of total costs as linear functions of distance is a prerequisite for this type of network modelling. Nevertheless, the formulation of its coefficients can be as complex as desired in terms of its parameters: time of operations, crew wages, cost of fuel, capital cost, speed, insurance, rate of time opportunity cost, relative values of a means' quality attribute etc.' (Jourquin et al. 1999).

A different approach was taken by Standifer and Walton (2000), who developed a complete GIS network focused on the state of Texas, USA, and used it to examine impacts of price, time, location and policy on shipper routing. Two methods were used to assign costs to routes. First, costs were placed in the link attribute database, which is the case for rail, truck and barge movements and for two-mode intermodal facilities. The second method was to use a turntable to assign costs at a given node. The drawback of this assignment methodology in comparison with the 'virtual link' concept is the linkage of costs to the attribute data, which does not allow one to analyse different operating scenarios for a given link, for example the use of larger or smaller barges.

Southworth and Peterson (2000) developed a single, integrated digital representation of a multimodal and transcontinental freight transportation network in order to simulate some 5 million origin-to-destination freight shipments. This research, however, was somewhat different, as the modes used for each transport were known beforehand based on the 1997 Commodity Flow Survey of the United States. The model was developed to simulate the mileages with each transport mode based on the mode sequences reported (Standifer and Walton 2000). To this purpose, the routable single-mode networks were linked through a series of intermodal truck–rail, truck–water and water–rail terminals, with appropriate costs assignable to line haul, terminal access and egress, and within-terminal links for shipment routing purposes.

The virtual links concept as incorporated in NODUS seems to be a promising approach for the modelling of trimodal transport chains. The assumption of costs being proportional to the freight volume, however, is not necessarily valid within a more detailed analysis of transport chains. The introduction of a new transport service or a higher frequency leads to higher fixed costs, whereas the transport volume may not rise in the same way, leading to a lower load factor and thus higher transport costs. The list of cost coefficients presented by Jourquin shows that the definition of adequate cost functions in itself forms an interesting research field. To determine these costs, information about the available infrastructure and its attributes, for example the types of barges that can be used, should be available. However, a more detailed analysis of transport costs and times for different trimodal transport networks, as is the objective of the research project described in the following section, will limit the geographical scope of the model to a regional level. This approach follows the three-stage modelling approach proposed by van Duin and van Ham (1998), which consists of using different models according to the geographical scope of the model. They propose an OR model for the European and national level, a spreadsheet model for the national and regional level and a simulation model for the regional and operational level.

11.3 MODELLING OF SEAPORT HINTERLAND TRAFFIC

The research project 'Modelling of Seaport Hinterland Traffic' has been introduced as a new project within the collaborative research centre, Modelling of Large Networks in Logistics, financed by the Deutsche Forschungsgemeinschaft (DFG).[6] The modelling framework for description, design, visualization and analysis of logistic processes within the collaborative research centre is the process chain paradigm according to Kuhn (1999). The goal of the research project on seaport hinterland traffic is the investigation of the competitiveness of trimodal transport networks. Due to the high proportion of containerized goods and the advantages of containers as standardized load units, the project concentrates on container traffic, and more specifically on full container loads (FCL).

Despite the events of 11 September, for the world container traffic an ongoing yearly increase of 7 per cent is still expected, or in other words a doubling of the container flows every ten years (Lemper 2001). Therefore an increasing networking between the individual ports and their hinterland is mandatory to fulfil the high requirements placed on logistics processes in the future. Approximately 65 per cent to 80 per cent of the total costs for the transport of containerized goods via seaports result from landside activities, only about one-third from the sea transport itself (Breitzmann 1993). A high level of interest in improving the seaport hinterland traffic exists among port authorities, shipping companies and freight forwarders. Even so, the average time for a container to spend in the seaport terminal is about 3–4 days (UNICONSULT and ISL 1998), offering some possibilities for bundling freight volumes.

Concerning the spatial expansion of the hinterland of a seaport a clear definition of its scope is not normally given, since the size and position of the trading area are influenced strongly by infrastructural conditions and the appropriate transport services of a port. The trading area or hinterland of a port is generally counted as that space which receives the import goods introduced via the seaport or which supplies the goods intended for export. The range of the hinterland ends where the import and export processes can be operated at lower cost by another port (Woitschützke 2000).

11.4 TRANSPORT ALTERNATIVES FOR SEAPORT HINTERLAND TRAFFIC

The need to model seaport hinterland traffic is based on the wide variety of intermodal transport alternatives, as presented in Figure 11.1. Reasons for this situation are the bundling of large freight volumes in the seaport and the direct transshipment in the seaport terminal to rail or barge, reducing the intermodal chain by one drayage leg. Hence, compared with intermodal transport within Europe, a major cost reduction is achieved, as the pre- and

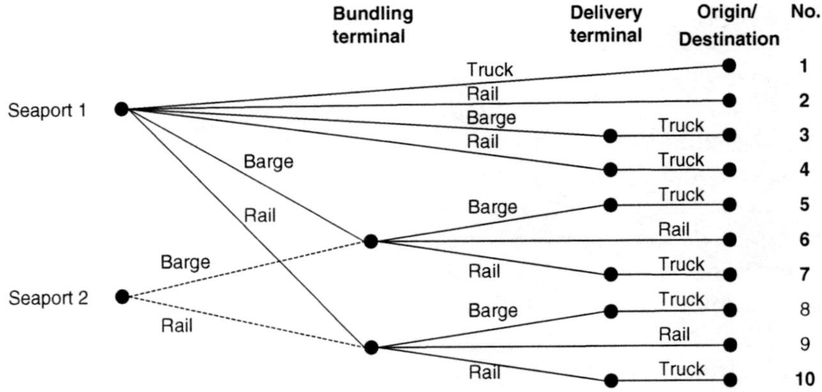

Figure 11.1 Transport chain alternatives for seaport hinterland traffic

end-haulage accounts for up to 47 per cent of the overall transport costs for intermodal transport chains, according to calculations of the Fraunhofer IML (Fränkle and Schwarz 2000). Therefore intermodal seaport hinterland transport can be competitive to road transport over shorter distances than other European intermodal transport.

Direct truck or rail transport and intermodal transport chains including one mode (alternatives 1 to 4 in Figure 11.1) are widely in use and therefore not explained in more detail. Remarkable, however, is the successful developments of container transport by barge, which rose from 452 000 TEU (twenty-foot equivalent unit) in 1991 to 917 000 TEU in 1997 for all German inland ports, whereby about 80 per cent of the volume comes from the ARA ports Antwerp, Rotterdam and Amsterdam (Planco GmbH 1998).

Barge transport in the form of hub-and-spoke networks with intermediate transshipment, alternative 5, has also been able to prove its competitiveness with road or rail transport, especially for smaller rivers flowing into the Rhine. Specially designed barges of the JOWI type (the name of the first ship of that kind) with cell guides for the storing of containers, the same system as usually in place in container ships for deep-sea container transport, and a capacity of up to 400 TEU are employed for the main transport relations, for example from Rotterdam to Mannheim and vice versa, while feeder barges are used to link smaller rivers, like the Mosel or the Main. For alternative 6, combined barge–rail transport, only a few examples are known. A train connection is operated for a chemical plant from Hamm to Duisburg, where containers are transshipped for barge transport to Rotterdam. Similar connections exists between Ludwigshafen and the port of Germersheim.

Alternative 7, combined barge–rail transport with trucking, might look like a quite theoretical alternative, first of all because rail and barge normally are seen as competitors in similar market segments of goods transport, and secondly because of the additional transshipment compared to direct train transport. However, transport chains of this type are already offered in the market, for example barge transport from Rotterdam to Mannheim and ongoing rail transport to Munich.

In fact, this type of transport chain is given a high potential for increasing the mode-share of rail and inland navigation in the hinterland container traffic (Schuh 2001). A major hub in the hinterland, for example Duisburg or Mannheim, could bundle freight coming by barge from several seaports, in order to be able to offer more and/or more attractive rail connections from this inland hub to the more distant hinterland.

The same principle could be applied for alternative 10, where the transport from the hinterland hub to the seaport(s) is done by rail instead of barge. Transshipment or shunting at the bundling node could be avoided when smaller trains are only divided or coupled, as is the case with the German NECOSS train system between Bremerhaven and Kornwestheim/ Germersheim. This train coupling and sharing (TCS) concept was also the basis for the design of the German Cargo Sprinter, a self-driving rail transport unit for 10 TEUs. In the NECOSS case, however, the system is performed with traditional trains. The TCS-concept would also be one possibility to realize transport chains like alternative 9, where smaller trains, coming directly, for example, from the production site of a shipper or going to a large distribution centre, would be bundled at a terminal in order to build one large train for the long-distance transport to or from the seaport.

Alternative 8 is probably the least likely for the time being. It could become interesting, however, in connection with increasing transport volumes to Central and Eastern European countries. To avoid too-long transport times and infrastructure restrictions, for example on the Rhine–Main–Danube channel or the Danube itself, rail transport from the seaports of the Hamburg–Le Havre range to an inland navigation terminal at the Danube, for example in Austria, and ongoing transport by barge on the Danube could be feasible.

This examination of the transport alternatives for container hinterland traffic shows that:

- a wide variety of transport alternatives exists, which makes an efficient planning tool necessary in order to determine the best transport alternative for given origin–destination flows; and
- the optimal transport alternative depends largely on the existing infrastructure, especially for rail and barge transport.

The latter is actually not surprising, as the layout or topology is one of the determining factors for every logistics system. For transport networks, however, the topology is largely predetermined by the available infrastructure, like roads, railway tracks, inland waterways and terminals for the linking of the transport modes. Hence, while the influence of the topology on the transport network is quite high, the possibilities to change or adapt the topology are very limited from an operator's point of view.

However, the use of GIS to provide the necessary information for the strategic/tactical planning of intermodal transport services is still a quite new approach. Detailed, structured information about infrastructure constraints (for example costs for infrastructure use, possible speeds, necessary traction power, diesel or electric traction) would enable a faster and more reliable planning of new transport services. At the moment, this information is usually available only within the actual transport operators. But these are not necessarily involved in the strategic/tactical planning for new intermodal networks, which could be performed for example by ports to attract new transport volume or by shipping companies to provide better and/or less expensive services.

Furthermore, the processes associated with container transport have to be considered in order to discover potentials for an optimized operation of the networks. Based on project experience at the Department for Transportation Logistics, huge optimization potentials still exist within intermodal transport chains. This could be proven in a project for the reduction of transport time between Munich and Verona from 12 to six hours. In particular, the utilization of rolling stock could be optimized by better round-trip planning and minimizing idle times of the resources, for example waiting at terminals.

Hence, the methodological approach for this chapter is to combine infrastructure information and process information for the modelling of intermodal transport networks. This approach should allow analysts to consider different options for combining transport modes in seaport hinterland traffic. At the same time, the influences and interdependencies of different performance indicators, like transport costs, times, capacity and frequency and so on, can be studied. For this purpose, databases are developed with the key performance indicators of the different parts of the transport network, like terminals, rail and barge transport, and pre- and end-haulage.

11.5 INFRASTRUCTURE IMPLICATIONS FOR THE TRANSPORT MODES

Introduction

In this section the implications of the available infrastructure on the different transport modes and the choice of the transport vehicle are described. This is done separately for the three transport modes road, rail and inland navigation, as well as for the terminals. In the final section of this chapter a few remarks are made about the availability of this infrastructure information.

Road Infrastructure

In principle, road infrastructure has the least influence on the actual transport operation. Vehicle limits regarding length, width and load capacity are standardized throughout Europe, with very few exceptions, for example in Sweden longer vehicles are allowed than in the rest of Europe. Even so, the availability of digitized road map information has had a huge influence on better transport planning and disposition, as it allows for optimized routing and an easy estimation of transport times. The road map information available normally contains the road network divided into nodes and links. The node data contain the geographical location and the characteristics of this node, for example if it is a junction (exit) or an intersection, the city and/or postal code area. The link data contain the nodes that are linked, the road length, the type of road and the road name. For each type of road an average speed for different types of vehicles can be defined (for example 60 km/h for a truck on a highway). As the same vehicle can be used throughout Europe, a calculation of transport times and costs for container transport, based on the distance, is easily possible. Only the weight and type of container must be known, as heavy 20 ft containers limit the capacity of a truck to 1 TEU, while its normal capacity is 2 TEU. Additionally, for longer distances limitations due to labour regulations have to be considered.

Rail Infrastructure

Due to the poor interoperability of European railways, detailed information about the railway infrastructure is necessary for the planning of railway operations, as shown in Figure 11.2, which is still far from being a complete list.

The technical information listed on the left side of the figure is necessary to determine the appropriate type of transport means, consisting of locomotive and wagons. Speed and distances are necessary to calculate transport times and costs. A huge influence on the transport costs is the track access

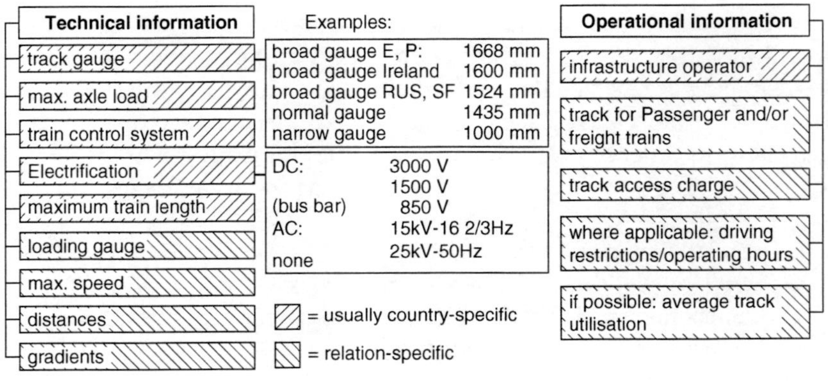

Figure 11.2 Necessary information about rail infrastructure

charges, which often depend on the type of rail track used, for example whether it is a main line or a branch line. Considering the development to separate passenger traffic from goods traffic on the European rail network to utilize its capacity better, it is also necessary to know whether a track is reserved for goods and/or passenger traffic. Infrastructure operator, driving restrictions or average track utilization are also important for the actual implementation of a rail service.

Inland Waterways

Within inland navigation, the influence of the available infrastructure on the capacity of the transport means is even greater than for rail transport. While on the Rhine large vessels with a width of up to 15 m and a length up to 135 m are allowed, on most channels only a length of 85 m and a width of 9.50 m is possible. Also, the available draught decides a ship's capacity. Most European waterways are classified according to a standardized classification system, which describes the maximum dimensions of ships that are allowed on the waterway. For container transport, however, the height of bridges, which is not included in the classification system, is also important. In fact, in Germany the limited heights of bridges in the canal regions, which allow only for two-stack container transport, are the major obstacle for an increase of container transport services by inland navigation. Even so, some early successes of barge transport in this canal region have been reported (Zimmermann and Matheja 2000).

Depending on the type of inland waterway and the direction of transport, huge speed differences exist. While most canals are subject to a speed limit, on many rivers the speed is determined only by the power of the engine and the direction of the ship. In some situations the operating hours of the locks may also have an influence on the transport time, as they are usually not operated 24 hours a day, and thus waiting times may arise. The fees for locks are included in the fees for canal or river use. Apart from the Rhine, Elbe and Danube, fees have to be paid for all rivers and canals in Germany. In order to examine the possibilities for container transport on a given waterway, specific information is needed, as shown below:

Point-related data:

- Location of ports and container terminals
- Connections between rivers/canals
- Location and height of bridges
- Location and dimensions of locks
- Time schedule of locks

Table 11.1 Infrastructure information for terminals

Technical information	Operational information
Location of container terminals	Capacity of transshipment devices
Type of terminal (barge, rail, both)	Operating times of the terminal
Number of berths	Additional services available:
Maximum width of ships	Container repair and cleaning
Storage area	Container stuffing and stripping
Distance rail-barge transshipment	Container depot
Number and length of rail tracks	Customs

Link-related data:

- Name and classification
- Distances
- Speed limits for each direction
- Average draught available
- Access fee

Terminals

Terminals as connecting nodes between the transport modes have a major influence on the possible network configurations. Especially for the connection of barge and rail transport, some specific information about the terminal is necessary, for example the length of the tracks inside the terminal, or whether a direct transshipment from barge to rail is possible. Table 11.1 presents a preliminary list of necessary terminal information.

11.6 AVAILABILITY OF INFORMATION

As explained before, digitized road map information is already present at the Fraunhofer-Institute for Material Flow and Logistics. For inland waterways detailed information is available from the national authorities, for example the German authority for rivers and canals. This information has been structured in order to create a database containing all relevant information on inland waterways, as specified in the section before. Because of the limited complexity of the inland waterways network, this task could be performed with a reasonable manual effort.

Regarding intermodal terminal information, for the German ports an extensive study was performed in the year 2000, funded by the German Ministry for Transport (Planco GmbH 2000). This information is available via the Internet and is being used for the construction of a database on terminal infrastructure. For other countries information exists for example from the UIRR (International Union of Combined Road–Rail Transport Companies), which has a database of more than 150 terminals in Europe.

It is more difficult to gather information about the international rail network. Information in digital format is available only from the national rail infrastructure operators, that do not have a common data formatting standard. A more practicable approach is taken by the North-South-Freight-Freeways, a network of ten European railway infrastructure operators dedicated to the promotion of international rail freight business (see http://www.freightfreeways.com/). This organization provides information on European rail tracks, with available time slots and quite detailed information about the infrastructure restrictions (timetable, infrastructure charge, axle load, loading profile, brake type and effort, maximum train length, maximum train load and required traction, energy supply).

With the sources named above, it is possible to build databases with the necessary infrastructure information for the modelling of trimodal transport networks in seaport hinterland traffic.

NOTES

1. The basic network structures identified within TERMINET are: begin-and-end network, line network, hub-and-spoke network, trunk-collection-and-distribution network, trunk-feeder network.
2. The Logistic service provider Danzas, for example, operates a special, high-quality intermodal service called Parcel Intercity between Hamburg and Munich; the rail transport itself for this service is operated by DB Cargo AG.
3. Usually a distinction is made between carrier's haulage, in the case that the shipping company organizes the transport to or from the seaport, and merchant's haulage, in the case that other actors organize the transport.
4. Shipping companies P&O Nedlloyd and Maersk Sealand have founded the railway undertaking European Rail Services (ERS) to provide rail transport from the seaports to the hinterland.
5. The APAS (*actions de préparation, d'accompagnement et du suivi*) studies were carried out in 1994–95 in order to prepare for the future Transport RTD programme of the European Commission.
6. The objective of the collaborative research centre is the development of a theory for the design, organisation and management of large networks in logistics. The Chairs of Transport and Warehousing Technology, Industrial Management, Factory Organization, Mathematical Statistics and Industrial Applications, Theoretical Informatics, Applied Computer Science, Systems Analysis and the Department of Logistics at the University of Dortmund in cooperation with the Fraunhofer Institute for Material Flow and Logistics work together to contribute to new initiatives in the field of logistics.

REFERENCES

Breitzmann, K.-H. (ed.) (1993), 'Containerlinienschifffahrt: Strukturen und Perspektiven des seewärtigen Containerverkehrs aus technisch-technologischer, organisatorisch-informationeller, wirtschaftlicher und kommerziell-rechtlicher Sicht', Rostock: University, p. 76.

Buchholz, J., U. Clausen and A. Vastag (1998), *Handbuch der Verkehrslogistik*, Berlin: Springer Verlag.

Crainic, T.G. (2000), 'Service network design in freight transportation', *European Journal of Operational Research*, **122**, pp. 272–88.

Crainic, T.G. and M. Florian (1990), 'Strategic planning of freight transportation: STAN, an interactive-graphic system', *Transportation Research Record*, **1283**, pp. 97–124.

Deutsches Institut für Normung (DIN) (ed.) (1984), *DIN 30781 – Transportkette*, Teil 1, Berlin, Köln: Beuth Verlag.

European Commission, Directorate-General Transport (1996), *Transport Research – APAS – Transport Strategic Modelling*, Luxembourg: Office for the Official Publications of the European Communities.

Fränkle, A. and F. Schwarz (2000), 'Eiserner Rhein – die Entwicklung eines neuartigen Schienenverkehrsangebotes', *Distribution*, **10**, pp. 63–5.

Janic, M., A. Reggiani and P. Nijkamp (1999), 'Sustainability of the European freight transport system: evaluation of innovative bundling networks', *Transportation Planning and Technology*, **23**, pp. 129–56.

Jourquin, B. and M. Beuthe (2001), 'Multimodal freight network analyses with NODUS, a survey of several applications', *Transportation Planning and Technology*, **4** (3) pp. 1–30.

Jourquin, B., M. Beuthe and C.L. Demilie (1999), 'Freight bundling network models: methodology and application', *Transportation Planning and Technology*, **23**, pp. 157–77.

Kreutzberger, E. (2002), 'Strategies to achieve a quality leap in intermodal rail or barge transport', paper at the FTAM conference, Delft, 23–24 May.

Kuhn, A. (ed.) (1999), *Prozesskettenmanagement – Erfolgsbeispiele aus der Praxis*, Dortmund: Praxiswissen Verlag.

Lemper, B. (2001), 'Die Wachstumsprognose muss nicht korrigiert werden', *Deutsche Verkehrs Zeitung (DVZ)*, **147**, pp. 9–10.

Macharis, C., and Y.M. Bontekoning (2002), 'Intermodal transport modelling research: a review', E-trans logistics conference, 28/29 November, Liège.

Newman, A.M. and C.A. Yano (2000), 'Scheduling direct and indirect trains and containers in an intermodal setting', *Transportation Science*, **34** (3), pp. 256–70.

Nozick, L. and E. Morlok (1997), 'A model for medium-term operations planning in an intermodal rail-truck service', *Transportation Research A*, **31** (2), pp. 91–107.

Planco GmbH (1998), 'Prognose des kombinierten Ladungsverkehrs der Binnenschifffahrt bis 2010', commissioned by the German Transport Ministry, http://www.planco.de/downloads/SCHLUSSBERICHT.pdf.

Planco GmbH (2000), *Terminalkonzept für den kombinierten Güterverkehr der Binnenschifffahrt*, Final Report, commissioned by the German Ministry for Traffic, Number 30.308/1999.

Schuh, G. (2001), 'Trimodalität schafft Wachstum', *Internationales Verkehrswesen*, **53**, p. 489.

Southworth, F. and B.E. Peterson (2000), 'Intermodal and international freight network modeling', *Transportation Research Part C*, **8**, pp. 147–66.
Standifer, G. and C.M. Walton (2000), *Development of a GIS Model for Intermodal Freight*, Research Report SWUTC/00/167509-1, June National Technical Information Service, (NTIS) Springfield, VA.
STREAMS (2000), 'Strategic transport research for member states. Final report for publication', funded by the European Commission under the Transport RTD programme of the 4th framework programme.
Study team ME&P and others (2002), 'Review of freight modelling, Report B2 – Review of models in Continental Europe and elsewhere', ME&P, June, http://www.roads.dft.gov.uk/roadnetwork/heta/resresult/freightmodel/pdf/b2.pdf.
Trip, J.J. and E. Kreutzberger (2002), *Complex Bundling Networks and New Generation Terminals: A Synthesis*, Delft: TRAIL Research School, Delft University Press.
UN/ECE (2001), 'Terminology on combined transport', prepared by UN/ECE, ECMT and EC, http://www.unece.org/trans/new_tir/wp 24/documents/term.pdf, accessed 19 June 2003.
UNICONSULT and ISL (1998), 'Attraktivitätssteigerung der deutschen Seehäfen durch Verbesserung der Hinterlandanbindung', Final Report, commissioned by the German Ministry for Traffic, Number 96515/97.
van Duin, R. and H. van Ham (1998), 'A three-stage modelling approach for the design and organization of intermodal transportation services', in *IEEE Systems Management and Cybernetics*, San Diego, CA, pp. 4051–6.
Woitschützke, C.P. (2000), Verkehrsgeographie, Köln: Verlag Stam, 2nd edn.
Zimmermann, C. and A. Matheja (2000), 'Erster Containerdienst auf nordwestdeutschen Kanälen mit Erfolg', *Binnenschifffahrt*, **55** (9), pp. 56–62.

PART III

Implementation and policy

12. Critical success factors: interconnectivity and interoperability

Bryan Stone

12.1 INTRODUCTION

Barriers to Intermodal

Intermodal transportation challenges each of the conventional transport modes to consider how it does what it does. Suddenly, every mode has to compete for its place in an intermodal service. Some rise to the challenge; others fail. Some embrace intermodal opportunities, and change their operations fundamentally. Others have regarded intermodal as disruptive, making little change, and that only reluctantly. Barriers emerge and remain.

This chapter looks at particular barriers to efficient intermodal. These are interconnectivity between the modes, and interoperability within the modes. In Europe, these barriers are frequent, reflecting national and local thinking. They are no longer tolerable. They lower efficiency and limit choice. They demand attention. They are often critical. Some improvement has come from within the modes themselves; we will see examples. In other cases, notably with European rail, this has failed. Since rail is fundamentally important to on-land intermodal, and features in policy, we will look in more detail at why this is so, and what, especially in the EU, is being done about it. We will learn that if the cost of failure is high, so is the cost of restoration; this has serious ongoing consequences for inland intermodal.

How we Choose

Creating an intermodal freight service has to be better, for a given demand, and in ways to be defined, than using a single mode. That is obvious; but let us think it through. A homely example demonstrates how choices are made, and suggests that barriers interfere with choice and efficiency.

I go to work every weekday. I walk to the nearby station, and take the train. If it rains I take a bus to the station. Naturally if I walk to work, past the station, I have lower costs, but a different outcome; it takes two hours. But I could cycle to work in 30 minutes. Yes, but it often rains; the traffic is dangerous, and sometimes I have a lot to carry. But what if the train is unreliable, dirty and full, and you wait in the rain, and bus connections are poor, and late home comers are occasionally assaulted? So perhaps I go by car, and make the traffic even worse. We quickly see that choices are multiple and open to creativity.

This example illustrates that choices will be made by users, details are significant, discontinuity can spoil the best plan, cash outlays are only part of costs, quality counts, and alternatives may be accessible and physically relevant. Someone has to think it out and make the chosen combination work. Interconnectivity increases the choices; its absence prevents choices. Interoperability is here less obvious, but might seriously impede individual modes from competing in the chosen process.

Freight intermodal contains all these elements. But what should it achieve, and who puts it together? Freight is inert. It cannot act for itself. Arrangements have to embrace the eventualities before they occur; the equipment has to be in place. The 'integrator' who puts it together and serves the user, must know it will work, and know what each mode contributes. Now the barriers of interoperability and interconnectivity have to be overcome by deliberate measures. Overcoming them demands a price, which burdens each mode and the whole.

The Price of Diversity

Europe was not planned to be efficient. Its peoples are diverse, with a history of conflict even as population, trade, wealth and industry grew. They keep their individuality, despite commitment to a single Europe. Intermodality draws on modal resources formed in diversity. It uses railways which, after political changes, reconstruction and technical renewal, are still fragmented and subject to national influences. Its highways and ports reflect a long history.

The 'integrator' has to sort it out. If he tries, it means subcontracting, or making flanking investments including locations, equipment and key personnel; or it may mean investing to control the action. In each case there are historical and conceptual barriers. They are inevitable. When an integrator, creating intermodal services, has to overcome the problems of interconnectivity and interoperability, the costs and risks are going to be higher, and the incentive to create intermodal operations will be less.

When arrangements, risks and investment for the move are out of control, costs increase. In the end, competitivity fails, and this is ultimately a burden on European trading efficiency.

Intermodality is complex, and complexity raises risks of failure. Failure is costly, and easily fatal. The integrator is therefore likely to choose carefully his opportunities, and modes, and even customers, because the object of his involvement is profit. This choice is distorted by issues of interconnectivity and interoperability. But whose problem are they anyway?

Who Cares?

On our journey to work, we learn to live with trivial incidents. We make an economic and a qualitative choice. This is paralleled in freight intermodal choice; users may entrust their business and living to those who provide the integrated service. But the brutal reality is that intermodal is of no interest to most European users; trucking is the norm. Note that this is not automatically so in the USA; many shippers know that intermodal is itself a choice, and insist in its appraisal. Indeed, Wal-Mart, the nationwide store chain, awarded its intermodal service award in 2002 and 2003 to Schneider National, a national US trucking company which makes extensive use of intermodal operations to serve Wal-Mart. In Europe, few shippers would be so aware.

There are two major European areas of freight intermodal: global ocean liner trade and domestic (inland) trade. One is highly successful, the other much less so. Liner shipping has established advanced intermodal systems, which have enjoyed 30 years of notable success. By contrast, domestic applications have lagged far behind.

The distinction between the two is fundamental. Their individual characteristics are not comparable. Integrating them is also physically, and certainly logistically, difficult, and often not relevant because they reflect quite different demand patterns. Interconnectivity and interoperability do not affect them equally.

12.2 DEVELOPMENT OF INTERMODAL TRANSPORT: DIFFERENT PERSPECTIVES AND ATTITUDES

From Modal to Intermodal

Although from the nineteenth century small containers (on small wagons) for freight were well known, this was only expediency, not intermodality. No one thought in system terms. 1960s visionaries saw the potential of intermodal systems; but first actions were mainly to address the new hardware.

With each mode, it is significant, whether the mode changed itself, as did liner shipping; or simply put another page in its catalogues, as did railways; or observed with interest, as did trucking; or acted opportunistically, as did inland waterways. In some ports the attitude in the 1960s was, 'Fight it at all costs', and curiously that became part of the maritime success; intermodal was strong enough to bypass traditional ports when these endangered the vision. One loser, unprepared for change, was notorious. The Port of London, after two years of strikes, saw the new Australia service diverted permanently to Southampton. The port collapsed, and today to Londoners the expression 'Docklands' means only real estate.

Maritime Containerization and Intermodality

For self-driven radical change, we look at liner shipping, which in 1967 was still ordering conventional freighters. Within five years, second-generation container ships dominated on the principal east–west trade routes of the northern hemisphere. With the conventional ships went the accumulated equipment to work them at the berth, to handle and store cargo, and to carry it inland. Casual dock labour was ended. It was a painful social upheaval. Port cities changed; ships and terminals became industrialized systems dependent upon sophisticated information management. Technology, but also the software of a world of trading, making, assembling, distributing, choosing and buying, have changed, together with our notions of costs and values. Container shipping has brought this about.

The example is so commonplace that we no longer think of the upheaval it caused, and the huge risks involved. It is still successful today. There has been unprecedented rationalization of the liner shipping industry, a massive fall in real rates to users, and transportation to a largely standard physical operation, where logistic aspects like control, tracing and support are the keys to competitive differentiation.

The revolution demanded that each new threshold be overcome, in four waves of development, at their most basic:

- making it work;
- handling the growth of demand;
- reducing the system costs;
- managing the performance.

Each wave built on the others, which themselves remained. Interestingly, at the first stage, intra-mode interoperability was ruthlessly imposed; exceptions were minimal. This rigour was upheld through the subsequent stages.

Today, handling the volume and reducing the costs go with raising quality, stimulating new but compatible technologies. Container shipping lines make harsh demands on ports and terminals, because cost and performance go with the economics of the ship as well as the flow of cargo. Ship costs are well under half the total costs of providing door-to-door maritime intermodal services to shippers.

This then was intermodal imposed by one mode, as a production system. The unnerving reality is that it resulted from Malcolm MacLean's insight, not in liner shipping, but in highway transportation, when he created SeaLand in 1955. MacLean was a trucker. His concern was not to be a new kind of steamship line, but a better trucker. He seamlessly integrated cheap, available vessels into his trucking operation. This was intermodal thinking. This was the vision: intermodal could drastically change the economics and performance of freight transport.

MacLean was an innovative integrator. He integrated, into his door-to-door business, all the various modal elements which gave him overall performance. He had to create them himself. His ships came from US military reserves. His containers were trailer bodies. His support services were subcontracted. He only wanted what served the overall purpose of better business. He provided an integrated service, into which sea voyages and ports were seamlessly integrated.

This bypassed the clumsy traditional interconnectivities of ships, cargo, ports and procedures. The result was dramatic; the whole historical concept, physically in ports, ships, stevedoring, warehousing, cranes and slings, forwarding and inland transport, and institutionally in tariffs, customs, insurance, rules and practices, was out of date. MacLean created interconnectivity and imposed interoperable equipment, in his own closed system. The remarkable thing is that he thereby imposed it, beyond his own system, on the world of liner shipping and ports, something which for other modes never happened.

Certainly there were some liner shipping companies who thought it was enough to carry 'containers' as well as their usual cargo. This added interfaces, increasing complexity in their existing operations, in their existing places and practices. These people added complications, but had no concept to realize the advantages. They would soon think again.

Real change was led by the Australian–European Conference. The leading members set up their own custom-built integrated operation, to achieve the performances which MacLean had shown to be possible. Forming new consortia, they converted the Europe–Australia trade to integrated container operation in 1969/70. They imposed standards and built the first integral container ships, the 'Encounter Bay' class. They bought standard containers, optimized schedules and port calls, planned inland moves, introduced container logistics and introduced through rates, under revolutionary tariff concepts. It was immensely courageous. And they shared the advantages with the trade.

They could afford to. Within months this was the only economically justifiable way to conduct liner trade. Within five years the major trades between Europe and East Asia had been 'containerized', to the form we recognize today. Liner shipping became intermodal, together with the support functions it required.

Railways and highways were outside liner companies' direct control or influence, and railways especially failed to see the lessons. They were not ready to change. The impact still contained the potential for revolution, but was seen rather as a curiosity, or a threat, or an option among many. There was little unanimity, and no vision.

The Road Haulage Industry

Trucking, fragmented and creative, did not need to worry greatly. New equipment to haul containers, and a new customer base, were not disquieting. Most port truckers, reacting to the new need, moved readily into hauling chassis and boxes, embracing new locations and procedures.

To the general road haulage industry, hauling maritime containers is a specialist job. Most are involved in general European trade where road is the almost universal manner of inland transportation. They could now look to domestic intermodal, and some did.

Some road hauliers have become intermodal integrators. They adapted their operations and their equipment. Some today have moved into management of the rail part of the operation. This may include terminal ownership and management, ownership of railcars, contract trains and even becoming rail undertakings. Like Schneider National, quoted above in the USA, such a haulier must remain user-focused, adopting intermodal only where real end-user advantages emerge. Obstacles like inadequate interoperability are therefore a major deterrent to a deeper commitment in the markets.

Even so, truckers in Europe came earlier to intermodal than in the USA partnerships, where new relationships awaited deregulation, to replace the confrontation. In Europe, by 1970, a true pioneer was Trasporti Ambrogio of Candiolo, Torino, today one of Europe's leading domestic intermodal operators with a network of block trains.

Road Haulage and the UIRR

Around 1970, truckers and forwarders in most European countries started to cooperate with national railways, forming national companies such as

Kombiverkehr, HUPAC and Novatrans in the Union Internationale des sociétés Rail-Route, UIRR. This launched a search for operational and technical concepts. It was an uphill struggle, but important results have been obtained. The UIRR found itself, with its essentially national membership of trucking interests, with almost entirely domestic operations. The background is described in the UIRR's excellent 30th anniversary book.

Interoperability was always critical for the UIRR. They relied on technical advances to carry heavy goods vehicles and swap bodies on the European rail network, with its restricted and varying loading gauges. The standard European semi-trailer, slightly under 45 ft long, swap bodies at 7.15 m, 7.42 m and 7.8 m, all practically demand custom-built railcars. Most constraining is the limited loading gauge. A 2.90 m high swap body or a 4 m high trailer is almost everywhere an exceptional load, requiring special, costly railcars and restricting choice of routes. This problem is unknown in the USA, where the economics of double-stack car operation, requiring about 6.73 m above rail level, have been a major incentive to certain national trucking companies to adopt intermodal.

Other obstacles such as documentation practices, service quality and information discontinuity have also been a severe handicap. The UIRR companies are not 'integrators' but take on the tasks of shaping the rail mode into usable form, providing rolling stock and schedules, creating information and managing terminal operations. They are acutely aware of interoperability issues. They have taken steps to overcome these obstacles. Many truckers use rail-based intermodal in a way which, left to themselves, they would not have found possible; but many weaknesses remain.

Rail services for intermodal are inherently more costly in Europe for three reasons associated with the limited track and clearance specifications. These are:

- the capital costs of specialized rolling stock, severely inflated by the need to run at high speeds and with extreme technical solutions such as low floors or small wheels;
- the poor use of available train length with various types of unit load or trailer (and influenced by the previous point, of design compromise for extreme situations);
- inability to optimize train loads due to limitations of European technology (intermodal cargo tends to be heavy, reaching maximum train load before length of train limits are reached).

In general, compared to International Standards Organisation (ISO) containers, swap bodies and trailers result in lower train load efficiency, but are the most desirable and realistic units for domestic trade.

Further on in this chapter there will be a further brief reference to the Rolling Highway, a technology which was largely entrusted to the UIRR companies but which is not truly intermodal in concept. Since, however, it illustrates some aspects of interconnectivity and interoperability, it will be noted in passing.

European Railways and Intermodal

European railways, in the 1970s and later, were interested in intermodal, and not only in the UIRR context. There was an awareness that the old patterns of wagons and shunting, freight stations and sidings might not survive. Traditional port-based rail traffic was already threatened by the influence of marine containers. But the inertia of a conventional, if declining, pattern of freight operations, with immense fixed assets and serious productivity problems, prevented more than a passing gesture. That gesture, at once visionary and timid, was the creation in 1967 of a European marketing company, Intercontainer. Timidity won. Potentially it was a catalyst for revolution, but it proved not to be. Largely held back by fears of self-competition of its European state rail owners, it made big investments and carried many containers, but itself never offered or achieved the intrinsic system benefits of integrated intermodalism. Intercontainer for 20 years carried substantial traffic of maritime containers, for which its relatively unsophisticated service approach was more effective. It lost this business as it failed to achieve cost reductions and to lead service development, for an increasingly critical market sector.

Certain national state rail companies, particularly in France, Germany and Italy, developed systems, mainly for maritime containers. In Britain, there was a special stimulus, as road haulage was already partly deregulated in 1964, and rail deregulation was in hand. The 'Re-Shaping of British Railways' Reports in 1964 contained a radical proposal for a high-productivity system of fixed-formation shuttle trains, running at passenger train speeds between dedicated road–rail terminals.

This was Freightliner, which in 1966 was as near as European railways would come in two generations to emulate liner shipping. For almost 40 years Freightliner, now a private company, has carried significant traffic and made modest profits. But neither Freightliner nor Intercontainer, although they still exist, changed the world of railways.

There was still a fundamental weakness in conventional rail commercial thinking. This weakness held back rail's effectiveness, and reinforced political frustration which led ultimately to the present liberalization legislation. This was the failure of national 'network' state rail to practice market and cost segmentation, and to disaggregate income streams. Intermodal suffered severely from this. To compete with through road haulage, intermodal takes local and regional collection and delivery by road, which is expensive, and combines it with ruthlessly streamlined long-haul rail from which all unnecessary costs and operations, delays, marshalling, and so on have been stripped away. If this clean-and-mean self-contained intermodal operation is not achieved, the exercise is in vain. But if it is achieved, and cannot be separated from the general costs and overheads of the standard rail freight business, with its low productivity and poor performances, then a sound business justification for intermodal involvement will never show. If the line haul is then charged for, on a basis of traditional general freight tariffs, the position will go from bad to worse. This was the case on most European railways until the late 1990s and beyond. Ill-informed rail commercial attitudes have prevented creative and sound intermodal growth.

It required the new entrant rail undertakings of the 2001 rail liberalization in Europe to offer market-relevant charges to users and intermodal operators, justified by specific costing of planned, high-performance operations. This has demonstrated in certain cases (not in all) that a line haul for intermodal can be profitable, at rates which justify rail as a legitimate part of a throughout intermodal operation.

US Railroads and Intermodalism

With deregulation of US rail through the Staggers Act, 1980, run-down railroads responded to the intermodal opportunity. Intermodal permitted a productivity breakthrough in the USA similar to that of liner shipping 20 years before. This, based upon double-stack high-productivity operations, and a new approach to market charging, supported by a cost-reduction model, all quite different to traditional European practice, became the rail intermodal revolution of the 1990s. Carrying some 11 million loads per year, and generating around a 15 per cent profit margin overall, intermodal is today the largest revenue source of US railroads, having overtaken coal in 2003. Steady growth continues.

This chapter will not analyse US intermodal in detail; for that, see elsewhere; reference to David De Boer's book, *Piggyback and Containers*, of 1992, and to *Intermodal Freight Transportation*, compiled by Gerhardt Muller (1999) in various editions by the ENO Transportation Foundation, Washington, DC, is essential.

The stimulus of deregulation led to a substantial user pressure on rail to play a greater intermodal role. The story of double-stack development is linked with this. It took some three years to obtain authority for trial running of the first double-stack train, for American President Lines; ongoing investments are required to obtain the 6.73 m (23 ft) vertical clearance needed for unrestricted double-stack operation on more routes. This investment has mostly been funded by the railroads, as private joint stock companies owning their right of way; in one or two cases public funding has been provided, especially in the north-east states where infrastructure is much older and congested, to increase clearances to permit double-stack. In 1984, just one double-stack train weekly left the US West Coast, for one destination. In September 2002, 241 weekly double-stack trains, with individual capacity around 400 TEU (twenty-foot equivalent unit), were scheduled from the West Coast to all major eastern markets. Interoperability is, also in the USA, still a problem, and affects axle loads, clearances, operating rules and equipment authorization. Recent trials in competition for the UPS South California contract show, however, what can be achieved. In April 2003, Union Pacific ran west- and eastbound trial trains between Chicago and Los Angeles. Average speeds throughout for the around 3600 km were 90 km/h and 96 km/h. Since maximum running speeds are 113 km/h, and there are many sections run at reduced speed and (by European standards) extremely severe gradients, this was remarkable. But these trains also ran for 1212 km on the tracks of competitor BNSF, 34 per cent of the line-haul. This meant that UP standard SD70MAC locomotives, used throughout, had to be interoperable over BNSF in the best European sense, respecting signalling and train-stop devices, driving, fittings and equipment. Interoperability is not easy, but it is not a dream.

Feedering: An Intermodal Success

Intermodalism created a new European coastal feeder business. As new dedicated vessels were built, interoperability was not a serious obstacle, and interconnectivity was mainly an issue of use of space and of service connections in ports. The growth of a flourishing feeder trade gave the new container ships in their hub ports such as Rotterdam and Hamburg access to regional distribution to secondary ports. The hubs in the Mediterranean, Gioia Tauro, Malta, and others still emerging, are entirely dependent on integrated feeder services and port operations, to achieve their purpose of regional distribution to serve a large long-haul vessel stopping briefly in transit.

If such concepts are to work (and they might appear vulnerable, and cost-intensive), the critical success factors will be those of successful intermodalism everywhere, that the part must be integrated into, and interoperably support, the whole. Scheduling of hub and feeder calls has to permit the effective connections of in- and outbound main route vessels with the local distribution and collection services. When this is well planned, and operates smoothly, a new range of secondary ports can enjoy a high-quality service the equal of a main port elsewhere. This depends, in the last resort, upon interoperability, reliable punctual main services and good management. The whole cannot work without its parts, and competes through total system costs.

A variation on this has been the re-emergence of the principal inland waterway axes to Rotterdam and Antwerp, and at a lower level the Danube, Seine and Elbe, as carriers of intermodal equipment, primarily deep-sea containers connecting with the big ships. This has brought new life to inland ports and operators, attracted substantial private investment, and given new choices to shippers in the regions served. Rhine shipping has an interesting problem of interoperability, where standard vessels can carry up to six 40 ft ISO containers side by side, 2.44 m wide, stacked four high, to the middle Rhine. Above Strasbourg to Basel, lock dimensions limit this to only four wide, and three units high. However, domestic units such as swap bodies are 2.50 m wide, so being restricted to only three units side by side. Costs of carrying domestic units are therefore inevitably higher through the Rhine. Rhine shipping also depends upon vertical transshipment by spreader, of stacked containers, with top access; only a small number of domestic units meet this requirement. Although, therefore, Rhine shipping has become a successful competitor of road and rail for deep-sea containers, with about 1.6 million TEU annually, it carries very few domestic units.

The Danube navigation has the potential, from Bavarian and Austrian ports downstream, to develop a substantial inland waterway operation to the Black Sea, using the same basic approach. However, the overall potential is clearly less, since connections with large deep-sea global lines are less relevant.

It is clear overall that the critical sector of domestic intermodal in Europe is lagging behind. Something has failed to be understood. Intermodal in Europe has not been brought up to the level of economic dynamism which occurred in such a short time, and on such an uncompromising scale, in liner shipping. In addition, it has not demonstrated the economic vigour which has made it a profitable, when specialized, land transportation mode in the USA.

12.3 INTERCONNECTIVITY AND INTEROPERABILITY

This brief commentary on intermodalism, described more fully elsewhere, is of course designed to show interconnectivity and interoperability obstacles. If we compare European Union policies, white papers and pressures to get trucks off the highways, these obstacles are a source of failure. Their impact is relative, depending on the objectives of our efforts. In inland domestic intermodal, they are certainly critical to success. In deep-sea business, they do not greatly impede users, but they certainly prevent the modes, especially rail, from being optimally involved.

We might recall that liner shipping did agree, at an early stage, with governments and the UNO, to determine certain features through ISO standards. Remarkable was that these quickly left behind the tentative starting standards, such as SeaLand's 30 ft long container, and the 8 ft height; nor are there binding standards in all features and everywhere today. Interconnectivity emerged by concensus; and today a feeder ship in South-East Asia, and a double-stack train in California, can both be part of an intermodal service concept operated by a European container ship line. Certain common equipment and fittings, dimensions and tolerances, respecting ISO 668, and other standards such as marking and numbering, are therefore essential, and have not changed in 35 years.

Yet we observe that although this was achieved, other simple organizational and technical obstacles prevent integrated systems from operating within Europe, and that today expense and delay are involved in overcoming these discontinuities. Also, and quite separately, we note that a normal domestic intermodal load unit in Europe is not compatible, in length, weight, strength, width and height, or fastenings, with any equipment designed to work in the liner shipping context. Clearly this also has to be addressed, and the EU has issued a draft Directive which starts to resolve this conflict, not for the first time.

The reader may by now suspect that we are leading to two separate sets of conclusions on critical success factors. One of these is the quality and robustness of the intermodal vision, and the effectiveness of its conversion into reality. The other is the tools available, the role of the various types of hardware and infrastructures, and their discontinuity of development. We may conclude that a too-simple expectation, as in political policy, that intermodal will emerge and flourish through top-down encouragement, is not justified. But two additional complications have to be addressed. One is control of the integrated intermodal service, and the other is the structure of investments throughout the chain. Some important divergences have arisen, critical now in a new liberalized European trading environment.

Interconnectivity is a good starting point, because issues always arise where systems meet, but fail to match. There is a lot of this. We should not imagine that Europe comes as a well-running industrial and infrastructure machine. It is a disorderly accumulation of mixed assets. European transportation infrastructure results from 150 years of perceived needs, private and public initiatives, wars, availability of funding, and national policies of support or intervention. The result of different rival national economies, it could not, in retrospect, have been otherwise. All states have suffered abrupt changes of policy and priorities. Populations have increased by several times. Wealth and its distribution have changed. Base industries like coal and steel have flourished, found markets, been undermined and disappeared.

Railways formed complex networks, and supporting infrastructure of stations, junctions and yards which would later frustrate rationalization. They had a high professional ethic and a tradition of service within a strict framework of rules. After 1945 successive financial crises and reductions of staff and duties went with a rapid modernization of the core networks. Unsurprisingly, since the equipment was paid for by national funds, the suppliers and standards were local. To the outsider, each railway looked very different and individual.

Interconnectivity, which was seldom an issue until recent years, suffered too. The rail networks in Europe were, and are, only in the most general sense continuous. They have national nodes, usually central, around which they are planned. They meet to exchange at borders. These are at the extremities of national systems with different interests and plans. There was little historic reason to do better. Now, under Directive 2001/14, the infrastructure of each state is separated from rail operations in order to make it available to competing train operators. The intention is that these can run services using the infrastructure as appropriate. This is only meaningful if the separate infrastructure managers consciously provide a coherent network, with common technical features and similar access rules for undisturbed through running. This aim is central to the White Paper, a *Time to Decide*. But unfortunately the infrastructure managers, collectively held to certain behaviour by Directive 2001/14, have financial and territorial mandates of national parliaments, and are accountable to national policies. They cannot synthesize a European network when this is not their mandate, and when international freight is only a small part of their claim upon scarce resources.

The practical result is that the networks cannot make equal commitments to paths and capacity, nor can they provide comparable physical conditions. Serious efforts have been made on some shared routes by the 'one-stop-shops' set up by some infrastructure managers to plan schedules and paths on common trunk routes; but the fundamental interoperability deficit is not thereby overcome.

The highway network suffers less from this problem. The motorways of Europe were almost all built after 1945, and, while they certainly reflect national priorities, the connections between national networks are mostly effective. The 'E' network of European highways is also a practical reality.

Heavy private and commercial traffic uses the EU network without serious discontinuity, although network gaps still remain, and construction standards vary.

Highway and rail suffer from a further aspect of interconnectivity, that they are not from the start designed to complement one another, but to compete; and both are, in Europe, mostly dedicated first to passenger transport. This means that they do not meet naturally, and integrated use of both has to overcome this obstacle. Their connections into major centres of freight generation and exchange such as ports are not generally complementary or optimal, although this is improving. Many road freight journeys start and finish on suburban streets in heavily congested areas. The opposite is also familiar; the location and land use planning of modern industry and distribution is often determined by a highway layout or intersection, and no thought is given to intermodal optimization.

In the USA, this was first addressed with the ISTEA (Intermodal Surface Transportation Efficiency Act) legislation of 1994, with public funding of connectors for intermodal operations. Highway authorities had ignored intermodal operations in their planning; freeway connections to access rail yards were outside their authority; and private railroads had constructed terminals, open to local neighbourhood roads, hoping that trucks would find it. Dangerous and ecologically objectionable situations had grown up around intermodal rail yards. Under the ISTEA, and follow-up legislation (presently TEA-21), funds were provided specifically to facilitate road–rail location synergy and access. While insufficient, this demonstrates an awareness of the issue of consciously bringing road and rail together, if intermodal is taken seriously by policy makers.

Interconnectivity for former, older infrastructure such as inland waterway ports is still usually today at a low standard, with rail access over industrial sidings and low-speed branches, and with road approach often through unsuitable industrial quarters. This is likely to present increasing problems, since limited space and increasing traffic will render conflicts more acute.

Modern container ports have been often situated some distance downstream from traditional city and estuary ports, often 30 or 50 km and sometimes more, partly to assure adequate draft (depth of water) and partly to obtain the large land surfaces needed by the port terminal operations. This has led to a replanning of highway and rail access which has not always been optimal. New infrastructure has been built, which has not always facilitated high-performance land transportation. Highway access over links to a city ring road may be adequate, but rail connections have often, being more costly, been minimal. This is a mistake when major ocean terminals may be handling enough traffic to justify block trains direct to inland points, but where terminal rail capacity is limited, shuttle trains cannot be stabled, and local operating is still tied to a regional classification yard of freight station on the 'old railway'.

In US ports, the issue of an 'on-dock' rail terminal, as opposed to an on-street shuttle of containers on trailers to a strategically placed inland rail yard, has been controversial. Some terminal operators wish to use all their space for streamlined operations to turn vessels round. Examples of both are found, but older port areas such as New York–New Jersey seem generally to suffer from their lack of efficient direct rail terminal access. In Long Beach, the publicly funded construction of the Alameda Corridor, a new 20 km dedicated rail route for direct line-haul trains from the port terminal areas onto the mainline rail networks of Los Angeles, is proving operationally and commercially effective. However, demands will still grow and a new joint initiative between steamship lines, local communities, terminals and rail companies has been set up in Los Angeles to tackle jointly the demands of another decade of normal trade growth. Intermodal is here a victim of its own success; and remember, there was one double-stack train a week in 1984. Interconnectivity will take on new dimensions here which go beyond short-term inconvenience and move over to the optimization of flows through regional multi-mode systems.

In Europe the system is vulnerable because individual states finance infrastructure through national programmes, often subject to non-transportation political influences. The rail network is at the mercy of local national policies on funding infrastructure for rail freight, including intermodal. The liberalization programme so far does little to bind individual governments into a coherent European network policy, but with heavy public funding required just to keep rail infrastructure at an adequate standard of availability, this will cause difficulties in some countries. The legislative basis is however now in place, with the implementation of Directive 2001/16. The adoption and implementation of the second railway package in 2004, including the creation of a European Railway Agency, have carried interoperability a significant step further.

Interoperability: How Railways are not, but May Become, European

In April 2001 the European Parliament adopted Directive 2001/16 on the interoperability of conventional rail operations. It became EU law in April 2003. To achieve interoperability for conventional rail, it sets procedures which determine priorities; sets, by consultative process, new standards for rail equipment and procedures; and makes these standards binding upon member states under European law.

The lack of interoperability is a major and recognised barrier to European rail. In future, European standards will be applicable, set by consultation and endorsed in the EU. These will be mandatory. Safety requirements, authorizations and licensing will also be harmonized. It will be a huge task, lasting decades, at a cost still undetermined. It is necessary but, given technical and competitive evolution, may never be complete.

Historic Overview: Railways Did Not Start with a European Vision

Railway interoperability was always the challenge when moving from 'small and fragmented' to networks. Before the mid-nineteenth century, scattered lines were being concentrated. The question of harmonization already had to be faced, before the nation states of Europe reintroduced new diversity.

There are many ways to be incompatible. Early lines were built to different gauges, with different clearances and profiles, with differing technologies. Loading gauges, once adopted, were difficult to change; even today, there is no single clear statement of what is possible on many European trunk routes.

External demands for safety ensured national, but at first still very different, standards for brakes, operating disciplines and signalling. Each country imposed different legal requirements, and fulfilled the needs in different ways. It is little better today, though further complicated by reconstruction and new technologies. One day, this would inevitably become a pan-European concern. That day has now arrived.

Railway Organization and Ownership Changes

Political influences also imposed change. European wars changed territories and led to new 'state railways' created in haste out of often incompatible private and local rail systems. Many historic anomalies remained, often still with us today.

Subsequent technical development, even up to the present day, has introduced new barriers, not only at borders. With electric traction, the different power systems developed by national and regional industries became a serious handicap. There are now five major power systems in use in Europe, some 16 automatic signalling systems, and as many automatic train stop systems with differing installations and functions.

The Union Internationale des Chemins de Fer, UIC, achieved a significant level of technical interoperability between railways. Much freight and passenger rolling stock, though not all, runs freely on much of the network. Some well-known barriers remained, such as track gauge in the Iberian peninsula, Finland and Eastern Europe, and loading gauge in Britain. Indeed, when the Channel Tunnel opened in 1994, there was almost no interoperable freight equipment; 1200 new intermodal freight cars had to be built from scratch.

There had been no incentive until the late twentieth century to think in European terms. Each railway and state extended the barriers to interoperability, unwittingly or not, with historic legacies, new technical variations, and local design and approval standards. There is no point in lamenting this situation, but it will have to be overcome. There is today no European railway.

Integration of national railways with their national supply industry led to captive suppliers, working to the specification of the home railway. Differing licensing practices in each country remained a costly deterrent to creativity, which Directive 2001/16 specifically replaces by a European approval system, still however to be implemented in member states.

For railcars, UIC standards came to impose 'lowest common denominator' technologies. European rolling stock costs compared to the USA are exceptionally high, and utilization is often poor; in 1995 we estimated that to provide wagon capacity for one TEU-km in Europe was some five times more costly than in the USA.

Europe also suffers from high-cost, high-specification motive power, produced in small uneconomic series and not interoperable. The contrast to road haulage vehicles, constantly improved and made cheaper by competitive innovation, could not have been sharper. National railways have bred their own albatrosses of expensive, underutilized equipment, a burden round their necks in any international competition.

Interoperability of Working Practices and Information

Operating practises, the 'software of interoperability', are a particular problem area, as standards of safety are imposed and sustained differently in each state. Safety invigilation of railways is usually entrusted to an independent national authority. The effect of this has been to prescribe, in national law, different working practices, licensing, training and recruitment, and the recognition of professional competence.

IT systems have also grown up nationally, and do not talk to one another. But contemporary users expect information, standards of service and data integration Europe-wide, just as they may receive in trucking. They find inadequate, incompatible rail data and quality control. These issues are even more difficult to identify and to put right. The software obstacle is critical for intermodal integrators. These need information to optimize various dissimilar activities, loading, trucking, terminals, train loading and movements. The enhancement of risk, by the failure of railways to manage information flow, has been a serious obstacle to intermodal effectiveness. It is therefore a deterrent to involvement.

12.4 STEPS TOWARDS EUROPEAN INTEROPERABILITY

The Key to a European Railway

Today, it is the view of both users and policy makers that interoperability obstacles now prevent rail from meeting qualitative demands for transportation. Rail freight reinvigoration, of which intermodal is a part, is hindered by a lack of interoperability.

The EU's Transport White Paper of September 2001, *Time to Decide*, recognizes this. It demands a coherent market-orientated European rail system, to serve European trade and movements. Measures to reinvigorate rail freight, including opening the networks progressively to competitive service provision by different rail operators, cannot be effective until conditions of construction and use of rolling stock, of access to the infrastructure, and the necessary business processes such as data exchange, are defined so as to become interoperable.

There is a tendency to confuse liberalization with interoperability. Achieving interoperability is a separate and urgent practical task to permit rail to be effective at a European level. Whatever we think of Open Access, nothing can be improved without the imposition, with legal authority, of interoperability. It is a key to economic operations on a European scale. There are therefore now two processes in progress simultaneously, separate but closely interrelated. One is to provide interoperability on a coherent European rail system. The other is to create new market-based structures for rail service provision, in line with demand and with European economic policy.

It took great political courage to admit that improvement would not come from within the rail industry. The consequence is now that, in a single Europe, the European Union is empowered, with legislative endorsement, to address the revitalization of European rail, of which interoperability is one condition, so that rail operators can exploit their new competitive freedoms.

Interoperability Legislation

The EU Council demanded the Commission in October 1999 to propose specific interoperability legislation for railways, with:

> A strategy on improving the interoperability of rail transport and reducing bottlenecks with a view to eliminating technical, administrative and economic obstacles to the interoperability of networks, while guaranteeing a high level of safety as well as personnel training and qualifications.

> In particular to improve interlinking and interoperability of the national rail networks, as well as access thereto . . . implementing any measures . . . necessary in the field of technical standardisation, as provided for in Article 155 of the Treaty.

The Preface of the Directive stated:

> The commercial operation of trains throughout the trans-European rail network requires in particular excellent compatibility between the characteristics of the infrastructure and those of the rolling stock, as well as efficient interconnection of the information and communications systems of the different infrastructure managers and operators.
>
> Performance levels, safety, quality of service, and cost, depend upon such compatibility and interconnection, as does particularly the interoperability of the trans-European conventional rail system.

The Directive applies to any relevant aspect of rail interoperability; these include infrastructure, rolling stock, information systems and data exchange, working conditions and training, social and environmental issues, operating practices and rules.

Interoperability for conventional rail imposes a mandatory EU legislative process in a sector of railway management which has up to now been the responsibility of individual railways and national governments, coordinated by the UIC, and supervised only by safety inspectorates accountable normally to national parliaments.

The issue is complex. It involves scientific, technical, operational, economic and institutional measures. The process has to be effective in all parts of Europe, without distortion, but without ignoring realities of the present diversity. The adoption of harmonised standards must not mean adopting the lowest acceptable common denominator, but encouraging the achievement of higher common standards. This has been done, with great difficulty, in the development of European Train Control systems for cab signalling, but cost of implementation is still high and implementation requires replacement of existing national systems. Part of the complexity lies in the selection of priorities, to achieve the greatest benefit without delay or disruption. There will inevitably be cultural conflict in implementation.

The process therefore requires a broad consultative basis, with recourse to many skills in various disciplines. There are five critical features:

- The concept of Technical Standards of Interoperability, TSIs, drawn up by a neutral, expert body.
- The 'Joint Representative Body', which coordinates work on agreed priorities and draws up TSIs. The Directive refers to a Joint Representative Body of railway companies, industry and infrastructure managers, and 'other parties likely to be affected'.

- TSIs have European validity. On adoption by the EU Council they become mandatory. TSIs overcome existing variations in railway practice or national legislation in the past.
- Each member state must appoint its own independent neutral body to carry out verification and authorization, in accordance with TSIs. The Directive calls these 'Notified Bodies'. They are subject to invigilation to prevent divergences of practice.
- Finally, a product of experience: under penalty of sanctions, member states must ensure that rail operators, infrastructure managers, and others, take no new actions which impede interoperability.

The European Commission monitors results, reporting periodically to the Council of Ministers and European Parliament.

The process of actually achieving interoperability is still open to debate. A first group includes telematics for freight, train guidance and signalling, freight wagons, noise measures, and driving and traffic management (including training). Issues such as axle loads and clearances are still a Europe-wide problem for which costs and funding have not been identified.

EU policy includes rapid and coordinated introduction of European Rail Traffic Management, ERTMS, to leapfrog the existing barriers of different signalling systems and associated train stop systems. This is as much a facilitation of interoperable motive power as it is a harmonization of signalling systems, because locomotives have to carry the equipment appropriate to every system they encounter, a complex and expensive issue also requiring testing and licensing in every case. Clearly, a substantial part of costs, as yet unquantified, will fall upon infrastructure managers, whose owners are member states. The latter are collectively responsible for the adoption of the interoperability legislation, and could be considered liable for the costs involved. This is however an oversimplistic view, since member states already have difficulties in most cases in funding rail infrastructure to an adequate standard today, without the burden of possible major additional public works for the European network.

Normal methods of financial appraisal at national level do not help such collective projects. Since, additionally, freight is only a part of the traffic involved, but the demands of intermodal traffic demand extreme solutions of profiles, speeds and high axle-loads, and perhaps longer and heavier trains, it will be difficult for individual governments to address this issue. It may be that only the European Infrastructure Managers Association (EIM) can undertake this task, to focus and define the demands of interoperability and of simultaneous improvement of the core network. It seems possible that the Commission will have to adopt this issue as part of its rail policy.

Intermodal and Interoperability

Intermodal involves more than railways, and the distinction between maritime and domestic intermodal complicates the issue even more. But it also shows how vital it will be to allow individual specialists, with vision in a market or a business sector, to set out to overcome the obstacles, by the use of creativity within the standards set through the interoperability process.

Maritime interests have, first, a set of priorities imposed by their own system needs. This concerns vessels, overseas and European terminals, global balances of cargo and equipment, and a restricted selection of networks. Their principal land intermodal concerns are links between economic hinterlands and port terminals, with inland distribution centres, usually involving further third parties. These links are subordinate to a much bigger business. Within that business they are however disproportionately expensive to provide, and therefore constantly under scrutiny. Their marketing significance cannot be underestimated, because the inland links are the face of the steamship line to its customers; that is, they are the place where the company actively competes. Interoperability is here a servant, which makes things work.

Liner shipping equipment is a clearly defined range of maritime containers which, if not completely standardized, are at least in defined families. The constraint is the integration with the vessel to give the throughout service reliably. Although this summary must not give the impression that a very efficient and cost-sensitive operation is simple, it at least has some clear characteristics. One of these is volume, and another is the need to have predictable, regular, high-quality performance accommodating all normal expectations. Loads, gross weights and mixes of container types can be anticipated. Other modes, rail, road and barge, have to handle inland flows. On rail, shuttle trains are usually used today; inland waterways have custom-built barges. Road means chassis availability.

Rail interoperability for intermodalism will obviously concern hardware such as railcars, requiring clarity over clearances, authorised speeds, axle loads, tolerances, but also encouraging better payload-tare ratios, and better use of loading services and overall train length. All this must also help to raise terminal efficiency. This shows that harmonisation for interoperability must also not just be technical, but must be system-relevant.

Interoperability means that equipment must be available, independent of country, infrastructure manager and owner, to do the planned job with maximum efficiency and productivity, without outside or arbitrary interference and without contradictory or intrusive certification or maintenance regimes.

Experience has told us in the past that such an apparently reasonable requirement is not easily met by limited-scale private operators. The needs are wider. A shuttle link between port and inland terminal may be complemented by another route involving another port, and perhaps a range of terminals. That would not be unusual, given the nature of the maritime container trades. There must therefore be a maximum interchange freedom between the container rail car fleets used in the different routes. But these may involve the networks of more than one infrastructure manager. Licensing of high-efficiency railcars, today a severe obstacle, and the standard clearances and operating parameters, must therefore be resolved at a European level. This is foreseen in the Interoperability Directive 2001/16. It is an urgent need.

Interoperability and Domestic Intermodal

For domestic intermodality, which will be a significant part of the expectations of a new invigorated rail freight activity, the situation is much more complex.

First, the geographical freedoms are greater. Intra-European trade flows may occur anywhere. Then, challenges arise with the equipment to be hauled. Equipment will be adapted, not to the railway, but to the cargo and the highway mode. Clear identification with the highway mode has already led to a range of trailers and European swap bodies of distinct dimensions. These reflect road vehicle capacity, as offered to the shipper. They require appropriate railcars and profiles, or the intermodal exercise becomes invalid.

If the intermodal integrator is providing his own complete service, including load units and railcars, there will be some scope for play-offs, but not much. Requirements for rail car design, length, authorized speed and other characteristics limit severely the freedoms available. If the railcar is provided by a rail operator or integrator such as a UIRR company, this introduces a further interface of interests, and tolerances will fall; options may be reduced. There are real physical limits: 4 m high standard semitrailers can be carried on low-floor cars, but at a tare weight and length penalty which affects the economics of train working severely. Unsuitable route characteristics cannot normally be changed quickly, since heavy engineering is involved. The direct route from Brig (Simplon) to Novara has been under reconstruction for at least four years, just for this purpose, to accommodate 4 m high trailers on given railcar types. Improvements on this very restricted route, of single track and limited clearances and rudimentary signalling, took over 6 years in all, and yet permitted from 2005 the through running of licensed locomotives and rolling stock from Freiburg im Breisgau to Novara. This was an interoperability success, but a costly one, associated with the Swiss policy of diversion of road traffic to use of intermodal rail services.

Domestic intermodal, demanding accommodation within the limits of tolerance of the loading gauge, authorized axle loads and speeds, challenges interoperability possibilities. We could, all other things being equal, reduce the space taken below the loading platform. But intermodal is a demanding customer, with priority traffic running at maximum freight train speeds to achieve path priorities. Average loads are often heavy. Since technical specifications determine the relation between wheel size, axle load and speed, freedoms are seriously inhibited. This is typical of intermodal everywhere.

There is some pressure, well justified, for heavier axle loads in Europe on priority freight routes. Zeta-Tech Inc. of New Jersey, the leading US authority on track user cost allocations, has demonstrated (Paris 2003) that heavier axle loads lower overall payload costs, despite an inevitable increase in material and maintenance costs. This result led to 30 tonne axle loads on the Kiruna–Narvik iron ore line in Sweden. Similar calculations seem to show a benefit for intermodal, but the wheel performance within limited profile clearances is still a serious constraint. Since the overall size of the load is always a challenge in domestic intermodal, we expect considerable engineering creativity in this aspect in coming years. The EU SAIL Project (Uni Aachen and IBM AG, Au-Wädenswil Zürich) demonstrates an approach completed and approved within present constraints. In France, the Lohr system cars for highway trailer loading were approved for use first on the Mont Cenis route between France and Italy. However, these cars and the terminal installations are not compatible with other intermodal technologies.

Creative design encounters serious limits. First, it cannot change engineering constraints. Second, it is being developed in parallel to open access and on-rail competition, which will reduce freight rates and therefore render costly solutions unacceptable, and interoperability standards as approved under TSIs will not allow reduced safety; they could, in the interests of simplicity and universality, be more restrictive than today. But there will certainly be a stimulus to do better. This will also enhance the divergence between maritime and domestic intermodal.

The Software of Interoperability

Here we might anticipate for intermodal a significant improvement, as TSIs for data exchange, obligatory message forms, operating rules, train loads and scheduling, and so on, become available. More intermodal integrators themselves may move into the sector of licensed rail undertakings, managing their own quality and data flow under TSI standards. There is scope for serious improvement.

The UIRR in 2000 conducted a transportation quality study under the EC PACT programme, and demonstrated that software obstacles of interoperability were in part responsible for their ongoing difficulties in obtaining reliable service. These ranged from foolish issues such as different dates in each country for timetable changes, to widely divergent practice in determining authorized train lengths and weights, giving rise to en-route interference with supposedly block trains. A fundamental obstacle which led to frequent follow-on delays was the inability of national rail authorities to exchange information on train running; the consequence was to accentuate other interoperability issues such as the need to change locomotives and drivers, where a delay without information led to resources being reallocated to other work and trains at borders left stranded.

The UIRR report stated: 'The in-transit and border disruptions are probably one of the most critical aspects of the whole . . . quality challenge . . . the interface between two railways is problematical'. The UIRR identified total costs of rail-caused delay of around €41 million on 1999 results, about 6 per cent of revenues. Yet the UIRR itself takes, as do operators like ICF, serious action to uphold quality, as with an independent information transmission system. Without such action, costs would be much higher, affecting both the end-users' interests, and the intrinsic waste of poorly used rolling stock and personnel because of delays. Since European equipment, wagons and locomotives are already relatively expensive as a result of a lack of interoperability in specifications and tendering, it may be imagined that Intermodal in Europe carries a heavy, if still partly concealed, cost burden through the failure of rail in Europe to achieve interoperability.

However, new forms of trading and transporting companies will emerge, with new models of cooperation. A more open and flexible market creates new opportunities for intermediaries such as leasing companies to supply rolling stock and other equipment, and to manage statutory and other inspections and maintenance.

This all implies resolution of interoperability issues because offers must be integrally valid to be able to compete. Clearly, we have not seen the end of such developments.

Existing operators and rail undertakings have equal opportunities to become more effective, and they undoubtedly will. Their organizations contain considerable skill and experience, which, with greater interoperability, may stimulate new forms of competition. That surely is one of the objectives of the total legislation. There is nevertheless an issue of fair competition arising from the coexistence, in a liberalized market, of state-owned, usually unprofitable, undertakings, and new entrant entrepreneurs. Undoubtedly intermodal operators, new and existing, will observe the development of competitive practices as the process continues.

Rolling Highway: An Interoperability Puzzle

One significant area where a curious distortion occurs is in the sector of the Rolling Highway. Here, interoperability issues will be very difficult to address. Road trucks travel on specially designed rail platforms with very small wheels, in four-axle trucks under low-floor flatbeds, which permit drive-on/drive-off loading and give clearance (when coupled with special measures to increase loading gauge) for heavy goods vehicles, usually up to 4 m corner height. They in no way represent an intermodal freight concept, and are not intended to; they are simply a means of carrying road vehicles on rail through an area of congestion or a physical barrier, such as the Alps, usually under heavy subsidy. Unfortunately they are often counted among intermodal traffic, creating occasional confusion; but they are no more so than a ferry carrying a lorry over a river. Their economic justification is curious; they cannot compete on direct costs, since their full costs, of usually relatively inefficient and short-distance rail haul, heavily outweigh the short-term marginal savings of the trucker's distance saved. They are used where there is political value, as an alternative to the costs of Alpine tunnels and other difficulties, and where external costs in sensitive environments may justify political intervention and subsidy. The rail vehicle may cost around €150 000, and each platform carries one highway vehicle. Train length and weight, and therefore train paths, are not optimally used.

These rail vehicles are however in no way universally approved, being only licensed locally and not allowed to operate in many parts of Europe. They are unlikely to fall under interoperability TSI conditions. They have their place, under strictly defined circumstances, but demonstrate how we are dealing with technical challenges which are not capable of universal resolution.

Other Modes: Inland Waterways

The particular success of intermodal on inland waterways on certain routes since 1970 suggests that interoperability was not a particular obstacle. In fact, it might have been; apart from the question of vessel hold and container width referred to earlier, there have been some issues to overcome.

The hold–container issue, briefly, resolved itself very quickly. Although early container carriage on the Rhein was with redundant bulk carriers, there quickly emerged a custom-built concept of container carriers, which as described, could carry within the standard vessel dimensions, available at different parts of the system, containers in a parallel side open hold. The proviso was top lift, as with deep-sea vessels. Rapid installation of light transfer equipment at river ports ensured this continuity. Even the relatively few 45 ft maritime containers in European use can be carried, more effectively by barge than on road. Height is a problem in the upper Rhine, where bridges do not allow more than three-high stacking. These issues are less significant in the lower Rhine, where pusher barge combinations can operate at high productivity and low cost. Here it is unlikely that rail or truck can compete with reliability and low costs of the efficient barge mode, for maritime ISO containers.

Domestic containers are however wider, at 2.5 m, and usually only have bottom lift, making them unsuitable for open-hold barges. Serious efforts were made in 1999–2000 to link Rhine shipping and rail in the EC PACT project 'ART', for traffic with Italy, using early multipurpose domestic containers 2.5 m wide but with top lift and stacking capability; but the market acceptance was not demonstrated. The technical and economic obstacles, coupled with non-competitive rail, were still too great at that time. Since most markets for domestic intermodal are strongest on routes where inland waterways have few natural affinities, no rapid change is expected, but an area of interest exists where inland waterways can interact with short-sea vessels for European coastal and regional services.

12.5 CONCLUSIONS

As has been shown, interoperability and interconnectivity issues can create serious additional burdens for intermodal freight operations. Since, within Europe, the economic and performance limits of land intermodal inhibit its competitivity severely, it seems clear that it also suffers from the additional costs, delays and risk of failure which interoperability, especially on railways, causes.

Significantly, as liner shipping moved rapidly to intermodal operations over 30 years ago, interoperability within the chosen system was achieved rapidly. Technical norms are enforced by international conventions and by usage. Interconnectivity was an issue since ports and terminals represented interfaces with a basically incompatible hinterland, but this has not hindered the growth of a worldwide and effective low-cost tradition of high-quality service.

As inland waterways have integrated into these operations, they have largely accepted the standards of liner shipping, thus reducing interoperability issues voluntarily and aligning investments.

We return to railways, where the biggest obstacles remain. If intermodal, in the maritime trades and in the much more contested sector of domestic intermodal, is to be as effective as is hoped (and believed possible), rail interoperability in the letter and spirit of the current EU legislation is urgent. Much of this will be costly to realize, but even first and simple steps to align working practices, raise quality, increase transparency and realize effective open competition would significantly improve business prospects, thereby attracting greater investment and commitment.

BIBLIOGRAPHY

De Boer, J.D. (1992), *Piggyback and Containers*, San Marino, CA: Golden West Books.
European Commission DG-TREN (2001), White Paper, *Time to Decide*, EC Brussels.
EU Official Journal (2001), Directive 2001/16, 'Interoperability for Conventional Rail', EC DG-TREN Brussels, March.
Intercontainer (various years), *Annual Report*, Basel: Intercontainer.
Muller, Gerhardt (1999), *Intermodal Freight Transportation*, Washington, DC: ENO Transportation Foundation.
UIRR (2001), *Developing a Quality Strategy for Combined Transport, PACT B99-B2 7060*, Brussels: UIRR.
UIRR (various years), *Annual Report*, Brussels: UIRR
Verband Deutscher Verkehrsunternehmen (2002), *Freight Railways, Sustainable Mobility*, Düsseldorf: Alba.

13. Interorganizational coordination: the role of information technology

Mariëlle den Hengst

13.1 INTRODUCTION

In the New Economy, organizations must continuously change due to ongoing changes in the environment (Donaldson 1996). In trying to improve the performance of the organization, the focus has shifted from the organizational level towards the interorganizational level (Malone and Rockart 1991; McGrath and Hollingshead 1994). This growing interest in interorganizational coordination can be illustrated by several interrelated business trends, such as globalization, outsourcing of secondary activities, and technological developments. This chapter concentrates on the impact of technological developments on interorganizational coordination.

Developments in information and communication technology (ICT) such as the World Wide Web, electronic data interchange and electronic mail can be seen as enablers to cross organizational boundaries more easily when dealing with information-intensive processes. In the beginning, the focus was on supporting existing interorganizational processes, for example the exchange of documents between organizations. One rapidly growing trend today is the emergence of new ways to do business, replacing the current businesses. Examples of this are the introduction of electronic trading markets, electronic auctions and electronic bookstores. This shows that ICT has developed from a minor force supporting interorganizational coordination into a dominant force for changing it (Buxmann and Gebauer 1998).

Interorganizational coordination is an important element in intermodal transport. Many organizations with different interests, cultures and core businesses are involved in intermodal transport. The processes of these organizations must increasingly be tuned to meet the ever-growing requirements of transport. Despite some successful initiatives to introduce ICT to support interorganizational coordination, there are also many failures. The several attempts to introduce a centralized database in the port of Rotterdam are just an example. Although there are many reasons for these failures, one of the reasons addressed in this chapter is the lack of a proper understanding of the impact of ICT on interorganizational coordination and vice versa.

In this chapter the impact of ICT on interorganizational coordination in intermodal transport is discussed. First, a theoretical framework on interorganizational coordination is presented. Second, this framework is applied to the container transport practice as an example of intermodal transport. Third, an ICT-based system is proposed to support interorganizational coordination in container transport. Finally, the possible impact of this system on interorganizational coordination in container transport is discussed.

13.2 INTERORGANIZATIONAL COORDINATION THEORY

The need for coordination arises as a logical consequence of the division of labour in and between organizations (Mintzberg 1993). A general definition of coordination is proposed by Malone and Crowston (1994): 'coordination is managing dependencies'. Coordination processes are required to manage dependencies. Processes are, however, not the only mechanisms to achieve coordination. The structure of a group of organizations can also be seen as a mechanism for coordinating activities (Jablin 1987). Both interorganizational coordination processes and interorganizational coordination structures are discussed below. This section is concluded with paying attention to the impact of ICT on interorganizational coordination. The theory presented in this section will be applied to intermodal transport in the next section.

Interorganizational Coordination Processes

In this chapter the focus is on two types of dependencies that must be managed in interorganizational coordination (Alexander 1993; Malone and Crowston 1994; Thompson 1967): those concerning competitive or shared resources and those concerning sequential added value or supplier–buyer relationships. To manage these two types of dependencies two different interorganizational coordination processes are distinguished: strategic and operational.

Strategic coordination focuses on managing competitive resources. Decisions must be made as to what processes are needed for the fulfilment of a customer order and which organizations are selected for the execution of these processes. A contract between the organizations is detailed. The output of the strategic coordination processes is a blueprint specifying, among others, the preconditions for the operational coordination processes. For intermodal transport, the blueprint specifies which transport services are combined for a certain transport request and under which conditions.

Operational coordination focuses on managing sequential relationships. It takes place during the execution of the customer order and focuses on the flow of goods or services through the sequential processes. The transfer of goods from one modality to another and the information exchange required for this form the main part of operational coordination in intermodal transport.

This chapter pays special attention to strategic coordination processes. Operational coordination processes already receive a great deal of attention in practice, and strategic coordination processes are far behind, as will be shown in the next section. Strategic coordination is divided into three smaller steps, based on Guttman and Maes (1998):

- The information step mainly involves information collection about competitors, suppliers, clients and environmental changes.
- During the preparation step, negotiations are prepared for by defining requirements to specify what is needed and by selecting possible suppliers that can meet these requirements.
- During negotiation, one tries to reach an agreement with one or more of the suppliers selected. Negotiation can be seen as the iterative communication of offers and counteroffers. The negotiation process terminates when a consensus is reached or a willingness to negotiate vanishes.

Interorganizational Coordination Structures

Besides the processes described above, interorganizational structures can be seen as mechanisms to achieve coordination. A structure, at an abstract level, can be viewed as a collection of elements and the set of relationships that connect these elements (Monge and Eisenberg 1987). In an interorganizational structure, the elements are the organizations and the relationships are coordination related.

Many different forms of interorganizational coordination structures exist, but they can be categorized into three basic coordination structures (Malone and Crowston 1994; Powell 1991; Thompson et al. 1991). A hierarchical coordination structure is characterized by long-lasting relationships between organizations with fixed rules of behaviour and clear authority relationships. The market as a structure coordinates fully autonomous organizations via bidding and pricing systems. Hybrids or networks vary between the extremes of pure markets and pure hierarchies.

The division between hierarchies, markets and hybrids is insufficient to describe individual situations as they include more complex developments. Four characteristics of coordination structures are proposed for dealing with this (Hengst and Sol 2002):

- Coordination structures can be classified into decentralized and centralized structures (Malone and Crowston 1994). In a decentralized structure, all buyers are able to contact all sellers to negotiate transactions, whereas in a centralized structure transactions between buyers and sellers are negotiated indirectly through a broker.
- The characteristic of the coordination structure being dominated or neutral takes into consideration the power of setting prices and rules (Bodendorf and Reinheimer 1997). In a dominated structure, one organization sets the prices and rules and it is up to the other organization either to accept this or not to agree on the deal. In contrast, a neutral structure enables organizations to introduce their prices and rules and to negotiate them among each other.
- The third characteristic takes into consideration the number of buyers or sellers that take part in the coordination and can vary between one organization and the total number of buyers and sellers in the network. The term 'participant' is introduced to refer to the buying and selling organizations. A distinction is made between the number of participants with whom agreements are negotiated (strategic coordination processes) and the number of participants with whom agreements are settled (operational coordination processes). The number of participants during negotiations can influence the results of the negotiations (Kalakota and Whinston 1996; Porter 1980): the more participants that take part, the better supply and demand can be coordinated.
- Organizations make agreements about a certain good or service. This agreement could be valid once only (short term) or for a longer period of time in which the good or service is required more than once (long term) (Williamson 1985). This is captured in the fourth characteristic, the duration of agreements.

Impact of ICT on Interorganizational Coordination

It is widely believed that the use of ICT reduces costs and increases capabilities and, therefore, enables people to shape coordination (Benjamin and Wigand 1996; Bodendorf and Reinheimer 1997; Chircu and Kauffman 2000;

Kornelius and Ekering 1994; Malone and Crowston 1994; Malone and Rockart 1991; Malone et al. 1987). Here we elaborate on the impact of ICT on the four characteristics of coordination structures (Hengst and Sol 2002):

- Coordination structures will become more centralized thanks to the use of ICT. At first glance it seems to be the other way around. As a result of a reduction in coordination costs, more decentralized structures will come within reach of buyers and sellers (Bakos 1991b; Cramton 1991; Lee and Clark 1996; Malone et al. 1987). An additional result, however, is that more and more information becomes available. The more information becomes available, the more difficult it gets to find the right information. Eventually, a centralized structure is preferred in which one or more brokers can satisfy the need for information required for coordination (Bailey and Bakos 1997; Bakos 1998; Kornelius and Ekering 1994; Malone and Rockart 1991; Moore 1996).
- The use of ICT is not expected to influence the aspect of dominated versus neutral.
- The number of participants during negotiations will increase thanks to the use of ICT (Bakos 1991a). The optimal number of participants to contact is determined by trading off coordination costs for further searches for new participants against the expected benefit from identifying a better participant (Bakos and Brynjolfsson 1993). The use of ICT reduces the costs of coordination and as thus leads to more participants (Kalakota and Whinston 1996).
- The use of ICT can also influence the duration of agreements. To build a relationship with an organization requires some investments, for example in information systems to share information. If the investments are high, it is not profitable to do this over and over again. Long-term agreements are settled in which the good or service can be supplied more than once. With the ongoing developments in ICT, the investments required will become lower. This could eventually lead to agreements for a shorter period of time.

In the expectations discussed above ICT is considered to be the driving force. There are, however, other aspects that have an influence on interorganizational coordination structures (Bailey and Bakos 1997; Rosenschein and Zlotkin 1994). Summarized below are six aspects that can be considered of importance:

- The first aspect concerns homogeneity and describes the number of factors needed to distinguish goods or services from each other.

When too many factors are required, this job is left to a third party, a broker, resulting in a more centralized structure (Bodendorf and Reinheimer 1997). Malone et al. (1987) add to this that the greater the number of factors needed, the longer the relationships will last and the lower the number of participants will be.

- The aspect of specificity refers to the degree to which the relationship between a buyer and a seller will produce an asset that is dedicated to a special purpose with poor alternative uses (Williamson 1986). If the degree of specificity is low, the buyer should adopt the maximum feasible number of sellers (Bakos and Brynjolfsson 1993), or the seller should adopt the maximum feasible number of buyers. Besides the number of participants, the duration of agreements is also influenced. The more specific the investments to be made, the longer the period of agreement will be.
- Time pressure exists for all goods and services since if it does not matter when the good or service is sold, it would not matter whether they were sold at all (Cramton 1991). The degree of time pressure, however, can differ among different goods and services. Under no time pressure the possibility exists to contact a large amount of sellers or buyers, where under pressure no time might be available to do this. Time pressure also influences the duration of agreements. When time pressure is quite high, negotiating could take up too much time. Long-lasting agreements are more preferable in that case.
- Goods or services can have a high value for an organization, for example where a critical purchase is concerned. Trust in the relationship is an important factor in these situations (Levacic 1991). Sellers or buyers are inclined to only a few participants and long-lasting relationships to build a relationship of trust.
- Frequency refers to how often a good or service is required, either occasionally or recurrently (Williamson 1986). The duration of an agreement and the number of participants are influenced by the frequency. The greater the frequency, the better long-term contracts are with only a few participants, since it would become too costly if agreements must be settled each time a good or service is required.
- Uncertainty is defined as the difference between the information at hand and the information needed to make a decision (Galbraith 1977). Long-lasting relationships with only a few participants prevail in uncertain situations (Williamson 1975).

The use of ICT and the aforementioned aspects are interrelated as well. Using ICT support it becomes easier to deal with low homogeneity, high

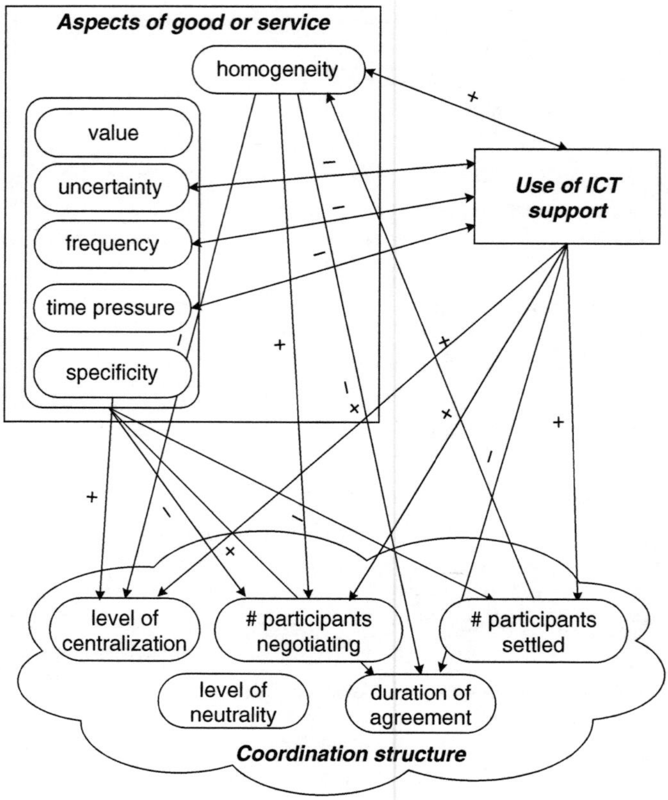

Figure 13.1 Interorganizational structures

time pressure, high frequency and high uncertainty: more information can be processed faultlessly in a shorter period of time. This indirectly increases the possibilities for more participants and shorter agreements; see also Figure 13.1.

13.3 INTERORGANIZATIONAL COORDINATION PRACTICE

Today, well over 60 per cent of the world's ocean-going general cargo is transported in containers (Muller 1995). The percentage of containerized cargo is even higher between economically strong and stable countries, approaching 100 per cent in some cases. There are around 400 ports all over the world that have the capability to handle containers. Though some of the

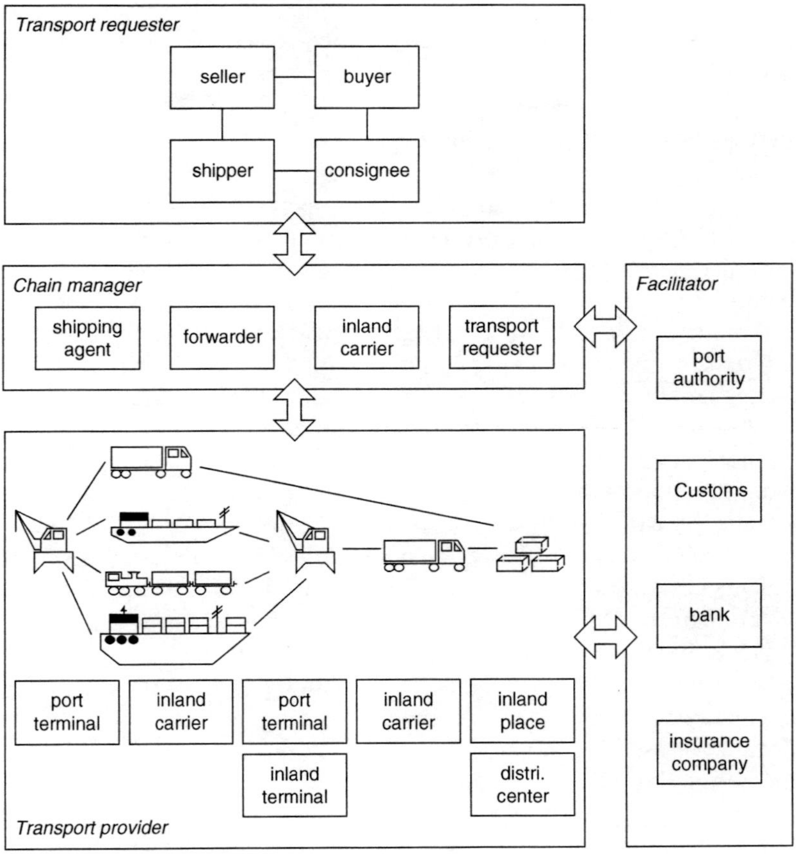

Figure 13.2 Organizations in inland container transport

containers are delivered to these ports and collected again from these ports by ocean-going vessels, the majority arrive and depart by road, rail or inland shipping. For the port of Rotterdam, for example, 85 per cent of the containerized goods have their origin or destination somewhere in Europe (GHR 1996). Inland container transport, therefore, is important. Inland container transport is the transport of containers between a port and a place in the hinterland. Many organizations are involved, with different interests, cultures and core businesses. These organizations include forwarders, rail and barge operators, trucking companies, terminal operators, Customs, and insurance companies. Figure 13.2 shows the different organizations in the possible role they can play in inland container transport. The processes of these organizations must increasingly be tuned to meet the ever-growing requirements for container transport. Interorganizational coordination is important here and it is described below by focusing on the processes and the structures.

Interorganizational Coordination Processes

The chain manager fulfils an important role in the coordination of container transport. This role can be carried out by different organizations: forwarder, shipping agent, carrier, and even by the shipper. During the operational coordination level, the chain manager, on behalf of the transport requester, takes care of the documents and formalities that are required for different activities in the container transport chain. ICT-based systems have been, and still are being introduced to improve the information exchange: less errors, faster exchange and in-time delivery.

During the strategic level, however, little ICT support is used. The chain manager supports the transport requester in selecting those transport services that have the best fit with the requirements of the requester. The chain manager must, therefore, know the possibilities and follow the latest developments in the transport network. Close contact with transport providers is a prerequisite. Information and communication are important in this. Conventional technologies such as fax and phone are used to support coordination. This limits the strategic coordination processes in several ways: information is scarcely available and mainly on paper only, the amount of information used is limited since processing this information by hand is time-consuming, the tariff is the most important factor taken into account whereas other important factors are neglected, decisions about with whom to do business are made by playing it by ear, and subjective preferences of the persons in charge dominate the choice of business partners.

It is believed that the situation described above is not adequate any more as a result of today's developments. First, it is getting more difficult to make the right selection of transport services offered, because the container transport network is getting wider and more dynamic: information about the network today is outdated tomorrow. Second, given the increasingly competitive transport market, transport requesters ask for cheaper transport and more possibilities to choose from, but still with a high level of reliability. It becomes increasingly important to process the increasing amount of information and to settle competitive agreements with the partners.

Interorganizational Coordination Structures

The coordination structures of inland container transport can be characterized using the four characteristics mentioned in the previous section.

First, the coordination structure is neither centralized nor decentralized: transport requesters can negotiate directly with transport providers and vice versa without the intervention of a broker, and transport requesters and transport providers can be represented by a broker. Second, a neutral coordination structure exists in inland container transport. Prices and rules for which and by which a container is to be transported are part of the negotiation and are not preset by one of the organizations. Third, the number of participants in inland container transport has the potential to be quite high. In practice, however, only a few organizations participate in a specific negotiation process and settle agreements. Finally, the coordination structure of inland container transport is characterized by long-term agreements between participants. Agreements are settled for a period varying from three months to a year and after this time they are almost always renewed for the next period of time.

The use of ICT to support the interorganizational processes (proposed in the next section) can influence the interorganizational coordination structures currently used. The directions of these changes are shown by describing the impact of ICT as well as the impact of the aspects mentioned in the previous section.

In inland container transport, the homogeneity of the transport service is quite low. There are many factors involved as it is not only origin and destination that influence the pricing of the transport service, but also other factors such as the type of goods, the weight of the goods, the departure and arrival times, the transport mode being used, the reliability, the administrative and physical complexity, the environmental effect and additional services. Relationships in inland container transport require hardly any relationship-specific investments in physical assets. The container is a standardized unit so no organization has to invest in equipment for the physical handling. Investments in ICT, however, are often relationship-specific. With the ongoing developments in ICT, it is expected that this specificity will vanish. Time pressure in inland container transport is often high. A transport service cannot be stored for later use, but is carried out at a specific moment. The goods that must be transported are often also under time pressure, because they must be available on time at the receiver for further processing. The value of a transport service in inland container transport depends on the type of goods that are transported. When the goods concern a critical purchase the value is high, but it could also concern goods of a low value. The frequency of transactions in inland container transport is quite high. Occasional transport of containers does happen, but only rarely. Most transport has a recurring nature. Inland container transport must deal with different types of uncertainties. One type of uncertainty is that economic trends are unknown. This makes it difficult to forecast the flow of products and goods in size and in direction, that is, to which regions products will be transported. Furthermore, it is not known in advance when a transport requester will have a container ready to be transported and how many containers the transport requester is going to transport.

To resume, the coordination structure can be described as either centralized or decentralized, neutral, with a few participants and long-term relationships. The use of ICT support is described above as having the potential to change coordination structures: more centralized, more participants and more short-term relationships. Furthermore, because of the low homogeneity, the high time pressure, the high frequency and the high level of uncertainty in the inland container transport chain, a centralized coordination structure is favoured in which transactions between buyers and sellers are negotiated indirectly through a broker. The number of participants should be kept low to avoid complexity during coordination and to build a relationship of trust. This is true both during negotiations and for settlement. There are also reasons to prefer long-term relationships to short-term ones. Using ICT support, however, it becomes easier to deal with low homogeneity, high time pressure and high frequency: more information can be processed faultlessly in a shorter period of time. This again increases the possibilities for more participants and shorter agreements.

Taking the above-mentioned notions into account, the following coordination structure can be 'prescribed'. The coordination structure of the inland container transport chain should be neutral and centralized through several chain managers, just as is the case in the current situation. The number of participants will increase compared to the current situation. However, long-term agreements are expected instead of short-term agreements, so that a relationship of mutual trust can be built in an uncertain environment.

13.4 INTERORGANIZATIONAL COORDINATION SYSTEM

An ICT-based system to support the strategic coordination processes could have added value as well as making a major impact on the inland container transport industry. A chain manager takes the leading role in strategic coordination and could be supported by the ICT-based system proposed below. Strategic coordination is carried out in three steps. First, detailed information about the inland container transport industry should be collected during the information step. An information structure is designed to support this. Next, during the preparation step, transport solutions have to be designed that are a match between transport requests of shippers and transport services offered by carriers. A model base is designed to support this. Finally, the transport solutions that result are used as input for the negotiation step. There is no support proposed for the negotiation step; because of the importance of trust, personal communication is preferred over ICT-supported communication.

Information Structure

Information must be collected about the inland container transport industry. The great challenge in this is to find a good structure for storing information about different elements of the container transport system: trains follow a time schedule, trucks can drive at any moment in time, tariffs depend on the type and weight of the container and the weight of the good, tariffs for transshipment depend on the time of day, and so on. The information structure is presented in Figure 13.3 and stores information on three main elements: transport providers, transport requesters and competitors.

First, information about transport providers is stored. Two types of providers are of importance: carriers and terminal operators. A terminal operator operates at one or more terminals. Two services are carried out at a terminal: transshipment and storage. The storage of a container costs a certain amount of money. The transshipment of a container also costs a certain amount of money, but this amount depends on the transport mode and on the time transshipment takes place. The carrier is the other type of transport provider, which operates a transport service on a connection between two terminals. A connection has a certain distance, which can be crossed using a specific transport mode. A transport mode causes some

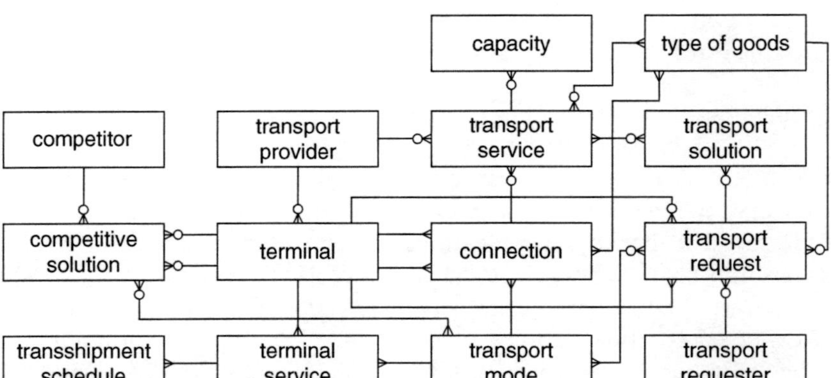

Figure 13.3 Information structure

environmental costs when used, for example air pollution. A list of the types of goods that are allowed on this connection is added to the information structure. The transport of highly explosive goods, for example, is prohibited on certain connections. Furthermore, a connection has a start time and an end time. The reason for this is that transport may not take place at every time of the day or week, for example during nights or weekends it might be prohibited. A transport service starts at a certain moment in time, has a certain frequency such as daily or weekly, and takes a certain time to complete. In case of a truck service, which does not follow a schedule, start time is not relevant, but information about the duration time is relevant. Furthermore, the transport of a container costs a certain amount of money. Finally, a list of the types of goods that are allowed to be transported with this transport service is added to the information structure: for the transport of some types of goods, a qualification is required and not every transport provider has the right qualifications.

The second element concerns transport requesters. A transport requester can have one or more transport requests. A transport request contains information about the number of containers which the transport requester wishes to transport, the type of goods in the containers, the origin and destinations of the containers, the total transport time allowed, and the preferred transport modes. Furthermore, a request comes with certain criteria that must be met, for example concerning costs, transport time, physical and administrative complexity, environmental effect, reliability, safety, after-sales service and quality.

The third element is about competitors. Competitors are other chain managers offering services to transport requesters. They provide transport solutions between two terminals. A competitive solution has a certain tariff, starts at a certain moment in time, takes a certain time to complete, uses one or more transport modes, and has possibly extra services that come with the transport solution.

Model Base

The model base mainly consists of an algorithm to find a transport solution that matches a transport request. Several criteria are being used to indicate the degree in which the transport solution meets the requirements of the transport request. The number of criteria taken into account should not be restricted: the more criteria there are under consideration, the more a better comparison between alternatives is enabled and the more the outcome of the negotiation is improved (Roloff and Jordan 1992; Schermer 1997). Some criteria are transport-related: costs, time, environmental effect, physical complexity, administrative complexity and extra service. Other criteria are participant-related: quality, reliability, personal relationship and after-sales service. The algorithm should meet several requirements:

- Multiple transport modes. Inland container transport is characterized by intermodality, meaning that more than one transport mode can be used for the transport of containers. The algorithm must work with trains, trucks, barges and coastal vessels.
- Multiple time aspects. The algorithm should deal simultaneously with three different time aspects. The first aspect is the transit time of transport services without taking scheduling into account. Trucks that can travel at any time are an example of this. The second time aspect takes into account time schedules according to which a transport service is carried out, for example in the case of trains. The third time aspect concerns time windows in which no transport is allowed, for example a driving ban during weekends for trucks, or tides in the case of coastal vessels.
- Multiple criteria. It is important to take into account multiple criteria for the design of a transport solution.

Several algorithms exist for similar problems (Buis 1996; Dijkstra 1959; Floyd 1962; Tulp 1991). Unfortunately, most algorithms lack some aspects required for use in inland container transport. Buis's algorithm meets the requirements best and is used as a starting point for the algorithm. The requirement for using multiple criteria is not met by his algorithm and this needs to be adapted in the algorithm. The algorithm is based on the shortest path algorithm described in Dijkstra (1959) and elaborated in Buis (1996). Dijkstra's algorithm is often considered to be the best algorithm to search a finite, directed graph whose links have non-negative lengths. For a detailed description of the algorithm see Hengst (2002).

Prototype

The information structure and the algorithm are translated into a prototype to show the possibilities of ICT support to strategic coordination processes.

When looking at the entry screen (Figure 13.4) several elements in the user interface can be detected. The transport request is elaborated into great detail. Besides asking for the origin and destination as well as the preferred transport modes, elements like the type of container, type of goods and time preferences can be entered (on the left side of the screen). On the right side of the screen, the criteria for the transport request can be set to a value. For the criteria tariff, for example, a limit is asked for as well as a

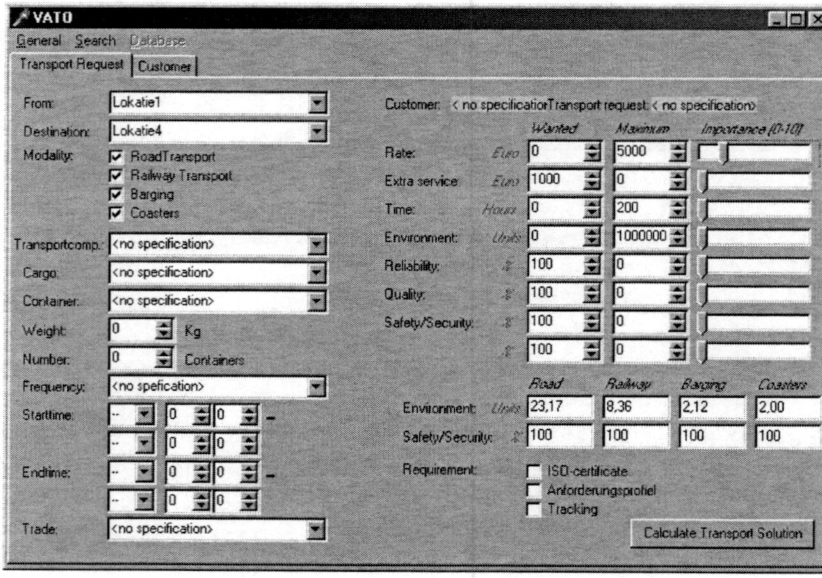

Figure 13.4 Entry screen for transport request

desired value. After defining the transport request, the best transport solution is shown to the user. The scores of the transport solution on the different criteria are presented. Besides this global level, a more detailed level of the transport solution in which more information is presented can also be shown. If the best solution shown is not chosen, one can search for the next-best solution.

13.5 DISCUSSION AND CONCLUSIONS

ICT offers great opportunities for changing and supporting interorganizational coordination. This chapter has given insight into interorganizational coordination and the theoretical impact of ICT and has also provided a design for an ICT-based system to support interorganizational coordination at a strategic level. The prototype and theory were used in four steps for evaluation.

First, the framework of Figure 13.4 was filled to see whether the elements of the framework correspond with practice and are sufficient for the purpose of the framework. Almost 75 people were consulted from 45 different organizations in inland container transport. Although practitioners understood the elements and used them properly, it was difficult to come

Table 13.1 Entry screen for transport request

Proposition	Completely agree	Agree	Disagree	Completely disagree	No opinion
The number of transport providers with which a relationship exists will increase (operational).	2	6	1		
Negotiations will be carried out with a wider range of transport providers than at present (strategic).	4	3	2		
There will be fewer long-term relationships compared with the current multiyear relationships.	–	1	8		
Information and communication technology is going to play an increasingly important role in interorganizational coordination.	2	6	1		

up with one 'value' for most of the elements. This was usually caused by exceptional situations. Nonetheless, the elements could be filled and appeared to be sufficient for an overview of interorganizational structures and the related aspects.

Second, the suggested interorganizational coordination structure was presented to nine experts for evaluation, five from the container practice and four from the consulting practice. After a thorough presentation on the research, the framework and the suggestions, the experts were asked to react to a number of propositions. The propositions and their responses are presented in Table 13.1. The responses are in line with the suggestions derived from the framework.

Besides their opinions on the elements presented above, the experts were asked to translate the situation sketched by the framework and the prototype into practice. They all believed that a situation like this would arise in inland container transport. They also thought, however, that it would take quite a while, perhaps a decade or more, to evolve. Implementing the system described in this chapter is just one step towards improving interorganizational coordination. Interorganizational processes and structures must change accordingly to gain maximum advantage of the usage of ICT. Coordination structures cannot be prescribed, but have to evolve over time, and investments in ICT in the inland container transport industry might take some time.

Third, a simulation model was developed to measure the performance in interorganizational coordination, making use of the ICT-based system proposed. The simulation model focused on matching supply and demand. Supply was modelled with more than 7500 transport services offered by transport providers, demand with slightly more than 10 000 transport requests from shippers. The simulation model was used twice: once according to the current situation and once according to the system designed. The results show that transport requests and transport services can be matched significantly better in the suggested interorganizational coordination system than in the current interorganizational coordination system. For a more detailed analysis of the performance, the reader is referred to Hengst (1999).

The fourth step of the evaluation concerned a real-life implementation of the ICT-based system. It showed that filling the database with the right information is a time-consuming activity. This is because most of the information is available only on paper at this moment, and because some information elements are not known in the current situation and must be collected explicitly. Although this activity is considered time-consuming, it is expected that most of this information will be made available in an electronic format in time. The use of Internet and software agents can then take over a great part of the work now done by human beings.

REFERENCES

Alexander, E.R. (1993), 'Interorganizational coordination: theory and practice', *Journal of Planning Literature*, **7** (4), pp. 328–43.

Bailey, J.P. and J.Y. Bakos (1997), 'An exploratory study of the emerging role of electronic intermediaries', *International Journal of Electronic Commerce*, **1** (3), pp. 7–20.

Bakos, J.Y. (1991a), 'Information links and electronic marketplaces: the role of interorganizational information systems in vertical markets', *Journal of Management Information Systems*, **8** (2), pp. 31–52.

Bakos, J.Y. (1991b), 'A strategic analysis of electronic marketplaces', *MIS Quarterly*, **15** (3), pp. 294–310.

Bakos, J.Y. (1998), 'The emerging role of electronic marketplaces on the internet', *Communications of the ACM*, **41** (18), pp. 35–42.

Bakos, J.Y. and E. Brynjolfsson (1993), 'Information technology, incentives, and the optimal number of suppliers', *Journal of Management Information Systems*, **10** (2), pp. 37–53.

Benjamin, R.I. and R. Wigand (1996), 'Electronic markets and the virtual value chain on the information super highway', *Sloan Management Review*, **36** (1), pp. 29–40.

Bodendorf, F. and S. Reinheimer (1997), 'Offer evaluation in an electronic air cargo market', *Proceedings of the Fifth European Conference on Information Systems (ECIS'97)*, Cork: Cork Publishing Ltd.

14.2 ACTIONS ALREADY TAKEN FOR INTERMODAL TRANSPORT DEVELOPMENT

The major focus of initial EU efforts was on the development of free competition and interoperability of transport systems, including the promotion of necessary infrastructure and consistency in Member States' laws. In addition, the EU identified priority investment projects that would best enhance the connectivity and interoperability of the European transport system. The EU has developed a Common Transport Policy that places emphasis on sustainable mobility. Currently, however, there is considerable debate on how to link transport goals with sustainability and related to that, energy goals.

In the transalpine areas, as well as in Great Britain or Scandinavia, where the haulage industry is highly fragmented, intermodal transport becomes a tool for opening the international trade to small-sized firms by the implementation of large logistics centres (interports, freight villages or Euroterminals), which offer the small and medium-sized enterprises (SMEs) accessibility to foreign markets.

Market pressures are triggering service rationalization strategies aimed at increasing economies of scale: Given the capital-intensive nature of many freight operations, and the fact that possible savings could occur only when costly infrastructure is shared by many, there were cases where large-scale investments were made to develop facilities that consolidate operations. By developing what might be called 'hub' operations, the per-unit cost of transport is lowered. A number of indicative examples related to intermodal centres (inland and maritime) and service providers are presented below (US Department of Transportation 2002).

Quadrante Europa/Verona Freight Village. This freight village covers a surface area of more than 2.5 million square metres, making it one of the largest European freight villages, operated by one entity. It is ideally located at the intersection of the key motorways and rail lines in the northern part of Italy. Hence it serves mainly international intermodal traffic (approximately 10 per cent of the country's total, of which 80 per cent is international). Most traffic is transported to Northern Europe, especially to Germany (and in particular to Munich) mainly through the Brenner Pass. Apart from intermodal transshipment it offers a range of services including custom procedures for non-EU cargo, logistic services, warehousing and ancillary services for all stakeholders of the supply chain, that is, shippers, freight forwarders and operators.

Kombiverkehr. Kombiverkehr was established in 1969 in Germany and it is one of the largest providers of overland intermodal services in the world. It provides 'one-stop-shop' services for intermodal freight transport, at the lowest possible costs. The services offered to customers are mainly block train services to German ports and to the EU (28 block trains daily serving approximately 60 terminals in European cities) and rolling highway services throughout the EU. The German government has promoted the widest possible participation of private capital in the company, and hence more than 250 European transport companies and freight forwarders are shareholders. To expand further the vertical provision of intermodal services, Kombiverkehr is a partner of two German ports, and thus it increases its handling capacity for intermodal freight.

Port of Gioia Tauro, Medcenter Container Terminal. The Port of Gioia Tauro in south-west Italy in the region of Calabria started its operation in 1995. It has become the key freight transshipment node in a network of more than 50 ports within the wider area of the Mediterranean and Adriatic Sea, as well as the Black Sea. Approximately 95 per cent of the total freight handled at the port is for transshipment. Transporting a shipment from South-East Asia to Rotterdam or Hamburg by sea would require 20 days or 22 days, respectively. However, shipping the containers to Gioia Tauro and employing its intermodal services via northern Italy and Switzerland would reduce the total transportation time to 14 days. Its services in 2006 include two trains departing weekly to Milan from Gioia Tauro, and nine weekly departures from Milan to Rotterdam. Hence, expansion of such services is imminent, associated with the development of a free trade zone in the port area.

Hupac/Trans Alps Service. The fact that Switzerland is not a member of the EU, and is located among the Alps, which form a natural barrier to the transport of goods along the north–south European axis, renders its national transport policies crucial for European north–south traffic. In any case, additional capacity at this particular location is needed. Until 2000, Switzerland had a weight limit of 28 metric tonnes for trucks in transit, while the corresponding limit in Europe was 40 metric tonnes. Moreover, two-thirds of freight through Switzerland was transported by rail, whereas the same percentage of freight through the French and Austrian Alps was transported by road. Following continuous pressure from the EU member states, the truck weight limit in Switzerland was raised to match that of the rest of Europe. Nevertheless, the Swiss government doubled the road tax fee (from €90 per truck to €200 per truck) in order to account for the additional road damage. Despite this road charge increase, the transport cost for German–Italian road freight was still lower through Switzerland, and thus attracted high demand, resulting in significant congestion at the Swiss borders and in some road tunnels, following strict safety measures to avoid road accidents. Therefore, the option of intermodal services became very attractive. The Hupac Group, an intermodal transport provider with a fleet of 2300 rail cars and locomotives and an operator of terminals, provides a range of intermodal transport services, including that of a rolling highway service that transports trucks across the Alps with a €300 per truck subsidy from the Swiss government. Hupac services transport approximately 40 per cent intermodal containers. The revenues from the road tax will partially finance the construction of a new rail tunnel in the Alps and further improvements to the railway system. The EU has agreed to contribute financially to such investments. When the new rail connection is operational, it will facilitate a direct rail service from Milan to Frankfurt.

Flughafen/Cargo City, Frankfurt, Germany. Frankfurt Airport ranks as the busiest cargo airport in Europe. It is ranked ninth worldwide. It is also advertised to be the primal nodal centre in the world combining all transport modes (air–road–rail–inland waterways). Needless to say, it provides direct links to the German motorway (autobahn) network, access to inland ports along the Rhine, and air links to more international destinations than any other airport in Europe. The German government owns 71 per cent of its management operator, named Fraport, whilst the rest belongs to private investors and airport employees. Fraphort manages all leasing and investment operations of Cargo City, which was established in 1996 as the airport's main freight transshipment centre offering handling and transshipment services.

In addition, the European Commission is promoting the Framework 'Freight Transport Logistics in Europe – the key to sustainable mobility' (COM(2006) 336 final), with measures like simplification of multimodal chains and co-modality, with the aim of securing sustainable transport.

14.3 BARRIERS AND STRATEGIES FOR INTERMODAL TRANSPORT DEVELOPMENT IN EUROPE

Historically, national transport systems were designed in part for national defence purposes, thus the physical design (for example the rail track gauge) and operations strategies (for example the ability to use locomotives across national boundaries) have often been incompatible. There are 37 different combinations of rail gauge, tunnel clearance and power systems in Europe. This legacy has left a significant challenge to modern Europe to provide a compatible transport network that is interoperable. Similarly, the historical development of individual national transport systems has resulted in a variable level of transport infrastructure development.

Distances beyond 400 km are presently regarded as the minimum for intermodal transport to remain competitive – though there are exceptions.

The two major exceptions to this rule are short transalpine links for complete trucks, namely Rollende Landstrasse, and the special case of container transport between the seaports of Rotterdam and Antwerp. The challenge of European intermodal transport is to compete on the medium transport distances below 500 km, where freight volumes are considerably higher than those in long-distance links.

Small-size intermodal shipments are now largely transported by truck. If they could be integrated into the intermodal system, intermodal transport would increase its transport volume share. Researchers (Trip and Bontekoning. 2002) have explored the possibility of implementing innovative bundling models and new-generation terminals as a means to integrate small-size shipments, mainly from outside the economic core areas, into the intermodal system. It has been found that it is possible to apply the concept of complex bundling with new-generation terminal operations, at least in theory. The general advantages of such theoretical concepts can be shown in that a higher loading degree of transport means higher frequency of services or a larger geographical coverage of the network.

In the context of research regarding intermodal transport, there have also been proposed strategies for European innovation policy in intermodal transport (Van Klink and Van den Berg 1998; van Zuylen and Weber 2002). It has been concluded that there are a multitude of factors fostering innovation in freight intermodality technology, for example the transport of empty containers (Choong et al. 2002); the development of integrated centres for the transshipment, storage, collection and distribution of goods with the aim to offer high-quality intermodal services (Konings 1996); and the provision of integrated transport service with the use of intermodal transport (D'Este 1996). A set of interdependent actions is proposed, composed of regulatory changes, pilot actions and demonstrations, research and development (R&D) (especially in new rail systems), new terminals and perhaps stimuli for the creation of intermodal service providers, that is, of organizations that have an intrinsic interest in intermodal solutions.

It has also been suggested that seaports are in an excellent position to stimulate intermodal transport, given the scale advantages they can generate in inland transport. In practice, it has been found (Van Klink and Van den Berg 1998) that the supply of intermodal services can enable seaports to create new hinterland connections and extend their hinterland potential.

Successful integration of the operators in complex intermodal transport chains needs to be supported firstly by adequate, harmonized European regulations. Hence, it is imperative that the harmonization of the legal and technical framework for international intermodal transports is implemented. Lack of European harmonization in infrastructure characteristics; in charging systems for use of infrastructure to cover its costs, regardless of transport mode; in operations rules; in regulations and standards and their implementation; appears as a major obstacle to full interoperability in international intermodal transport.

Technical specifications for transport means are often regulated differently by country and by mode, which also raises questions on integration. In addition, individual operators have a tendency to acquire the rolling stock that suit their operations and choice of loading units. Handling the variety of vehicle types for different operators is a source of congestion at terminals, which in turn causes inefficiency.

In order to eliminate such problems in intermodal transport, three types of integration may be introduced:

- Spatial integration: considered as a way to create cohesion between European regions. Although most European regions have access to a terminal, it cannot be advocated that a Continent-wide cohesion exists. On the one hand, there are regions generating high traffic density for which intermodal transport can be very efficient and already contributes to the opening-up and the unblocking of areas. However, it is pointed out that the accessibility of the remote regions by intermodal transport is not fully convincing. For these regions there is a need to promote intermodal transport as part of a policy of regional development and, in a transitional phase, a need for the implementation of gateways.
- Professional integration: aims at making use of the customers' knowledge and requirements and elaborating the ways to get the transport actors involved, interested and informed about intermodal transport.
- Technological integration: stresses that if a technological innovation is a way to increase the quality of a particular function, it is also clear that technology alone cannot be the solution to a global problem. This type of integration, therefore, involves a method of implementation that creates the required synergies between technological innovations and the operating systems they are applied to.

The EU research project 'IQ' has identified and proposed several development policies for intermodal transport (IQ 2000):

1. Sustainability. This aims at promoting the development of intermodal transport to achieve more sustainable mobility patterns and environmental improvements.
2. Pricing policy. According to this, intermodal transport will be developed through cost-efficiency improvement of transport, reduction of external costs and improvement of quality.

3. Integration. The aim is to improve the interoperability and functioning of transport modes by the efficient operation of transport interchanges, access to and from interchanges, and supporting telematics information systems.
4. Competition. The aim is to improve the competitive position of intermodal freight transport through improved organization, technique and control of transfer on medium distances.

The above policies need to be applied. In this context, in the same research project, three scenarios regarding the development of intermodal transport in Europe were elaborated and they are presented here as possible development strategies for the implementation of the development policies:

1. Open corridors. This strategy refers to the development of intermodal transport in limited but important flows over specific transport corridors. These are flows on hinterland links of major seaports and services provided to a restricted number of large shippers for inter-plant transport. The crossing of natural barriers will potentially increase demand and, therefore, transalpine corridors are considered as a possible part of the limited 'network'.
2. Highly efficient core network. Intermodal transport is developed along major national and international corridors. The quality of rail services should be significantly improved and the relevant costs decreased, in order for rail transport to be able to compete with road transport, which is also constantly improving its performance. Innovative solutions for flow concentration are required, such as gateways and hubs, supported by better performances of railways.
3. European-wide network. Under this scenario, intermodal services are offered to European regions, under attractive commercial conditions. Intermodal transport becomes a European-wide alternative mode to road transport. For this to be successful, it needs strong public involvement in terms of infrastructure investment and continuous support.

The EU research project PROMOTIQ provided guidelines for promoting intermodal transport (PROMOTIQ 2000). The elements presented in Table 14.1 are recognized as the most important ones for the promotion of intermodal transport. The proposed actions to lift barriers refer to actions for the alleviation of the respective barrier by any actor, public or administrative body, and so on.

The findings of the two projects mentioned above are combined to produce a coherent action plan for the development of intermodal transport, as presented in the following.

Table 14.1 Elements and actions for intermodal transport development

No	Crucial elements for intermodal growth	Barrier	Action to lift barrier	Supplementary actions by policy makers	Expected results
1	Pricing of intermodal services	Freight pricing system is not harmonized across member states, especially for rail/terminal/port operations	Create harmonized pricing system for freight transport in EU	Promote the new pricing system as a fair and transparent one among potential users	Fair and efficient pricing system. New operators will enter the market
2	Insurance/liability	Different principles govern different modes in the intermodal transport chains	Establish harmonized procedures/principles for insurance/liability across different modes	Enforce the use of new harmonized procedures	Current and potential customers of intermodal will be feeling much more confident on procedures (will be known everywhere) and will also save time and costs
3	Labour hours and practices at intermodal terminals	Different labour practices are followed in terminal operations across member states	Harmonization of pan-European labour hours and practices at terminals	Decide upon standards of terminal operations and enforce new practices Promote the harmonized labour system in terminal	Knowledge of standard operating hours and easier calculation of costs across EU for operators

Table 14.1 (continued)

No	Crucial elements for intermodal growth	Barrier	Action to lift barrier	Supplementary actions by policy makers	Expected results
				operations to potential users	
4	Operating costs	Diesel fuel tax different in different EU countries	Harmonization of diesel fuel tax between member states	Set a minimum reasonable fuel taxation in all member states	Reduction of total transport costs
5		High costs for intermodal operations	Tax exemption for those road vehicles used in intermodal transport operations	Enforce tax exemption in all member states	
6	Employment costs	High total operating costs due to high employment costs	Reduce employment costs by applying more automated systems	Promotion (among operators) of ways to reduce employment costs. Organize related seminars	Reduction of employment costs and therefore attraction of new operators
7	National monopolies	Small-sized new entrants do not have opportunities due to national monopolies	Monopolies should be restricted by the legal framework and monitored by a pan-European regulator	Promote the benefits of becoming an intermodal operator	New (small) operators will be created
8	Human resources in intermodal operations	Personnel are not trained for intermodal terminal operations	Offer training for intermodal jobs (mainly at terminals)	Organize training activities	Availability of personnel trained in intermodal operations

		Small operators/new entrants cannot meet the cost for training their employees for intermodal operations	Provide funds to small operators/new entrants to train their staff (technically and operationally)	Promote staff training and funding opportunities to potential operators	Trained personnel available, especially for small/new operators in order to enter niche/specialized markets
9	Terminal location	The terminal location is not always financially and operationally viable	Identify the optimum relationship between viable intermodal traction provision, terminal density and network	Promote the strategic location of terminals to potential operators Offer training to terminal operators on choosing the right terminal location	Optimization of operations Reduction of time and cost
10		Transshipment systems used are not the same in every terminal/transfer point	Use integrated systems for transshipment systems	Communicate the use of common transshipment systems to operators. Enforce the use of integrated systems	Operators will not have to choose transshipment points by the handling systems available criterion. Therefore optimization of cost can be achieved
11	Transshipment systems	Intermodal terminals are not well placed in relation to the shippers' premises location	Create terminals within industrial zones (and not only within distribution centres)	Organize seminars and encourage shippers to create intermodal terminals within the industrial zones they are operating by explaining the benefits of intermodal transport	Short-distance intermodal growth

Table 14.1 (continued)

No	Crucial elements for intermodal growth	Barrier	Action to lift barrier	Supplementary actions by policy makers	Expected results
12	Real-time information	Real-time information systems used are not always reliable and adequate	Apply efficient real-time information systems	Promote the use of a reliable real-time information system and advertise it to potential customers	Real time information will be provided to customers, especially in the case of irregularities, therefore optimization of operations will be achieved
13	Integrated services	Different services are offered to operators in different locations	Create 'one-stop shops' for the entire intermodal chain	Advertise 'one-stop shops' (and their advantages) to potential customers	Reduced operational time and cost, optimization of operations
14	Terminal opening hours	Terminal opening hours are not always suitable for operators	Wider terminal time windows for pickup and delivery of loading units	Advertise the new opening hours of terminals	Optimization of operations. Attraction of new customers.
15	Terminal operations	Terminal operation and management is not always effective under the control of the government and the operational costs are also high	Partnership between public and private sector in the terminal development, management and maintenance.	Advertise the benefits to private companies in owning and/or managing intermodal terminals	Optimization of terminal development and management

16	Rail gauges	Different rail gauges between terminals and network, or between neighbouring countries	Construct new/improved infrastructure to homogenize rail gauges across member states	Enforce member states to change rail gauges	Faster services and lower operational costs
17	Intermodal loading units handling systems	Appropriate handling systems are not available at every transfer point	Equip terminals with new handling systems	Subsidize terminal operators. Promote the use of all transfer points by advertising to potential customers the new/improved handling systems	Optimization of transfer point use
18	Information systems and the use of EDI for information exchange	Efficient information systems are not used in all cases	Apply modern information systems and use EDI systems widely	Advertise the existence of modern information technology	Higher-quality services
19	Transit time	Transit time is sometimes high	Offer competitive transit time to allow high frequencies of services	Advertise the high frequency of services	Higher-quality services
20	Interoperability	Lack of interconnection and interoperability of networks and equipment	Introduce uniform networks and handling equipment	Communicate information on modernization and/or investments for rail infrastructure to rail	Compatibility between the European standards enabling the free movement of the freight trains

Table 14.1 (continued)

No	Crucial elements for intermodal growth	Barrier	Action to lift barrier	Supplementary actions by policy makers	Expected results
				traction providers, intermodal transport operators and customers (industries, integrators)	(without border stops) and facility of introduction of new entrants
				Plans for investment have to be communicated in order for operators to establish their commercial plan	Progressive homogenization of the European standards (at technical and operational level)
				Encourage management cooperation between transport companies to enhance the free movement of transport modes at a European level	Train waiting time at border crossings little or none
				The new control rules have to be communicated to the railway operators, the rail infrastructure managers and the intermodal operators.	

21	Frequency of services	Lack of flexibility of transport services with regard to the scheduling and the frequency of services	Introduction of a freight dedicated network or a freight priority network or freight priority windows	Improvement of intermodal services (transit times, frequencies) and easier slot connections	Introduction of the freight-dedicated or priority network or windows within the dense areas, combine conventional and intermodal freight trains to ensure the profitability of the system
22	Current management practices at terminals	Time-consuming operations	Promotion of new management methods at terminal interfaces	Inform (through seminars) terminal operators on new management methods at the terminals and in the networks	Develop a generic tool adaptable to the specific requirements of each actor and establish links between actors
23	Operations at terminals	Lack of flexibility regarding the cut-off time of the services	Increase of the terminal opening hours and days	Enforce terminal operators to follow the new rules of opening days and hours.	Improvement of flexibility with regard to the cut-off time and pickups of boxes
24	Specialized markets	Intermodal rail operators are not confident to enter the small and specialized markets	Identify specialized niche markets	Encourage small operators to enter the niche markets by subsiding them	New market opportunities and intermodal growth opportunities

Table 14.1 (continued)

No	Crucial elements for intermodal growth	Barrier	Action to lift barrier	Supplementary actions by policy makers	Expected results
25	Dimensions of loading units and vehicles	Frontal loading of the pallets impossible in the containers	Redefinition of the container standards	Enforce the use of standards	Intermodal transport units and containers adapted to the traffic (groupage and air connection)
26		Rail container standards different from air container standards		Advertise the use of new loading units to current and potential customers and promote their advantages	

Some of the actions presented above have already been considered by the European Commission, and others are planned in the near future. With Decision No 884/2004/EC, the Decision No 1692/96/EC on Community guidelines for the development of the trans-European transport network is amended. It focuses on measures to create a rail network giving priority to freight, as well as the introduction of the Motorways of the Sea. Also, rail links to ports are recognized as the means to make the most of the complementarity between rail, sea and inland waterway transport.

Much progress has been made through Directives 2001/12 (on access to railway infrastructure), 2001/13 (on licences to railway operators) and 2001/14 on railway capacity. On the lack of interoperability, progress has been made on high-speed services. Now the European Commission intends to do the same on the rest of the network, particularly for freight services. On the high-speed network, under Directive 96/48 related to interoperability harmonization, experts are working on adoption of Technical Specifications for Interoperability (TSIs). For the rest of the network, similar work has started under Directive 2001/16 for conventional rail interoperability. Recently, both Directives have been amended by Directive 2004/50/EC on the interoperability of the trans-European high-speed rail system and Directive 2001/16/EC on the interoperability of the trans-European conventional rail system. There is also Directive 2004/51/EC of the European Parliament and of the Council of 29 April 2004 amending Council Directive 91/440/EEC on the development of the Community's railways, which provides for opening the rail market.

14.4 NEW AREAS FOR INTERMODAL TRANSPORT DEVELOPMENT

Introduction

Areas (markets) for which potential exists to develop intermodal transport have been identified (PROMOTIQ 2000). These areas provide opportunities for intermodal transport to grow and at the same time raise its share in the freight transport market. These are presented in the following. Five new areas where the development of intermodal transport could be successful are identified.

The Role of Railways as Traction Providers

Rail traction plays the most important role in intermodal transport chains, since rail is the most commonly used mode in intermodal operations.

There are still many barriers affecting rail operations, but the European Commission has already taken legislative action for their alleviation. However, there are still actions to be taken. Harmonization is a very crucial element in optimizing intermodal rail operations and affects all aspects of these operations. The most important step towards the promotion of rail in freight transport in Europe is the commitment from the Commission to create the Rail Freight Freeways (RFF), and the opening of the market (Directives 2001/12, 2001/13, 2001/14).

There is a strong potential for intermodal transport if the railway companies across the EU form alliances and collaborate on a pan-European level. They will then be able to achieve economies of scale and also offer better quality services to their customers across Europe. There is also a new role to be played by the specialized railways which offer services to small and niche markets, and this applies especially to short-distance rail services.

Another important issue is that of the train paths. Train paths (slots) can be allocated in a number of ways. It would be preferable to establish a dynamic process, which makes every company concerned aware that any given path entails a certain cost. So far the infrastructure provider is in a monopoly position. It is important to introduce an ad hoc structure for this purpose. It would be contrary to the trend of liberalization to provide the traditional railway operator with preferential rights. Significant steps have been taken by the European Commission since 1991, but the fully open market in railways has only been effective since January 2006, following the provisions of Directive 2004/51/EC of the European Parliament and of the Council of 29 April 2004 amending Council Directive 91/440/EEC on the development of the Community's railways.

Short-Distance (< 300 km) Intermodal Services

The main critical elements for creating obstacles to the development of short-distance intermodal transport in Europe are the unfavourable traction rates compared to the long-distance services, the inappropriate infrastructure for intermodal services at terminals (mainly this applies to the rail gauge and the inland waterways facilities at maritime ports) and also the access to infrastructure for short-distance services.

The only action that is feasible to be realized in a short time period and with a comparatively low cost is the adjustment of the freight train rates according to the distances they are operating. Responsible for taking this action are mainly the national governments and the European Commission in coordination with the national authorities. The same policy makers should monitor and control the application of the action in the long term with the help of a pan-European regulator.

The actions to lift the barriers that exist in this domain should first be focused in Northern and Central Europe, where dense freight flows exist and there is more potential for short-distance intermodal services to be created and be profitable as well. In areas where heavy freight traffic flows exist, the alternative of short-distance intermodal services has the advantage of avoiding road congestion and this should be communicated to potential customers as a marketing tool. Pilot projects should be carefully designed and selected and R&D activities would assist towards that direction.

Intermodal Services for Small Shipments

Small shipments markets are related to groupage and express transport services. Intermodal transport services and actors exist in these market segments and, in particular, for the groupage activity. The development of new services and actors is limited by technical, operational, commercial, social and regulatory barriers. The groupage and express services are important for the development of intermodal transport in a market dominated by road transport, whereas their share, when compared to other types of freight transport, will be intensified by the development of e-commerce.

In order to develop intermodal transport in the small shipments market segment, consensus has to be found between the policy makers, in order to introduce fair competition conditions in the market. At the same time, the intermodal and railways operators have to develop pan-European cooperation to promote rail networks and provide high-quality services to integrators.

Intermodal transport could be developed in this market by:

- using rail intermodal services for groupage and express parcels to provide transport services at national, European and international levels;
- using high-speed freight or freight–passenger trains, to provide express transport at short distances (between 150 and 300 km).

In order to be efficient and due to the weight–volume ratio of the parcels, intermodal transport has to consolidate the flows and hence, there is a possibility for developing services within dense areas, where logistics and industrial zones are well implemented. The small shipments segment is characterized by high-value goods, which is one of the target market segments of intermodal transport. On a pan-European scale there are barriers that do not permit interoperability in the small shipment sector, for example remaining postal monopolies; border crossing, especially for intra-European transports in transit through Switzerland; time schedules in intermodal transports and remaining customs regulations within Europe.

Integration of Air Transport into the Intermodal Transport Chains

If intermodal services are to attract the air cargo market they must respond to the same customer needs that air cargo does, and if possible enhance the attributes of a door-to-door service integrating both rail and air transport legs. Airfreight's major advantage is that of speed of the air leg. Users are prepared to pay a premium cost for the benefits of lower overall door-to-door times.

The integration of air transport within the intermodal chain covers two essential points of the transport policy:

- the enhancement of environment-friendly transport means and reduction of the road congestion in the main corridors, hence an improvement of the citizens' lifestyle and mobility;
- the improvement of the physical and commercial accessibility of the remote regions to European and outbound trade markets for SMEs.

The air–rail cargo services combination is not widely used at present for serving airports and inland European destinations. The strong market position of road transport for the pre- and end-haulage has until now been difficult to displace by intermodal operations. The introduction of rail pre- and end-haulage can be envisaged for specific transport markets, geographical areas, transport actors and commodity types. Freight transport by road adequately fulfils the requirements of a surface transport system and, therefore, constitutes the dominant means of transport that is coordinated with airfreight transport.

The planning of the proposed measures to ensure the integration of air transport within the intermodal chain is related to two types of actors:

- The institutional bodies (European Commission and member states), which have produced a report with recommendations on the ways to develop combined use of rail, in particular high speed services and air. The European Commission has established the Rail Air Intermodality Facilitation Forum, which has produced a report with recommendations on ways to develop combined use of rail, in particular high speed services and air.
- The operational actors (airlines, rail traction providers, rail infrastructure managers, intermodal operators and users as the integrators), who are in a better position to define the needs and to apply,

within a cooperation process with the institutional bodies, the measures to improve the competitiveness and the performances of the intermodal transport.

New Trends in Short-Sea Shipping Services

Short-sea shipping (SSS) should be promoted as an environment-friendly and safe alternative mode of transport, particularly to the congested road or rail one. There is a certain need for integrating short-sea shipping in the intermodal transport chain and, therefore, offering door-to-door services. The main actions to be taken refer to the connectivity of ports with intermodal chains, the interoperability with other modes participating in the chains, the standardization of loading units, the use of modern and efficient information technology in SSS operations, the port infrastructure which is sometimes not adequate or non-existent for intermodal operations, the procedures at ports, and finally, the use of new technology at ships for more efficient operations on the sea leg.

Two very important elements for the promotion of short-sea shipping are the change of its image and the creation of dedicated infrastructure for short-sea shipping operations in ports. Hence, SSS should be considered as a fast and reliable transport mode, which is competitive to road in terms of quality of intermodal services.

Regulatory measures should also be taken, which will:

- Prevent distortion of competition between ports.
- Simplify existing customs procedures and other related administrative formalities which arise at ports.
- Encourage the use of information technology for the best development of short-sea shipping.
- Make EDI more widely available, particularly in the smaller ports used by SSS.

14.5 PRIORITY ACTIONS AND ACTION PLAN MODEL

Introduction

Given the analysis of the actions needed to be taken in order to promote intermodal transport in Europe, as presented previously, the present section deals with the main policy recommendations to the policy makers for implementation. Thus, guidelines for the creation of new intermodal services and operators are included in the Policy Action Plan, which is analysed below. The proposed actions are prioritized in relation to the time-frame of their implementation. Possible conflicts between the proposed actions are also presented.

Priority Actions

Several key priority actions are presented, based on existing tendencies and the analysis provided in the previous sections.

Action No 1: Fair and efficient pricing

Context Charging systems have developed differently for different forms of transport. It is, therefore, now difficult to create a European-wide, integrated, sustainable transport system that is vital to the free movement of goods in the Single European Market. The most important action is the creation of a fair and transparent pricing system. This will lead to increased competition within intermodal freight transport and, therefore, to a lower investment risk for intermodal operators and investors. Rail infrastructure charges should be harmonized with other freight transport modes stimulating competition between rail, road and water transport. Rail freight infrastructure pricing should also be harmonized internationally.

Implementation The new pricing system should be promoted to the current and potential customers of intermodal transport as an additional benefit. This is a supplementary action to be taken by the policy makers apart from the one establishing the fair and efficient pricing system. The main expected result is that new operators will enter the intermodal market and, therefore, competition will take the place of the current situation of monopoly characterizing most cases. The new pricing system should be monitored by the European Commission and regulated by the pan-European intermodal regulator, which is proposed to be created as a supplementary action.

Action No 2: Establish pan-European regulator for intermodal transport

Context The regulator will exercise his functions in a manner that will promote the use of the network for the carriage of goods, exactly as it is done in individual countries, for example in the United Kingdom (NERA 2000). The policy of the regulator should have as its main objective the increase of intermodal transport within and between EU member countries. Supportive regulation can help. The pan-European regulator should fully understand the market needs and also work closely with the European

Commission and with the national governments for a growth in intermodal transport flows. It should regulate the infrastructure providers and also control them and making sure they meet the capacity needs of freight, including routing strategy, network enhancements and sharing investment risk. More specifically, it should take action to reduce freight transport costs, help improve reliability of intermodal services, allow open access for new operators (and new business in general) and manage its property taking into account freight needs.

Implementation Although it is an action to be taken with very careful steps, its urgency is so high that it makes it a short-term action. The cost of establishing the pan-European intermodal operator is not high.

Action No 3: Establish intermodal standards

Context The variety of loading units has been recognized as one important barrier. Harmonization of loading unit standards across modes will bring efficiency in intermodal operations and will also admit higher loading factors and avoid empty hauls. The creation of working groups for setting the standards of loading units as announced by the European Commission in COM(97)243 is a good step towards harmonization and should be continued until standardization and harmonization are complete.

One of the main barriers identified in all aspects of intermodal transport is the different procedures followed and documentation required between the member states, mainly at terminals. One way to promote intermodal transport is to harmonize these procedures, as this would cause faster and more reliable services. A lot of paperwork can be transferred to electronic form through the use of EDI, which should be extended to include more actors.

Implementation This varies according to the standards to be set. For example if a best-practice handbook is to be produced for a medium-sized terminal it should not take a long time, but in the case of a large port, it could take a long time for the standards to be established. Setting the standards of the loading units is not a time-consuming procedure, but the transfer from the current loading unit sizes to the new standard ones could be of significant duration. The associated cost could be high as well, particularly in the cases of countries with dense flows, in which operators regularly change loading units. Nevertheless, this is not the case for the countries with lower intermodal freight traffic flows.

Action No 4: Promote interoperability of intermodal operations

Context Interoperability of intermodal operations is not a single action, it rather signifies a concept and in order for it to be fulfilled, several actions need to be taken simultaneously. Interoperability in intermodal operations mostly refers to interoperability at interfaces (transshipment points). It is directly related to Action No. 3 (harmonization of intermodal operations standards). Interoperability will be promoted mainly by enforcing intermodal actors to follow the standards by applying a relevant regulatory framework.

Implementation A long-term action is required with a high cost due to the need to change the relevant technology and the standards of loading units.

Action Plan Model

Actions regarding implementation are needed in order for the EU to introduce measures to overcome the identified barriers for the creation of new intermodal services and operators. These barriers involve commercial, social and operational issues. The aim is to find the way (with the assistance of the introduced Policy Action Plan) to alleviate the barriers that might exist together with their sources. The 'non-value added' activities have to be removed. The Policy Action Plan is a systematic procedural framework for the readjustment of the intermodal transport policy by the EU, with the objective to overcome the barriers and enhance opportunities for increasing the share of intermodal transport.

For the development of an action and in order to make it appropriate for application, the following checklist has to be elaborated:

- What are the action's objectives?
- Consensus issues among interested parties for a new intermodal service.
- Added value from the introduction of such a service.
- Barriers for implementation.
- Risk assessment.
- Data requirements.
- Budget restrictions.

As the planning of an action progresses, the stages and linkages between the checklist items need to be established. The actions suggested are related to the general transport policy and they address issues that include among others:

- environmental;
- economic; and
- social integration of Europe.

Based on the above, an action (regardless of the area it is applied to) has the following general objectives:

- Transport objectives. These aim to ensure the effective functioning of the Community's transport system and the protection of the environment. They also aim at advancing the state-of-the-art of an intermodal transport system or creating a new one.
- Sector objectives. These refer to objectives, which lie within a single transport sector.
- Area objectives. These refer directly to the areas of major policy interest within each transport sector. They support a policy decision and they aim at implementing a new concept.
- Application objectives. These address the implementation of an action and they also aim at building a consensus among different actors of intermodal transport chains.

The basic origins of an action are:

1. A transport measure solution to an existing situation (top-down approach).
2. The existence of a policy implying the introduction of a transport measure (top-down approach).
3. The development of a technology, technique or other transport measure (bottom-up approach).

The overall implementation plan refers to the organization for applying the actions identified. It is a general overview of the process that should be followed by policy makers in order to apply the proposed actions. It leads to the Policy Action Plan, which is a decision tree for policy makers to enable rational decision-making, as far as new and improved services and actors in the intermodal transport market are concerned. The actions are also related to the target group of customers for the new opportunities (intermodal services), as well as with their implementation period.

In order to evaluate the results of an action or of a series of actions for the promotion of intermodal transport, certain tools can be used, such as:

- cost–benefit analysis (CBA);
- multi-criteria analysis (MCA);
- cost effectiveness analysis (CEA);
- goal achievement methods (GAM).

In the context of the Policy Action Plan and in order to decide if an action needs to be taken, the following steps have to be followed.

First step

Four selections of targets need to be made first: transport market, geographical area, intermodal transport market actors and commodity types. This selection is not required to be made for all four targets at once. Any necessary combination can be undertaken, depending on a particular case.

Second step

The second step is to examine whether intermodal transport services and actors exist in the identified target markets.

Third step

If intermodal transport does not exist at all, the various barriers have to be examined. Institutional, infrastructural, commercial, economic, technical and operational, and social barriers should be investigated. If one or a combination of these barriers exist, then action should be taken for their alleviation. If they do not exist, one should proceed to the next step.

Fourth step

If intermodal transport exists, the objectives for promoting it further and increasing its share in the freight transport market should be set, that is, transport, sector, area and application objectives.

Fifth step

This step is the final one and constitutes the implementation plan. The appropriate groups of people should be involved in consultation before any action is taken. The necessary data for comparing the possible alternatives to the action should be gathered carefully and analysed. Prior to the full implementation of the action, a pilot implementation should be undertaken. If the action leads to the creation of a new service or the establishment of a new intermodal transport operator, this should be carefully monitored in order to examine its rate of success. If it is not proved to be successful, then it should be withdrawn. Figure 14.1 presents the policy action plan described.

14.6 CONCLUDING REMARKS

The way forward for the development of intermodal transport in Europe is the combination of the top-down approach (European Commission policies, legislation, and so on) and the bottom-up approach, which is the identification of the intermodal transport market actors' needs. Strategies have been identified and enforced by the Directives and the weak points of the intermodal market have been identified and analysed through extensive research. What needs to be done next is to proceed to a combination of the above, in order to apply the optimum solutions to the identified problems and offer these solutions to the intermodal transport market actors.

All the measures and actions recommended cannot be fully effective unless each of the parties concerned in the transport chain does everything necessary to ensure the development and efficiency of intermodal transport. A framework under which freight infrastructure investment can take place should be produced. Investment decisions should be made by public bodies in collaboration with experts. The development of intermodal transport in the European Union is a long-term exercise. The impact of the current efforts towards the increase of the share of intermodal transport should be evaluated on a pan-European scale over a long time perspective. The European Commission should continue reviewing developments that will lead to an increase in the share of intermodal transport.

The role of mergers and alliances between intermodal transport actors in the development of new operators should be highlighted. There is a need for greater collaboration between the main actors of an intermodal transport chain, especially the active involvement of the shipper. This trend exists and its development should be supported by organizing pilot cases, round tables and other marketing actions that will inform the participants on the benefits of such a scheme. The collaboration of actors will have as a result the development of pan-European operators, which will achieve economies of scale.

Intermodal transport should be maintained in the political agenda. More publicity should be given through campaigns promoting the advantages of intermodal transport. Quality improvement is the key for increasing the share of intermodal freight transport and for enabling intermodal transport to play a role in European cohesion, integration, harmonization, economic efficiency, competitiveness and sustainability. Actors within the industry should undertake the implementation of most of the required actions using their own resources, especially if provided with tools to pinpoint improvement possibilities. However, much also depends upon the political level of ambition and on the policies used to assist intermodal transport to fulfil its potential with regards to setting appropriate framework conditions for competition and cooperation within the transport sector.

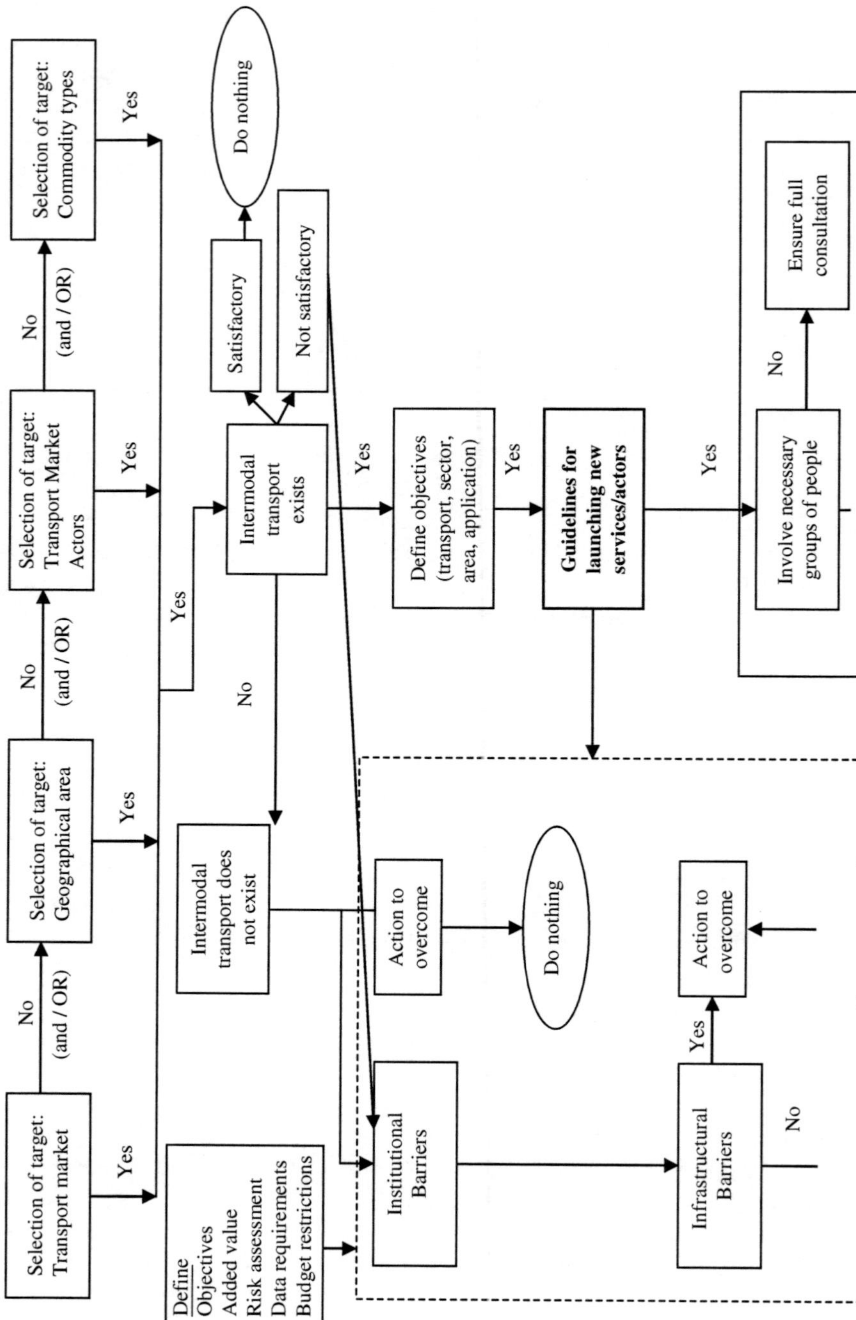
Selection of target: Transport market
Yes
No
(and / OR)
Selection of target: Geographical area
Yes
No
(and / OR)
Selection of target: Transport Market Actors
Yes
No
(and / OR)
Selection of target: Commodity types
Yes
Yes
Intermodal transport exists
Satisfactory
Not satisfactory
Do nothing
No
Yes
Define objectives (transport, sector, area, application)
Yes
Guidelines for launching new services/actors
Yes
Involve necessary groups of people
No
Ensure full consultation
Intermodal transport does not exist
Action to overcome
Do nothing
Define
Objectives
Added value
Risk assessment
Data requirements
Budget restrictions
Institutional Barriers
Infrastructural Barriers
Yes
Action to overcome
No

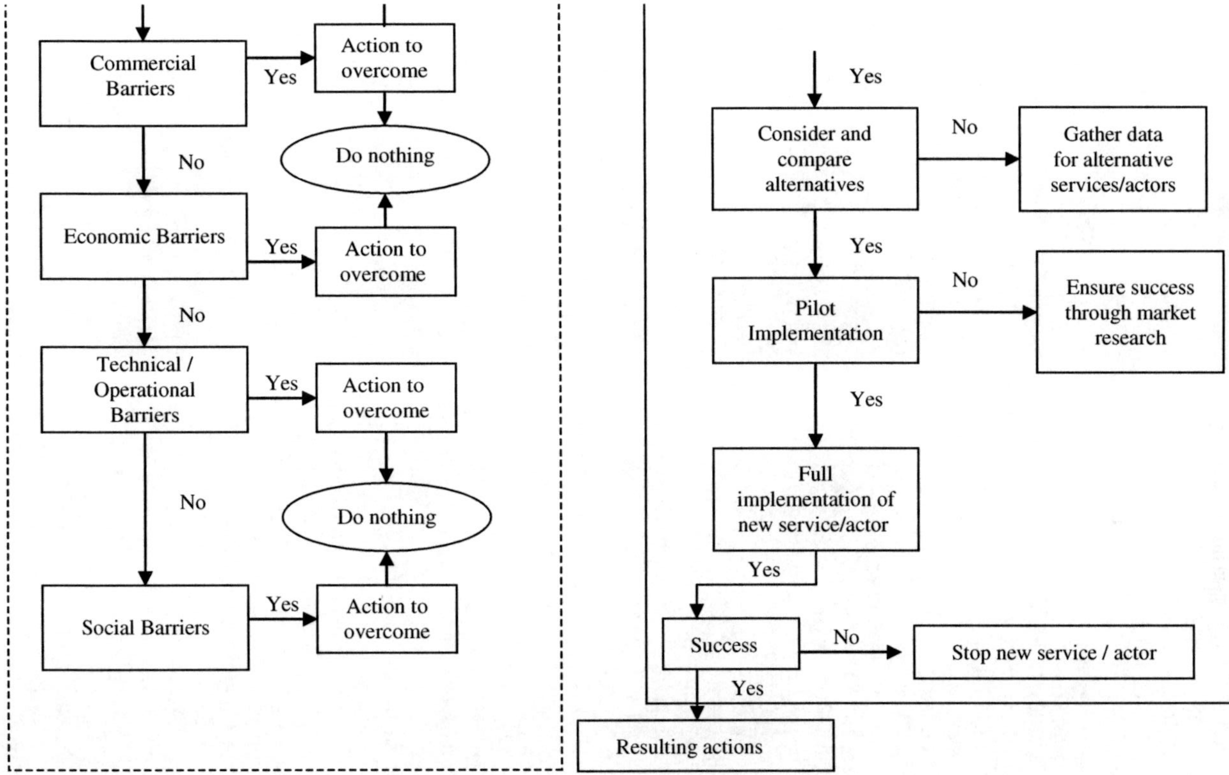

Figure 14.1 Policy action plan for intermodal transport in Europe

REFERENCES

Choong, S.T., M.H. Cole and E. Kutanoglu (2002), 'Empty container management for intermodal transportation networks', *Transportation Research Part E*, **38**, pp. 423–38.

Council Directive 96/48/EC of 23 July 1996 on the interoperability of the trans-European high-speed rail system.

D'Este, G. (1996), 'An event-based approach to modelling intermodal freight systems', *International Journal of Physical Distribution and Logistics Management*, **26** (6), pp. 4–15.

Directive 2001/12/EC of the European Parliament and of the Council amending Council Directive 91/440/EEC on the development of the Community's railways.

Directive 2001/13/EC of the European Parliament and of the Council of 26 February 2001 amending Council Directive 95/18/EC on the licensing of railway undertakings.

Directive 2001/14/EC of the European Parliament and of the Council on the allocation of railway infrastructure capacity and the levying of charges for the use of railway infrastructure and safety certification.

Directive 2001/16/EC of the European Parliament and of the Council of 19 March 2001, on the interoperability of the conventional rail system.

Directive 2004/50/EC amending Directive 96/48/EC on the interoperability of the trans-European high-speed rail system and Directive 2001/16/EC on the interoperability of the trans-European conventional rail system.

Directive 2004/51/EC of the European Parliament and of the Council of 29 April 2004 amending Council Directive 91/440/EEC on the development of the Community's railways.

Decision No 884/2004/EC of the European Parliament and of the Council of 29 April 2004 amending Decision No 1692/96/EC on Community guidelines for the development of the trans-European transport network.

European Commission (1996), *A Strategy for Revitalising the Community's Railways*, European Commission White Paper, Brussels.

European Commission, (1997), COM(97)243, 'Communication on intermodality and intermodal freight transport in the European Union', Brussels.

European Commission (2001a), White Paper, *European Transport Policy for 2010: Time To Decide*, Brussels.

European Commission (2001b), COM(2001)264, Communication on 'A sustainable Europe for a better world: A European Union strategy for sustainable development', Brussels.

European Commission (2004), COM(2004) 453 final, Communication on 'Short sea shipping', Brussels.

European Commission (2006a), COM(2006) 380 final, Communication on 'Mid term review of the Programme for the Promotion of Short Sea Shipping', Brussels.

European Commission (2006b), COM(2006) 336 final, Communication on 'freight transport logistics in Europe – the key to sustainable mobility', Brussels.

IQ (2000), 'Intermodal quality', European Commission, DG TREN (previously DG VII).

Konings, J.W. (1996), 'Integrated centres for the transshipment, storage, collection and distribution of goods', *Transport Policy*, **3** (1–2), pp. 3–11.

NERA (2000), 'An economic analysis of the freight market', report to the office of the Rail Regulator, London.

PROMOTIQ (2000), 'Conditions for the promotion of a new generation of intermodal transport services and operators', European Commission, DG TREN (previously DG VII).
Trip, J. and Y. Bontekoning (2002), 'Integration of small freight flows in the intermodal transport system', *Journal of Transport Geography*, **10**, pp. 221–9.
US Department of Transportation – Federal Highway Administration (2002), 'Freight transportation: the European market', International Technology Exchange Program.
Van Klink, H.A and G.C. Van den Berg (1998), 'Gateways and intermodalism', *Journal of Transport Geography*, **6** (1), pp. 1–9.
van Zuylen, H. and J. Weber Matthias (2002), 'Strategies for European innovation policy in the transport field', *Technological Forecasting and Social Change*, **69**, pp. 929–51.

15. The role of government in fostering intermodal transport innovations: perceived lessons and obstacles in the United States

José Holguín-Veras, Robert Paaswell and Anthony Perl

15.1 INTRODUCTION

Freight transportation systems all over the world make significant contributions to the world, regional and local economies. The importance of these contributions is clearly evident in the American case, which provides a good example of the economic importance of freight.

In 1997, business and industry transported cargo worth $6.9 trillion and weighing 11 billion tons. This caused 2.7 trillion ton-miles of goods to be transported across the continental United States (USDOT 1999a). Truck transportation accounts for 71.7 per cent of the value of cargo transported and 69.4 per cent of its tonnage (ibid.). At the personal level, Americans spend more on transportation, freight movement and commuting, than they do on clothing, operating the household, recreation and intercity travel put together. Transportation costs account for 11 per cent of disposable income, the fourth largest item in family budgets (USDOT 1999b). Using 1994 gross national product numbers, freight transportation made up 6.3 per cent of total expenditure, which could go up to 10–11 per cent of total expenditure if revenues spent on inventory, warehousing, and logistics services are included (ENO 1998). As a percentage of total expenditure, freight transportation represents 38.52 per cent of the total, while passenger transportation accounts for the rest (USDOT 1999b).

The impact of freight on the US economy is considerable. Overall, it is estimated that one out of every ten jobs in the American economy is either directly or indirectly related to transportation (ENO 1998), which could increase to one out of four jobs if jobs in logistics and warehousing are taken into account. These numbers roughly translate into 4 million jobs directly attributable to transportation. Three million of these jobs are freight related (USDOT 1999a).

The extent and rapid pace of globalization has placed an increasing burden on the entire freight industry. In the new global economy, the freight transportation system, originally designed to operate across national boundaries, will be expected to operate as if national boundaries do not exist. The American freight transportation system is becoming an ever more important piece of the global network. This growth adds pressure to the freight transportation system to increase capacity. Symptomatic of this growth in demand are the needs customers now place on freight services: increasing reliability, cost effectiveness, higher efficiency and, more importantly, a service tailored to their specific needs (Holguín-Veras and Thorson 2003). Not only will the freight transportation system have to increase capacity, but it will also have to increase the variety of services provided to meet customer needs.

The freight transportation system is also the subject of significant and justifiable concern by environmental and community groups. Epidemiological studies (for example Ostro 1987) indicate that particles less than 2.5 μm in aerodynamic diameter ($PM_{2.5}$), a size that can reach deep into the lower respiratory tract of the lungs, create significant health problems. Since nearly all diesel particles fall within the $PM_{2.5}$ range (Godlee 1993), health considerations demand the implementation of transportation policies aimed at ameliorating the negative air quality impacts of truck traffic. These concerns are backed by an increasing number of studies that have specifically analysed the health impacts of truck activity (for example Bhatia et al. 1998), and by community-based environmental research that provides indication of the relationship between truck traffic and environmental impacts (Lena et al. 2002).

The confluence of the trends discussed above seems to provide strong reasons to implement proactive policies to foster intermodal transport innovation and, ultimately, enhance the competitive edge of the American economy, foster the role of freight transportation as an agent of economic development and the efficiency of the freight system, as well as reduce the negative environmental and health externalities, and congestion, produced by freight transportation activity. Interestingly enough, both at the international level and in the USA, such intermodal innovation policies, more often than not, are absent at the policy table with only a handful of good examples (for example Singapore, the Netherlands) where far-reaching freight transportation programmes, including the area of freight automation, have been in place for a long time.

In one of the few publications on the subject, Boske (1998) provides a succinct description of 'best practice' in multimodal and intermodal planning, which, by definition, does not represent the typical situation. A separate publication (Boske 1999) provides in-depth analyses of best practice in the US. The analyses of the findings in Boske (1998) highlight a number of interesting patterns. Across the board, in Europe, the United States and Latin America, the main focus of multimodal and intermodal planning is on the definition, programming and investment for projects that foster an efficient and seamless intermodal transportation system. In the US, a handful of states have implemented exemplary planning practices that routinely gather input from the stakeholders about intermodal projects. For the most part, initiatives intended to foster intermodal innovation are not considered to be within the scope of responsibilities of even the most progressive state planning departments. The same applies to the Latin American countries (Boske 1998). In Europe, both at the supranational and the national level, there appears to be an enhanced recognition of the need to foster intermodal innovation. European policy makers appear to have made a linkage between the interconnection of their transport modes and the integration of their economies.

The main objective of this chapter is to conduct a comprehensive analysis of the factors that explain the absence of intermodal innovation initiatives in the US. Since the American situation is symptomatic of the state of affairs in most developed (and some developing) countries its analysis may provide insights into how best to tackle the problem of defining and implementing intermodal innovation initiatives. Among other things, analysis of the relatively well-documented American case provides some insights into how best to overcome the typical challenges associated with defining policies and programmes to foster intermodal innovation.

This analysis provides supporting information to assess the role of government in fostering intermodal transport innovations through the implementation of a consistent set of policies, programmes and projects, referred to in this chapter as intermodal innovation initiatives. It should be implicitly understood that research is a necessary and vital element supporting such initiatives.

The chapter is comprised of three major sections. Section 15.2 entitled 'Effects of institutional diversity and durability on intermodal innovation' provides a brief description of the institutional structures that influence intermodal innovation initiatives. 'Challenges' (section 15.3) presents an analysis of the main obstacles to the implementation of a meaningful set of such initiatives. Section 15.4 entitled 'Towards a systematic policy of intermodal innovation' presents an outline of policy steps aimed at the creation of a set of intermodal innovation initiatives. Section 15.5, 'Conclusions', summarizes the main findings.

15.2 EFFECTS OF INSTITUTIONAL DIVERSITY AND DURABILITY ON INTERMODAL INNOVATION

As befits the world's most mobile society, the United States is a major producer of transportation research and innovation. However, amidst this bounty of analytical output, it is not easy to identify a consistent or coherent focus on the systemic challenges of freight transportation. Part of the reason for that can be found in the institutional diversity and durability of American transportation finance, planning and operations.

American transportation innovations have traditionally reflected the institutional structure of transportation planning and development. When the private sector took charge of railroad development in the nineteenth and early twentieth centuries, it took the lead in creating proprietary technical, and to a lesser extent economic, research that facilitated innovations in moving freight and people by rail. When state and federal government agencies began developing America's national highway network, their technical and socio-economic research was similarly focused on that mode, but public dissemination of results became a means of diffusing technical and administrative innovations. A longer time horizon was also introduced to US transportation research, with at least some investigations corresponding with state and national 'master plans' for road, and later public transportation programmes.

Through the course of the twentieth century, the scale of research efforts by universities, governments and private industry has grown considerably, and with it has come a growing diversity of issues in, and perspectives on, improving mobility. Each sponsor of transportation research brings different objectives, timeframes and techniques to their work. Such diversity is not, in itself, problematic.

However, when this tendency toward such fragmentation is combined with the American propensity to create exceptionally durable transportation institutions, the ability to advance the understanding of systemic issues that cut across organizational boundaries and to integrate findings from disparate investigations into innovative results becomes limited. Intermodal innovation is constrained by this durability in transportation policy – the tendency for American government to create administrative and financial arrangements that 'lock in' particular organizational arrangements and relationships between politics and technology (Perl 1991).

This institutional durability, and its modally based nature, has a significant impact on the freight transportation research priorities. This can be appreciated in the way in which research funding has been approached by the different agencies. The list of agencies that, in one way or another, engage in freight transportation research encompasses federal, state and local agencies. This section identifies the major agencies that sponsor or directly conduct freight transportation research in the United States, and highlights their influence and role.

The National Science Foundation (NSF) has sponsored a number of research projects on different facets of freight transportation. For the most part, the projects sponsored by the NSF are those with potential to make significant contributions on basic research across multiple disciplines. A partnership between the United States Department of Transportation (USDOT) and the NSF has opened new opportunities for funding of high-risk, high-pay-off basic transportation research. This partnership fills a void in transportation research because high-risk, high-pay-off basic research has not been considered a priority by traditional funding sources in transportation, for example Departments of Transportation. The NSF is interested in expanding the partnership with the USDOT, as well as others based upon the successful model of public–private research partnership in the semiconductor industry.

The United States Department of Transportation spent a total of $192 million on research and development contracts in 2001 (US Office of Management and Budget 2001, p. 27). Although no budget breakdown is available, a number of agencies within the USDOT do conduct research with a more or less explicit focus on freight transportation.

The Federal Highway Administration (FHWA) is the largest and best funded of the USDOT agencies dealing with surface transportation. The FHWA is responsible for managing the Federal Aid Highway Program which distributes revenues collected from automotive excise taxes to designated road-building programmes in the states, as well as the Federal Lands Highway Program which directly constructs roads on federal lands. The Research, Development, and Technology Service Business Unit at FHWA oversees direct and sponsored research on highway technology, management and planning innovations. Much of this research is technically oriented, focusing on materials and design of road infrastructure and carried out by the Turner-Fairbank Highway Research Center. But some of it also addresses operational and administrative questions.

The FHWA's Office of Freight Management is the agency within the US government that is most focused on research that can contribute to enhancing the movement of goods. The FHWA is pursuing a Freight Productivity Program to examine the needs of freight mobility and begin to offer support for new policies. A freight analysis framework has been created to offer:

> a methodology to estimate trade flows on the Nation's infrastructure, seeking to understand the geographic relationships between local flows and the Nation's

> overall transportation system. The framework will help identify areas of improvement to increase freight mobility, including highlighting regions with mismatched freight demand and system capacity, and encouraging the development of multistate and regional approaches to improving operations. (USDOT 2002)

The FHWA has also sponsored a 'National Freight Dialogue', which is aimed at fostering dialogue among public and private participants in the movement of freight (see http://www.icfhosting.com/fhwa/nfd_disc.nsf/Splash?OpenPage). It is replete with discussion of the need to give freight transportation a higher priority, and to build understanding of obstacles and opportunities to freight transport innovations, presumably through research. However, a detailed research agenda that encompasses a systemic analysis of how to enhance the productivity and sustainability of America's freight transportation system remains to be added to this dialogue.

The Federal Motor Carrier Safety Administration (FMCSA) was split off from the FHWA in 2000, with a 'primary mission . . . to prevent commercial motor vehicle-related fatalities and injuries'. While the FMCSA conducts research into safety-related topics such as operator fatigue whose results have a significant influence on freight transportation, there is little attention paid to how alternative practices and new technologies like automation might transform freight system performance and hence safety. The Federal Railroad Administration (FRA) also conducts research primarily in the area of safety, and also organizes this around particular challenges and risks posed by current operating patterns and technology.

The Bureau of Transportation Statistics (BTS) is America's primary repository of data on all aspects of mobility. In cooperation with the US Census Bureau, the BTS conducts a Commodity Flow Survey (CFS) approximately every five years (since 1993). Unfortunately, the reductions in the sample size of the CFS (from 200 000 in 1993, to 100 000 in 1997, and 50 000 in 2002) have severely undercut its ability to produce detailed tabulations of commodity flows. The BTS provides periodic analytical overviews of the trends in goods movement, with an emphasis on encapsulating the outcomes of system performance. In addition, the BTS does support a relatively small number of freight transportation research projects through its normal research funding programme.

At the state level, departments of transportation (DOTs) tend to support and participate in applied transportation research aimed at improving maintenance or enhancing their operations. An important vehicle for such efforts is the National Cooperative Highway Research Program (NCHRP), which is administered by the Transportation Research Board under the guidance of the Standing Committee on Research of the American Association of State Highway and Transportation Officials (AASHTO).

The NCHRP ranks research proposals based on state and federal input. The state DOTs also periodically fund freight research projects, usually through local universities and the federally sponsored University Transportation Centers (UTCs). These projects tend to focus on either specific operational issues or freight transportation modelling to support statewide planning efforts (for example Sorratini and Smith 2000).

Additional locations for American transportation research may be found in Metropolitan Planning Organizations (MPOs) which, by law, must focus on transportation and land use issues in the US urbanized areas. As might be imagined from the diverse geography found across these MPO jurisdictions, only some of them would identify freight movement as a significant transportation activity worth monitoring. This tends to occur in MPOs with a significant concentration of airport, maritime, and/or rail terminals or transfer facilities. In such cases, attention to traffic flow, environmental impacts and economic contribution of freight movement is identified and tracked. Local challenges, such as road congestion or poor interconnectivity between modes, can be assessed and suggestions for improvement can be developed. An example of this type of project is the one funded by the New York City MPO, the New York Metropolitan Transportation Council (NYMTC), to define a strategic plan for the development of a regional freight transportation model (Holguín-Veras et al. 2001).

Problems that lend themselves to a local solution can be approached with innovative solutions. The Alameda Corridor project, one of the most innovative in the US, is a new 22 mile urban rail freight corridor across Los Angeles. However, when freight mobility is constrained by problems that extend beyond a given MPO's jurisdiction, the prospect of these organizations generating research that will stimulate innovation to address these problems declines considerably.

America's configuration of transportation agencies offers the opportunity to generate many important research initiatives. Working directly, and in partnership with industry and universities, government sponsors numerous initiatives that draw upon many disciplines including pure and applied science, engineering, social science, planning and management. The components and capacities of a world-class freight research programme are certainly available within this context. Yet institutional diversity and durability have, to date, made it difficult to organize analysis that can transcend modal, administrative and geographic jurisdictions. As a result, potential freight transportation innovations are less likely to get stimulated by current institutional configurations. Under favourable circumstances, such as certain MPOs' implementation of responsibilities created by the Intermodal Surface Transportation Efficiency Act, publicly supported exploration of freight transportation opportunities has enabled intermodal planning and project development to become a central focus of federal and state transportation agencies' work.

15.3 CHALLENGES

Introduction

Even where research generates the raw ingredients for innovation, implementation of a set of intermodal innovation initiatives in the United States faces a number of challenges. This section highlights some of the most significant ones so that insights could be gained on how to overcome them. This analysis highlights four major factors that constrain innovation: (1) government–private industry dynamics; (2) size, geographic factors and industry structure; (3) lack of identification between private industry success and national economic objectives; and (4) mismatched planning horizons.

Government–Private Industry Dynamics

One of the most important distinctions between the passenger and freight transportation systems is related to the nature of their relationship with the government. This is the result of the different paths that passenger and freight transportation systems have taken over time. The factors conditioning these dynamics are briefly discussed next.

Since its early beginnings, in the United States, freight has been moved by private carriers and has been dominated by private companies that operate various components of the system. In some cases, for example inland water transportation and trucking, the private companies do their businesses using a public right-of-way (rivers and channels in the case of inland water transportation, and public roads in the case of the trucking industry), while in others, most notably railroads and pipelines, the companies integrate ownership of the right-of-way, the facilities and operating carrier. Quite often, these rights of way were obtained from the public in return for the provision of certain transportation services. This has created a not unexpected tug-of-war. The government, representing the public and its investments, wants to regulate those investments. The private companies want totally unregulated operations to ensure maximization of their profits. The relationship between freight companies and the government has even had periods of open hostility, such as in the late nineteenth century that saw the enactment of anti price-discrimination laws preventing railroads from using price differentiation schemes. These laws were repealed in the late 1870s after the financial situation of the railroads deteriorated so dramatically that the very existence of the railroads and the service they provide was threatened (Holguín-Veras and Jara-Díaz 1999). US takeover of all railroads in World War One and some Northeast and Midwest railroads following the Penn Central bankruptcy in 1969 were other periods of costly confrontation.

When freight companies use a public right-of-way, the prevailing perception among those companies is that their interests are not best represented by the US or State Department of Transportation, or any other transportation agency for that matter. This is particularly evident in the trucking industry, where truckers tend to believe that DOTs are 'out there to get them' and that they are unjustly portrayed by DOTs as pavement destroyers, congestion producers and the like, while their contributions to the success of the American economy are not acknowledged and appreciated. This is undoubtedly a reflection of long-held views among traditional engineers, who think of the freight industry, particularly truck transportation, as something to control tightly. One of the professionals interviewed during this research termed this as the 'ban the truck' attitude.

The net result is a situation in which the government agencies do a minimal amount of policy intervention (usually in the areas of safety and the environment) that purposely avoid policy measures and legislation that may be perceived – by any segment of the industry – as altering the 'level playing field of competition'. In turn, instead of relying on transportation agencies to do transportation policy on their behalf, freight companies try to influence transportation policy by means of modally based trade groups (for example the American Trucking Association, ATA; Association of American Railroads, AAR; American Association of Port Authorities, AAPA; Intermodal Association of North America, IANA). These influential organizations lobby the executive and legislative branches of federal, state and municipal governments for support of specific programmes, projects and pieces of legislation of interest to their trade group. As may be expected, the resulting transportation policies and programmes are the reflection of modally based priorities that fail to account for system considerations of intermodal and multimodal aspects. As shall be seen later, this has important implications for the definition of intermodal innovation policies.

In contrast, the relationships between government agencies and the different components of the passenger transportation system have taken a different path. Passenger transportation systems have been implemented using two major modalities. The first one is the use of the public right-of-way by individuals or transportation companies that contribute directly through fees and tolls, and indirectly through taxes, help pay for the facilities' upkeep, while retaining ownership of the vehicles, for example private car owners. It has been assumed and customarily accepted that the public interest is best represented by the State Departments of Transportation and elected officials. Indeed, it has been observed that elected officials and transportation officials are fairly responsive to the wishes and expectations of car owners, as they represent a significant fraction of the population that votes. In fact, most elected officials, if presented with a situation in which they have to choose among alternatives that benefit one sector at the expense of the other (which occurs frequently in resource allocation problems), would tend to favour passenger transportation, as well as the road modes, over other options. The consequence of this is to reinforce the prevailing perception in the trucking industry that their interests are not represented, or are minimally taken into account, by transportation and elected officials, in spite of having a similar arrangement to car drivers, that is, public right-of-way and private ownership and operation of vehicles. This seems to give credence to the old saying used by freight transportation professionals to explain the low priority given to freight transportation: 'freight does not vote'. For their part, railroads seem to react with a similar disdain of transportation officials for responding to passenger demands, which usually translate into either support for road building that can aid their truck competition or demands for increased passenger rail operations that constrain rail freight capacity.

A second modality of implementation of passenger transportation delivery can be found in the case of quasi-public transit agencies that provide transportation service with subsidies from public funds while using a public right-of-way. Because of their quasi-public character, these agencies have traditionally had close ties with the political leaders, which translates into a rather cooperative relationship with elected officials. As a result of the empowerment of transportation agencies to represent car drivers and the close relationship between transit agencies and the political elites, transportation agencies have been able to undertake a relatively proactive role in defining and implementing passenger transportation policy. In some extreme cases, transportation agencies have even been able to implement policies and programmes that may negatively affect small pockets of individuals and companies, which is accepted as long as it is done for the greater good.

The nature of the dynamics of the relationship between government agencies and the freight industry weighs heavily in the minds of the individuals in charge of setting research priorities. One of the top concerns cited to the authors of this chapter about advancing innovation through a freight transportation research programme is the possibility that such a programme could have differential impacts upon the freight industry, that is, that the programme upsets what is considered to be a level playing field of economic competition. This line of thought is based on the fundamental assumption that efforts to stimulate freight transportation innovations should be neutral, from the standpoint of any differential impacts that they might produce. This stands in sharp contrast with the passenger transportation case, in which there is widespread recognition among transportation officials about the need to implement proactive 'interventionist' policies, for example to reduce car usage. In cases like this, the government's role in fostering a more rational use of resources is acknowledged.

The differential impacts that concern transportation officials could reveal themselves in a number of different ways, for example by altering the geographic pattern of commodity flows and trade, or by altering the relative volumes of inter- and intramodal freight flow. Freight transportation research that may result in giving an advantage to the Port of New York and New Jersey will undoubtedly concern other port authorities in the East Coast, for example Baltimore. Similarly, freight research that stimulates a disproportionate advance of innovation in the trucking industry would undoubtedly generate opposition from the railroad industry, where such research would be viewed as government intervention that favoured the competition. The trucking industry and its advocates would similarly oppose research that sought to advance new technology and more productive techniques that generated a high pay-off for freight railroads. The dynamics between the freight industry and the government have resulted in a state of affairs in which: (1) there is very little tradition of collaboration and partnership between the rail and road modes; and (2) the policy and research initiatives that stimulate innovation are, in essence, modally determined. The latter is particularly important in light of the fact that – in spite of the ambitious and far-reaching goals first set by the Intermodal Surface Transportation Efficiency Act of 1991 – the institutional structure of transportation decision making in America remains modally based. In this context, both the institutional structure and the trade groups reinforce each other, which result in the perpetuation of the modally based modus operandi. A recent example of this perspective on innovation is the proposed 'Commercial Traffic Effects Institute' (TRB 2002) that would be chartered to 'develop federal (truck) size and weight standards and related highway management practices, recommend regulatory changes, evaluate the results of the implementation of new regulations, and support state implementation of federal regulations'.

Size, Geographic Factors and Industry Structure

Introduction

One important element that poses a challenge to the implementation of federal policies to foster intermodal innovation is related to the geography of freight transportation in the United States, in particular the size and complexity of the system. This section provides a brief description of the main components of the American freight transportation system: rail freight, truck transportation and the port system. Air freight, pipelines and the inland water system are not discussed here for the sake of brevity, and because they have relatively unique issues not directly related to the issues affecting the three main freight modes.

Trucking

Truck transportation in the United States is an activity of massive size. According to the 1997 Vehicle Inventory and Use Survey (VIUS) (USDC 2000), there are close to 72.8 million trucks. In terms of size, these trucks could be classified as: (1) light trucks, that is, weight less than 10 000 pounds; (2) medium trucks (weight between 10 001 and 19 500 pounds); (3) light-heavy trucks (weight between 19 501 and 26 000 pounds); and (4) heavy-heavy trucks (with weight exceeding 26 001 pounds). Light trucks are, by far, the most numerous (68.1 million), followed by heavy-heavy trucks (2.54 million), medium trucks (1.44 million) and light-heavy (0.73 million).

In terms of industry structure, trucking has been, it is, and probably it will be, an activity in which there exists a significant number of owner-operators. As shown in Table 15.1, 53 per cent of the units surveyed by the 1997 VIUS belonged to owners of only one truck. The trucks owned by companies with five trucks or less represent 70.5 per cent of the total. A significant portion of those are doing full-truckload (FTL) operations, usually intercity travel,

Table 15.1 Structure of the trucking industry

Number of trucks in company	Number of units	% of total	% of respondents
1	18 553 557	25.49	52.70
2–5	9 790 007	13.45	27.81
6–9	1 490 431	2.05	4.23
10–24	1 660 380	2.28	4.72
25–99	1 479 723	2.03	4.20
100–499	988 021	1.36	2.81
500–999	287 938	0.40	0.82
1000–4999	361 648	0.50	1.03
5000–9999	128 665	0.18	0.37
10 000 or more	462 627	0.64	1.31
Not reported	37 597 254	51.64	–
Total	72 800 252	100.00	100.00

because of the relative ease with which they could enter the market. On the other hand, the number of individual operators in the less-than-truckload (LTL) market is much less, because LTL operations usually require expensive distribution terminals strategically located in major metropolitan areas, from where the FTL shipments can be sorted out and redistributed.

The trucking industry is represented by the American Trucking Association (ATA) and numerous state and local trucking organizations (for example the New Jersey Motor Truck Association, the New York Motor Truck Association). The ATA focuses, for the most part, on issues affecting the trucking industry at the national level, though it sometimes engages states in fighting for policy measures that benefit its membership. The local and state trucking associations, for the most part, focus almost exclusively on local issues. The relationship between the ATA and the local and state trucking associations is highly uneven and dynamic.

Rail freight

The American rail freight system is the world's largest. It is comprised of approximately 128 000 miles of active tracks. For comparison purposes, Canada (second-largest) has 59 000 miles and Russia (third-largest) has 54 000 miles (Muller 1999). The different railroads are classified, on the basis of their operating revenue as: (1) Class I, which are those with operating revenues exceeding $253.7 million; (2) Class II, those with operating revenues between $20.3 and $253.7 million (most regional railroads belong to this class); and (3) Class III, that are those with operating revenues less than $20.3 million (Muller 1999).

Following deregulation, the number of Class I railroads has consistently declined from 35 in the 1980s to nine (1998). The Class I railroads as of 1998 were: Burlington Northern and Santa Fe, Union Pacific, Consolidated Rail Corporation, Norfolk Southern, CSX Transportation, Canadian National, Canadian Pacific, Florida East Coast and Illinois Central. By 2002, consolidations and acquisitions had reduced this number to seven carriers, of which just five were headquartered in the United States.

As of 2001, the four largest railroads in the United States were: Burlington Northern and Santa Fe, CSX Transportation, Union Pacific and Norfolk Southern. A unique feature of the American rail freight system is the lack of a sole national carrier that dominates the others. The East of the Rocky Mountains is dominated by CSX Transportation and Norfolk Southern, while the West is the realm of Burlington Northern and Santa Fe and Union Pacific. Given the wide range of social and economic conditions across the different states it is extremely likely that, in spite of the policy makers' best efforts, any significant freight transportation research initiative would have differential impacts across the different states.

Ports

The American port system is complex and dynamic. The proliferation of major ports on the East Coast – many of them originally supported through local public funds – has led to a situation of overcapacity that has translated into severe competition among the different port authorities. Since a significant portion of port demand is discretionary in nature – because it depends on the decision of shipping companies about the ports of call – the outcome of this competition is perceived by port managers as a matter of 'life or death'. Since most of the energy of port managers is spent on this struggle for survival, basic or applied port research (an area in which freight automation would have a significant impact, as demonstrated by the examples of the ports of Singapore and Rotterdam) is a low priority. Ports do research for highly specific needs and often incorporate these studies as parts of environmental impact or planning studies, for example on the impacts of dredging. Needless to say, the overcapacity on the East Coast heightens the concerns among port managers about research that may provide a competing port with a leading edge. On the West Coast, although until the downturn of the global economy in 2000 there were port capacity problems, these were usually addressed by means of infrastructure capacity enhancements, which is the traditional approach. In an expanding global economy, these pressures to add capacity may provide additional incentives to speed up freight automation research in port operations.

Lack of Identification Between Private Industry Success and National Economic Objectives

As discussed in this section, the size and complexity of the American freight system poses a challenge to the implementation of a significant freight research programme. The multiplicity of frequently conflicting objectives of the different freight modes are a reflection of the fact that they, in essence, compete with each other. This competition takes place across modes and across the geography of the country.

In this context, the success of a particular company is perceived by its competitors as something achieved at their expense, as part of a zero-sum exercise. More importantly from the policy standpoint is that there is not a close identification between the financial well-being of a given freight company and the success of the American economy. The expression 'What is good for the country is good for General Motors, and what's good for General Motors is good for the country' does not ring true in the American freight transportation system (the statement is attributed to Charles E. Wilson, former head of General Motors and Secretary of Defence under

President Dwight Eisenhower, who allegedly said it at a Senate subcommittee in the 1950s). It should be noted, however, that local and state transportation and elected officials tend to recognize the role of ports as engines of local and regional economies, probably more than any other freight mode (with the notable exception of New York City in the 1950s and 1960s, where political leaders must share in the blame for the disappearance of the port's operations on the New York side). This is driven by the fact that ports have a fixed location in contrast to trucking and railroad companies that operate across the country. At the national level, however, there is no evidence of any identification between the success of the port system and national economic objectives. This situation stands in sharp contrast with the case of countries that lead the world in intermodal innovations such as freight automation (for example Singapore, the Netherlands) where there exists a close association between the success (or failure) of a particular freight enterprise (that is, the Port of Singapore and the Port of Rotterdam) and the economic development of the country. This closeness translates into a heightened awareness of the importance of freight transportation and intermodal innovation, and a more cooperative working environment between private industry and the government.

Mismatched Planning Horizons

A factor that deserves mention is related to the significant differences between the planning horizons of the system's operators – virtually all of which are a part of the private sector, where day-to-day operations keep the time horizons short – and the public agencies responsible for planning, financing and implementing transportation projects. These public agencies, with extended planning cycles and complex decision-making and implementation procedures, think of 'short term' as within two years. 'Medium term' may be between two to five years, while 'long term' can mean a 10-, 20- and even 50-year planning horizon. Private firms, on the other hand, have much shorter planning cycles, where 'short term' may be as little as two weeks. 'Medium term' could be anything within six months, while 'long term' may refer to the next year.

As expected, this significant disparity in planning horizons complicates the process of trying to define common goals between transportation agencies and the freight industry. On the one hand, transportation agencies are not designed to respond with the speed required by the private sector for even 'long-term' decisions. On the other hand, the freight operators are not interested in long-term projects with potential pay-offs far off on the horizon. This disparity needs to be taken into account when attempting to advance the innovations stemming from freight transportation research.

There is one point where the 'short-term' understanding of public and private entities may coincide. While the public planning and investment processes are by necessity longer term, transportation projects supported with public funds must be reported on annually. This takes place under the auspices of the Metropolitan Planning Organization. The instrument is the annual Transportation Improvement Program (TIP), which is an annual listing of projects, and the resources to support them. It is signed onto by the member organizations of the MPO. It is at this forum that short-term needs can be expressed and that freight needs can be placed on the table as essential components of meeting regional and local transportation, land use and environmental objectives. What is needed to launch this process is a representative of the freight industry to sit at the MPO table. Such a representative can be either elected by the freight industry, which is the ideal situation, or represented by an 'Office of Freight Transportation' set up in an appropriate public organization. Since the multiple obligations of freight industry leaders often prevent them from attending meetings with public officials – as the experience in the Freight Transportation Working Group in New York City indicates – designating a staff member to collect input from the industry and present their points of view in planning meetings may a pragmatic solution.

15.4 TOWARDS A SYSTEMATIC POLICY OF INTERMODAL INNOVATION

Implementing systemic freight transportation innovations requires taking into account the unique challenges to translating research findings into new practices that were discussed in the previous section. Careful consideration of these factors would help maximize the chances of implementing such research programmes. Table 15.2 shows the key challenges identified before, as well as a preliminary list of the potential approaches that should be considered.

As shown in Table 15.2, three of the key issues identified before (issues 1, 2 and 3) are related, in various ways, to the way in which the government agencies interact with the freight industry. The fourth and the fifth issues are, to a great extent, related to the key features of the freight industry structure, that is, the significant intermodal and intramodal competition that takes place in the US. Not surprisingly, there is a significant amount of overlap among the approaches identified to overcome these issues.

In terms of policy implementation, the order in which the different types of new technology and/or techniques are adopted does matter. It seems clear that the research community and the freight industry must

Table 15.2 Challenges and approaches to implement freight transportation innovations

Challenge	Approach
1. Lack of cooperative tradition between government and the freight industry	• Enhance current broad industry based initiatives (e.g. TRB, National Freight Dialogue) • Create and foster new public–private partnerships
2. Mismatched planning horizons	• Identify research topics that integrate operational concerns with infrastructure planning, thus generating interest among the largest number of stakeholders • Partner with consulting firms and freight industry to identify research topics
3. Modally based priorities (the result of modally based agencies and trade groups)	• Politically empower the agencies and offices with broad industry impact, and make them accountable for transcending modal perspectives • Employ the 'Golden Rule', i.e. 'the one who has the gold, rules'
4. Lack of identification between private industry success and national objectives	• Educate decision makers on the importance of freight to the nation's economy • Conduct research on broader socio-economic impacts of freight activity
5. Concerns about differential impacts of freight research	• Develop a research agenda of broad industry appeal

join forces and work together to elevate the consideration of freight issues to a level commensurate to the importance of freight to the nation's economy. In this context, the National Freight Dialogue is an important first step.

The leaders of the freight industry must play a critical role in raising the level of awareness among transportation and elected officials about the need to increase funding for transportation research, education and training. It is very likely that the executives of all major freight companies, across all modes, together with the leaders of the different trade groups (for example the ATA, AAPA, AAR, IANA) will set aside their differences and support such effort. An industry-led coalition is also likely to garner congressional support from those states in which freight transportation has a visible and recognized role in the local economies (for example New York, New Jersey, Texas, Pennsylvania, California and Illinois).

Success, even at a relatively minor scale, breeds success. In this context, should this coalition succeed in calling the attention of transportation and elected officials to the need to do more work on freight research, it may open the door to other forms of public–private partnerships. This, in turn, will contribute to a better working relationship between all sides.

The proactive participation of the freight industry may be the only way to bring about much-needed institutional changes that foster a comprehensive and truly intermodal freight transportation research programme. Key components of this would be: (1) the political empowerment of agencies and offices with broad (intermodal) mandates; and (2) the allocation of the funds needed for systematic and long-term freight research. The importance of the latter is best captured by the phrase coined by one insightful professional interviewed for this chapter, who mentioned: 'the Golden Rule, i.e., the one who has the gold, rules'. In other words, aligning adequate funding to implement organizational and technological outputs with a freight research programme focused on intermodal innovation could overcome some of the institutional obstacles identified in this chapter.

The mechanism by which this process could be implemented could take different forms. Ideally, an industry-led coalition with academia could try to obtain a congressional mandate (and the corresponding funds) to establish a freight transportation research programme managed by either the National Science Foundation or the National Academy of Sciences' Transportation Research Board (TRB). Among other things, this would benefit from the fact that the TRB is already a forum for discussion of freight transportation issues, in which there is significant participation from almost all stakeholders on a regular basis. A less ideal alternative, though more in tune with the inherent desires of members of Congress to enact pieces of legislation that directly favour their constituents, would be to create freight transportation research centres in the major metropolitan areas. Among other things, this mechanism is more likely to generate local and industry support, because it would make a more direct connection with their needs. One of the multiple paths that could be used to move these ideas forward is shown in Figure 15.1.

It is also important to highlight that – putting aside the obvious differences in size – the American case shares some key similarities with the cases of smaller and even developing countries that have made significant intermodal advances: (1) there is no widespread recognition at the highest decision-making levels of the synergies generated by intermodal innovation; and (2) funding decisions are often made on the basis of a modally based focus, which is the consequence of having modally based institutions

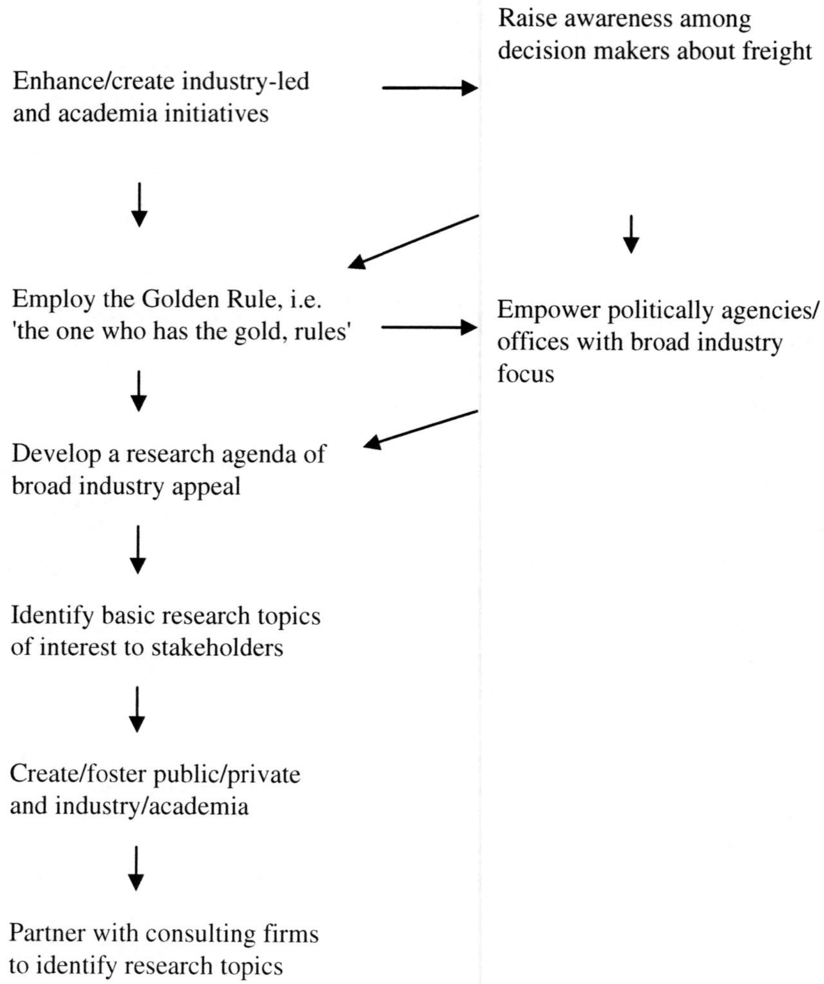

Figure 15.1 A possible implementation path for intermodal innovations

and trade groups. They differ in that in countries where the transportation system is far from being fully developed, there is often a heightened awareness of freight transportation's significant contribution (or potential for contribution) to the national economy. In this context, the issues identified in this chapter, as well as the implementation path suggested in Figure 15.1, may be applicable to these socio-economic environments with proper modifications. Cases such as the Netherlands, Singapore and Hong Kong, where freight transportation is recognized as an economic engine to be protected and enhanced, are in the opinion of the authors nothing more than the exceptions to the rule.

15.5 CONCLUSIONS

This chapter has presented an overview of the main challenges to implementing a comprehensive research programme that would stimulate intermodal innovations in freight transportation. The analysis focused initially on the American case from which a set of conclusions and recommendations, of more general applicability, were extracted. The analysis then identified challenges related to the institutional setting, as well as those related to the unique features of the American freight transportation system and the dynamics of the relationship with the government agencies. The chapter identified four major sets of factors: (1) government–private industry dynamics; (2) size and geographic factors; (3) lack of understanding about the relationship between private industry success and national economic objectives; and (4) mismatched planning horizons. The chapter also highlighted a number of the different approaches that could be used to overcome the identified challenges. The authors also put forward a preliminary implementation path that would help generate the new technology and techniques that would enhance the freight transportation system's performance.

In spite of the suggestions for launching research that would stimulate innovation here, there should be no doubt that this is a problem of considerable complexity and difficulty. The public and private policy participants that must be engaged to implement such efforts possess asymmetrical dynamics of interest and organization that inhibit change. For that reason, the modest findings of this chapter should be interpreted as nothing more than a small step in the long march toward using research as a springboard for intermodal transport innovation.

ACKNOWLEDGEMENTS

This chapter has benefited greatly from the insights generously provided by a distinguished set of experts, none of whom is to blame for any shortcomings of the chapter. All of the latter remain the sole responsibility of the authors. The authors would like to express their gratitude to Ms Priscilla Nelson, Former Director of the Division of Civil and Mechanical Systems at the National Science Foundation, and to Professors C. Michael Walton (University of Texas at Austin), Michael Meyer (Georgia Institute of Technology), George List (Rensselaer Polytechnic Institute), Arnim Meyburg (Cornell University) and Arun Chatterjee (University of Tennessee at Knoxville). Mr Gary Maring, former Director of the Federal Highway Administration's Office of Freight Management and Operations, Ms Kathleen Quinn and Mr

Bob Davis, both from the FHWA's Office of Freight Management and Operations, also provided invaluable insights as did Ms Christina S. Casgar, Former Executive Director of the Foundation for Intermodal Research and Education.

Anthony Perl would like to thank the City University of New York's Institute for Urban Systems, which supported his work on this chapter during his residency as a visiting scholar.

REFERENCES

Bhatia R., P. Lopipero and A.H. Smith (1998), 'Diesel exhaust exposure and lung cancer', *Epidemiology*, **9**, pp. 84–91.

Boske, L. (1998), *Multimodal/Intermodal Transportation in the United States, Western Europe, and Latin America: Government Policies, Plans and Programs*, Lyndon B. Johnson School of Public Affairs, Policy Research Project Report Number 130, Austin, TX: University of Texas at Austin.

Boske, L. (1999), *Case Studies of Multimodal/Intermodal Transportation Planning Methods, Funding Programs, and Projects*, Lyndon B. Johnson School of Public Affairs, Policy Research Project Report Number 132, Austin, TX: University of Texas at Austin.

ENO Transportation Foundation, Inc. (1998), *Transportation in America*, Washington, DC: ENO Foundation.

Godlee, F. (1993), Air Pollution II. Road Traffic and Modern Industry, *British Medical Journal*, **303**, pp. 1539–43.

Holguín-Veras, J. and S. Jara-Díaz (1999), 'Optimal space allocation and pricing for priority service at container ports', *Transport Research Part B*, **33** (2), pp. 81–106.

Holguín-Veras, J. and E. Thorson (2003), 'Modeling commercial vehicle empty trips with a first order trip chain model', *Transportation Research Part B*, **37** (2), pp. 129–48.

Holguín-Veras, J., G. List, A. Meyburg, K. Ozbay, R. Paaswell, H. Teng and S. Yahalom (2001), *An Assessment of Methodological Alternatives for a Regional Freight Model in the NYMTC Region*, New York: Metropolitan Transportation Council (NYMTC).

Lena, T.S., V. Ochieng, M. Carter, J. Holguín-Veras, and P. Kinney (2002), 'Elemental carbon and PM2.5 levels in an urban community heavily impacted by truck traffic', *Environmental Health Perspectives*, **110** (10), pp. 1009–15.

Muller, Gerhardt (1999), *Intermodal Freight Transportation*, Washington, DC: Eno Transportation Foundation.

Ostro, B.D. (1987), 'Air pollution and morbidity revisited: a specification test', *Journal of Environmental Economic Management*, **14**, pp. 87–98.

Perl, A. (1991), 'Financing transport infrastructure: the effects of institutional durability in French and American policymaking', *Governance: An International Journal of Policy and Administration*, **4** (4), pp. 365–402.

Sorratini, J.A. and R.L. Smith (2000), 'Development of a statewide truck trip forecasting model based on commodity flows and input–output coefficients', *Transportation Research Record 1707*, Washington, DC: Transportation Research Board.

Transportation Research Board (TRB) (2002), 'Regulation of weights, lengths, and widths of commercial motor vehicles', Special Report #267, prepublication copy, Washington, DC.

US Department of Commerce (USDC), Economics and Statistics Administration, US Census Bureau Service Sector Statistics Division (2000), *Vehicle Inventory and Use Survey 1997*, January, CD-EC97-VIUS (in CD ROM).

US Department of Transportation (US DOT) Bureau of Transportation Statistics (1999a), *1997 Economic Census. Transportation: Commodity Flow Survey*, Publication ECT97CF-US from the Economic Census of the US, issued December.

US Department of Transportation (US DOT) Bureau of Transportation Statistics (1999b), *National Transportation Statistics*, Washington, DC: US Department of Transport.

US Department of Transportation (US DOT) (2002), 'Operations: freight analysis framework', http://www.ops.fhwa.dot.gov/freight/adfrmwrk/index.htm, accessed 29 March 2001.

US Office of Management and Budget, Budget Review and Concepts Division, Budget Concepts Branch (2001), *Object Class Analysis*, Washington, DC: US Government printing Office, available at http: www.whitehouse.gov/omb/budget/fy2003/pdf/objclass.pdf (accessed 31 October 2007).

Index